FLANNERY
at the
GRAMMYS

FLANNERY
at the
GRAMMYS

Irwin H. Streight

University Press of Mississippi / Jackson

The University Press of Mississippi is the scholarly publishing agency of the Mississippi Institutions of Higher Learning: Alcorn State University, Delta State University, Jackson State University, Mississippi State University, Mississippi University for Women, Mississippi Valley State University, University of Mississippi, and University of Southern Mississippi.

www.upress.state.ms.us

The University Press of Mississippi is a member of the Association of University Presses.

Any discriminatory or derogatory language or hate speech regarding race, ethnicity, religion, sex, gender, class, national origin, age, or disability that has been retained or appears in elided form is in no way an endorsement of the use of such language outside a scholarly context.

Cover concept: Irwin H. Streight and daughter Flannery Evangeline
Cover design: Jennifer Mixon

Copyright © 2024 by University Press of Mississippi
All rights reserved
Manufactured in the United States of America
∞

Library of Congress Cataloging-in-Publication Data

Names: Streight, Irwin Howard, 1959– author. | O'Connor, Flannery.
Title: Flannery at the Grammys / Irwin H. Streight.
Description: Jackson : University Press of Mississippi, 2024. | Includes bibliographical references and index.
Identifiers: LCCN 2024011658 (print) | LCCN 2024011659 (ebook) | ISBN 9781496825940 (hardback) | ISBN 9781496850218 (trade paperback) | ISBN 9781496850225 (epub) | ISBN 9781496850232 (epub) | ISBN 9781496850249 (pdf) | ISBN 9781496850256 (pdf)
Subjects: LCSH: O'Connor, Flannery—Criticism and interpretation. | O'Connor, Flannery—Influence. | O'Connor, Flannery—Musical settings. | Music and literature. | Popular music—History and criticism. | Popular music—Philosophy and aesthetics.
Classification: LCC PS3565.C57 Z876 2024 (print) | LCC PS3565.C57 (ebook) | DDC 813/.54—dc23/eng/20240424
LC record available at https://lccn.loc.gov/2024011658
LC ebook record available at https://lccn.loc.gov/2024011659

British Library Cataloging-in-Publication Data available

In Memoriam

R. Neil Scott
1952–2012

O'Connor Scholar ✒ Generous Mentor ✒ Good Friend

CONTENTS

3   **INTRODUCTION**

16   **CHAPTER 1** Bruce Springsteen: "The Flannery O'Connor of American Rock"

39   **CHAPTER 2** Lucinda Williams: Chasing Flannery's Peacocks

71   **CHAPTER 3** Mary Gauthier: The Brutal Hand of Grace

88   **CHAPTER 4** Kate Campbell: "Equal Parts Emmylou Harris and Flannery O'Connor"

103 **CHAPTER 5** Sufjan Stevens: In Flannery's Territory

127 **CHAPTER 6** Nick Cave: "In the Bleeding Stinking Mad Shadow of Jesus"

155 **CHAPTER 7** PJ Harvey: Uh Huh, O'Connor

166 **CHAPTER 8** *Wise Blood*, Punk, and Heavy Metal

188 **CHAPTER 9** Everything That Rises

229 **CODA** "Gonter Rock, Rattle and Roll"

234 **BONUS TRACK** Stage Names from O'Connor's *Wise Blood* and Characters

239 **ACKNOWLEDGMENTS**

243 **NOTES**

293 **CREDITS**

299 **INDEX**

FLANNERY
at the
GRAMMYS

INTRODUCTION

Flannery at the Grammys

Flannery O'Connor had little interest in or appreciation of music: "All classical music sounds alike to me and all the rest of it sounds like the Beatles," she once memorably remarked. On another occasion she referred to herself as possessing "the Original Tin Ear," completely unattuned to the pleasures and purposes of music, and added, "I like music that is guaranteed good because I have no way of finding out for myself." O'Connor would surely be surprised and perhaps enjoy the irony that she has had a marked influence on the works of some notable contemporary American and British singer-songwriters and bands, among them Bruce Springsteen, Lucinda Williams, Mary Gauthier, Sufjan Stevens, PJ Harvey, Nick Cave, R.E.M., U2, and Tom Waits. These artists have individually received numerous awards and accolades from American and British music academies—enough to be "guaranteed good."

Titling this book *Flannery at the Grammys* on the one hand recognizes that, to date, among the major artists discussed are two multiple Grammy Award–winning songwriters who widely acknowledge the shaping influence of O'Connor's fiction on their art and vision, Springsteen and Williams, multiple Grammy-winning supergroups R.E.M. and U2, and four Grammy nominees: Gauthier, Stevens, Cave, and Harvey. Added to this list is double Grammy-winner Tom Waits, who acknowledges O'Connor's influence on his songwriting. The title also alludes to the fact that O'Connor has indeed been mentioned at the Grammys, the annual televised awards ceremony for the American music industry. At the 1988 Grammys, the Irish rock band U2 was awarded the Album of the Year for *The Joshua Tree* and a second Grammy for Best Rock Performance by a Group. In his acceptance speech, after several thank-yous, U2's guitarist The Edge read out a list of inspiring individuals the band wished to thank, beginning with Nobel Peace Prize honorees Desmond Tutu and Martin Luther King Jr., followed by Bob Dylan and—fourth from the top—Flannery O'Connor. As for O'Connor's influence on the lyrics of U2's celebrated recording, it is at least evident in an allusion to one of O'Connor's story titles, "The Enduring Chill," in the first line of the elegiac "One Tree Hill," which refers to mourners at a funeral who "turn away to face the cold, enduring chill" of lives doubtless filled with some degree of guilt and sorrow.

This book presents chapter-length critical commentaries on six major singer-songwriters and a seventh of some repute whose song craft and artistic sensibilities bear an evident and acknowledged arc of Flannery O'Connor's influence. Rock music icon Bruce Springsteen, country-blues artists Lucinda Williams and Mary Gauthier, folk gospel singer Kate Campbell, and indie composer and singer-songwriter Sufjan Stevens have each acknowledged O'Connor's considerable influence on the content and, for Springsteen and Gauthier, the narrative form of their songwriting. Australian Nick Cave and Brit PJ Harvey each deliberately draw on O'Connor's art in creating their own. Individual works by these songwriters either consciously reflect or present the "startling figures" and Christ-haunted misfits found in O'Connor's fiction. A further chapter examines the curious case of O'Connor's first novel *Wise Blood*, a grotesque satire on contemporary irreligious American society that has had an ironic influence on songwriters in punk, heavy metal, and alternative rock genres. The penultimate chapter is a gathering of short commentaries largely on individual works by both major and minor players that borrow content from O'Connor's fiction or are inspired by her artistic vision. The closing coda spotlights the one rock 'n' roll rebel found in O'Connor's fiction: the delinquent fourteen-year-old Rufus Johnson in "The Lame Shall Enter First," one of her Christ-haunted prophets-in-waiting and thus a kind of metonym—a symbolic stand-in—for the likewise Christ-haunted, truth-telling singer-songwriters and pop groups discussed in the chapters that follow.

The significant presence of Flannery O'Connor in contemporary music and in other products of popular culture begs and perhaps beggars explanation. A celebrated—and in some quarters controversial—American writer, O'Connor was a devout Catholic whose active faith informed everything she wrote. A native of Georgia, she had an uncanny gift for creating compelling fiction about the world of the southern Baptist Bible Belt spanning the postwar years leading up to the civil rights advances of the mid-1960s. She died in 1964 at age thirty-nine from complications of disseminated lupus, a debilitating immune-deficiency disease that claimed her father when she was a teenager and from which she suffered for the majority of her writing life. In her brief lifetime, O'Connor published two short novels featuring southern religious fanatics, *Wise Blood* (1952) and *The Violent Bear It Away* (1960); a collection of ten short stories, *A Good Man Is Hard to Find* (1955); and seven personal essays, mostly on the art of writing fiction—her brand of fiction. O'Connor's second collection of nine stories, *Everything That Rises Must Converge* (1965), was published posthumously. Her corpus of short fiction, including published chapter excerpts from her novels and stories from her MFA thesis, was issued in 1971 as *Flannery O'Connor: The Complete Stories* and won a National Book Award for Fiction—an exceptional conferring of this honor for a work by a deceased author. O'Connor's complete corpus of published fiction, along with selected essays and letters, is available in the Library of America series (no. 39) in a single volume, *Flannery O'Connor: Collected Works*, one of the publisher's best-selling volumes.

Why a devout Catholic woman writer of southern gothic stories and novels, featuring largely unlikable characters and with plots invariably marked by violence and murder, would have such strong stock and visibility in contemporary popular culture is surely a matter of considerable curiosity and significant import. O'Connor's religious orthodoxy and seemingly regressive views on matters of race and gender, so counter to the ideologies of present times, would tend to make her more a cultural pariah than a kind of contemporary prophet figure as some regard her. Why then have highly influential and successful pop music stars—Bruce Springsteen, R.E.M., and U2 among them—invoked her as an influence on their art and vision? The chapters in this book attempt to answer this question.

Christ-Haunted

Flannery O'Connor published her literary manifesto "The Fiction Writer and His Country" early in her career in an edited book of statements by writers on their art, *The Living Novel: A Symposium* (1957). In this essay, O'Connor states her case as a writer who holds strongly to theological truths: "I see by the standpoint of Christian orthodoxy. This means that for me the meaning of life is centered in our Redemption in Christ and that what I see in the world, I see in its relation to that." O'Connor recognized that this was not an easy position to take in a post-Christian era, nor one easy to make evident in realistic fiction. As she remarks in her reluctantly added author's note to the second edition of *Wise Blood*, reissued in 1962, "That belief in Christ is to some a matter of life and death has been a stumbling block for readers who would prefer to think it a matter of no great consequence."

It is not overly reductive to say that O'Connor wrote two novels and published nineteen short stories all ultimately intended to reveal to secular readers and to nominal Christians alike that humanity is in need of redemption through Christ. Everything she wrote converges on the figure and fact of

Jesus. In her widely anthologized short story, "A Good Man Is Hard to Find," after a crucial car accident that begins a chain of deadly events, her character Bailey exclaims, "We're in a terrible predicament!" Yes, O'Connor appears to say, an existential, ontological predicament. And Christ is at the center of it. She puts the matter into the mouth of The Misfit, her conflicted serial killer in that story: "If [Jesus] did what He said, then it's nothing for you to do but throw away everything and follow Him, and if He didn't, then it's nothing for you to do but enjoy the few minutes you got left the best way you can." For The Misfit, committing an act of meanness against someone is all the pleasure and purpose he can find in a life lived outside of experiencing the redemptive presence of Christ.

While O'Connor the writer is Christ-centered, folks in the postwar southern society she writes about are, in her phrase, "Christ-haunted" and thus subject to a conflicted religiosity. She was mindful that many of her readers were like Mrs. May in her story "Greenleaf," a "good Christian woman" with "a large respect for religion, though she did not, of course, believe any of it was true." To be Christ-haunted is to be conscious of the salvation story of the Christian gospel, to have known and perhaps encountered its transforming truth, yet rejected its mystical personal imperatives ("You must be born again" [St. John 3:7]) and creedal claims. The story of the incarnation was central to O'Connor's core beliefs and fictional practice. In her art, she uncompromisingly addresses the spiritual vacuity she observed in secular society.

It is fair to say that the major singer-songwriters in this study, with perhaps the exceptions of Kate Campbell and Sufjan Stevens, are Christ-haunted, as O'Connor uses the term. Each of them has had some form of religious formation within a denominational strain of Christianity, although only Campbell and Stevens identify as Christian. The religious elements in their song art are neither dogmatic nor suggestive of a personal system of belief. While Springsteen may be the most Catholic of the lot and therefore most closely aligned with O'Connor's religious beliefs and sacramental worldview, he does not regularly attend mass, is raising "pagan babies" (as he tells the *VH1 Storytellers* audience) and has constructed a "personal" Jesus who does not possess "godly power" (as he notes in his 2016 autobiography *Born to Run*). Lucinda Williams is the most evidentially Christ-haunted of this subset of songwriters. Her religious heritage, from a line of southern fundamentalist preachers, including some fanatics, parallels the spiritual inheritance of O'Connor's reluctant prophet figures Hazel Motes and Francis Marion Tarwater. In explaining the perspective she brings to her songs about fundamentalist southern religion, "Atonement" and "Get Right with God," Williams has remarked, "My life reads like a southern gothic novel. It really does." In performance, she often tells her audience to read O'Connor's fiction in order to better understand these songs. Springsteen too has on occasion referenced O'Connor's novel *Wise Blood* from the stage.

Another of the Christ-haunted is Nick Cave, who might have stepped out of the pages of *Wise Blood*, a novel he was obsessed with while writing his own first novel, *And the Ass Saw the Angel* (1989). In his considerable song corpus and his biographical/philosophical prose pieces, Cave conducts a conflicted and sometimes tortured monologue directed at God—a theodicy of sorts: an effort to make sense of the fallen world and of the human condition in light of what might be known of the God of Abraham, Isaac, and Jacob, and how the person and work of Christ is to be comprehended. The paradoxically named "Holy Church of Christ Without Christ" that O'Connor's charlatan preacher Onnie Jay Holy proposes in *Wise Blood* would be a fit place in which to expound on the gospel according to Cave.

Does O'Connor's Christ-haunted fiction attract the Christ-haunted artist? Is this what drew Springsteen to *Wise Blood* and the O'Connor stories he read around the time he was telling his dark tales about desperate characters in *Nebraska*? O'Connor's Christ-haunted protagonist and blaspheming preacher-gone-wrong Hazel Motes certainly attracted Nick Cave, and Lucinda Williams has declared on numerous occasions over the years that *Wise Blood* is her favorite book. Mary Gauthier may not be consciously *Christ*-haunted, yet across the soulscape of her songs wanders a tortured individual struggling with personal demons and looking for some form of lasting redemption. As an always-recovering alcoholic, assisted through AA's Twelve-Step program, Gauthier appears to be more grounded in faith in a Higher Power than in the Christ of the New Testament.

The Sacred within the Profane

Two circus freaks and a ubiquitous offensive lawn statue become embodied means through which the sacred is manifest in O'Connor's art. In "Parker's Back," fourteen-year-old O. E. Parker's vision of a tattooed man at a local fair presents him with an image of Adamic wholeness, of human completeness, though he does not know it at the time. The transformation of his soul at the story's conclusion is predicated on his ultimately realizing and recognizing this image of wholeness in himself once the signifying presence of Christ has been incarnated in his own flesh in the sacred image tattooed on his back. In "A Temple of the Holy Ghost," a hermaphrodite in an adults-only circus tent lifts their dress to display a bisexed body in like manner to a priest celebrating mass, raising the lid of a monstrance to reveal the sacramental bread of the Host within. Sacred shock is O'Connor's preferred method of revealing the profane means of grace in her stories. For Mr. Head and his alienated grandson, Nelson, in her controversially titled story "The Artificial Nigger," this shock comes as they stand in the presence of a piece of racist lawn statuary, lost in the big city of Atlanta and far from their country home, and feel touched by "the action of mercy."

O'Connor shocked many of her readers, particularly her coreligionists, by suggesting in a parable-like way in her stories that the sacred may be mediated through the profane—simply defined as that which is not considered sacred or related to any form of religious practice. A nymphomaniac is the embodied presence of a divine love that desires consummation; pigs "pant with a secret life"; and an artificial leg is symbolically associated with a character's "soul." The wideness of mercy and grace, the manifold, odd, and often violent ways in which the divine is encountered in human experience—these are O'Connor's concerns as a storyteller who confesses to orthodox Christian beliefs. Art is about the human, she emphasized in her talks to students and writers' groups, and the artist should not ignore any of the stuff of lived experience. She shows a readiness in her art to let an unlimited grace abound, and a dogged obedience to her artistic calling to tell about the meanness in this world and how it might be met with unorthodox means of redemption. Perhaps part of the attractiveness of O'Connor's art and vision to the contemporary musicians discussed in this study is that, like her, they desire to be truth-tellers in their chosen mediums.

Whether consciously or not, all the singer-songwriters discussed at length in this study share some sense that the sacred may be revealed in the profane. In Springsteen's "Matamoros Banks," for example, the decaying and dismembered body of a drowned Mexican migrant grotesquely figures as a symbol of heavenly transformation. Mardi Gras revelers, including drag queens, prostitutes, and a voodoo priestess, form a "soul parade" that "winds its way down Eternity Street" in Mary Gauthier's O'Connor-inspired vision of a heavenbound procession in "Wheel inside the Wheel." In the songs of Nick Cave, sex and the sacred are intimately linked, sometimes blasphemously, sometimes not. The motif of the sacred enfleshed in or envisioned as an alluring woman runs through his extensive corpus, distilled in a song that borrows lyric substance from a Methodist hymn:

Just a closer walk with thee
Come back, honey, to me
Then I'll be moving up close to thee
O let it be, O Lord, let it be

While O'Connor's stories have a limited range of character types and settings, her intent is to show that the action of grace is boundless. Accessing the sacred is not limited to codified sacraments, though the act of baptism and hunger for the elements of the Eucharist figure strongly in her narratives. She invokes St. Augustine for a principle that informs her own sacramental art: "that the things of the world pour forth from God in a double way: intellectually into the minds of angels and physically into the world of things." Like the mystical English poet William Blake to whom she has been compared, O'Connor saw the mystery of the divine on every face and in every grain of red Georgia soil. Perhaps this aspect of her art also attracts the spiritual but not religious singer-songwriters included in this study.

A Prophet *with* Honor in Her Own Country

I write her name with honor, for all the truth and all the craft with which she shows man's fall and dishonor.
—THOMAS MERTON

From the beginning of her writing career, Flannery O'Connor had a sense of a divine source and purpose behind her writing. A prayer journal she kept from January 1946 to September 1947 while attending the University of Iowa's prestigious Writers' Workshop reveals her mindfulness of the spiritual grace informing whatever abilities she might have or might develop as a writer. "You have given me a story," she writes prayerfully. "Don't let me ever think, dear God, that I was anything but the instrument of Your story." She would later come to identify this spiritual gift as "prophetic vision," a necessary quality of the writer concerned with plumbing the mystery at the heart of human meaning, what she refers to repeatedly in essays and letters as "ultimate reality." In several of her letters, O'Connor intimates that her writing proceeded through a kind of divine enabling. "Ultimately, you write what you can, what God gives you," she tells one correspondent. In another letter she alludes to seeking divine assistance while working "in the realm of the impossible" on her dramatically and structurally complex second novel, *The Violent Bear It Away*.

Living as a literary anchorite with the "habit of art," O'Connor was in every respect a servant of the word/Word. She did not outline her novels or stories before beginning to write but wrote to discover what she had or was meant to say. "I certainly have no idea how I have written some of the things I have, as they are things I am not conscious of having thought about," she confesses in a letter. Hers are understandably ghostwritten stories, perhaps Holy Ghost–written and inspired. A mystery at the heart of their creation may account for the "preternatural power" of her fictions that the late esteemed literary critic Harold Bloom identifies.

In her youthful prayers, O'Connor appeals to God to make her a mystic and to enable her to be the best artist she can be. Perhaps the singer-songwriters in this study recognize that mystic, prophetic voice in O'Connor's art and are compelled by it. It might be that Bruce Springsteen said something to this effect when he exclaimed of O'Connor, "She's just incredible!"

✎ ✎ ✎

Bruce Springsteen, more so than other songwriters examined in this study, shares a spiritual formation with O'Connor. Like O'Connor, he is a cradle Catholic, raised in the teachings and rituals of the Church. For O'Connor, the facts and acts of her faith informed her artistic vision—so much so that she claimed she would not be a writer were it not for the shaping and directing influence of her Catholicism. Springsteen too has a Catholic way of understanding the human condition. Though he confesses not to hold to Catholic orthodoxy in his personal life, Springsteen the writer indisputably thinks in theological terms, as the considerable biblical imagery and religious language in his songs attest and numerous commentators have observed. What he calls the "internal landscape" formed by his Catholic upbringing has shaped his artistic outlook and sensibilities. Certainly, this includes the doctrine of original sin for a boy well catechized in the early 1950s at St. Rose of Lima parochial school in Freehold, New Jersey. This fundamental Christian doctrine Springsteen discerned as central to O'Connor's fictions. In a revealing interview in the now-defunct arts magazine *DoubleTake*, he talks about O'Connor's influence on the content and craft of his songwriting: "There was some dark thing—a component of spirituality—that I sensed in her stories and that set me off exploring characters of my own. She knew original sin—knew how to give it the flesh of a story." Human drama, O'Connor once wrote, "usually bases itself on the bedrock of original sin, whether the writer thinks in theological terms or not." She saw her own stories as being about free-willed human souls in action, struggling to find satisfaction and meaning in the sway of what she called "the general mystery of incompleteness." She described the initial manuscript of her first collection of short fiction, *A Good Man Is Hard to Find*, as "Nine stories about original sin."

So, along with a Christ-hauntedness that may draw him to O'Connor's art and vision, there is for Springsteen in particular an artistic/theological influence grounded in her fictional dramatizations of the reality of original sin. He wrote the dark-spirited *Nebraska* songs and a number of songs that appear on *The River* after being profoundly affected by reading her stories and viewing John Huston's film adaptation of *Wise Blood*. O'Connor once reflected in a letter that on the journey of faith, "You arrive at enough certainty to be able to make your way, but it is making it in darkness." The older Springsteen has likewise asserted, "I always wanted to base the heart of my work in the dark side of things and then find my way." His lyric explorations of a "something" or a "more" that gnaws at the souls of the troubled characters who appear in songs on *The Ghost of Tom Joad*, *Devils & Dust*, and *Western Stars* continue the themes and characters he began to explore in *Nebraska*. Chapter 1 follows Springsteen as, with O'Connor as his guide, he writes song after song about characters who descend into the American heart of darkness. As in O'Connor's often dimly redemptive narratives, even in Springsteen's dark songs the careful listener can as well discern a hopeful "pin point of light."

Lucinda Williams has the distinction of being the only songwriter in this study to have met Flannery O'Connor. She was four years old when her family moved to Macon, Georgia, thirty miles down the road from the O'Connor farmstead outside of Milledgeville. Her father, Miller Williams, who would become an acclaimed poet, was then making a meager living as a traveling book salesman, which gave him the opportunity and excuse to call on O'Connor. Lucinda Williams remembers waiting with her father on the porch outside the farmhouse until O'Connor flashed the blinds on her study window—a signal that her morning writing session was over and she was free to receive visitors. While her father enjoyed one of his monthly conversations with the author, young Lucinda would chase the many ducks and peacocks that roamed freely on the O'Connor farm property, known as Andalusia.

Thus, Lucinda Williams grew up with knowledge of O'Connor. Her father assigned her O'Connor's stories and novels to read when she was a teenager, and she claims to have read everything the author wrote. Repeatedly, she has told interviewers that O'Connor's *Wise Blood* is her favorite book and director John Huston's film adaptation of it her favorite movie. The *Rolling Stone*

Encyclopedia of Rock and Roll records her acknowledgment that O'Connor is "a major influence on her songwriting."

Williams was raised in the shadow of the hellfire religion of southern Pentecostalism, the ethos of O'Connor's fiction. Her two grandfathers were Methodist preachers, on her mother's side of the rabid sort—like Hazel Motes's "waspish" circuit-riding grandfather who preached "with Jesus hidden in his head like a stinger." And for a time Williams was fascinated with the extreme expressions of southern religious fanaticism, experiences that inform the content of the uncomfortable lyrics to her songs "Atonement" and "Get Right with God."

Much of Williams's life and writing resonates with O'Connor's art. She has compared her carefully crafted, darkly redemptive songs to O'Connor's short stories. Agonizing moments of grace that are central to O'Connor's fictions occasionally break through in Williams's pained song narratives, "in the silence of the roses" and like "broken butterflies." And like O'Connor, she does not hesitate to give the devil his due. Chapter 2 explores O'Connor's influence on Williams's vision and craft as a songwriter and traces the overarching theme that both southern writers share, expressed in the refrain of Williams's Grammy-winning rockabilly gospel song, "You got to get right with God."

Mary Gauthier suggested the subtitle of her chapter here, "The Brutal Hand of Grace," in conversation following a performance at Hugh's Room in Toronto, Canada. Gauthier's concerns and methods as a songwriter have much in common with O'Connor's. Like Williams, she has "read everything" the author has written and acknowledges O'Connor's influence on her own artistic sensibilities and her courageous and painstakingly crafted narrative songs. Though raised a Catholic and sent to parochial school by her adoptive parents, Gauthier does not identify with a specific religious tradition; nonetheless, a deeply compassionate spirituality informs her work.

Of the songwriters discussed in this study who acknowledge O'Connor's influence, Gauthier comes closest in her often-confessional songs to presenting O'Connor's sense of the expansive, all-encompassing agency of grace and divine mercy in fumbling human affairs. Grace, O'Connor indicates, is costly—imaginatively in her story art, and polemically in her published talks and essays. Gauthier knows this personally and likewise relays this truth in her songs and in her 2021 autobiography, tellingly titled *Saved by a Song*.

Though not as commercially successful or well recognized as other chapter-worthy musical figures in this study, **Kate Campbell** is a sort of inverse double to O'Connor as a songwriter. The Mississippi-raised daughter of a Baptist preacher, Campbell has been telling stories in song about the

South in, to date, sixteen albums of original work since her self-recorded 1994 debut *Songs from the Levee*. Most of her work is folk and gospel, with a strong strain of blues featuring that Muscle Shoals sound of her close collaborator, Country Music Hall of Fame legend Spooner Oldham. Campbell's *Rosaryville* collection (1999) takes a southern Baptist perspective on the piety, religious practices, and eccentricities of the South's Catholics. Like O'Connor, whose influence she acknowledges in interviews and in the liner notes of two of her recordings, Campbell's artistic milieu is solely the South—its social codes, its fraught history, its religiosity, its oddball outsiders. Her narrative songwriting style aligns with that of Mary Gauthier, with whom she shares a birthplace and similar latecomer status to her artistic vocation—at age thirty. Campbell is a gifted songwriter and storyteller who has toured with Emmylou Harris and the late Guy Clark, and recorded her compositions with contributions from Rodney Crowell and the late John Prine and Nanci Griffith, among other Nashville notables. Chapter 4 examines a selection of Campbell's songs of the South with their "mix of believability and darkness" that echo what she sees in O'Connor's fiction, her similar interest in southern religious eccentrics and extremists, and her O'Connoresque comic send-ups of southern manners.

Sufjan Stevens, once one of the darlings of indie pop music, aspired first to be a fiction writer like his "idol" Flannery O'Connor. While enrolled in an MFA program at New School University in New York in his mid-twenties, he produced a volume of short stories. Set in a region of his native Michigan that might be described as a northern version of the Bible Belt, Stevens's stories feature religious extremists and undercurrents of the diabolical that strongly echo elements found in O'Connor's tales of the southern grotesque. Despite his recognized talent as a fiction writer, Stevens found the American market for short fiction "impenetrable" and moved on to his "Plan B"—a career as a composer and songwriter that has taken him to the forefront of contemporary music and to the stage at the 2018 Academy Awards. Chapter 5 follows Stevens as he translates his O'Connor-inspired short fiction into his first song cycle, *Michigan* (2003), and directly references O'Connor's works in songs on *Seven Swans* (2004). Moreover, as a devout Christian, Stevens shares O'Connor's belief that all human endeavor is played out "in territory held largely by the devil." His songs court that spark of incarnate evil that sometimes ignites in a serial killer and, as Stevens sings, can smolder in the heart of a successful pop artist.

Nick Cave might have stepped out of the pages of O'Connor's fiction as one of her Christ-haunted characters. The Australian-born songwriter and successful novelist—among other writerly accomplishments—was for a time obsessed with O'Connor's *Wise Blood* and its blaspheming, sin-seeking protagonist Hazel Motes. Cave's faux southern gothic first novel *And the Ass Saw the Angel* (1989), which has sold more than one hundred thousand copies, borrows plot elements and character types from both of O'Connor's novels.

Songs on *The Boatman's Call* (1997; 2011 Remastered Edition, LP), the most highly regarded album by Nick Cave and the Bad Seeds, collectively present a quest narrative, a kind of profane *The Pilgrim's Progress*. Across the six songs on the A-side of the reissued record, the narrator's position moves from unbelief in "an interventionist God" to a questioning expectancy that echoes the words of John the Baptist regarding the Christ: "Are you the one that I've been waiting for?" The narrator of these songs might be understood in light of O'Connor's affirmative statements about "unbelieving searchers" in her essay "Novelist and Believer." He longs to believe in some transcendent truth, yet is caught in an age of unbelief, unable to find what he's looking for—much like O'Connor's character The Misfit. Cave's pilgrim journeys toward the sacred through the carnal, envisioning a number of female figures as embodying the divine life or a divine presence.

Unlike Cave's art, little critical attention has been given to the sexual and erotic imagery in O'Connor's works. Her own prurience about this "lacking category" in her fiction seems to have somewhat hushed scholarly attention to the use of sex in her stories. Yet she concurs with a scholar who finds "a strong kind of sex potential" in her first story collection. Indeed, a kind of erotic theology is evident in *Wise Blood* and in her later stories "A Temple of the Holy Ghost" and "The Comforts of Home," and these works make congress with the sacral-sexual themes in Cave's songs. Chapter 6 explores Cave's irreligious religious quest and underscores the Hazel Motes–like nature of his spiritual journey as evidenced in his song narratives and several polemical works.

British alt-rock diva **PJ Harvey** sought inspiration and lyrical support from O'Connor's short fiction for three songs on her 1998 recording *Is This Desire?* Reviewers at the time did not notice that she drew on O'Connor's stories in forming her song narratives. Upon close examination, the lyrics to these songs are largely pastiches of descriptive phrases and bits of dialogue from individual stories—*found* lyrics of a sort. No other songwriter in this study has so informed his or her work with O'Connor's own words. Harvey's lyrical bricolage in these songs raises interesting issues of artistic inspiration and influence. Commentary on Harvey in chapter 7 follows the discussion of Nick Cave, with whom she had an intense though short-lived romantic relationship in 1995–1996, and who presumably introduced her to O'Connor's works.

Punk and Heavy Metal: O'Connor's first novel, *Wise Blood*, has had an uncanny appeal to songwriters on the extremes of popular music, in the genres of punk, heavy metal, and forms of post-punk and alternative rock. This odd comic novel has had a significant though limited currency in these gothic modes of music, and probable explanations for this are just that. Though the influence is often hard to trace, mainstream metal bands Ministry and Corrosion of Conformity have released major works influenced by the novel, and the alternative music artist JG Thirlwell, sometimes known as Wiseblood, has branded with O'Connor's book title his own Hazel Motes–like blasphemous and degenerate stage persona as well as a small, highly offensive set of recordings.

Chapter 8 develops the argument that representations of O'Connor's novel *Wise Blood* and its protagonist Hazel Motes in punk and metal works reflect unironic misreadings of the book's religious satire (or perhaps of John Huston's film adaptation of the novel). For O'Connor, Haze's blaspheming and dissipation and existential frustration ultimately leads him to become "a kind of Protestant saint." For the purveyors of the more extreme popular music examined in this chapter (and, as well, for some censorious reviewers of O'Connor's novel), he is a type of licentious anarchist, promoting an anti-Christian self-determinism—not unlike the antiauthoritarian doctrines widely expounded by performers and fans of these forms of music.

Everything That Rises: Everything that rises to critics' attention as being influenced by O'Connor's art and vision, or sharing some features of her gothic fictions, is not verifiably so. It may be that the point of similarity is "only southernness," as R.E.M.'s Mike Mills somewhat disingenuously remarked about connections between the catalog of the Athens, Georgia–based band and O'Connor's artistic vision and works. However, a number of songwriters and groups across musical genres and at all levels of commercial recognition have deliberately referenced O'Connor's stories and novels or person in individual songs or have acknowledged her shaping influence to some extent. Chapter 9 is a collection of short commentaries on these artists and their O'Connor-inspired recordings. It also includes analysis of songwriters and bands that have referenced O'Connor or one of her stories in a song or song title, or who have declared themselves fans of O'Connor's fiction in published interviews. Completing the gatherings in this book is an annotated short lineup of performers and bands whose stage names are derived from the title of O'Connor's first novel or the name of one of her characters.

Chapter 1

BRUCE SPRINGSTEEN

"The Flannery O'Connor of American Rock"

Most prominent among the contemporary singer-songwriters who acknowledge Flannery O'Connor's shaping influence on their writing is American cultural icon and multiple Grammy Award winner Bruce Springsteen. To date of this publication, Springsteen has won twenty of the coveted music awards over his long recording career. In an interview with actor Edward Norton at the 2010 Toronto Film Festival before the premier of *The Promise*, a documentary on the making of Springsteen's fourth song cycle, *Darkness on the Edge of Town* (1978), Springsteen recalled his early musical influences and the widening effect of his reading at the time, which included the works of Flannery O'Connor. "All the writers we love," he reflected, "put their fingerprint on your imagination, in your heart, and in your soul."

Springsteen was introduced to O'Connor's art and vision through a copy of her *Complete Stories* given to him by Barbara Downey, the wife of his then new manager and cultural tutor, Jon Landau. Springsteen read a number of O'Connor's stories and was profoundly affected. He later viewed John Huston's film adaptation of *Wise Blood* when it was released in theaters in the fall of 1979. He was then in the process of recording the songs for his double album *The River* (1980). As a songwriter he was consciously moving into a darker vision of American life and a narrative style of songwriting that was more character-centered, away from the more expressionistic lyrics of his earlier, largely autobiographical albums. Something in O'Connor's vision and skillfully wrought short fiction resonated with the young songwriter, who already sensed he had a story to tell and was looking to hone his craft. According to his first biographer, Dave Marsh, Springsteen was particularly in awe of the "minute precision" in O'Connor's storytelling, "the way O'Connor could enliven a character by sketching in just a few details." Further, there were "mysteries he wanted his music to help him reconcile," mysteries grounded in the "claustrophobic lower-class Catholic guilt" he had been raised in that he recognized in some of O'Connor's characters and, as Marsh implies, in himself.

In a 1998 interview with Will Percy, nephew of novelist Walker Percy, published in *DoubleTake* magazine, Springsteen recalls the transforming effect on his songwriting of reading O'Connor's fiction:

> I'd come out of a period of my own writing where I'd been writing big, sometimes operatic, and occasionally rhetorical things. I was interested in finding another way to write about those subjects, about people, another way to address what was going on around me and in the country—a more scaled down, more personal, more restrained way of getting some of my ideas across. So, right prior to the record *Nebraska*, I was deep into O'Connor.

O'Connor's Catholic vision and the spiritual landscape in the fallen world of her fiction have had a deeply informing and lasting influence on Springsteen's sensibilities as a storyteller. In interviews with music journalists since 1980, he has frequently acknowledged the influence of O'Connor's fiction on his songwriting. As late as a 2014 interview published in the *New York Times Book Review*, Springsteen continued to single out O'Connor's collected stories as the "one book" that has most profoundly informed his artistic sensibilities. He mused philosophically on the effect that reading O'Connor's works has had on his consciousness: "You could feel within them the unknowability of God, the intangible mysteries of life that confounded her characters, and which I find by my side every day. They contained the dark gothicness of my childhood, and yet made me feel fortunate to sit at the center of this swirling black puzzle, stars reeling overhead, the earth barely beneath us." In his autobiography, *Born to Run* (2016), Springsteen further acknowledges O'Connor as a "model" of an individual artist who, like himself, "worked on the edges of society" and whose art had been "assimilated and become part of the culture at large."

O'Connor's influence on Springsteen's art is most pointedly evidenced in the style and content of songs on his first solo recording, *Nebraska*, released in 1982. The older Springsteen regards it as one of the best records he has made, along with the multiplatinum *Born in the USA*. As he observes of O'Connor in the Percy interview, Springsteen well knows "original sin" and, in his words, "how to give it the flesh of a story." Indeed, a number of the lyrics for the *Nebraska* songs are directly influenced by his reading of O'Connor's short fiction and her novel *Wise Blood*, and even bear evidence of quotation from her works. The influence appears to be as much on matters of form as on the thematic content: "I was interested in writing kind of *smaller* than I had been, writing with just detail," Springsteen comments. And he specifically connects the sudden transformation in his songwriting style with his reading of O'Connor's stories, exclaiming to a *Rolling Stone* interviewer, "She's just incredible."

What Springsteen appears to have learned from O'Connor in his more "scaled down" and "restrained" narrative songs is the breadth of meaning-making that story affords, how the materials of fiction—character and incident—most effectively present the human and social truths that he wanted to write and sing about. Songwriting of this kind, he discovered, "has a little in common with short-story writing in that it's character-driven." The characters in his songs, he told Will Percy, "are confronting the questions that everyone is trying to sort out for themselves . . . moral issues, [and] the way those issues rear their heads in the outside world." Both the mystery of our condition and the manner in which we respond to lived experience are as much the stuff of popular song lyrics as of fiction, Springsteen suggests. He adds, "In some fashion that's my intent: to establish a commonality by revealing our inner common humanity, by telling good stories about a lot of different kinds of people."

Springsteen in the early 1970s had been heralded as the new Dylan. And his songwriting style on the early albums owed much to what one critic calls Dylan's "narrative impressionism." A well-known example of Springsteen's early style of songwriting is the lyrically dizzying pop tune "Blinded by the Light," from his first album, *Greetings from Asbury Park, N. J.* (1973), a song that has been described as presenting "characters doing strange things that just happen to rhyme." A cover version by the British group Manfred Mann and His Earth Band made it to the top spot on the *Billboard* pop charts in 1977, the only Springsteen song to achieve this distinction. One of its memorable verses goes,

> Some silicone sister with her manager's mister told me I got what it takes
> She said "I'll turn you on sonny to something strong if you play that song with the funky break"
> And go-cart Mozart was checkin' out the weather chart to see if it was safe to go outside
> And little Early-Pearly came by in her curly-wurly and asked me if I needed a ride

This early "minor masterpiece," as Springsteen wryly comments, was written "with a rhyming dictionary in one hand and a notebook in the other." He confesses that the song is cryptically "on the autobiographical side." Explicating his own lyrics in 2005 to the audience of the *VH1 Storytellers* TV music series, he jokes, "That's a song that explains why I never did any drugs: I don't think I could have stood it. My mind was already reeling."

Around the time he began writing songs for *The River*, leading up to the *Nebraska* album, Springsteen was shifting away from the abstruse, Dylanesque lyrics of his earlier songs toward more character-centered narratives. The haunting, dark, folk-style and rockabilly songs on *Nebraska*, accompanied by acoustic guitar, complemented occasionally with harmonica and a fair amount of whooping and wailing, are quite unlike the lyrically dense, anthemic songs of the earlier albums, with their party-like atmosphere and wall-of-sound production. There are no pop-inflected rock anthems, no driving guitar solos or catchy piano riffs that define the E Street Band sound of a Springsteen song. Springsteen's manager Jon Landau hesitated to call the new songs out and out folk music. Rather, the songs on *Nebraska* are, according to Landau's nuancing, performed in "a folk-related style." Reflecting on the transformation in his songwriting style at that time, Springsteen comments in a 1992 interview, "I wanted to have my own vision and point of view and create a world of characters, which is what the writers I admired did." He has remarked that this album is "very influenced by Flannery O'Connor stories."

Reason to Believe: The *Nebraska* Songs

Flannery O'Connor describes her first collection of short fiction, *A Good Man Is Hard to Find*, as "nine stories about original sin." That is, stories that confront a world in which an individual feels alienated from God, from fellow beings, and ultimately from his or her true self. Like the allegorically named character of the collection's title story, O'Connor's characters are all misfits, social and spiritual outcasts, in need of grace and love and purpose, and convinced, like Hazel Motes in *Wise Blood*, that all they require is a good car and their broken, stalled lives will be mended and set in motion. Springsteen's *Nebraska* songs present a cast of O'Connoresque characters, leading lives of sometimes quiet, sometimes vocal desperation, and introduce a new breed of characters into his songs.

Critical commentary on the title song "Nebraska" invariably remarks on the influence of Terrence Malick's 1974 film *Badlands*, which gives a fictionalized account of serial killer Charles Starkweather and his girlfriend Caril Fugate, who in 1958 went on a killing spree from Lincoln, Nebraska, through to eastern Wyoming, senselessly murdering ten people in eight days, including Fugate's parents and infant sister. After viewing Malick's film, Springsteen was interested enough in the details of the story to call author/broadcaster Ninette Beaver, who had written about the murderers in a biography entitled

Caril. Originally titled "Starkweather," "Nebraska" presents a monologue by a serial killer as he faces execution by electric chair.

But Springsteen acknowledges he was also "deep into O'Connor" in the months of intense songwriting that led to the *Nebraska* recording. In fact, the title song both borrows from and echoes a theme of the title story from O'Connor's first collection—her most widely anthologized work, "A Good Man Is Hard to Find." Devoid of conscience and of any sense of remorse, the narrator of "Nebraska" remarks coldly, matter-of-factly, about the string of murders he has committed, "I killed everything in my path." In a briefly dramatized moment of confession with a sheriff before he is executed, he remains unrepentant: "I can't say that I'm sorry for the things that we done / At least for a little while, sir, me and her we had us some fun." Springsteen's imagined monologue draws some of its details from Beaver's book: a noted criminal psychologist who interviewed the real-life Starkweather remarked that to an abnormal degree he showed "no sign of true remorse" for his murders.

Moreover, the listener familiar with O'Connor's story might recognize here the concluding words of The Misfit's accomplice, Bobby Lee, who after senselessly shooting a holidaying family remarks, "Some fun!"—to which The Misfit, in the last line of the story, replies tellingly, "It's no real pleasure in life."

Like O'Connor's The Misfit, Springsteen's killer is a man who feels "unfit" for human society. A jury has found him guilty, and he is sentenced to death. And like O'Connor's character, he appears to be remarkably unaware of the nature of his transgressions. The Misfit remarks to the grandmother of the family that he cannot even remember the offense that sent him to prison: "I set there and set there, trying to remember what it was I done and I ain't recalled it to this day." Failing to find any meaningful reason for being or believing, he states his credo with a snarl: "No pleasure but meanness." Springsteen's Starkweather character likewise remarks about his impulse to murder, "They wanted to know why I did what I did / Well, sir, I guess there's just a meanness in this world."

A key word from O'Connor's story, *meanness* here comes to denote for Springsteen—as well as for O'Connor's The Misfit—a response to a world that has lost meaning. O'Connor's understanding of the source of this *meanness* appears to have influenced Springsteen's own exploration of this theme in his music, as he tells Will Percy:

> There was something in those stories of hers that I felt captured a certain part of the American character that I was interested in writing about. They were a big, big revelation. She got to the heart of some part of meanness that she never spelled out, because if she spelled it out you wouldn't be getting it. It was always at the core of every one of her stories—the way she left that hole there, that hole that's inside of everybody. There was some dark thing—a component of spirituality—that I sensed in her stories, and that set me off exploring characters of my own.

A meanness born out of a sense of meaninglessness informs the haunting sixth song on *Nebraska*, "State Trooper," whose narrator, driving late at night along a New Jersey turnpike, appears to have committed some heinous deed or is about to do so. In the song's refrain, he pleads with an invisible state trooper:

> License, registration, I ain't got none
> But I got a clear conscience 'bout the things that I done
> Mister state trooper, please don't stop me

In this arguably most menacing song on the album, Springsteen appears to quote O'Connor directly: the narrator's imagined reply, "I ain't got none" to a request to see his license and registration from a yet-to-be encountered state trooper, echoes Hazel Motes's remark to the patrolman in chapter 13 of *Wise Blood* after cold-bloodedly running over Solace Layfield, the preacher who has been mimicking him. Asked "Where's your license?" Haze eventually responds, "Well I ain't got one." Springsteen's character too is on a desperate drive, his mind, to quote a telling adjective in the song's third stanza, getting "hazy" while he tries to make sense of the many voices coming at him as he twists the dial of the car radio through the early morning "talk show stations." The song concludes with this lone-ranging narrator's desperate last prayer, "Hi ho silver-o deliver me from nowhere." Here again an image of Hazel Motes is perhaps invoked: "Was you going anywheres?" O'Connor's patrolman asks an anxious Haze, after his car is pushed over an embankment. "No," Haze replies.

To say that Springsteen's characters are consciously Christ-haunted, like so many in O'Connor's fiction, is perhaps to attribute too much spiritual self-consciousness to Springsteen's own cast of misfits. The *Nebraska* characters appear unrelentingly caught in deep existential crises, facing the stark awareness that their lives are devoid of meaning, and desperate, as is the narrator of "State Trooper," to be delivered "from nowhere." In his prefatory notes to the *Nebraska* lyrics in the revised and updated *Bruce Springsteen: Songs* (2003), Springsteen reflects on the ideas and sensibilities behind his songwriting at the time: "If there's a theme that runs through the record, it's the thin line between stability and that moment when time stops and everything goes to black, when the things that connect you to your world—your job, your family, friends, your faith, the love and grace in your heart—fail you." In a finishing comment that seems informed by one of O'Connor's central images, Springsteen declares, "I wanted the *blood* on [the recording] to feel destined and fateful" (emphasis added).

Whereas several songs on *The River* and *Born in the USA* present characters who look for deliverance from their sense of isolation and despair by jumping into a fast car or the arms of a lover, Springsteen angles in the closing song of *Nebraska* at another possible resolution to a search for meaning. Perhaps invoking one of the inspirations for the song, Dave Marsh comments that the images in "Reason to Believe" "are as bizarre as anything in *Wise Blood*." Marsh reads this and the rest of the songs on the album as offering revelations of utmost despair, as Springsteen staring "straight into the void" of human meaning and purpose and finding "nothing at all." This is surely a fundamental misreading of the album's arcing themes. Rather, this final song seeks to resolve the litanies of meanness, desperation, hopelessness, and longing recounted in the preceding stories, and to resolve them in a decidedly Catholic fashion.

Each verse of "Reason to Believe" presents a scene of expectation. And the expected event or action has a theological, even eschatological turn. The third verse presents O'Connoresque images of a child baptized in a river and an old man dying in a derelict building:

> Take a baby to the river, Kyle William they called him
> Wash the baby in the water, take away little Kyle's sin
> In a whitewash shotgun shack an old man passes away
> Take the body to the graveyard and over him they pray

From our first days to our last—and all of life in between—the narrator of this song asks, "Lord won't you tell us, tell us what does it mean / At the end of every hard-earned day people find some reason to believe."

In the first verse, the narrator regards a man poking a dead dog lying in a ditch, seemingly expectant that it will come back to life. The abandoned woman in verse two waits at the end of a dirt road for her prodigal lover, young Johnny, "to come back." Christian mysteries of sin, baptism, and the life ever after are all invoked in the third verse. The song concludes with an image of a groom standing waiting for his bride, even after all the congregation is gone—inversely suggesting the classic image in Christian eschatology for the expectation of Christ's ultimate union with *his* bride, the Church. Tellingly, Springsteen at one point considered titling the album *Reason to Believe*, which would certainly have put a more hopeful gloss on the collected songs. However, Warren Zanes records Springsteen's remark that a "hopeful" reading of "Reason to Believe" is "a common misinterpretation" of what he considers "one of the darkest songs on the record." Nonetheless, to invoke the final phrase in O'Connor's *Wise Blood*, there are "pin point[s] of light" in these songs that point to Springsteen's own sustaining reasons to believe.

It's Hard to Be a Saint in the City: Springsteen's Catholicism

As a storyteller, Springsteen shares with O'Connor a vision informed by a Catholic faith and upbringing. While this faith is not specifically foregrounded in his songs, his way of seeing, like O'Connor's, is nonetheless filtered through the lens of Catholic doctrine and belief. As Jim Cullen observes in *Born in the U.S.A.: Bruce Springsteen and the American Tradition* (2005 edition), "At the core of Springsteen's Catholicism is an 'analogical imagination' . . . a distinctively Catholic way of understanding the world." Cullen remarks that Springsteen's Catholicism is "never far from the surface" of his songs, and though he is certainly "no one's idea of a saint," no other contemporary popular American songwriter has a corpus so grounded in a religious sensibility or so pervaded with the language of the Christian faith. Close examination of his collected lyrics confirms that the Springsteen lexicon is replete with a host of religious terms: *sin, grace, hope, mercy, atonement, salvation, heaven, hell, holy, God, Jesus, angels,* and, most prevalently, *faith* and *prayer*. He sings about religious realities of temptation, sin, guilt, forgiveness, mystery, baptism, new birth, and the struggle of belief. A consciousness of wrongdoing and redemption, of the intrusion of divine mercy and grace, a holding on to and holding out for faith—these themes are found in Springsteen's music from his early "It's Hard to Be a Saint in the City" (1973) to the gospel anthems on *The Rising* (2002), his artistic response to 9/11, and the more explicit expressions of his Catholic faith on *Devils & Dust* (2005) and *Wrecking Ball* (2012). As George Yamin demonstrates persuasively in his essay "The Theology of Bruce Springsteen," Springsteen's "message . . . is primarily a theological one"; his song narratives are often concerned with recasting, and to some extent reinterpreting, "the Judeo-Christian story of salvation history."

One of the first commentators to note the Catholic overtones in Springsteen's songs, particularly in reference to his 1987 album *Tunnel of Love*, is the Catholic novelist and sociologist Father Andrew Greeley. In a review article in *America* in February 1988, "The Catholic Imagination of Bruce Springsteen," Greeley refers to Springsteen as "a Catholic Meistersinger" and maintains that because he was raised a Catholic and attended Catholic school, Springsteen's "work is profoundly Catholic . . . because his creative imagination is permeated by Catholic symbolism he absorbed, almost necessarily, from the Sacraments." Greeley explores the Catholic sacramentalism that informs the album's title song, "Tunnel of Love," and other songs including "Two Faces," "Spare Parts," and the concluding track "Valentine's Day." For Greeley, Springsteen's symbolic use of images of rebirth and renewal charges his songs with a Catholic piety through which, to invoke a line from the closing song, "God's light [comes] shinin' on through." Without his necessarily being aware of it, Springsteen is a kind of "liturgist" for the Catholic faith, Greeley argues, and concludes that "without a Catholic perspective" one would have great difficulty understanding these songs.

O'Connor makes similar remarks about her own Catholic imagination in a letter to John Lynch: "I write the way I do because and only because I am a Catholic. I feel that if I were not a Catholic, I would have no reason to write, no reason to see, no reason ever to feel horrified or even to enjoy anything."

She ends definitively, "I have been formed by the Church." Springsteen appears to echo O'Connor's assertions and to confirm Greeley's view in his comments made to the *New York Times* following the 2005 release of *Devils & Dust*. Asked to account for the prevalent "Christian imagery and concepts" in this collection of songs, Springsteen wryly replies with a trinity of reasons: "Catholic school, Catholic school, Catholic school." Springsteen, then in his late fifties, acknowledges that his Catholic upbringing and faith was something that he "pushed off for a long time," but adds that he has been "thinking about it a lot lately." He observes, "I realized as time passed that my music is filled with Catholic imagery. It's not a negative thing. There was a powerful world of potent imagery that became alive and vital and vibrant, and was both very frightening and held out the promises of ecstasies and paradise. There was this incredible internal landscape that [the Catholic faith] created in you. As I got older, I got a lot less defensive about it." As *New York Times* writer Jon Pareles notes, "Thoughts of redemption, moral choices and invocations of God have been part of Springsteen's songs throughout his career, but they have grown stronger and more explicitly Christian on his 21st-century albums." Songs on *The Rising* (2002), *Devils & Dust* (2005), and *Wrecking Ball* (2012) well exemplify Pareles's claim. In a 2020 interview with producer Rick Rubin and author/podcaster Malcolm Gladwell, Springsteen acknowledges, "I basically consider myself a spiritual songwriter."

Springsteen's spirituality also sparked the interest of Catholic novelist and cultural critic Walker Percy, who, after reading Greeley's article in *America*, wrote "a fan letter—of sorts" to Springsteen in February 1989, expressing his admiration for his songwriting and commending him as "one of the few sane guys" in the rock music business. Having learned through Greeley's article that Springsteen is a fellow Catholic, Percy writes to inquire further about Springsteen's "spiritual journey." As Catholics, he writes, the two of them "are rarities in our professions: you as a post-modern musician, I as a writer, a novelist, and philosopher," and he remarks on Springsteen's reported admiration for Flannery O'Connor, whom Percy calls "a dear friend of mine, though . . . a much more heroic Catholic than I." Percy notes that he is suffering from cancer and taking radiation treatments and is quite ill. He succumbed to cancer in May 1990 before Springsteen found occasion to reply. But his unanswered letter eventually led to the interview with Percy's nephew Will, in which Springsteen talks candidly about his spirituality and particularly about O'Connor's influence on his artistic sensibilities. At Will Percy's urging, Springsteen eventually wrote a reply—eight years later—to Walker Percy's widow. In that four-page handwritten letter, reproduced in part in *DoubleTake*, Springsteen offers a response to Walker Percy's inquiry: "The loss and search for faith and meaning have been at the core of my own work for most of my adult life. . . . Those issues are still what motivate me to sit down, pick up my guitar and write."

As a songwriter raised a Catholic, Springsteen shares with O'Connor a set of theological assumptions about human nature, about what O'Connor refers to in one of her essays as "the general mystery of incompleteness," by which she means humankind's separation from God. Springsteen's lyrics are often infused with biblical language and allusions and usually subtle but occasionally explicit expressions of Christian doctrine. He is not afraid to use the word *sin*, for example, a word that appears nearly a dozen times in his lyrics, and most frequently denotes the theological notion of *original sin* rather than the decidedly venial sins many of his characters are given to. Significantly, the word is often used in concert with the act of, or reference to, baptism. Baby Kyle William is baptized in a river in *Nebraska*'s closing song "Reason to Believe" in order to "take away little Kyle's sin." The doctrine of original sin is the explicit subject of the biblically grounded "Adam Raised a Cain" from *Darkness on the Edge of Town*, which begins with a scene of a young boy's baptism as his father looks on, and repeats the Church's doctrine: "You're born into this life paying / For the sins of somebody else's past . . . You inherit the sins, you inherit the flames." In "My Father's House," a song with biographical as well as anagogical overtones that precedes "Reason to Believe," the narrator laments the "unatoned" sins that have separated a father and son. Springsteen's compelling song stories recall O'Connor's credo that "Where there is no belief in the soul, there is very little drama" and her complementary assertion that the best stories are based "on the bedrock of original sin, *whether the writer thinks in theological terms or not*" (emphasis added).

One of the most Catholic themes in Springsteen's songs is that for every wrongdoing there is a price to pay. In a number of early songs, the central character is an unmarried teenage mother or a couple forced to wed as the result of a teenage pregnancy. In one of Springsteen's most poignant song narratives, "The River," the young male narrator atones for getting his high school sweetheart pregnant by enduring an unhappy marriage and a dream-wrenched life. A companion song on the record, significantly titled "The Price You Pay," fuses an allusion to Moses denied entrance to the Promised Land with an aimless "little girl" holding a "pretty little baby in [her] hands"—a single mother facing the prospect of a life of denials. While the sins of the flesh exact their due from Springsteen's characters, some mode of redemption is often held out or realized. The abandoned young mother in "Spare Parts," for example, despairing of her lot, takes her infant son to the river seemingly intending to drown him. As she stands in the water, she is transformed, her love confirmed in what is in effect a baptism of both child and mother—most certainly an indelible O'Connoresque scene:

> Mist was on the water, low run the tide
> Janey held her son down at the river side
> Waist deep in the water, how bright the sun shone
> She lifted him in her arms and carried him home

The mystery of grace enacted through the sacrament of baptism is perhaps the most explicitly Catholic element in Springsteen's songs. However, as in O'Connor's fiction, specific elements of Catholic culture and practice rarely surface in Springsteen's lyrics. Though in his early songs "Lost in the Flood" and "If I Was the Priest" (only recently released on *Letter to You* [2020]) he makes disparaging references to nuns and priests and the Virgin Mary, there are scant if any direct references to expressly Catholic elements of the Christian faith in Springsteen's song narratives. His subject, like that of O'Connor, is the individual soul lost in the badlands of fallen human nature, whose capacity for grace and need of redemption transcend the particulars of creed and denomination.

O'Connor once remarked, "For the fiction writer, to believe nothing is to see nothing" adding that her beliefs are what give her work "its chief characteristics." While Springsteen does not share O'Connor's morality nor, to the same extent, her Christian commitment, his artistic vision and spiritual perception have been inescapably shaped by his Catholic upbringing and beliefs. Like O'Connor in her fiction, Springsteen writes the kinds of songs he does because he is a Catholic. In an often-cited letter to Betty Hester early in her writing career, O'Connor discusses the informing power of her Catholic faith on her artistic vision and work: "I won't ever be able entirely to understand my own work or even my own motivations. It is first of all a gift, but the direction it has taken has been because of the Church in me or the effect of the Church's teaching, not because of a personal perception or love of God . . . I am not a mystic and I do not lead a holy life." Her words could as truthfully be Springsteen's.

Telling Violent Stories Quietly

Along with a Catholic faith that informs his artistic vision, Springsteen shares with O'Connor a thematic of violence as symptomatic of, and agent of revelation in, a world where everything has become increasingly off balance. He remarks in the *DoubleTake* interview that his songs "tell violent stories very quietly." This is especially so in his trio of folk-inflected recordings: *Nebraska*, *The Ghost of Tom Joad*, and *Devils & Dust*. These albums form a distinctive subset within Springsteen's corpus, and, it might be argued, present his most authentic voice and vision as a songwriter. Like O'Connor's The Misfit, Springsteen's violent characters act out of a meanness born of meaninglessness. They have lost hope and deny any possibility of transcendence—of their individual, social, or existential condition. In their quietly violent stories, he and O'Connor reflect a common understanding of evil as it is played out in the lives of individuals who are driven to the extremes of their own natures, and ultimately to acts of violence.

For O'Connor, violence is usually a means of alerting or converting her characters to the big-R Reality of her Christian worldview. In reflections on the art of story writing collected as "On Her Own Work" in *Mystery and Manners*, she remarks, "I have found that violence is strangely capable of returning my characters to reality and preparing them to accept their moment of grace." Similarly, Springsteen remarks in the *DoubleTake* interview that the violent circumstances and impulses of his characters allow for a degree of intimacy and insight that "[takes] you inside yourself and then back out into the world." As with O'Connor's stories, the quiet strain of violence in Springsteen's songs probes at the reality of the evils, of the "devils" (his word) that manifest themselves in desperate human hearts and in the territory of contemporary America.

Set against the economic recession in America in the early 1980s, the *Nebraska* songs to some degree acknowledge that dire socioeconomic realities underlie the impulse toward violence. Both the speakers of "Atlantic City" and "Johnny 99" are out of work and remark similarly, "I got debts that no honest man can / could pay." The unnamed narrator of "Atlantic City," who appears to have agreed to a contract as a hired killer, explains, "I been lookin' for a job but it's hard to find." In his concluding remark, he tells his lover and would-be accomplice, "I'm tired of comin' out on the losin' end / So honey last night I met this guy and I'm gonna do a little favor for him." Similarly, in "Johnny 99" Springsteen's character Ralph is jobless after an auto plant closure and unable to find work. Despairingly, he gets raging drunk one evening and, for some unstated reason, shoots a hotel night clerk. In his statement before the judge, he initially defends himself as a desperate man, deeply in debt: "The bank was holding my mortgage and they was takin' my house away." But, he confesses, "It was more 'n all this that put that gun in my hand."

Springsteen's probing of the heart of darkness in modern American society is concerned with that "more" that motivates violent deeds. Like O'Connor, he presents the impulse to do evil—in signature acts of violence—as something more than simply a socialized behavior or, in O'Connor's words, "this or that psychological tendency." As Jim Cullen observes, Springsteen's *Nebraska* songs are largely concerned with "the problem—the nature—of evil. . . . Springsteen posits evil as a force that defies demographic specificity or rational explanation." Indeed, in Springsteen's song stories, a character's impulse to do evil is often a mystery to him. An unmotivated urge scratches at his consciousness, and he tries in some way to explain his dark desires. (Springsteen's violent characters are always male. Not so for O'Connor: her violent female characters include nine-year-old Mary Fortune Pitts in "A View of the Woods," who kills her grandfather with her fists; the troubled Wellesley girl in "Revelation," who throws a book at good-natured Ruby Turpin and then tries to strangle her; and O. E. Parker's broom-wielding wife, Sarah Ruth, seen thrashing him across the back in the closing sentences of "Parker's Back.") In the *Nebraska* songs, Springsteen explores the mystery of evil as incarnated in characters driven to violence. Like a fiction writer, he is intent in these songs on drawing the listener into his characters' hearts and minds: "I wanted to let the listener hear the characters think," he remarks in notes to his published song lyrics, "to get inside their heads, so you could hear and feel their thoughts, their choices."

In *The Ghost of Tom Joad* (1995), recorded more than ten years after *Nebraska*, Springsteen picks up his exploration of the mystery of "meanness" in the human heart. This second collection of folk songs offers, like *Nebraska*, a set of character studies of individuals whose lives are marked by violent incidents and impulses. Here, as storyteller, Springsteen again lets his violence-driven characters speak for themselves, his own voice "disappear[ing] into the voices of those [he's] chosen to write about." The ex-prisoner Charlie in "Straight Time" has found a job at a meat-packing plant and has been walking the "clean and narrow" for eight years. Though he appears to be settled, has married a Mary, and tells us that he spends his evenings playing with his kids on the kitchen floor, "tossin' my little babies high," Charlie still can "feel the itch" to do some wrongful deed, and observes,

> Seems you can't get any more than half free
> I step out onto the front porch and suck the cold air deep inside of me
> Got a cold mind to go tripping 'cross that thin line
> I'm sick of doin' straight time.

Charlie is making a life and has an outward appearance of stability but reflects that he is only "half free" of his criminal impulses. In the refrain he warns the listener that he is tired of going "straight" and is preparing to pull off another job. The song's last stanza offers a vignette of Charlie in his basement, sawing off the barrel of a gun, and later returning after apparently committing a violent crime. He is stained with the sin of his deed: "Can't get the smell from my hands," he says as he contemplates a fugitive future.

"Straight Time" is followed on *Tom Joad* by the more graphically violent "Highway 29," both songs exemplifying Springsteen's claim to "tell violent stories very quietly." Here is another story of the mystery of evil in the human heart: how a shoe-store clerk turns into a violent bank robber after a night of illicit sex with a seductive customer. "Highway 29" is a simple ballad with a seesaw melody, played gently on an acoustic guitar as a song of lament. The action and emotion in the lyrics are undercut by Springsteen's subdued matter-of-fact delivery of the song. His narrator muses nonchalantly on his violent crime: a bank robbery in a small town that goes horribly wrong and results in gunshots and a bloody "mess" before the couple make their getaway. As his story continues, the narrator probes his inner compulsions, leading to a kind of existential reflection:

> I told myself it was something in her
> But as we drove I knew it was something in me
> Something that'd been comin' for a long, long time
> And something that was here with me now
> On Highway 29.

That repeated and inexplicable "something" in Springsteen's unnamed character is an impulse to do evil. This same impulse, a murderous meanness, is in O'Connor's The Misfit a response to a life that is "off balance" because it lacks the stabilizing hope of salvation from sin, offered by faith in the Christ of the Christian gospel. Springsteen's characters, though, do not appear to come to an awareness of their need for grace, as most of O'Connor's tormented characters eventually do, however imperceptibly and usually forcibly. Like young Tarwater after transgressing against his great-uncle's wishes for burial, O. E. Parker after his epiphany with the tattooed carnival artiste, or Mr. Shiftlet as he abandons the "angel of Gawd" and speeds ahead of a thundercloud on his way to Mobile, Springsteen's characters choose to escape after the violent shock that has altered their consciousness. Charlie ("Straight Time") imagines "driftin' off into foreign lands," and the fugitive pair in "Highway 29" try to outrun the law by fleeing to the Sierra Madres in Mexico.

The litany of violence reported and implied in Springsteen's songs matches the variety of destructive acts in O'Connor's stories, where, along with the cold-blooded murder of a grandmother and family of five on the way to Florida, her characters meet with brutal ends inventive enough to satisfy Quentin Tarantino. The violence in O'Connor's fiction is less quiet at times than that in Springsteen's songs—she describes violent acts; Springsteen's narrators mostly report them—but both writers intend the violence in their work to be disquieting to similar ends.

For Springsteen, like O'Connor, violence is not an end in itself but a means toward some form of revelation: about the depth of meanness the human spirit is capable of, about the desperate conditions of individuals who, to quote Springsteen, feel "alienated from their friends and their community and their government and their jobs," and ultimately from a sense of their own purpose. In a *Rolling Stone* interview shortly after the release of *Nebraska*, Springsteen remarks on his characters as emblematic of a kind of malaise in America: "I think you can get to a point where nihilism, if that's the right word, is overwhelming, and the basic laws that society has set up—either religious or social laws—become meaningless. Things become really dark. You lose those constraints, and then anything goes."

While violence in O'Connor's fiction is often seen as an agent of grace, as in the embrace of the bull-God that pierces the heart of Mrs. May in her story "Greenleaf," O'Connor is interested as well in the violence that results when the human heart is stripped of the forces that hold it in check. She remarks, "With the serious writer, violence is never an end in itself," and adds, "It is the extreme situation that best reveals what we are essentially." Like many of Springsteen's characters, a number in O'Connor's fiction react violently or meet with some form of violence within a world that has lost constraints, has lost its moral or ontological center. As Springsteen does in songs such as "Nebraska," "Johnny 99," and "Straight Time," O'Connor explores the descent into murderous "meanness" of characters who have rejected both the social and spiritual ties that bind them to living uprightly. Thomas, the egocentric and sexually repressed scholar in "The Comforts of Home," is perhaps her most outstanding example of the common man turned cold-blooded killer—a theme that fascinates Springsteen and that O'Connor plies to her own revelatory purposes.

Thomas is presented as a kind of case study of the bedevilment of a human heart—a *good man* eventually compelled to commit murder. O'Connor's near-clinical interest in his descent into the diabolical may account in part for the story's unfavorable reception among her critics and her own early disappointment with it. In *Flannery O'Connor: The Imagination of Extremity* (1982), O'Connor critic Rick Asals comments, "The plot of 'The Comforts of Home' is surely one of the least convincing O'Connor ever devised"; he finds the story "preposterous . . . implausible" and "only sporadically believable." This is harsh criticism indeed. Before the story was first published in the *Kenyon Review*, O'Connor herself confided in a letter to fellow writer Cecil Dawkins that she was worried about the ending, and after it appeared in print, wrote to novelist John Hawkes that she was "dissatisfied with" the story. Perhaps her dissatisfaction was related to the seemingly unredemptive act of violence at its conclusion.

Embarrassed by his do-gooder mother and affronted by the wayward girl she has brought into his home, Thomas responds with rage, casting aside any occasion for acting charitably, toward either the girl or his mother. He has intellectually rejected the notion that love is a transforming force, that it is grounded in "mystery" and the "mysterious"—words that jointly appear three times in the story—and refuses to accept that it might flow through "invisible currents entirely out of his control." Thomas must contain the world within his limited powers of analysis. Star Drake's nymphomania, he believes, is evidence that she is a "moral moron . . . Born without the moral faculty—like somebody else would be born without a kidney or a leg." She is beyond redemption in his eyes, her essence "the very stuff of corruption" yet paradoxically "the most unendurable form of innocence" he has encountered.

In his loathing for the girl who has disturbed his comfortable existence and unbalanced his emotional and social well-being, Thomas steps outside of common human moral constraints. He finds himself remarking at one point, "If she shoots herself, so much the better!" Thomas chooses the manners of meanness over abiding in the redemptive possibilities of mystery, rejecting the love enacted in and through his sibyl-like mother. Unconstrained by love, he is instead willing to be "guided by" the lies of his father—an unseen yet active presence: the father of lies. As he pulls the trigger on a handgun he has planted in Star Drake's purse, aiming to "bring an end to evil in the world," Thomas is cast into a fire of his own making, his own animating evil impulses revealing what he essentially is—no better than the girl, and, in fact, far worse. In an anagogical reading of this story, he murders love incarnate, whomever the bullet kills.

Thomas's entry into a world of violence and regret is signaled in a telling sentence-long paragraph in the story's final lines. Confronted by the fierce but "intimate grin" of Star Drake, who mocks him accusingly, "Thomas damned not only the girl but the entire order of the universe that made her possible." In this moment, he crosses what Springsteen calls "that thin line"—a nexus of the spirit where "you lose . . . constraints, and then anything goes." Both O'Connor and Springsteen are interested in characters who operate at the edge of such darkness.

It is worth noting that O'Connor's most famous story is also her most shockingly violent. Arguably, the violence in "A Good Man Is Hard to Find" is best understood as more symptomatic of The Misfit's despair and evil-heartedness than it is a dramatic vehicle for the grandmother's "moment of grace," O'Connor's comments on her story notwithstanding (*Mystery and Manners*, 108–14). Her only gun-toting central character, The Misfit is a man facing a sense of the unjustness and meaninglessness of his life. He is caught in an extreme existential crisis. His wanton killing of Bailey's family, and his other brutal acts, are his response to a world in which he perceives that "everything [is] off balance." With no reason to believe in the reality of the Christian story of redemption, or anything else that would give his life purpose, like so many of Springsteen's desperate-hearted characters, The Misfit has lost all constraint. His violence is motivated by the pure desire to vent his emptiness and despair by killing somebody "or doing some other meanness to him." The Misfit remarks famously, with a snarl, "No pleasure but meanness." He and his accomplices mercilessly murder a family of six with no other motive than possibly to steal their car.

Though we might want to believe that The Misfit's encounter with the grandmother of the family has had a transforming effect on him—as O'Connor comments she would "prefer to think"—the old woman's murder appears no more meaningful to him than those of the other family members: "Take her off and throw her where you thrown the others," he instructs his accomplices. As O'Connor would have us observe, the grandmother's reaching out to touch The Misfit, saying, "Why you're one of my babies. You're one of my own children!" is the "real heart" of the story. The perceptive reader may perhaps here apprehend, as O'Connor describes it, "the action of grace in the grandmother's soul." And her transforming moment is what makes the story "work," O'Connor has said. The Misfit cynically observes a flash of goodness in the grandmother, however extremely attenuated: "She would have been a good woman . . . if it had been somebody there to shoot her every minute of her life." Yet, while he is the catalyst for the grandmother's revelation of grace, The Misfit's alliance with evil and its signal acts of violence appears unmitigated, as O'Connor critic Stephen C. Bandy also argues, only now lacking in "pleasure."

In her prefatory remarks to a public reading of "A Good Man Is Hard to Find" (collected as "On Her Own Work" in *Mystery and Manners*), O'Connor declares, "I don't want to equate The Misfit with the devil." Yet she makes it clear that, like Thomas in "The Comforts of Home," The Misfit is animated by a cosmic Evil; his is the "specific personality" through which that evil plays out. He shoots the grandmother after her grace-giving touch because, as O'Connor explains in a letter, "This moment of grace excites the devil to frenzy." In the end, even the enjoyment, the "real pleasure," of his acts of "meanness" now seems denied him. The Misfit's darkness may grow even darker if he responds to every act of human compassion "as if a snake had bitten him."

Springsteen surely pays homage to O'Connor in a song that shares a title with her story. His ballad "A Good Man Is Hard to Find (Pittsburgh)" was recorded four months after the 1982 *Nebraska* album but remained unknown until it appeared on *Tracks* (1998), a collection of previously unreleased songs. Springsteen's ballad tells the story of a love-shorn woman who has lost her soldier husband in the Vietnam War. Though the story's details do not accord with O'Connor's life, the image in the song of a lone woman who "sits by the light of her Christmas tree / With the radio softly on / Thinkin' how a good man is hard to find" is resonant for those familiar with O'Connor's life and aware of the popular radio tune from which she took her story's title. Springsteen directly evokes O'Connor's story and perhaps O'Connor herself in the second verse, "She's gonna have to tell about the meanness in this world / And how a good man is so hard to find." The visionary art of O'Connor and Springsteen bears similar witness to the spiritual torment and violence that mark the lives of those who give themselves over to "meanness."

"I've Got God on My Side"

On the bonus DVD accompanying the *Devils & Dust* CD (2005), Springsteen performs five of the album's tracks: just the singer, his battered black Gibson acoustic, and a harmonica. The camera leads us up an old staircase in an Edwardian-style house to where Springsteen sits on a spindle-back chair in a partially renovated bedroom with baby-blue wainscoting. A Tiffany-style lamp glows on a stand in a far corner. Gilt-framed mirrors of different sizes and empty picture frames hang behind him on a wall stripped of paper. The framing and editing of the images have a deliberately amateurish, homemade feel, enforced by scratchy-lettered titling and credits for the video. The setting is metaphorically apt for the stripped-down versions of the songs he performs:

small-to-large portraits in "Reno," "Long Time Coming," and "Matamoros Banks"; mirrored moments of emotion and experience in "All I'm Thinkin' About" and the tone-setting title song, "Devils & Dust." The staging of the songs evokes the circumstances of the making of *Nebraska*: Springsteen in 1982 sitting on a creaking wooden chair in the bedroom of his rented house in Colt's Neck, New Jersey, with a four-track TEAC Tascam 144 cassette tape deck—the forerunner of home-recording studio hardware—recording haunting folk-style guitar and harmonica tunes for a demo that later proved resistant to a full band sound and resulted in his first album of acoustic folk songs.

Devils & Dust represents both a return and a departure for Springsteen. Following on his response to 9/11 in the highly successful *The Rising* (2002), which led to a reuniting of the E Street Band and a slew of typically energetic and emotion-filled stadium concerts, Springsteen returns to his Guthrie-style folk ballads: straightforward storytelling with a guitar and some minor accompaniment in the mix. Songs on this collection present a cast of diverse characters, sons and mothers and separated lovers who recount their stories of loss and longing and hoped-for reunion. Many of the album's songs were written and recorded in 1995 while Springsteen was composing material for *The Ghost of Tom Joad*.

Devils & Dust departs from Springsteen's earlier work in the degree to which the songs reflect a Catholic spirituality. Springsteen's Catholic upbringing, including the abuses he suffered in parochial school, has been the subject of some of the stories he tells from the stage, and is described at length in Marsh's biography, *Glory Days* (1987), and in Springsteen's autobiography, *Born to Run* (2016). Increasingly his songs have become more grounded on that "internal landscape" formed by his youthful religious indoctrination. Redemptive acts and expectations resound in the *Devils & Dust* songs. "I like to write about people whose souls are in danger, who are at risk," Springsteen tells a *New York Times* writer, a theme that resonates in O'Connor's short fiction.

In its opening track, *Devils & Dust* begins, metaphorically, and perhaps literally, in the desert. The narrator of the title song—who "could be a soldier in Iraq or America itself," according to one commentator—sings convincingly, evoking Bob Dylan's ironic folk anthem, "We've got God on our side / We're just trying to survive," but asks, "What if what you do to survive / Kills the things you love?" Sung, to the steady strumming of an acoustic guitar, accompanied by crescendoing strings, the song is a gentle jeremiad: its imagery of fields of "blood and stone" and "mud and bone" with the rising "smell" of death palpably invokes the senseless carnage of war and adds to the implied condemnation of American fearmongering in the song's prophetic and varied refrain:

> Fear's a dangerous thing
> It can turn your heart black you can trust
> It'll take your God-filled soul
> Fill it with devils and dust

The album's prophetic strains find fullest expression in the piano ballad "Jesus Was an Only Son," which focuses on the moment of Christ's passion and his imagined consoling words to his mother Mary: "Mother, still your tears / For remember the soul of the universe / Willed a world and it appeared." Explicating this song to the *VH1 Storytellers* audience, Springsteen, sounding like an evangelical, states that it "starts from a premise that everyone knows what it is like to be saved." Parsing the song's second line—"As he walked up Calvary Hill"—Springsteen can only remark to the audience, "Once you're a Catholic, there's no getting out. That's all there is to it." That Catholicism is more metaphorically expressed in "Maria's Bed," where the narrator, who has "walked the valley of love and tears and mystery" and has given himself "up for dead," finds life-giving "cool clear waters" and indeed "sweet salvation" in Maria's bed. (Springsteen's female characters are often, and perhaps figuratively, named Mary or Maria.) "Leah" expresses a similar spiritual longing, its third and final verse confessional:

> I got somethin' in my heart, I been waitin' to give
> I got a life I wanna start, one I been waitin' to live
> No more waitin', tonight I feel the light I say the prayer
> I open the door, I climb the stairs . . .

Lantern in hand, the narrator has been walking a road "filled with shadow and doubt," looking for "proof" of "a world where love's the only sound." The song's title and images invoke the biblical story of Jacob and his long-suffering love and the famous Holman Hunt painting of Christ, holding a lantern and knocking at a door. The personal nature of this song is overlaid by the artwork on the lyrics sheet that accompanies the CD, showing a monochromatic picture of Springsteen half visible through a half-open door, his right eye looking directly at the viewer or a visitor.

Fittingly, this most Catholic collection of Springsteen's songs ends with the eschatological overtones of "Matamoros Banks," a song that figuratively describes a soul's thwarted journey across a river to the Promised Land, and literally, recounts, backward, the journey from death to life of a Mexican man drowned attempting to swim the Rio Grande from Matamoros to Brownsville,

Texas. As the song opens, we see his body "rise to the light without a sound." We follow his journey back as his corpse is carried on the current for two days. The water strips him of his earthly identity, of his clothes, disfiguring the flesh of his face, as Springsteen gently sings, "'Till every trace of who you ever were is gone / And the things of the earth they make their claim / That the things of heaven may do the same." A song that fuses themes of both spiritual and earthly reunion, "Matamoros Banks" is voiced in quiet liturgical tones, its longing and twice-repeated concluding refrain like an invocation to the listener: "Meet me on the Matamoros / Meet me on the Matamoros / Meet me on the Matamoros banks."

✒ ✒ ✒

"More than anything else, I wanted to be just a good storyteller," Springsteen tells an audience gathered at a Netflix event in May 2019 to promote the film version of *Springsteen on Broadway*, his long-running and, post-pandemic, revamped and reprised one-man show. The narrative-style of songwriting that is evidenced in the *Nebraska* and *The Ghost of Tom Joad* recordings is further emphasized by the unusual typography of two of the songs in the lyrics booklet included with the *Devils & Dust* CD: the sexually explicit story in "Reno" appears as a single typed prose paragraph; "Black Cowboys," a story of a boy's escape from a progressively dysfunctional mother and her drug-dealing boyfriend, is sung in largely rhyming couplets but typeset in six short paragraphs—a form that has not appeared on a Springsteen lyrics sheet before. Form follows function, for this is largely a collection of stories and character studies, influenced, as ever, by what he learned through reading Flannery O'Connor's fiction. This style of songwriting Springsteen confessedly prefers over the energetic pop anthems that have built his reputation and fortune. Indeed, the Boss appears to want to transcend the ranks of a mere singer-songwriter: in a number of interviews, he has referred to his corpus of songs as "my ongoing novel." The official video for Springsteen's 2020 single "Letter to You," shot in his home recording studio just before the COVID-19 pandemic, features in quick cuts as many images showing acts of writing as it does shots of Springsteen and aging E Street Band members playing instruments; it ends with an image of Springsteen's hand putting pen to paper.

Bruce Springsteen is a writer whose songs seek both to reflect and to remediate the social and spiritual malaise of America. His Catholic faith, however faltering, informs his artistic vision. Like O'Connor, as a storyteller he regards the craft of songwriting as "an incarnational art." His songs are largely peopled with desperate-hearted characters on hopeful journeys to a promised land of reunion and renewal, longing for and occasionally finding their "beautiful reward"—or with restless misfits who sever the ties that bind them to lovers, friends, family, communities (and at times to any sustaining grace) and descend into darkness or give themselves over to a mysterious meanness. "The Catholic sacramental view of life is one that sustains and supports at every turn the vision that the storyteller must have if he is going to write fiction of any depth," writes Flannery O'Connor in her essay "The Church and the Fiction Writer." And, it might be added, as Springsteen bears witness to in his works and in his own words, that same sacramental view supports the vision of this storyteller in song.

Chapter 2

LUCINDA WILLIAMS

Chasing Flannery's Peacocks

The late poet Miller Williams tells a story of visiting Flannery O'Connor at Andalusia, the family farm outside of Milledgeville, Georgia, in the company of his preschooler daughter Lucinda. In the fall of 1957, Williams had moved with his family to nearby Macon, where he was barely paying the rent by working as a traveling book rep for Harcourt Brace—a pretext he used for calling on O'Connor, whom he calls in his remembrance, "one of the finest writers in English in our time." He continues the story: "At her invitation, I began to drive over from Macon at least once a month—whenever I was off the road—often taking along my four-year-old daughter Lucinda, who laughed and fell and laughed and fell again as she chased Flannery's peacocks. When I scolded her for it, Flannery told me to let her go: 'She won't catch them unless they want her to.'" Lucinda Williams, now a three-time Grammy Award winner, is in effect still chasing Flannery's peacocks. Her often raw, confessional songs have won her a devoted audience, though only modest commercial success in the more than forty years she has performed as a singer-songwriter—this despite *Rolling Stone* declaring her "America's greatest songwriter" in 1998 and *Time* hailing her "America's best songwriter" in 2001. From her 2001 Grammy Award–winning *folk* song "Get Right with God" to the agonizing refrain of "Unsuffer Me" on her 2007 release *West*, and the lengthy, Pentecostal-like "Faith and Grace" gospel chant that concludes 2016's *The Ghosts of Highway 20*, she charts her own rocky road to righteousness in an admired canon of songs that speak frankly of heartbreak, loss, loneliness, sexual desire, and an achingly lyrical pursuit of a hoped-for "real love."

Born in 1953 in Lake Charles, Louisiana, to a literary father with a taste for the Delta blues and the songs of Hank Williams (no relation), and a mother with aspirations of being a concert pianist, Lucinda grew up in a household filled with poetry and story and eclectic music. A precocious child like the young Flannery O'Connor, she began writing her own poetry and stories at age six. She recalls, "I wrote for fun the way most kids would be out playing ball." Her family moved from Macon to Baton Rouge when she was nine, where her father, though a biologist by training, and without yet having published a volume of verse, was offered a position teaching English at Louisiana State University—largely, Miller Williams says, on the strength of a reference written by his friend Flannery O'Connor. Lucinda started playing guitar and writing songs in 1965 at twelve years old, inspired by listening to Bob Dylan's *Highway 61 Revisited*. She played her songs for her father's poet friends—frequent visitors included James Dickey, John Ciardi, Allen Ginsberg, Howard Nemerov, and Charles Bukowski—who commented on them.

At sixteen, Williams was expelled from her New Orleans high school for her involvement with a group of students arrested after staging a protest against acts of racial injustice by school administrators. She spent the following year in Mexico, under the tutelage of her father, who was there on a Fulbright scholarship. He gave her a list of a hundred great books to read that included works by major American authors, among them Flannery O'Connor's novels and story collections. Williams credits her poet father with infusing her with a sense of the power and pleasure of words and for teaching her how to use words with precision and economy when crafting her song lyrics. She also widely acknowledges her youthful reading of O'Connor as having a shaping influence on her songwriting sensibilities. Reflecting on her formative years and the reading that has lent a rich literary quality to her lyrics, Williams remarks in a 2016 interview in *Rolling Stone*, "I have a certain Southern Gothic sensibility. I related to Flannery O'Connor at a young age. My mother's father was a fire-and-brimstone Methodist preacher. I saw a lot of that kind of thing growing up, and I read about it in O'Connor. Her writing was really dark but also ironic and humorous. It informs a lot of my songs."

Along with an early interest in peacocks, the years growing up in Georgia, and a youthful identification with O'Connor's form of southern gothic, Lucinda Williams connects with O'Connor in a number of other ways in her life and work. Like O'Connor's, Williams's southern identity "lies very deep" in her art. Her songs are thoroughly soaked in an ethos of back-road juke joints, the practices of southern religiosity, and the southern towns and cities she has lived in or escaped to—Lafayette, Baton Rouge, Lake Charles, and Austin—often heartbroken over a lost lover, departed or dead. As one reviewer has noted, Williams's writerly gift for evoking a sense of place and for presenting vivid characters and situations, her cast of "Pentecostal weirdos" . . . "make her just as much Flannery O'Connor as Loretta Lynn in terms of her songwriting." Her brief biography in the *Rolling Stone Encyclopedia of Rock and Roll* notes that she acknowledges O'Connor as "a major influence on her songwriting." She has named *Wise Blood* as her favorite novel and its film adaptation by famed director John Huston as her favorite movie. At the Carolina Theatre in Durham in January 2015, Williams hosted a screening of Huston's *Wise Blood* film and discussed the connections between some of her lyrics and O'Connor's novel. Consistently over the course of her career, in interviews, in blogs on her website, and in her 2023 memoir *Don't Tell Anybody the Secrets I Told You*, Williams has repeatedly attested to O'Connor's shaping and abiding influence.

Like Bruce Springsteen in his 1999 *DoubleTake* interview, Williams too has publicly acknowledged specific ways in which her artistic vision and songwriting art have been influenced by reading O'Connor. In a 2014 interview-memoir for the literary music magazine *Radio Silence*, she talks about her father's friendship with O'Connor and of accompanying him on his regular visits to Flannery's family farm. (An excerpt from this interview is included in a critical casebook on O'Connor in the Pearson anthology, *Literature: An Introduction to Fiction, Poetry, Drama, and Writing*, edited by X. J. Kennedy and Dana Gioia.) Here is how she understands O'Connor's writing as influencing her own:

> When I was about fifteen and sixteen, I discovered her writing and read everything I could get my hands on, which wasn't that much. But I read everything, and I also devoured Eudora Welty's stuff. But for me, Flannery O'Connor was to writing what Robert Johnson was to the blues. That might be the best way to say it. There was something about her stuff that was just a little more crooked, a little more weird, a little more out there.

Later in the interview, Williams acknowledges O'Connor's influence on particular songs and relates the way her own life experience resonates with O'Connor's character Hazel Motes: "My song 'Get Right with God' and my song 'Atonement,' I got a lot from her novel *Wise Blood*. I was sleeping on a bed of nails," she explains.

A sense of knowing what she wants as an artist enabled Williams to walk out on her first record deal with a major label, RCA, when she was forty and so broke she could barely keep herself fed. It drove her to spend six years making her first commercially successful album, rolling through three sets of producers and countless rerecordings of her songs for her 1998 breakthrough release, *Car Wheels on a Gravel Road*. The result was a Grammy and a reputation for being difficult to work with. Similarly, O'Connor, at twenty-three and looking to publish her first novel, stood up against her first editor, John Selby at Rinehart, insisting that *Wise Blood*'s unconventional form and peculiar content were its chief virtues. She responded adamantly to Selby in a letter, "I am amenable to criticism, but only within the sphere of what I am trying to do. I will not be persuaded to do otherwise." For this she was accused of being "stiff-necked, uncooperative, and unethical" and "prematurely arrogant." Williams had a more colorful response to a noted musician who was interested in recording one of the songs from her self-titled 1988 album but first requested that she change the lyrics and add a chorus. Though at the time she was singing on street corners and in bars and desperately needed the royalties, Williams recalls, "my response was, basically, you can kiss my Dixie white ass."

Eight years passed between the release in 1980 of Williams's debut album of original songs, *Happy Woman Blues*, and her self-titled album, another four years before *Sweet Old World* appeared in 1992, and a further six years before *Car Wheels on a Gravel Road*. She has had a run of recordings in the twenty-first century, with nine studio albums released since 2001's *Essence*. Her highly praised *The Ghosts of Highway 20* was released in December 2016, and the Trump-era angry rock songs on *Good Souls, Better Angels* came out in 2020. Following a severely debilitating stroke in November 2020, Williams regained her form as a songwriter and performer and released her fifteenth studio album in the summer of 2023, *Stories from a Rock n Roll Heart*, with Bruce Springsteen and Patti Scialfa on backing vocals for the album's lead single, "New York Comeback." Known for working slowly, and for "legendary perfectionism" in the recording studio, Williams over a more than forty-year career has released her songs at about the same rate that O'Connor wrote stories—about two songs per year since she began writing and recording her own compositions.

Williams's musical genre is hard to define. A genius as a songwriter, according to such musical luminaries as Emmylou Harris and Steve Earle, Williams has developed her own sound, her own form—a "music gumbo," one critic calls it. But in a music industry all about labels, her hybridity has been a liability. For executives at Columbia Records, Williams was too much blues and rock for country, too much country for mainstream rock, and a folksinger only by a stretch. The interspaces of her style largely explain her lack of commercial success, however admired and remarkable her songwriting gifts. Her three Grammy awards are illustrative: 1993 Best Country Song for "Passionate Kisses" as recorded by Mary Chapin Carpenter; 1998 Best Contemporary Folk Album for *Car Wheels on a Gravel Road*; and somewhat ironically, a Grammy for Best Female Rock Performance on what might best be described as a rockabilly gospel song, "Get Right with God," from her 2001 release *Essence*. She is, according to one reviewer, "in a class of her own . . . beholden to blues, folk, country, and rock without swearing full allegiance to any of them." One description of her musical genre reads like something that would appear on the back label of a wine bottle: "bright, contemporary roots rock sound with strong country and blues flavors."

Get Right with God

Themes of violence, child abuse, sexual obsession and exploitation, alcoholic dereliction, and religious fanaticism thread through Williams's corpus of songs and particularly describe those on her acclaimed 2003 release, *World without Tears*. Her songs are edgy and occasionally raw and even shocking. Like O'Connor, she is interested in exploring human experience at its sometimes terrible extremes. This exploration includes the practices and perspectives of southern religious extremists who, like Hazel Motes, torture and maim themselves, even risk death, in penance for their sinfulness or in their manic pursuit of righteousness. Indeed, elements of a kind of Motesian Christ-hauntedness inform several of Williams's song lyrics, completely unironically, as in O'Connor's fiction, and as with O'Connor are cast without irony in the garb and language of southern Bible Beltism.

Open the CD case to *Essence* and on the inside cover is a full-spread photograph of a sign standing in a harvested, wet field, with an imperative message painted on white boards in red and black block letters: "GET RIGHT WITH GOD." The long shadow it casts in what appears to be an evening sun forms a proportioned cross on the stubbly ground. Is Williams out to mock southern religious extremists with this collection of songs—as early reviewers thought was O'Connor's intent in *Wise Blood*? What does Williams intend by confronting the listener with this ubiquitous roadside slogan from the Bible Belt—not once but twice, including on the cover of the enclosed lyrics booklet? An interviewer on National Public Radio in 2001 asks, "Is this song a satire?" assuming that the stark religious content of a song that takes its title and chorus from a cliché of old-time religion cannot be taken seriously. Williams responds frankly, "Well, I do want to get right with God," and offers that the best way to explain the song—which she calls a folk song—is that it describes "the lengths to which someone will go to get right with God." Her remark is not unlike one that O'Connor relished from a neighbor lady in response to her stories: "Well, them stories just gone and shown you how some folks would do."

Here are the words of the first verse and chorus of Williams's Grammy-winning rockabilly gospel song:

> I would risk the serpent's bite
> I would dance around with seven
> I would kiss the diamondback
> If I knew it would get me to heaven.
> 'Cause I want to get right with God
> Yes, you know you got to get right with God

Subsequent verses offer a litany of self-mortifying acts the singer would perform if by doing so she could "walk righteously again": burn the soles of her feet and the palms of her hands and sleep on a bed of nails, "Till my back was torn and bleeding"—all of this resolving in a plea to God to then "take me as one of your daughters." Like O'Connor's hapless preacher-gone-wrong Hazel Motes, after he has killed his false-prophet double, the narrator of "Get Right with God" appears willing "to pay" for a sense of righteousness by torturing her flesh and even risking her life. The images in this song recall Hazel's acts of mortification at the end of *Wise Blood*: overpowered by the sense that he

Photo credit Jeff Minton.

is "not clean," he blinds himself, walks in shoes filled with gravel and broken glass, and wraps his chest in three strands of barbed wire. In an interview in 2017, Williams states directly that the imagery in this song "was kind of borrowed from [O'Connor's] book *Wise Blood.*"

Williams is reportedly fascinated by practices of southern religious extremists, those brave and often misguided faithful who, believing that the righteous will suffer no harm, handle serpents and drink poison, testing the literalness of controversial verses in the sixteenth chapter of the Gospel of Mark. At the time she was recording the songs for *Car Wheels*, Williams became deeply interested in the spiritual practice of snake handling, following on Dennis Covington's book on the topic in 1995, *Salvation on Sand Mountain*. She collects books and photographs of southern Christians in religious frenzies as they handle snakes, sip strychnine, and succumb to the slaying power of Holy Spirit preachers—a fascination with an element of the southern grotesque that Williams claims originated in her youthful reading of O'Connor.

Williams's own Christ-hauntedness, as expressed in "Get Right with God" and, for some reviewers, her fanatical obsession with the Christ story in her own life, appears entirely genuine. According to a revealing *New Yorker* article of 2000, her home in Nashville at that time was decorated throughout in "Southern religious kitsch": glittery pictures of Jesus in heart-shaped frames adorned her bedroom, one hanging on the headboard of her bed. Images of Jesus painted on scallop and conch shells were mounted on the walls; bottle caps with minuscule Jesuses painted inside served as fridge magnets; and a night-light of Jesus of the Sacred Heart was plugged in above her kitchen sink. On another occasion, Williams admitted that she collects crosses and crucifixes not out of religious devotion but because she loves the symbolism. Yet Christ-haunted and Christ-obsessed she certainly was in 2001 when she recorded "Get Right with God."

But like O'Connor's hillbilly prophet Mason Tarwater in *The Violent Bear It Away*, at times Williams, too, cannot "stand the Lord one instant longer." Her raunchy, grating rock song "Atonement" from her 2003 recording *World without Tears* was written as a response to the presumptuous hellfire religion of southern Baptistry she encountered while living in Nashville. Explaining in part why she left it for Los Angeles for the second time in 2002 (she'd made a previous move there in 1984 following a lover), she says in an interview, "I got tired of people asking me what church I attended. It wasn't 'Do you go to church?' but 'Which one do you attend?' This [song] was written as a backlash to that." When introducing "Atonement" in performance, Williams often puts it in context by informing her audience that the song was influenced by her reading of Flannery O'Connor, particularly *Wise Blood*.

"Atonement" crowds all of southern religion into a single song that "Lock[s] you in a room / With a holy roller and a one-man band" listening to "Shouting with twisted tongues" from "Hell fire scorched lungs." It evokes the religion of O'Connor's southern family evangelists the Carmodys in *The Violent Bear It Away*, a raw and eviscerating style of preaching "the Word of God," which as the child evangelist Lucette cries out repeatedly, "is a burning Word to burn you clean." Williams (whose Christian name, like that of Lucette, means "bringer of light") voices this song as though both repelled and enraptured by the scene. For all its abrasive, pulsating assault on the listener, the song takes an O'Connoresque twist at the end and becomes more an invocation than a condemnation of the gospel of the grotesque, in what would appear to be the words of a preacher:

> Come on, come on
> Pay close attention to this
> Let me give you something good to eat
> Bite down hard 'til it sticks between your teeth
> Glory, glory we've killed the beast

O'Connor's moonshiner, backwoods prophet Mason Tarwater would be very much at home in Williams's locked room, and it is the kind of place O'Connor likes to put most of her unwittingly Christ-seeking characters. With its screeching guitar sounds and grating rhythms that proclaim "Glory, glory," Williams's song "Atonement" is in itself like a peacock's cry.

Williams's pursuit of the agonizing grace figured in O'Connor's symbolic peacocks is most viscerally evoked in "Unsuffer Me," a stand-out track from *West*. A dragged-out, bluesy song, given power and presence by Williams's drawling, pained voice against sustained, cutting guitar notes, it is a kind of palinode to "Get Right with God," with the singer's anguished appeal to divine mercy to be unbound, unbloodied, unsuffered after all she has gone through:

> Unsuffer me
> Take away the pain
> Unbruise, unbloody
> Wash away the stain
> Anoint my head
> With your sweet kiss
> My joy is dead
> I long for bliss
> I long for knowledge
> Whisper in my ear
> Undo my logic
> Undo my fear
> Unsuffer me

Williams once commented on a MySpace web page that "Unsuffer Me" is "a song of redemption—a spiritual song, to whoever your God is, whatever power it is that can come in and release your burden." It is an anthem of longing for wholeness, healing, love—and, yes, anointing—evoked through both words and music. Williams's spiritual quest, especially manifest in the songs on *West*, also informs her songwriting on *Blessed* (2011) and the consecutively recorded *Down Where the Spirit Meets the Bone* (2014) and *The Ghosts of Highway 20* (2016). As she writes in a blog, her "dark songs of redemption" have "something in common with Flannery O'Connor's short stories." That commonality is an honest, bared looked at the landscapes of the South and of the soul, a holding out for the possibility within human experience of a transforming revelation, and a belief in a paradoxical release from pain and longing through some form of redemptive suffering.

One of the plums from O'Connor's occasional papers, in an address entitled "Some Aspects of the Grotesque in Southern Fiction," is her anecdote about receiving a letter from "an old lady in California" who complained that reading O'Connor's stories did not give her the satisfying sense of having her heart "lifted up." To which O'Connor rejoined, "I think that if her heart had been in the right place, it would have been lifted up." In a posting on the website of her record company Lost Highway following the release of *West*, Williams echoes and at the same time invokes O'Connor: "I get tired of people looking at my songs and feeling that they're all sad and dark. There's more to them than that. Some people might read Flannery O'Connor and see that [her fiction is] simply dark, and it *is* dark and disturbing, but there's a philosophical aspect, even a comical aspect as well."

And a Little Child Shall Lead Them

O'Connor once reflected in a letter on the sense of heightened consciousness she had at a young age: "I was a very ancient twelve." Williams too privileges the sensibilities she had at twelve years old, the age at which she began creating songs: "I write songs a lot about life as seen through a child's eyes, because I think that's often the most beautiful, poetic way that life is looked at," she once remarked from the stage during a live recording. In individual stories and in songs about the experiences of children, both southern writers employ a technique that novelist Henry James termed a *center of consciousness*, a way of telling a story largely or wholly from the point of view of a single character—a child—although the narrative is written in third person. O'Connor greatly admired James's novels and literary theories, which she attempted in some respects to emulate in her fiction.

Howard Burkle argues in his article "The Child in Flannery O'Connor" that O'Connor's child characters often suffer because of some spiritual or moral flaw that informs the choices and lived reality of their parents or adult guardians. In her stories, adds Burkle, "O'Connor censures the moral-spiritual flaw implicitly by depicting the child as its innocent victim." The grieving and emotionally orphaned ten-year-old boy Norton in "The Lame Shall Enter First" is a prime example. His do-gooding father, ironically named Sheppard, shames and neglects him while seeking vindication of his own progressive theories and practices as a social worker with a hard-case juvenile delinquent named Rufus Johnson, whom he has unwisely invited into the family home. Sheppard's moment of revelation comes clearly and unconditionally: "He had stuffed his own emptiness with good works like a glutton. He had ignored his own child to feed his vision of himself." But the insight comes too late to save his desperate-hearted young son from hanging himself in order to be in heaven with his recently deceased mother. Similarly, nine-year-old Mary Fortune Pitts in "A View of the Woods" is a victim of her grandfather's greed. Grandfather Fortune wants to sell the cow pasture that Mary's father depends on for his livelihood and the adjoining woods as well. In service of progress, he envisions in their place cottage properties and a town with paved roads, a supermarket, gas station, motel, and drive-in movie theater—a town that he vainly imagines will be named Fortune, Georgia, after him. Young Mary resists her uncharitable, irascible grandfather for reasons beyond his comprehension: to preserve the sacramental pastoral world signified in "the lawn" and the "line of woods" that she views from her front porch. Eventually, her resistance turns to blind fury, and in her final physical assault on her grandfather, both die violently by the other's hand.

In her child characters, O'Connor dramatizes Christ's injunction that we must become like little children to enter the kingdom of heaven. The emphasis in "A Temple of the Holy Ghost," for example, is on child-like acceptance of this spiritual truth. The unnamed child in this story accepts instinctively the idea that she is "a Temple of the Holy Ghost." Repeating the phrase to herself makes her feel "as if somebody had given her a present." By the story's end she holds the symbol of the Eucharist in the same holy regard: the last image in the child's consciousness is the setting sun that appears "like an elevated Host drenched in blood." She gazes at a mystery that she appears in her child-like way inwardly to comprehend.

As she leaves the convent where her worldly cousins are attending school, the girl is literally and figuratively marked with a sign of the cross as a big nun suddenly clasps her in a smothering embrace, "mashing the side of her face into the crucifix hitched onto her belt." In a letter in which she discusses how her spiritual, religious sense coincides with the dramatic events in the last paragraphs of this story, O'Connor confirms her intentions here and affirms her own belief in Catholic doctrine: "Understand though, that, like the child, I believe the Host is actually the body and blood of Christ, not a symbol."

The O'Connor story that most resonates with Williams's childhood memories is "The River." Both the moral sense and the dramatic sense of this story intertwine with the childhood emotions and circumstances recalled in "Car Wheels on a Gravel Road." The title song for Williams's Grammy-winning fifth album is a blues-rock tune that presents a story of domestic tension as recollected through the consciousness of a child of "about four or five years," the approximate age of the hapless Harry Ashfield in O'Connor's story.

Like O'Connor's story, Williams's song appears to recount a singular event rather than present a montage of childhood memories (as she does in "Bus to Baton Rouge," the closing track on *Essence*). In "Car Wheels," Williams's child self sits in the kitchen of a house in Macon, Georgia—where she lived at that age—at breakfast time, smelling "coffee, eggs and bacon." A Loretta Lynn song plays on the radio. Readers familiar with O'Connor will be mindful that she begins both "The River" and "The Lame Shall Enter First"—stories featuring an emotionally neglected child—with a scene at breakfast time. The sound of "car wheels on a gravel road" announces the arrival of "Somebody somewhere I don't know" and signals the little girl's departure: "Come on now child we're gonna go for a ride." A cursing adult gathers keys and a dusty suitcase and slams the screen door, shouting out, "You'd better do what you're told." An adult drama is taking place the cause of which Williams's child narrator is somewhat aware, just as the child Harry in O'Connor's story is aware that his "sick" mother is in fact suffering from a hangover. Harry's likewise cursing father ushers him out of an apartment smelling of "dead cigarette butts" and into the care of a babysitter at six o'clock in the morning, without having fed him breakfast.

As in O'Connor's child-centered stories, in Williams's lyrics the human drama and interactions are filtered through the limited—but precocious—consciousness of the child, who rides in the back seat and hears a "Low hum of voices in the front seat" telling "Stories nobody knows." The only story the child has been told is that we "Got folks in Jackson we're going to meet." But Williams's child character is not deceived, just as the child Harry/Bevel, referred to by a friend of his parents as "old man," begins "gradually seeing" the nature of his domestic reality and what lies ahead of him. The most striking line in Williams's song is in the second to last stanza, where the child narrator remarks with deep self-awareness, "Could tell a lie but my heart would know." As Burkle notes the remarkably "perspicacious" child protagonists in O'Connor's fiction, who "seem old before their time," so too Williams's child narrator here is wise beyond her years. And like a number of O'Connor's children, the young child in the song suffers spiritual and emotional trauma as a result of the transgressions of her parents and other adults. The song concludes with a stanza written in third person:

> Child in the backseat about four or five years
> Lookin' out the window
> Little bit of dirt mixed with tears
> Car wheels on a gravel road

When Miller Williams first heard his daughter perform "Car Wheels on a Gravel Road" at Nashville's Bluebird Café, he came backstage with tears in his eyes and apologized to her for the domestic tensions and circumstances that occasioned the affecting childhood experience the song recounts.

The lyrics to the bouncy, bluesy "Car Wheels" are illustrative of the economy that Williams employs in her narrative songs, an economy that she credits to instruction by her poet father along with her wide reading of southern fiction. Miller Williams was his daughter's literary mentor; throughout her career she sent her song lyrics to him for his comments and occasional ameliorations of a word or phrase—"Just little things, but it's amazing what a difference it makes." Indeed, she regards her method of songwriting as much like that of a poet, eliminating all words not essential to the meaning, stripping language to enable expression of a song's naked truth. These are the principles of good writing that Miller Williams acknowledges O'Connor instilled in him over the course of their monthly conversations in the late 1950s. The skill here, as in minimalist poetry, is to remain lean lyrically while evoking a complete image or dramatic moment. What listener to "Car Wheels" does not see the perceptive child narrator "Pull the curtains back and look outside" and notice "Somebody somewhere don't know"? The next important moment in the narrative comes when the adult voice, likely that of a relative, speaks imperatively, "Come on now child, we're gonna go for a ride." Each verse has the same narrative economy, as the story moves from the kitchen to an angry departure through a slammed screen door, to the child sitting in the back seat of a car listening to the "Low hum" of adult voices in the front while a Hank Williams song plays on the car radio, watching "Telephone poles, trees and wires fly on by," to arrival at the "folks in Jackson," who live in a "broken down" shack with engine parts lying around and "dogs barkin' in the yard." Throughout the narrative there is the rhythmic hum and refrain of "Car wheels on a gravel road." The brief lyrical substance of this song tells a complete and complex story, with vivid sensory details, resolving in the child's emotional response to the tense, confusing adult drama she is caught in: "Little bit of dirt mixed with tears."

If, as Williams has said from the stage, "it's all true" in the songs about her experiences and those of her family members, then she has been deliberately anachronistic in the opening verse of "Car Wheels" for the sake of its subtext. When Williams was four or five years old in 1957–1958, it was not possible to hear "Loretta's singing on the radio." Loretta Lynn was first heard on the radio with her debut single "I'm a Honky Tonk Girl" in 1960. She had a string of hits between 1963 and 1966, including "Before I'm Over You," a song about a woman's response to hearing that her husband has left her for another woman, the self-explanatory "The Home You're Tearing Down," and "You Ain't Woman Enough (To Take My Man)," in which a wife confronts and insults her husband's lover: "Women like you are a dime a dozen / You can buy 'em anywhere." Loretta Lynn's songs, according to one commentator, are about "philandering husbands and man-stealing hussies." The reference to Lynn in this song may well be understood as literary license serving to signify the nature of the adult drama the child unwittingly witnesses.

The Hank Williams reference also invokes themes of marital discord and perhaps infidelity. Lucinda recalled hearing his music constantly through her growing-up years. Her father was obsessed with Hank Williams and once sat down for a drink with him after a concert, trading on the surname they shared to introduce himself. In 1957, quite possibly the year in which the song's story took place, the first compilation of Hank Williams's recordings was released, *36 of His Greatest Hits*. "Hank's voice on the radio" could be heard in such songs of heartbreak and domestic strife as "You're Gonna Change (Or I'm Gonna Leave)" and his classic "Your Cheatin' Heart." These two references to popular music in "Car Wheels" provide strong social and emotional subtexts to the song.

While little is known about the domestic tensions in the Williams household during Lucinda's growing-up years, her mother, Lucille, suffered from mental illness and alcoholism and was in and out of psychiatric hospitals, where she was treated with electroshock therapy. She would become hostile when her medication was not effective, and eventually became incapable of caring for her three young children. This is probably why four-year-old Lucinda went along with her father when he made his monthly visits to the O'Connor farm while the family was living in Macon. Around this time, one of Miller's students, nineteen-year-old Rebecca Jordan Hall, was acting as caregiver and housekeeper for the children under the same roof as their mother and eventually became Miller's lover. After divorcing Lucille in 1964, Miller married Jordan in 1969. Perhaps in this song Lucinda Williams is following the advice that O'Connor reportedly gave to her father on one of their Saturday afternoon visits: "Tell the truth, but understand that it is not necessarily what happened."

I'll Never Be Free from These Chains Inside

In her live recording of "Bus to Baton Rouge" at the El Rey Theatre in Los Angeles on 6 September 2007, Williams does something rather untypical and thoroughly Springsteenesque, inserting a brief biographical narrative into her performance of the song. She introduces the song as having been written about her childhood experiences in the house of the grandmother on her mother's side, and adds, "My life reads like a southern gothic novel. It really does." Williams has disclosed little about her mother, who died in 2004. Bill Buford's candid profile in the *New Yorker* in 2000 states that Lucille Williams was incapable of raising her children "owing to mental illness or depression or something the family is uncomfortable talking about." Lucinda Williams has talked about many uncomfortable subjects in her songs, the place she goes "to get things out of [her] system." Her most revealing statements about her mother are expressed in her stage patter recorded that evening at the El Rey. She inserts her mother's story into this slow, dream-like ballad of childhood remembrance, signifying that their lives are connected by what they both experienced in the house on Belmont Avenue.

Like so many of Williams's best songs, "Bus to Baton Rouge" is a personal narrative, one of her short-story songs. It is the longest track on the album, with a playing time of just under six minutes. Using techniques shared with works of fiction, the song begins with lines that evoke a strong sense of place, of the South, of Louisiana, where houses are raised on cinderblocks, "what with the rain and the soft swampy land," and camellia bushes and honeysuckle bloom. The twice-repeated single line of the chorus—"I took a bus to Baton Rouge"—adds little to the story other than to support the purposeful journey the singer takes to a place that holds mostly painful memories. Is she seeking expiation of something by her visit? Or simply confirmation of her perceptions from childhood?

The tone of this song shifts in the last line of the second quatrain of the opening verse, with reference to "switches" made from the honeysuckle vine that were used on Lucinda and her siblings "when we were bad." The house has an almost inhuman atmosphere as Williams describes it. Its interior is pictured as a place of oppression and repression, of denial and a kind of death:

> All the front rooms were kept closed off
> I never liked to go in there much
> Sometimes the doors they'd be locked 'cause
> There were precious things that I couldn't touch
> The company couch covered in plastic
> Little books about being saved
> The dining room table nobody ate at
> The piano nobody played

While performing the song to the El Rey audience, Williams breaks off at this point to talk about her mother, a memory invoked by the song's reference to an unplayed piano:

> My mother was born in a little town called Bonita, Louisiana. Her daddy was a Methodist minister. He was a hellfire and brimstone minister. She had four brothers: one of them died coming home from World War Two on his motorcycle. His name was Robert, and my brother was named after him. He was a poet and he played saxophone. My mother studied piano. She started taking lessons when she was four years old. And she wanted to go to music school and do all that kind of thing. But her family really did not give her a lot of support. She was from that generation where she was raised to get married and have kids. And she struggled with that all her life. So that is what this song is supposed to talk about.

The song is both a recollection of childhood memories and a coded narrative about the home her mother was raised in. Most of the song is rooted in memory, what *was* for the child Lucinda at the time and not what *is* revealed to the adult on her later visit by bus. The funeral atmosphere of the house, its "closed off" oppressiveness, is the dominant feeling of the song, relieved only briefly by a memory of childhood awe at a lamp with a rotating lampshade that bore a seaside scene. "Little books about being saved" alludes to the strict fundamentalist Methodist upbringing her mother endured. But the song registers the child narrator's own painful experiences there as well, matters that even a frank confessional writer like Williams finds "too hard" to tell. These life-stealing memories are figured as "Ghosts in the wind that blow through my life" and "Follow me wherever I go."

A reference to a fig tree that once stood in the backyard evokes vegetation of the South but, given the fundamentalist religion of Lucinda's maternal grandparents, might also allude to the one thing that Jesus is reported to have cursed during his ministry on earth. Two of the synoptic gospels tell the story of Christ cursing a fig tree that is not bearing fruit (Mark 11:12–14; Matthew 21:18–22). The traditional interpretation of this parabolic miracle is that the unfruitful fig tree is a metaphor for the people of Israel, who had the outward appearance of religiosity but had not produced anything of spiritual worth, what St. Paul later refers to as "the fruit of the Spirit" (Galatians 5:22). The fig tree in the backyard of her fundamentalist forebears perhaps symbolizes a carrying forward of that curse. In the song's anguished conclusion, Williams sings, "I will never be free from these chains inside / Hidden deep down in my soul." In this Hawthornesque confession, she presents a picture of herself as spiritually tormented, bound by blood to her stridently religious ancestors—somewhat like the character of Hazel Motes in *Wise Blood*. Indeed, in this song, Williams not only echoes O'Connor's themes but could be one of her Christ-haunted characters.

The suffering of children is a prevalent theme across Williams's recordings. Songs on 2016's *The Ghosts of Highway 20* revisit the childhood life that she wrote about so starkly in *Car Wheels on a Gravel Road*. As she reflects in her 2023 memoir, her songwriting has been to some degree a form of therapy for dealing with her childhood traumas. The *Highway 20* recording resulted from a tour in 2011 following the release of *Blessed* that led to Williams's first concert in Macon, Georgia, her childhood home when her father befriended O'Connor. Traveling with husband/producer Tom Overby in the tour bus westward to LA along US Interstate 20, Williams was struck by her many connections to the cities and towns along it: "It was literally a map of my life in many ways." US Interstate 20 is a major east-west highway that stretches fifteen hundred miles from the northwest corner of Texas to the center of South Carolina. It extends through Shreveport, Louisiana; Jackson, Mississippi; Birmingham, Alabama; and Atlanta, Georgia, like an asphalt curtain rod for the South, and forms an arterial base line to the places of Lucinda's childhood and youth, and to southbound highways leading to cities and towns that have cradled her life and consciousness:

Lafayette and Lake Charles and Baton Rouge and Macon. US Highways 129/441 also descend to Milledgeville off I20 just east of Atlanta. The white line of Highway 20 thus leads to the storylines of Lucinda's lyrics and the characters she writes about—"the ghosts of people we once knew but never quite forget," as Tom Overby has described them in a blog: "Like characters in a Tennessee Williams play or a Flannery O'Connor story, they never quite leave, maybe showing up in dreams or incidences that suddenly bring long forgotten faces back into the present."

The simply titled "Louisiana Story" that ends disc 1 of *Highway 20* is a childhood reflection in fifteen short verses that begins with a montage of conflicting memories, "looking back on the sweetness / Looking back on the rough." The lyrics are remarkable for their conversational simplicity underneath an alternating rhyme scheme with verse lines of mostly three or four words. The verbal economy and lyric craft express indelible memories and a child's awareness of emotional tensions with the force of a minimalist poem, and confirm that Lucinda Williams is heir to her poet father's gifts. She sings the song languorously, in the dreamy discourse of a child, the images thoughtfully paced and balanced between arpeggio instrumental phrases.

Recollections of childhood innocence, of "playin' / Barefoot in the street" and "Running and chasing after / The ice cream wagon," are soon overshadowed by memories of emotional abuse, a mother who would "cuss / When something got spilt." At verse 7, the song resolves into biographical fragments describing Lucille Williams's strict fundamentalist upbringing. Her father, a Methodist circuit preacher, was a severe man who "taught the Bible / From Lake Charles to Monroe / Shreveport to Slidell / Baton Rouge to Thibodaux":

> Her daddy's kind
> Didn't spare the rod
> Blinded by the fear
> And the wrath of the lord

O'Connor describes Hazel Motes's grandfather, also a circuit preacher, as "a waspish old man who had ridden over three counties with Jesus hidden in his head like a stinger." That description seems to fit Williams's maternal grandfather:

> He'd call her a sinner
> And say you're going to hell
> Now finish your dinner
> And tell 'em you fell

"The weight of centuries lies on children, I'm sure of it," remarks O'Connor in a letter. Her child protagonists are *all* weighed down with a burden of some sort: emotional neglect for Harry Ashfield in "The River" and ten-year-old Norton in "The Lame Shall Enter First." Both boys take their own lives in their innocent longing to be loved and to belong. For nine-year-old Mary Fortune, eventually violently killed by her grandfather in "A View of the Woods," the burden is the threatened livelihood of her family and her own spiritual sustenance. A near pathological prophetic calling torments fourteen-year-old Francis Marion Tarwater in *The Violent Bear It Away* and is exploited in the eleven- or twelve-year-old evangelist Lucette, who shrieks words of judgment at Tarwater's reprobate Uncle Rayber.

Williams's child characters, like O'Connor's, are highly perceptive and deeply affected by their life circumstances. They carry the weight of painful memories and may likewise have experienced some form of abuse or neglect—as Williams herself experienced in what she describes as "a difficult childhood." These children are like the kid in Williams's somewhat sentimental song "He Never Got Enough Love" from *Sweet Old World*; abandoned by his mother as a child and abused by an alcoholic father, he ends up committing murder because "He never got enough love / In all his life / He wasn't brought up right." Another song, "Sweet Side," from *World without Tears*, tells in frank detail the story of a lover who was physically abused in childhood: "You were screamed at and kicked over and over / . . . Hands that would feed you when you were two / Were the same hands that beat you black and blue." Williams's child characters bear the weight of their pain into adulthood or just as often meet with some form of tragedy—a life of dereliction or an early death. O'Connor's trapped or traumatized child protagonists are mostly spared the dire social or psychological outcomes of their dysfunctional upbringings by a quick trip to heaven. Of the child Harry/Bevel in "The River," who accidentally drowns himself in an effort to reach the kingdom of heaven, O'Connor has commented, "he comes to a good end," saved from further deleterious treatment by his godless, careless parents, "a fate worse than death." O'Connor's Catholic faith assures her, as she remarks of Harry/Bevel, "He's been baptized and so he goes to his Maker."

This Sweet Old World

O'Connor once said, "I'm a born Catholic and death has always been brother to my imagination. I can't imagine a story that doesn't properly end in it or in its foreshadowings." Indeed, in her two novels and in ten of the nineteen stories in her two collections, the lead character or a character of interest meets with death, usually a violent one, and usually at the hands of an individual aligned as an agent of divine grace or justice or mercy. (O'Connor restrains the Reaper's hand in two of her best stories, "Revelation" and "Parker's Back," written near the end of her life.) In her most widely read story, "A Good Man Is Hard to Find," a family of six, including an infant and a lively grandmother, are shot to death by an escaped convict and his accomplices for no other reason than "meanness" and perhaps to leave no witnesses to the theft of their family car. Glossing her story in a talk she gave to a student audience in the fall of 1963, not many months before her own death, O'Connor remarked that readers "should be on the lookout for the action of grace" in the story, "not for the dead bodies."

A thematic of death is another way in which Williams's art joins with O'Connor's. One would be hard pressed to find another contemporary American singer-songwriter with a canon of songs so pervaded with death. The dead in her songs are mostly fellow artists and former lovers, and mostly dead by suicide. Nonetheless, like O'Connor, Williams often treats death in a life-affirming way, if for different reasons. Two songs about death by suicide appear on *Sweet Old World* (1992), a collection one reviewer describes as "an unflinching meditation on death, loss, and regret." Death again—particularly that of her mother in 2004—is the subject of three songs of grief and loss on her 2007 collection *West*: "Mama You Sweet," "Learning How to Live," and "Fancy Funeral."

"Pineola" on *Sweet Old World* tells the story of the suicide of a brilliant young poet, Frank Stanford, whose infidelities and lies eventually led him in 1978 impulsively and dramatically to take his life with three gunshots to his heart. Stanford was an admired member of the circle of poets around Miller Williams and very attractive to women. At age twenty-five, Lucinda was one of many women with whom Stanford had a relationship, but in her 2023 memoir she dispels the belief that they had a two-month "tumultuous affair." In ballad stanzas, "Pineola" reads like a short story, telling of the responses of friends to the death of "Sonny" and reporting on the gathered mourners as he is laid in a grave in Subiaco Abbey Cemetery in Logan County, Arkansas. The lyrics are laden with incredulity that such a promising life has ended. Stanford's suicide and the suicide four years later of another friend inspire Williams's most affecting and familiar song about death (memorably covered by Emmylou Harris on her 1995 breakthrough album *Wrecking Ball*), the title track "Sweet Old World." Unlike the narrative reportage of Stanford's death and funeral in "Pineola," "Sweet Old World" is addressed directly to the dead friend, and the lyrics read like a list poem, detailing the sensual and emotional experiences that his suicide has denied him: "The breath from your own lips / The touch of fingertips / A sweet and tender kiss." The chorus repeats the lines "See what you lost when you left this world / This sweet old world." It is a beautifully crafted, melodic ballad that Williams sings with tender longing. She began writing it in 1979 shortly after Stanford's death but, given the vicissitudes of her career, did not record it for thirteen years. It is not so much a song about death as about life. As Williams has commented to music journalist Jewly Hight, "I don't look at ['Sweet Old World'] as a dark song. . . . Basically, it's saying, you know, 'Life is worth it.'" Williams's songs largely regard death from a this-worldly perspective. "Why would anyone willingly leave this sweet old world?" is a question she asks in several songs, including "Seeing Black," from her 2011 release *Blessed*, a song about the suicide on Christmas Day 2009 of wheelchair-bound songwriter Vic Chesnutt. "Drunken Angel" was written in response to the avoidable shooting death in 1989 of troubled Austin songwriter Blaze Foley.

Williams's 2016 *The Ghosts of Highway 20* offers one of her most stark, existential meditations on death in "Death Came," written in 2004 following the death of her mother. In biblical tones the lyrics consider Death as an animate force or being in play since Adam and Eve "tasted the fruit from the tree of knowledge." The opening verse echoes some plot detail from O'Connor's short story "The River":

> I was called to the rolling banks by the water
> to bathe in the river of truth
> The river tried to pull me under
> and refused to turn me loose

Williams may have had O'Connor's story in mind or even had it in hand as she wrote these lines. Her phrase "the river of truth" is of a kind with those describing the place of baptism in O'Connor's story. In his shouted words to the people gathered on the banks, O'Connor's young Reverend Bevel Summers refers to the waters he baptizes in as "the River of Life, made out of Jesus' Blood"; he continues with a string of related phrases capitalized in O'Connor's text: "the River of Faith . . . the River of Life . . . the River of Love" and later, as he is about to baptize five-year-old Harry Ashfield, "the river of suffering . . . the deep river of life." The child has just that morning learned "the gospel truth" from a picture book, *The Life of Jesus for Readers Under Twelve*, read to him by his caregiver, Mrs. Connin, been baptized in the river by the preacher, and told that "You count now." In his effort to rebaptize himself, Harry, like the character in Williams's lyrics, is "pulled . . . swiftly forward and down" by the river that carries him both to his death and to "the Kingdom of Christ."

As a Catholic, O'Connor had a firm belief in a heavenly home for the dead in Christ. Williams's view of the afterlife is, however, conflicted, and most elegiacally expressed in "Copenhagen," one of three songs about death on *Blessed*. She told a *Rolling Stone* interviewer that the song expressed her immediate and "very literal" experience upon hearing news of the unexpected death of her longtime manager and musical collaborator Frank Callari while she was on tour in Copenhagen in October 2010:

> You have disappeared
> You have been released
> You are flecks of light, you are mist
> Somewhere spinning 'round the sun
> Circling the moon
> Traveling through time, you are mist

Some website transcriptions of this lyric read "missed" for the deliberate homophone on *mist* at the end of the chorus tercets. The misprint is significant, since the idea and the state of death in the lyrics are expressed in the form of diffuse ethereal matter.

In another vein, Williams offers a simple roots blues gospel song, "Heaven Blues" on *Little Honey* (2008), that appears to affirm a popular Christian view of heaven:

> Gonna see my mother, gonna see my mother up in heaven (*Repeat four times*)
> I'll understand, I'll understand when I get to heaven (*Repeat four times*)
> Gonna talk to God, gonna talk to God up in heaven (*Repeat four times*) . . .

The songwriter's seeming belief in a heaven that is "a better place than this / Where I can go and receive my mother's kiss" is evident in the insistent blues hymn "Doors of Heaven" on disc 1 of *The Ghosts of Highway 20*. The confident eschatology of these songs is, however, offset by a later song on disc 2, "If There's a Heaven." The penultimate track on the recording, it was written in memory of Williams's father and addressed to him. She inquires of her father's ghost, "When you go, will you let me know / If there's a heaven out there[?]"

While O'Connor's fiction is heavenly minded, she has little to say about what she expects from heaven in either her letters or lectures. Notably, just weeks before her untimely death at age thirty-nine, she enclosed in a letter dated 14 July 1964, to her close friend and agent Janet McKane, a copy of a prayer to the Archangel Raphael, noting that she has recited it every morning for many years. The prayer reads in part,

> Raphael, lead us toward those we are waiting for, those who are waiting for us . . . we feel the need of calling you and pleading for the protection of your wings so that we may not be as strangers in the province of joy . . . in a land that is always peaceful, always serene, and bright with the resplendent glory of God.

Given her terminal illness and her deep personal and artistic credo of the necessity of salvation in Christ for all humanity, O'Connor was certainly fixed on death as a transition to an eternal life in a heavenly abode, free from the "separations and sorrows of life" referenced elsewhere in the prayer.

In contrast to Williams's response to death—largely *see what you've lost*—O'Connor in her fiction embraces the opposite viewpoint of *see what you've gained*. In her Catholic belief, she regards the deaths of her child characters in particular as a mercy rather than a tragedy. Harry Ashfield, Norton Sheppard, Mary Fortune, and the mentally deficient child Bishop Rayber have each been spared the soul-corrupting effects of their spiritually vacant parents or relatives. As in Ben Jonson's famous elegy "On My First Son," these children have, in O'Connor's accounting, "'scap'd world's and flesh's rage."

Something Wicked This Way Comes

For Williams as for O'Connor, the Devil is not "only a manner of speaking" but an animate force of cosmic evil that can take incarnate form. Perhaps Williams's hellfire and damnation preacher ancestors have given her this much. Williams's shuffling blues-rock song "Something Wicked This Way Comes," the opening track on disc 2 of *Down Where the Spirit Meets the Bone*, goes to remarkable lengths to present a kind of apology on the diabolical nature of the "something wicked" about which she writes. And that sinister *something* is a *someone*, an evil being, personified in the "he" pronoun in the lyrics. So it is for O'Connor, who explained her use of fictional Devil figures in a letter to novelist John Hawkes: "I want to be certain that the Devil gets identified as the Devil and not simply taken for this or that psychological tendency." O'Connor's Devil is "a real spirit who must be made to name himself, and not simply to name himself as vague evil, but to name himself with his specific personality for every occasion."

The evil presence Williams describes in "Something Wicked" follows a similar narrative arc to the sinisterly transforming "stranger" to "friend" that haunts young Tarwater in O'Connor's novel *The Violent Bear It Away*. Indeed, she has remarked that this song "is straight from Flannery O'Connor." Williams's wicked something begins as an unseen presence "hiding underneath / The grass beneath your feet," like the "disagreeable" voice inside Tarwater's head at the novel's outset that lures him away from his given task of burying his deceased great-uncle. The devilish dialectic continues in verse 2, which describes a kind of possession of an individual by an evil presence: "He will make you his home." O'Connor's belief in demonic possession is revealed in her letter to Hawkes, where she summarizes what she has learned through "reading about some cases of possession in the 19th century." As O'Connor makes clear in *The Violent Bear It Away*, young Tarwater soon finds his thoughts and words merging with the spirit of untruth that begins to inhabit and control him. That spirit eventually takes incarnate form in O'Connor's text as "the stranger," who picks up the hitchhiking Tarwater, offers him a drink of drug-laced whiskey, and after he loses consciousness, drives him to a wooded area and rapes him. Williams's third verse includes the O'Connoresque lines, "He invites you to come in / And drink with him / He won't leave you alone." The fourth verse opens with the warning, "You will fall from grace." Just as O'Connor's novel ends with a hellish image of "the grinning presence" of evil enveloped in flames, so Williams's wicked being is identified with Lucifer, the fallen angel, "cast out of heaven" (Williams's phrase echoes *Revelations* 12:9 [KJV]), with "No mercy / No love" for anything or anyone in Creation. The song concludes with a blues litany that underscores the abiding lack of mercy and love in this "mighty wicked" force and being. Clearly, Williams's Devil and O'Connor's are one and the wicked same.

Three Chords and the Ugly Truth

When she began writing songs, and up to the release of her breakthrough recording *Car Wheels on a Gravel Road*, Williams handed her lyrics to her poet father for his comments and ameliorations. His advice included this imperative: "Number one: stay away from overused clichés." Yet, as does O'Connor, Williams often uses clichés in her writing. In the mature songwriting on *Down*

Where the Spirit Meets the Bone and *The Ghosts of Highway 20* in particular, she seems to have abandoned her father's early advice. To what purpose? Both she and O'Connor appear to engage consciously with clichéd truths with the intent to redeem the sense of a seemingly exhausted phrase. O'Connor transforms—often comically literalizes—clichés and idiomatic expressions: Christ is idiomatically on Parker's back, in the weight of his spiritual disaffection and felt lack of wholeness, and ends up there diagrammatically as well; Hulga Hopewell loses her false leg and, symbolically, her false beliefs and thus is left both physically *and* philosophically without a leg to stand on; precious Ruby Turpin is forced to face her own hypocritical *hogwash* while hosing off a pen of dirty squealing hogs. Clichés and dead metaphors are raised to new literal and anagogical life in the events and symbolic transactions in O'Connor's stories.

Williams's lyrics glorify the cliché as well, but her plane of reference is to the imminent, the intimate, the immediate human truth that the cliché expresses. Songs such as "Fruits of My Labor" (*World without Tears*), "If Wishes Were Horses" (*Little Honey*), "Out of Touch" (*Essence*), and "Wrap My Head around That" (*West*) all take a cliché or proverbial saying at face value and build a story around it. For Williams, the cliché speaks the heart's truth in the language of the tribe; it links familiar emotional terrain with a familiar phrase or idiom that most listeners understand. Thus, the sense of her lyrics connects directly with her audience through a shared shopworn metaphor. A few lines from "Ugly Truth" on the *Blessed* recording illustrate Williams's method of layering her lyrics with pointed clichés and familiar figures of speech:

> Leave your husband, leave your wife
> Keep on runnin' your whole life
> Sweep your dirt under the rug
> Fix your hurt with a little love

The song continues with stock metaphors that express familiar and paradoxical human truths:

> Burn your bridges, burn your friends
> Blow 'em kisses and make amends
> . . . .
> Take the high road or take the low
> No one but you and God will ever know
> And you might play rough and win or lose
> Either way, love, you'll get the blues.

While Williams's cliché-marked song titles noted above are standouts on the albums in which they appear, in the highly O'Connoresque companion recordings *Down Where the Spirit Meets the Bone* and *The Ghost of Highway 20*, cliché phrases are more intensely and intentionally present in her lyrics. Indeed, on the *Spirit Meets the Bone* song cycle, *every* song includes a cliché or common expression, and many songs are built around the layering and repetition of such phrases. Here, by way of illustration, is the opening verse of the bluesy "One More Day"—the last original song on disc 2 (the final song is a version of J. J. Cale's "Magnolia"):

> Give me one more day
> To turn things around
> Give me one more day
> To get my feet on the ground
> To dig in my heels
> And settle down
> Give me one more day
> To turn things around

Williams's choice of the cliché over the poet's aesthetic of making something new is surely a deliberate strategy; she is too gifted as a lyricist simply to be pasting ready-made phrases together like some Tin Pan Alley hack. Rather, the intent of the cliché in her lyrics appears to be the directness of its truth-telling. The cliché title phrases of "Burning Bridges" and "Cold Day in Hell," for example, form repeating refrains in each song, as if to edge the metaphor into something more than merely figurative expression, to invoke some part of the literal sense behind each phrase as it applies to an occasion of human pain and tragedy. Though printed in a booklet included with each of these double CDs, Williams's lyrics as sung do not have the physicality of a printed poem, where the words on the page can play with indirection and suggest and obliquely carry the freight of their meaning. Listening to music while driving or making dinner or tidying up, the distracted contemporary listener may be best served by a song that dishes up its truth plain and simple and direct, as does "Temporary Nature (of Any Precious Thing)":

> Life's never fair and it can be rough
> And it can turn and play cruel tricks on us
> And just when we think we've had enough
> There's always one more river to cross

By overplaying a clichéd expression, Williams charges it with renewed emotional intensity. It is a rhetorical strategy she shares with O'Connor, whose fictional exposés of "good country people" and attitudes toward a "displaced person," or her disturbing story about "the comforts of home" or anagogical acknowledgment that "a good man is hard to find" push past the surface truth of these clichés to deeper, often ironic, liminal truths latent in these familiar expressions.

"Everything but the Truth" from *Down Where the Spirit Meets the Bone* is a pastiche of inspirational phrases and southern sermon-like imperatives that also includes a refrain which echoes one of O'Connor's well-traveled statements from her collected letters. In defending her Catholic beliefs, O'Connor wrote to her devoted correspondent Betty Hester, "The truth does not change according to our ability to stomach it emotionally." While Williams may or may not be directly echoing O'Connor's assertion in the refrain that dominates her preachy song "Everything but the Truth," the truth claim in her song is pointed in the same direction as O'Connor's comment in her letter. And there is little doubt that both artists intend the same meaning.

"Everything but the Truth" might be understood as a kind of blues sermon framed around a series of motivational statements moving from the mundane truisms of pop psychology to an ontological claim that invokes Bible Belt theology. The song opens with a blues verse layered with the positive assertion, "You got the power to make this mean old world a better place," and continues in the second verse with the inspirational slogan "Before you can have a friend / You gotta be one." The refrain moves into more preacherly assertions: "Everything's gonna change / Everything but the truth." That "the truth" for Williams is grounded in Judeo-Christian belief is signaled in a description of God-like nature that follows this repeated refrain: "He's not playing games, / He's taking names / And he is bulletproof." The refrain that opens verse 4 turns a theological corner with a homely southern fundamentalist-sounding phrase: "God put the firewood there / But you gotta light it yourself."

As these lyrics illustrate, Williams shares with O'Connor a penchant for framing and developing her art around an existential aphorism: a religious slogan, a social or philosophical truism, a truth pithily expressed. Williams's song titles similarly resonate with and are likewise generative of her stories in song. Consider the sources and significance of these O'Connor story titles: "A Good Man Is Hard to Find," "The Life You Save May Be Your Own," "You Can't Be Any Poorer Than Dead," and "Everything That Rises Must Converge." Each is a complete statement, a kind of truth claim. As O'Connor scholar Carole K. Harris has also observed, "O'Connor's most successful stories unfold as a working through (by means of repetition) of a single phrase, often catchy because cliché-like, that first appears as the title of the story." In O'Connor's use, the first three of these common or axiomatic phrases are lifted up from their profane origins to an anagogical plane of meaning. The fourth alludes to an intrinsically transcendent concept. Each assertion bears a seed of truth that O'Connor grows to its parabolic fruition in their respective stories.

Most famously, the catchphrase "a good man is hard to find" that titles her well-known story transcends its ostensible origin in the blues song written by Eddie Green in 1918 and made popular in the 1920s by Bessie Smith and Sophie Tucker. O'Connor scholar John Desmond argues that the phrase invokes "Christ's rebuke to Peter when Peter tried to call him good," as recorded in the Gospel of Mark (10:18). To this Jesus replied—certainly ironically given the Christian doctrine of the Incarnation—"Why do you call me good? No one is good except God alone" (NASB). Other commentators on the story have suggested that the phrase is proverbially related to Micah 7:2, which in the King James Version (KJV), widely read in the Bible Belt of the 1950s (and still so), contains the phrase "The good man is perished out of the earth." O'Connor's story certainly addresses the source of *goodness* in humankind. Matthew Henry's commentary on the KJV observes of Micah 7:2, "The good man is a godly man and a merciful man; the word signifies both." O'Connor's The Misfit knows he is neither godly nor merciful and responds to the grandmother's contrary assertion with "Nome, I ain't a good man." The title takes on a Christological meaning given The Misfit's struggle to reconcile himself to the truth of the life and salvific sacrifice of the good man / god man Jesus, who has "thrown everything off balance."

O'Connor asks the reader to apply a similar anagogical reading to the title of her short story "The Life You Save May Be Your Own." Her original title was "The World Is Almost Rotten." In a letter, O'Connor indicates that the final title was the choice of her friend and eventual editor, Sally Fitzgerald. Its source is in the story, when the con man on the run, Mr. Shiftlet, encounters a road sign warning "Drive carefully. The life you save may be your own." This slogan was used in a widespread campaign of road safety in the early 1950s. Of course, in O'Connor's story, the currency of that word *save* in southern fundamentalist discourses implies another, spiritual meaning. While O'Connor is on record suggesting that her character Mr. Shiftlet is "unredeemable" and is "of the Devil because nothing in him resists the Devil," she adds that the Devil is of interest to her comic storytelling "because he is always accomplishing ends other than his own." Like Ruby Turpin, who must be cleansed of her hypocritical hogwash, Mr. Shiftlet prays unwittingly, "Oh Lord . . . Break forth and wash the slime from this earth!" His prayer is followed shortly by an answering "guffawing peal of thunder" as the heavens open and "raindrops, like tin-can tops, [crash] over the rear of Mr. Shiftlet's car," like cans tied on behind honeymooners' vehicles, as he speeds into the spiritual gear that will take him from shiftless tramp to a new life in Mobile.

The title "You Can't Be Any Poorer Than Dead," given to the opening chapter of O'Connor's second novel when it was published discretely in 1955 in *New World Writing*, was considered as a possible title for the novel. Again, as with "A Good Man" and "The Life You Save," the title phrase is embedded in the story. This time its origin is indicated as diabolical: young Francis Marion Tarwater utters the phrase "in the voice of the stranger"—the evil presence that has begun to invade his consciousness and will later materialize—as he reluctantly works at digging a grave for his recently deceased great-uncle. The title has a literal sense: as the "voice" informs Tarwater, "The dead are poor." They no longer participate in human exchange; their demands are no longer heard nor obeyed. And so, says the "voice," the lifeless body of Mason Tarwater will "have to take what he gets." The literal sense of this claim must be balanced in O'Connor's Christianity with the teachings of Christ, whose Sermon on the Mount includes the statement "Blessed are ye poor, for yours is the kingdom of heaven" (St. Luke 6:20, Douay-Rheims). If "you can't be any poorer than dead," then, according to Christ's sermon, you also cannot be more blessed than in that condition. And it would follow, as for *the poor* in life, the *poorer* in death will be translated in spirit to "the kingdom of heaven."

O'Connor chose the title "Everything That Rises Must Converge" for her story about the social risings of Black Americans and the consequent "reducing class" of privileged white southerners. Her title is a translation of a mystical axiom coined by the controversial Jesuit paleontologist and theologian Pierre Teilhard de Chardin, from his masterwork of scientific philosophy, *Le Phénomène Humain* (*The Phenomenon of Man*), published posthumously in 1955. Teilhard's theory of a parallel biological and spiritual evolution of the human species, culminating in what he called the "Omega Point," an ultimate cosmic union with Christ, extrapolates from St. Paul's mystical remark in his *Epistle to the Colossians* (1:17b) that in Christ, "all things hold together" (ESV) or that "by him all things consist" (KJV and Douay-Rheims—O'Connor's preferred translation). Teilhard's theo-scientific vision of ordinary human history converging at a point in time with the divine appealed to O'Connor's fictional vision of the cosmic significance of events and exchanges in ordinary life—how the local participated in the universal. As her biographer Brad Gooch explains, O'Connor's choice of Teilhard's translated axiom "*Tout ce qui mont converge*" for her title "summed up the priest's notion of all life, from the geological to the human, converging toward an integration of the material and the spiritual . . . an integration of the scientific theory of evolution and the theological dogma of Incarnation, of God made man." Shortly after O'Connor read Teilhard's works in translation, his books and ideas were subject to a *monitum* (official reprimand) from the Holy Office at the Vatican, for ideas— "indeed even serious errors"—considered an offense to Catholic doctrine. Regardless of the Vatican's censure, O'Connor considered Teilhard the most important Catholic writer of her time and referred to him in her letters as not only "a man of God" but "a great mystic."

The philosophy behind Teilhard's proposition not only informs the title story of O'Connor's last collection of short fiction but also arcs throughout her collected stories in that volume and, indeed, her fiction as a whole. The stories in *Everything That Rises Must Converge* are ordered and projected along two lines that trace the social and spiritual risings that are the primary concern in all of O'Connor's fiction, and that ultimately converge in an Omega Point for the southern society that informs her sensibilities and is her fictional métier: the apocalyptic melding of race and redemption in the last story in the collection, "Judgement Day." In its generative potential, "Everything that rises must converge" stands as the apotheosis of O'Connor's use of axiomatic, truth-claim phrases as titles for her individual stories and collections.

Faith and Grace

"Faith and Grace," the standout track on Williams's *The Ghosts of Highway 20*, is an extended blues meditation that builds momentum like a Pentecostal prayer. This song is unlike anything in Williams's canon, and at twelve minutes and forty-five seconds is the longest track she has ever recorded. The original studio recording was nearly twenty minutes, and the session reportedly rolled along like a mystical train. (Titled "A Little More Faith and Grace," the original one-take recording [18:31] was released as a twelve-inch maxi-single on turquoise vinyl.) Working with two Jamaican musicians, one a Rastafarian minister, and the inspired playing of guitarist Bill Frisell, Williams transforms a traditional blues gospel song recorded by Mississippi Fred McDowell called "Just A Little More Faith and Grace" into a kind of improvised holy roller anthem.

"Faith and Grace" joins a subset of what might be considered Williams's song sermons: "Atonement," "Get Right with God," "Everything but the Truth," and the Beatitudes-like title song on *Blessed*. The tone of "Faith and Grace" is pastoral and affirmative; she adopts the persona of a revivalist preacher—but not of the hellfire and brimstone brand with "scorched lungs" breathing damnation and hard-bitten redemption featured in "Atonement." Tom Overby describes Williams during the single-take recording session, like one of O'Connor's prophesying characters, "completely letting go and going into something that could be called a gospel trance—I guess you could say she was full on testifyin'." The rhetoric in the third verse points to Christ's words in the Sermon on the Mount as recorded in St. Matthew's Gospel: "Ask, and it shall be given you; seek, and ye shall find; knock, and it shall be opened unto you" (7:7 KJV):

> When it seems like every door is locked
> I know he's gonna hear me knock
> And I know I'll be standing right
> 'Cause I'm standing on the rock

Williams also invokes St. Paul's athletic metaphor for living righteously:

> Just a little more faith and grace
> To help me run this race
> That's all, that's all, all I need

The soulful outro to the song as released on CD extends for 4:15 minutes. Over the gently distorted, atmospheric, phased notes of Frisell's guitar, Williams extemporizes like a southern Pentecostal preacher, repeating "That's all I need, a little more faith and grace," until, Van Morrison-like, the repetition becomes more intense and the Bible Belt imperative in the refrain of her Grammy-winning song "Get Right with God" is steadily, insistently added and repeated—twenty-five times! In this last song on the double CD, an ironic reversal is manifest: Williams takes on the persona of a southern evangelist, mouthing the kind of religiosity that drove her from Nashville in the 1980s. If "Atonement" reflects a resistance to the pull of southern religion in her life in her mid-thirties, the spiritual arc of songs written in her sixties appears to have led Williams along some way into the arms of her Methodist forebears.

Both *Down Where the Spirit Meets the Bone* and *The Ghosts of Highway 20* begin with musical settings of poems by Miller Williams, "Compassion" and "Dust" respectively. Her father's influence on her songs is thereby acknowledged and honored. In an interview late in his life with O'Connor scholar Marshall Bruce Gentry, Miller Williams (who died 1 January 2015) acknowledges the extent of Flannery O'Connor's influence on his writing and professional career. He credits O'Connor with giving him a sense that every word in a piece of writing matters, "to try not to have a word in a written work of art that could be taken out without damaging the other words." As O'Connor memorably defined her own accomplished art form, "A story is a way to say something that can't be said any other way, and it takes every word in the story to say what the meaning is."

Beyond the insights O'Connor offered Miller Williams on the craft of writing, and her role as "a mentor to him," as Lucinda remembers, O'Connor also had a hand in directing his professional destiny. In the Gentry interview, Miller states unequivocally, "I am where I am because of Flannery O'Connor," noting that a letter from her secured him his career-making job as an English professor at Louisiana State University, even though his education and teaching experience were in biology. O'Connor's uninvited intervention on behalf of her friend and frequent visitor may have enabled greater financial and familial stability in the Williams household following the move from Macon in 1961 and the subsequent dissolution of a tempestuous marriage.

That there is as well a trickle-down effect of O'Connor's influence on Lucinda Williams's lyric craft is plainly stated in the credits to *Down Where the Spirit Meets the Bone*. The liner notes for the double CD include this telling concluding acknowledgment:

> Dad—As Flannery O'Connor was to you, you were my greatest teacher. Thank you. —Lucinda

Chapter 3

MARY GAUTHIER

The Brutal Hand of Grace

Troubadour folksinger Mary Gauthier (pronounced Go-*shay*) acknowledges Flannery O'Connor as "one of the big influences" on her songwriting and on her consciousness and creative process as an artist. Gauthier, who lives in Nashville, participated in a roundtable discussion held at Vanderbilt Divinity School in February 2009, part of a series of lectures, panels, and presentations on the theological dimensions of O'Connor's art. Under the banner "The Enduring Chill: Remembering Flannery O'Connor," Gauthier, along with spoken-word artist Minton Sparks, songwriter and visual artist Julie Lee, and Lindford Detweiler and Karin Berquist from the band Over the Rhine, presented an evening of music as part of the event in the university's aptly named Mercy Lounge. The next morning, these artists gathered to talk about the place of O'Connor's visionary storytelling in their own works. Gauthier's comments during the panel discussion indicate her deeply grounded understanding of O'Connor's works and vision. She knows the journey through darkness toward some pinpoint of light that can be experienced reading an O'Connor story. The same holds true of listening to a Mary Gauthier song.

Gauthier first encountered O'Connor's fiction in a freshman English course at Louisiana State University and has since "read it all," including O'Connor's letters and the pieces collected in *Mystery and Manners*, from which she quoted on the Vanderbilt panel and occasionally refers to during media interviews. She remarked in a personal interview that as a woman and a writer she owes a debt to O'Connor for her willingness to be "an unladylike writer"— echoing an earlier reviewer in *Time* magazine. Flannery O'Connor, she added, gave her the "courage and permission" to go to places where, with "large and startling figures," she could tell stories about her own and others' experiences of "darkness," and to talk about these experiences in violent terms. Indeed, she readily connects O'Connor's often violent and shocking stories with her own songs about desperate and destitute characters.

Mary Gauthier's start to life almost seems to have come out of an O'Connor story. Born to an unwed teenage mother in 1962, she was abandoned as a newborn on the doorstep of St. Vincent's Infant Asylum in New Orleans, where she spent the first year of her life. She was adopted into an Italian Catholic family; her father was an alcoholic and her mother suffered severe mental health disorders. She was sent to a Catholic school and had a troubled youth, leaving home at fifteen and becoming caught up in drug and alcohol addiction that landed her briefly in jail at eighteen. She did not begin writing songs until she was thirty-five, after nine years as a successful, though seldom sober, restaurateur in Boston.

A central theme in Gauthier's songwriting is a deep longing for a home. Her abandonment as a newborn has left her with a desperate desire for human connection. She tells her life story in an achingly artful cycle of songs titled *The Foundling*, released in May 2010. Another theme running through Gauthier's songs is the need for redemption, for the touch of divine mercy and grace. Her most celebrated work, "Mercy Now," the title track from her 2005 recording, is a song of supplication that moves from the personal to the universal. Gauthier's characters, like those that people O'Connor's fictions, are all "looking for the grace from which they fell" ("Camelot") and finding it, though they "don't deserve it" ("Mercy"), in unlikely and often unlovely ways.

Like O'Connor, Gauthier is articulate about her creative process and the mystery of where her songwriting comes from. "It's a holy art," she says. "I think [my songs] come from the Creator; I think they come from the same place that the spirit comes from," she once remarked in a radio interview, adding, "The mystery deepens as I go forth as a songwriter." O'Connor expresses a similar notion in "The Nature and Aim of Fiction": "If a writer is any good, what he makes will have its source in a realm much larger than that which his conscious mind can encompass and will always be a greater surprise to him than it can ever be to his reader." As a writer of Catholic faith, O'Connor is very straightforward in acknowledging a divine source for her storytelling "gift," which she has said "comes from God" and may well be used to serve some holy purpose. As Gauthier translates this truth to her own calling, she believes "songs that heal come from a higher place."

O'Connor further remarks that writers with "the sharpest eyes for the grotesque, for the perverse, and for the unacceptable . . . may well be forced to take ever more violent means to get [their] vision across" to an unreceptive audience. Gauthier is such a writer. Like O'Connor, she is willing to offend and even to enrage her audience to get across her particular truth and vision. "If you don't offend, and you don't shock, and you don't scare, then you might as well write commercial songs in Nashville," Gauthier remarked in an interview.

Gauthier's subjects and her edgy, talking country-blues style is certainly not the stuff of commercial country music. She is fond of quoting Woody Guthrie's comment that the job of the artist is "to disturb the comfortable and comfort the disturbed." As she memorably defines her art, "Songwriting is just telling the truth and making it rhyme," and she works at finding the humility and courage to be what she calls "a truthteller": "Truthtellers are different than other songwriters. Truthtellers are always looking for the darkness, to try to shine some light. So we always have to go to the place where we don't know where we are and we don't understand what is happening. It's a treacherous way to write; it's a treacherous way to be." O'Connor likewise remarks that it is in the process of writing that she discovers what it is she has to say, commenting in a letter to her close correspondent Betty Hester, "I work from such a basis of poverty that everything I do is a miracle to me."

O'Connor was not in the business of writing uplifting stories, or stories of the kind that most readers—even her coreligionists—liked to read. One reader complained that one of O'Connor's stories had "left a bad taste in her mouth," to which O'Connor characteristically responded, "You weren't supposed to eat it." In her manifesto, "The Fiction Writer and His Country," O'Connor writes, "It requires considerable courage at any time, in any country, not to turn away from the storyteller." Gauthier expresses her affinity with O'Connor this way: "We are both willing to clear the room."

Mary Gauthier as Mary Grace

In O'Connor's short story "Revelation," we meet the plus-sized Ruby Turpin, one of a number of good Christian women in O'Connor's fiction who—for those familiar with her stories—are invariably headed for a violent, transformative comeuppance. Ruby, in name and authorial treatment, is evidently the most precious of these in the O'Connor canon. But as precious as she is, we discover that Ruby is bigoted, self-righteous, and given to thoughts and eventually to words that denigrate and diminish the humanity of others around her.

As she looms over a collection of southern stereotypes in a doctor's waiting room, Ruby becomes conscious of the ugly, smirking stare directed at her by a plump, pimply-faced girl of eighteen or nineteen sitting across the room, introduced by her affronted mother as Mary Grace. The girl sits silently scowling, reading a psychology textbook titled *Human Development*. At the point at which Ruby begins voicing her self-righteous, judgmental thoughts to the waiting room at large, Mary Grace explodes with rage, throws the book at Ruby, and then, with a howl, hurls herself at Ruby, grabbing her by the throat. Before she is subdued by the doctor's needle, the emblematically named Mary Grace delivers in a whisper her pointed message to *un*righteous Ruby: "Go back to hell where you came from, you old wart hog." O'Connor, in effect, does the same thing in story after story: she throws the book at her characters—and, perhaps, at the spiritually unaware or self-righteous reader. And in each case the revelation is the same: a painfully regenerative shot of God's grace finds its mark.

Gauthier too has figuratively thrown the book at characters in need of deeper human development, in need of the kind of grace that, after an initial shock, will both reform and redeem them. And, as in O'Connor's stories, this grace moment in Gauthier's songs is born out of pain and suffering and sometimes enacted with violence. On the Vanderbilt panel, Gauthier spoke about O'Connor's influence on her own vision and focus as a songwriter attuned to the concept of grace:

> You don't go to the dark place gratuitously. It's purposeful. You do it because without darkness there is no light. And that is what Flannery taught me. And it is all wrapped around the concept of grace, that without sorrow and suffering we have no use for grace. So, [my songwriting is] a purposeful journey into the sorrow and struggle and frailty of human nature. I think it's one of the only true ways to talk about grace that has a deep resonance. If not, you're talking about "a flesh-colored Christ that glows in the dark"—that Dylan line—the Jesus for sale. That's what I learned from Flannery's work that is deeply spiritual behind the struggle.

Both writers present us with examples of what theologian Dietrich Bonhoeffer calls "costly grace," which in his writings in *The Cost of Discipleship*, he defines in apposition to what he calls "cheap grace." "Cheap grace is the preaching of forgiveness without requiring repentance . . . Communion . . . [and] absolution without personal confession. Cheap grace is grace without discipleship, grace without the cross." Costly grace, however, "is *costly* because it costs a man his life . . . because it condemns sin, and *grace* because it justifies the sinner." It comes to those who have "a broken spirit" and "a contrite heart." Above all, Bonhoeffer concludes, costly grace is the incarnational, crucifying "grace of Christ himself." Gauthier's songs present hard, confronting encounters with "costly grace" in raw, often confessional lyrics.

Gauthier can sing compellingly about the costly, hard transforming nature of grace because she has experienced it firsthand. As she tells NPR's Terry Gross, she was in and out of rehab in her teens and twenties, struggling with heroin addiction. An adopted child raised in an unstable household, she felt hopelessly alone, always longing for a connection she never seemed able to make. She images her condition as "running around with a plug trying to find a socket to plug into." At twenty-eight, on the opening night of a restaurant in Boston of which she was part owner and chef, Gauthier was arrested for drunk driving and spent the night in a holding cell. In her interview with Gross, she describes this experience as a turning point in her life:

> On the floor of the jail cell, I left my body for probably a millisecond and looked down on myself and saw something pitiful. And it was that moment when the grace of God could enter—grace—that unmerited gift. I received it. I saw my condition as hopeless. And in that moment of surrender, I became willing to ask for help, and it changed everything. It changed everything.

The most compelling expression of a life-changing encounter with grace in Gauthier's work is the song "Karla Faye" on her 1999 recording *Drag Queens in Limousines*. The song briefly summarizes the real life of Karla Faye Tucker—"a junkie a whore living for the next high," who, while stoned on heroin, was an accomplice in the killing of two people in a robbery gone horribly wrong. Tucker was sentenced in 1983 to be executed for these grisly murders and came to Christian faith a few months after she was placed on death row in the Texas prison where she spent fourteen years. As the date of her execution approached, then Texas governor George W. Bush refused to commute her sentence, despite appeals from several world leaders, including Pope John Paul II. Karla Faye Tucker died by lethal injection on 3 February 1998, the first woman executed in Texas since the Civil War. Her life, especially her conversion story, has been the subject of several books and two feature films.

Gauthier was compelled by the story of Tucker's transformation from a desperate drug-addicted prostitute to a near-beatific figure who offered counsel and encouragement and the good news of the gospel to her fellow prisoners. "Karla Faye," cowritten with Crit Harmon, is based on testimonial from Tucker, told to her biographer Beverly Lowry. In the song Gauthier describes Tucker's moment of grace:

alone in her cell, no dope in her veins
the killer'd become little girl lost again
she fell to her knees, she prayed she would die
on the cold cement floor she finally cried
and love came like the wind
love whispered her name
love reached through and held her, love lifted her pain
fifteen years on death row, her faith deeper each day
Her last words were "I love you all"
Goodbye, Karla Faye

As for O'Connor's tattooed O. E. Parker, who has symbolically come to the end of himself in his efforts to make sense of his "botched" life, the moment of grace for Gauthier's Karla Faye comes unexpectedly, in a whisper, and has cost plenty. Here, as in most of O'Connor's stories, the action of grace occurs in the face of impending death. In fact, few of O'Connor's characters are touched by grace and live to testify. Rather, like Karla Faye Tucker at her moment of execution, they experience Bonhoeffer's costly grace as he *ultimately* defines it, as the crucifying "grace of Christ himself."

In Gauthier's slow, waltzing lament, there is the conviction of experience in her delivery of the grace lines: she too has known an infusion of grace on the floor of a jail cell. Yet while her Catholic upbringing imprinted Gauthier with some of the dogmas of the Church, there is little Catholic imagery in her work—unlike in Springsteen's art—save perhaps her own beatified "Our Lady of the Shooting Stars" on *Drag Queens in Limousines*, a private sainted figure both sensual and spiritual. Gauthier found the Catholicism in which she was raised "authoritarian and empty." Her spirituality and sense of the sacred is more grounded in the Twelve-Step program of Alcoholics Anonymous that rescued her from thirteen years of alcohol addiction and instilled in her a sense of a divine Presence watching over her. "There's more surrendering the will to God . . . than Catholic traditional gospel thinking," Gauthier says about her spiritual practice and belief.

Acts of grace in extremis are at the heart of many of O'Connor's stories. Mrs. May in "Greenleaf," for example, is in the same moment divinely embraced and impaled by the charging bull-god who has "come down to woo her." The liberal humanist social worker Sheppard in "The Lame Shall Enter First" experiences a transforming epiphany that opens him up to a *caritas* kind of love, only to find that the child he has neglected and now longs to nurture has hanged himself in a desperate attempt to be in heaven with his recently deceased mother.

The most palpable illustration of costly, extreme grace in O'Connor's fiction is in "A Good Man Is Hard to Find," in which a family of six is methodically murdered by an escaped convict calling himself The Misfit, who expresses his existential angst over his struggles to believe in the story of Christ's redemptive sacrifice. Absent of true meaning, The Misfit's life has devolved to the point where he can find no purpose or pleasure except in committing acts of "meanness." While the bodies pile up in the woods, and The Misfit shoots the pleading grandmother three times point-blank, O'Connor's advice to the traumatized reader is to overlook the bodies and the terror of the moment and to notice instead the "almost imperceptible" gesture of grace enacted when the grandmother reaches out to the hardened killer and says, "Why, you're one of my babies, you're one of my children." This is grace transacted with a gun to the head; costly grace indeed, for it costs the grandmother everything—her dignity, her family, her conception of herself, and her life.

Most of Gauthier's songs are connected in some way to her own life; her narrators and characters pursue a desperate hope of making a meaningful connection with someone or something. "Worthy," a song from *Trouble and Love* (2014), cowritten with Mary Chapin Carpenter, speaks to Gauthier's own story: a desperate life of addictions and emotional trauma saved by an amazing grace. To Terry Gross's question about how her jailhouse experience changed her life, Gauthier responds, "It means more to me, actually, twenty-four years later than it did at the time." "Worthy" recalls that transforming experience. It opens with an O'Connoresque line: "It took a mighty blow to crack me to the core." The action of grace is often manifested shockingly and only after great cost and struggle, as is attested in the words to the bridge that leads to the final chorus:

> I walked through a wall of fire
> Left behind the only life I knew
> No way back, no place to hide
> When a voice came through . . . Worthy
> Worthy, what a thing to claim
> Worthy, worthy, ashes into flame.
> Worthy.

Here, in this Methodist-hymn-like song—and in all Gauthier's songs where grace is evident—the reifying, self-affirming work of grace is recognized and accepted, though it has cost plenty. In this respect, Gauthier stands apart from O'Connor, whose fictional dramatizations of the Calvinist doctrine of "irresistible grace," as critics have pointed out, are presented with characters ill-prepared for or adamantly resistant to its usually violent incursions. The wannabe artist Asbury in "The Enduring Chill," for example, gets a severe dose of grace, though it is "the last thing [he is] looking for."

In O'Connor's essay "Some Aspects of the Grotesque in Southern Fiction," she has this to say about the nature of grace in literature and life: "There is something in us, as storytellers and as listeners to stories, that demands the redemptive act, that demands that what falls at least be offered the chance to be restored. The reader of today looks for this motion, and rightly so, but what he has forgotten is the cost of it . . . he has forgotten the price of restoration." Mary Flannery O'Connor's short stories and Mary Gauthier's song-stories remind us of the paradox of grace, of the brutal grace event transacted on a hill called Golgotha and offered freely from the wounded hands of God to all . . . but not without cost.

Snakebit

Gauthier's "Snakebit" is professedly her "most Flannery O'Connor inspired song," cowritten with Hayes Carll, the first track on her fifth collection, *Between Daylight and Dark* (2007). Gauthier acknowledges that she drew on O'Connor's The Misfit in shaping the sensibilities of her snakebit character. The song's title, she says, comes from an expression used by her father any time disaster struck or his earnest efforts to accomplish something were thwarted.

In both lyrical content and sonic form, "Snakebit" appears to owe as much to Bob Dylan's "Ballad of Hollis Brown" (1963) as to anything in O'Connor's fictions. The opening two verses blend third-person narration with a first-person account, both dealing with the sense of desperation felt by the "I" in the song: "The children are crying, they never got their supper / Where would you run to in the darkness of the night?" the lyrics begin, echoing the theme of Dylan's ballad—the desperate poverty and privation that leads to desperate acts. In answer, a first-person voice enters: "Even shadows fear to wander / They gather 'round me in the candlelight." In the second verse the outer narrator observes a broken crucifix, "bloody, sharp and shattered" on a bedroom floor, which the first-person narrator admits to smashing in response to an existence filled with "Pain and prayers and promises scattered." Like the desperate characters in Bruce Springsteen's *Nebraska* songs, whose sense of meaninglessness drives them to acts of violence, Gauthier's snakebit character has impulsively "pulled [a] pistol from [a] dresser drawer" to commit a deadly act—or has already done so. The chorus cries, "Oh Lord, oh Lord / Oh Lord, what have I done? / Everything worth holding slips through my fingers / Now my hand's wrapped around the handle of a gun."

O'Connor's influence in the song might be observed in the description of the distraught and remorseful first-person narrator, whose voice takes over the lyrics following the first chorus. Typical of Gauthier's characters, no gender is given, but he or she is forty years old, feeling put upon, "forsaken, forgotten, without love," and under the dark shadow cast by a deceased father, whose repeated foretelling of misfortune now replays in the narrator's mind: "Kid, I knew when you was born you'd end up snakebit like me." Thomas in O'Connor's story "The Comforts of Home" comes to mind in that stupefying moment after the gun he holds goes off in the story's concluding scene. O'Connor's snakebit characters respond with violence as a serpent evil touches them: Thomas fatally fires as though his hand were "guided by" the "hissed" imprecations of his lying father/the father of lies; The Misfit recoils from the proffered grace of the grandmother's touch on his shoulder "as though a snake had bitten him," and likewise murders with a gun. One possible reading Gauthier offers of her song is that her character makes "a decision to reject the holy and pick up the gun." Gauthier's haunting blues song reveals someone in an anguished inner state akin to those of O'Connor's two gun-wielding characters and likewise intimates a cosmic Evil that can animate human actions.

"Wheel inside the Wheel," from Gauthier's first commercially successful recording *Mercy Now* (2005), presents the listener with a vision of an eclectic procession of people marginalized by race, religion, and sexual orientation, all metaphorically winding their way heavenward. "The parade of souls" in Gauthier's banjo-driven, talking blues song invokes a vision (with the same implicit shocking intent) like that of the chastened Ruby Turpin in O'Connor's "Revelation." In Ruby's vision of a "vast horde of souls . . . rumbling toward heaven," the social order she hypocritically applies to all those she meets is inverted. The "bottom rail [is] on top." The "white-trash" she despises, the Blacks, and a whole company of "freaks and lunatics" who, "leaping like frogs," appear even further off balance than the temporarily mad Mary Grace, are all headed across that "vast swinging bridge" into heaven ahead of respectable good Christian folk like herself and her husband. But more important than the inverted hierarchy is the revelation that the vastness of divine grace includes them all, not just Ruby's better types. This is the shock of grace we are led to understand ultimately alters Ruby's pharisaical outlook.

Gauthier's song updates O'Connor's story of a bigoted, hypocritical good Christian woman, adding transsexuals, gays, and Indigenous peoples to the litany of Others who might have been included (or excluded) in Ruby's judgmental vision and thoughts. The song invokes the Mardi Gras parades in New Orleans that precede the season of Lent: flambeau dancers, French Quarter queens, Native Americans in "colored feathers and beads," and Black Americans led by New Orleans native Satchmo (Louis Armstrong) parade and chant behind a brass band playing "When the Saints Go Marching In." In Gauthier's heavenly procession, Marie Laveau, the famous voodoo queen of nineteenth-century New Orleans, who was eventually given a Catholic burial, "promenades with Oscar Wilde," who likewise died a baptized Catholic despite his sins against the morals of his age. All join in a "soul parade" that "winds its way down Eternity Street": "marching across the sky / Their heat and their light bathed in blue as they march by." The image recalls the streak of celestial highway that resolves in hue from lavender blue to purple in Ruby's visionary moment.

Like O'Connor's story "Revelation," Gauthier's song presents an image of the vast inclusiveness within the action of grace. The "wheel inside the wheel" phrase invoking Ezekiel's prophetic vision, aligns with the mystery co-involved with manners that distinguishes O'Connor's artistic and Catholic viewpoint. "I just stole this right from the Bible, as any good songwriter will do," Gauthier once remarked in introducing this song from the stage. She also acknowledges that it owes something to an old spiritual she heard Johnny Cash sing:

Ezekiel saw the wheel . . .
Way up in the middle of the air
Now the little wheel ran by Faith
And a wheel in a wheel in the wheel good Lord
Way in the middle of the air

There is gospel truth wheeling inside this song's truth. An elegy for a friend who had recently died, Gauthier's "Wheel inside the Wheel" may well owe its eclectic procession to Ruby's vision, and most certainly is intended to offer the same possibly "abysmal life-giving knowledge" to the sanctimonious and self-righteous that is transacted in and through O'Connor's story.

Our best works of art, says O'Connor in her essay "Novelist and Believer," "naturally involve the salvation or loss of the soul. Where there is no belief in the soul, there is very little drama." Gauthier's narrative songs might be defined as a collection of soul dramas, the characters whose stories she tells winding their way up "Eternity Street," like the "vast horde of souls . . . rumbling toward heaven" across the "vast swinging bridge" that Ruby Turpin envisions in the sky.

The Habit of Songwriting

O'Connor's manuscripts, housed in the O'Connor Collection at Georgia College & State University in her hometown of Milledgeville, bear evidence of her painstaking rewriting and reworking of drafts. She labored for five years on her first novel, *Wise Blood* (1952), thousands of draft manuscript pages resulting in a 232-page book. Her second novel, *The Violent Bear It Away* (1960), took seven years to complete. For O'Connor, writing meant rewriting and then compulsively revising what she had rewritten. This degree of attention to language and form, and her imaginative (and prayerful) pursuit of the story she needed to tell, resulted in a literary output of about two short stories a year, alongside her two novels, over the eighteen years of her writing life.

Gauthier shares O'Connor's painstaking approach to composition and the experience of writing as hard work and a process of discovery. "Songwriting is not easy for me," she has said. "I write about what I don't know and try to understand it"—a remark that echoes O'Connor. Like O'Connor, her style is simple and direct, using small details in her character-centered stories to reveal larger truths: "I want to tell a story and be done with it. But I want to tell it big." She spends months and even years honing the lyrics to a song to find the right words with the right sounds and syllables. Her autobiographical "career song" as she calls it, "I Drink," cowritten with Crit Harmon and rereleased in 2002 on *Mercy Now*, went through more than three hundred drafts. Its chorus illustrates the expansive simplicity of Gauthier's minimalist style:

> Fish swim birds fly
> Daddies yell mamas cry
> Old men sit and think
> I drink

Her carefully crafted, poetic lyrics have led to comparisons with Lucinda Williams and attracted the interest of Bob Dylan, who once played "I Drink" and explicated its lyrics on his satellite radio program, *Theme Time Radio Hour*.

Gauthier has mused about why people come to hear singer-songwriters: "One of the reasons is because they look good; one of the reasons is because they sing good; one of the reasons is because they have something to say and have stories to tell." She emphasizes that she fits into the third category and declares, like Bruce Springsteen, "I'm a writer; I'm a serious writer." In fact, like other O'Connor disciples Sufjan Stevens and fellow southerner Jim White, she has tried her hand at writing short fiction, O'Connor's preferred form. Gauthier's story "The Holiday Inn Again" appears in *Amplified*, a unique collection of mostly first-effort short stories by Americana artists—including Jim White—published in 2009. Gauthier's story is told through a familiar construct in O'Connor's short fiction, the point of view of a child, an eleven-year-old girl whose alcoholic adoptive father calls her an "ungrateful bitch" and threatens to return her to the orphanage. He is regularly abusive to his wife, forcing her to pack up her two daughters and flee to a Baton Rouge Holiday Inn. Tired of retreating to motels with her mother and younger sister each time there is domestic violence, the child narrator tries to convince her mother to move to an apartment with a swimming pool, to no avail. "It's just too dangerous to have you kids around water," the mother responds in the story's ironic last line. Like most of Gauthier's work, the story is partly autobiographical, partly imagined—an "amplified" version of the first verse of "I Drink"—artfully written and painful to read.

O'Connor was characteristically frank with the wannabe writers who gathered to hear her speak in college classrooms and antebellum parlors: only those gifted with "the ability to create life with words" should pursue the art of writing fiction. A short story is not an anecdote or a reminiscence but "a complete dramatic action," she emphasized. Moreover, in her art and vision, "A story always involves, in a dramatic way, the mystery of personality." And this is revealed, as she shows in explicating her story "A Good Man Is Hard to Find," in small descriptive details and some telling gesture that "indicates where the real heart of the story lies." In O'Connor's signature story, this moment occurs when the grandmother's "head clear[s] for an instant" and she reaches out and touches The Misfit in a gesture of sympathy and connection. This violent and puzzling story, says O'Connor, would be meaningless without the grandmother's signifying gesture: "If I took out this gesture and what she says with it, I would have no story," she explains. There would be no mystery.

Gauthier, like Bruce Springsteen, has a writer's gift to make her characters live and to create small dramatic incidents that, as O'Connor remarks about the essence of a good story, "can't be reduced, [but] can only be expanded." The individual vignettes in "Camelot Motel" from Gauthier's 2002 *Filth and Fire* are illustrative of some of the characters and circumstances she writes about and reveal the lyric economy of her songwriting. The point of view in this narrative song moves like a voyeur from room to room in a seedy motel. In one room, a woman "lights the day's first cigarette" after an implied extramarital tryst with a "self-assured lover" who looks on silently from the double bed; then she "picks up the phone and calls her kids from the motel kitchenette." In another room a man wakes to the ravings of an emotionally disturbed woman he picked up in a bar the night before, who turns out to be a religious maniac. Two gay men who "met in a chat room" and go by pseudonyms suffer from pounding hangovers as they quietly prepare to check out. In a fourth room, a pair of armed drug dealers count their money, nervously attuned to "every little sound"; one of them "keeps picking up his pistol and putting his pistol down." These characters come alive completely through the small deft details and gestures Gauthier's lyrics provide. Her cast of "cheaters, liars, outlaws and fallen angels" gathered in the song's chorus are all, like O'Connor's backwoods rednecks and band of misfits, consciously or not, "looking for the grace from which they fell."

The title song of Gauthier's 1999 *Drag Queens in Limousines* introduces other characters in her community of souls. Along with drag queens and "nuns in blue jeans" are AWOL marines, actors, barflies, and "drunks that philosophize." "These are my friends," Gauthier sings in the song's final line. Gauthier invokes the world of the "bad neighborhood" she once lived and worked in, flipping burgers "to cover the rent" and drinking shots of bourbon "at Happy Hour for 35 cents." The song is an invitation to understand those who, like the song's narrator, "do what [they] gotta do" and hope that people who love them will "catch up." One of them is the exotic dancer in "Evangeline," who is everything she wants to be when she is dancing—and she can "dance on air" on "the dirty stage." Others, like the narrator of "I Drink," sit alone and drink and eat TV dinners, and say that they "don't give a damn" when indeed they do.

A displaced person herself, Gauthier identifies with people on the social margins, who through addiction, rejection, or misfortune have found themselves cast out or unwanted, performers in life's sideshow. Two early songs about AIDS victims, "Goddamn HIV" and "Skeleton Town," describe the painful estrangement of gay people with the disease and their abandonment by family and even the medical system. Added to the marginal collectives in "Drag Queens in Limousines" and "Wheel inside the Wheel" are the Key West street people in "Christmas in Paradise" who celebrate the season by erecting an artificial Christmas tree on the bridge under which they live and cheerily shouting "Merry Christmas y'all!" to passing motorists. Gauthier's songs about displaced persons include the picked guitar and piano ballad "Can't Find the Way" about a shocked and impoverished survivor of Hurricane Katrina trying to find her way home. As well, Gauthier has worked with the SongwritingWith:Soldiers program, creating songs that poignantly bear witness to the experiences and responses of emotionally damaged Iraq War veterans, embracing an extensive community whose mental health has made them DPs to their careers and loved ones. Her Grammy-nominated *Rifles and Rosary Beads* (2017) features raw songs of war and home-front experience, cowritten with veterans and their spouses.

Uncomfortable songs about an abandoned infant, addiction, dereliction, the effects of HIV, suicidal urges, and street people are not the usual matter of Top 40 country music. Nor is Gauthier trying to shock or offend for effect, as a lesser artist might do. Rather, she writes the kinds of songs she does because her subject is humanity in all its incarnate forms. And within that humanity are extremists and psychopaths, the homeless and the desperate-hearted, the abandoned, the lost. Gauthier's songs speak for and about these people.

Though socially marginalized, these characters are far from marginal in their emotions and experiences. Gauthier's intent, as the great southern writer William Faulkner defined his concerns, is to discover and "write down the heart's truth out of the heart's driving complexity" for the sake of "all the complex and troubled hearts" that are our own. That troubled heart beats the same in an alcoholic, a hobo, or an Iraq War vet with PTSD. Like the desperate-hearted characters in Springsteen's *Nebraska* songs, or in Lucinda Williams's *World without Tears* collection, whose sense of meaninglessness, despair, and loss drives them to acts of violence and self-abuse, Gauthier's snakebit characters recoil in pain and anger, more often retreating than reacting violently. O'Connor once remarked of her backwoods, corn-whiskey swilling, shotgun waving, raving prophet figure Mason Tarwater, "I'm right behind him 100 per cent." Gauthier too is 100 percent behind her often broken, ill-fortuned characters. And no more so than the character The Foundling in her autobiographical cycle of songs.

Abandoned as a newborn, Gauthier has felt herself a displaced person all her life, and the cycle of songs on *The Foundling* (2010)—recorded in Toronto, Canada, far displaced from the South—tells some of her life story and her efforts to find and communicate with her birth mother. Songs on *The Foundling* are wrapped in pain, unraveled by despair, and aching with a sense of abandonment and loss, however bravely endured. Collectively, they form a kind of folk-blues musical in three acts, beginning with a theme song that introduces the central character, The Foundling, a name like O'Connor's The Misfit, with a big-T definite article. The Foundling's story of abandonment and search for home is narrated in a cycle of songs that blends first- and third-person narratives to suggest both individual and collective experience. The recording is structured into three groups of three songs. Acoustic guitar and violin create the sound in all but one song, and each trio is separated by a brief, ragged accordion interlude. The melodies and arrangements are "evocative of gypsy music," as music critic Jewly Hight observes, conjuring "images of wandering and rootlessness." The Foundling's story is completed with a "Coda" that repeats the chorus of the opening theme song. One can imagine these songs as part of a larger, dramatic narrative that might be staged, and in a sense, of course, they are: as Gauthier writes in the notes accompanying the CD, "*The Foundling* is my story."

On track 6, "Blood Is Blood," she sings about the universal experience of a foundling: the pain of not knowing where you come from, whose blood beats in you, whose face helped form the one that stares back at you from the mirror: "I don't know who I am / I don't know who I'm not," the lyrics bewail. In notes on the songs, Gauthier describes "Blood Is Blood" as "an adoptee identity crisis song," but it is more than that. It is an existential cry of a tormented being struggling to stay whole and alive: "I've got a heart that's ripped / I've got a soul that's torn / I've got a hole in me like I was never born." The pain in this song is palpable. Tania Elizabeth's violin drives the pain into the listener's soul in the raw, grating, dissonant instrumental bridge that begins in the exact middle of the song and lasts for an agonizing twenty-six seconds.

Before the listener can recover, on the next track, "March 11, 1962" (Gauthier's date of birth), we hear a voice in one side of a terrifying telephone conversation. The longest piece on the recording, this spoken-word song sits at the center of the album's thirteen tracks, as its story sits at the center of Mary Gauthier's being. "March 11, 1962" is about "the hardest thing" The Foundling has ever done: finally speak with her birth mother forty years after the fact. It took five hundred dollars and three days for a private detective to locate Gauthier's birth mother; it took Gauthier a further six months to muster up the courage to call her. It took thirteen years of honing her craft to produce this remarkable song.

Stories of children abandoned at birth who go through life unaware of their parentage are as old as the tales of Oedipus and Moses. They are a common trope in popular culture, from the comic-book icon Superman to *Star Wars* hero Luke Skywalker. In few if any of these stories is the discovery of one's true parentage a happy revelation. Oedipus blinds himself upon learning that he has unwittingly killed his father and slept with his mother, as the Delphic Oracle had prophesied, and Luke loses a hand in battle with the dark lord Darth Vader after hearing the words that now echo through popular culture consciousness, "I am your father." The Foundling discovers she is a "shameful secret" her birth mother has never revealed and does not want to remedy. As Gauthier sums up the conversation in her notes, "She had no desire to meet me. It was too much for her." Yet in the song The Foundling finds some point of resolution, some purpose for the search and the terrifying telephone call. The song ends on a note of affirmation that brings some sense of closure, however painfully muted, though little existential relief: "I had to thank you once before this life went by / Yeah, that's why I called. Goodbye."

Gauthier's notes say nothing about the inspiration for "Walk in the Water," the song that follows. And nothing speakable can be said. This song finishes the painful middle act, with the singer announcing a desire to commit suicide, apparently in response to the adult experience of her further rejection by her birth mother. Like the trapped and desperate Edna Pontillier in *The Awakening* by New Orleans writer Kate Chopin, or the mentally ill Virginia Woolf approaching the River Ouse with stones in her pockets, The Foundling declares, "I'm gonna walk in the water till my hat floats away." The numbing despair in this song is caught in the long, sustained bow strokes of the violin teasing out haunting notes that hover and dip between fundamental tone and harmonic—musically suggesting a kind of interspace in the self between being and not-being, that space in the consciousness of someone who has resolved to take his or her life. The song is only bearable in the knowledge that Act 3 is coming, with the song titles "Sweet Words," "The Orphan King," and "Another Day Borrowed" holding out promise that The Foundling has not foundered. Nonetheless, it takes "considerable courage" to stay in the room with songs so bravely created and so freighted with pain.

Mercy Now

T Bone Burnett once remarked, "The best songs are the ones that are so personal and small that they become universal and big." He cites Bob Dylan's "Blowin' in the Wind" and the Beatles' "All You Need Is Love" as examples. Gauthier's "Mercy Now" is such a song. While it deals with personal pain, loss, and fear, this is not a song that clears the room; rather, it embraces everyone in it. Gauthier's signature song proclaims that everyone is in need of "the action of mercy"—a key phrase in O'Connor's lexicon. Indeed, the two words in Gauthier's song title appear in O'Connor's description of Mr. Head's existential encounter with divine mercy as he gazes upon the "artificial nigger" in her story of that title. O'Connor once acknowledged that this fraught-titled story was her favorite and she thought one of the best stories she had written, because "there is a good deal more in it than I understand myself." Face to face with a mystery *incarnate* in plaster, after his denial of his grandson Nelson, we read, "Mr. Head had never known before what *mercy* felt like because he had been too good to deserve any, but he felt he knew *now*" (emphasis added).

"Mercy Now" is a standout song in Gauthier's canon. Among her many well-crafted, compelling works, it is the song she is best known for, and she often finishes her performances with it. Although she typically writes "more from perspiration than inspiration," as she said in a 2005 NPR interview shortly after her album *Mercy Now* was released, that song came suddenly, as a kind of "epiphany" that gave her a deep "sense of forgiveness." She attempted to capture that moment of insight as best she could. "It was more like I reeled [this song] in than I wrote it. I am absolutely sure it came *through* me not *from* me." Typical of her compositions, the song begins with a personal focus, its first two verses describing her father's decline from Alzheimer's and her brother Michael's incarceration (she dedicates the album to him). And then, atypically, the song opens out to embrace "my church and my country" and "every living thing." The personal, political, and social realities we all face, Gauthier sings, are all under the mercy of the divine in this life and the next. "Only the hand of grace" can sustain and keep us. The theological truths in this song are emphasized in the booklet accompanying the CD, where the lyrics to "Mercy Now" are overlaid on a black-and-white photograph of a graveyard marker featuring a life-sized stone carving of a woman, bowed with her hands clasped in prayer, leaning against a strong stone cross.

Gauthier's last verse in "Mercy Now" distills O'Connor's concerns in fiction: our need, "every single one of us," for the touch of grace and mercy, and our participation in a drama played out—as O'Connor describes young Tarwater's condition—between "Jesus or the devil." "We hang in the balance / Dangle between hell and hallowed ground," Gauthier sings. For the misfits who inhabit her songs, as in O'Connor's fiction, "everything [is] off balance," headed for a long fall, destined for a "walk through the fire," but with the possibility that the lost and lonely will find the way to their true home, that they will be found and no longer foundlings in the end.

In her 2021 memoir *Saved by a Song*, Gauthier joins hands with O'Connor as a storyteller in song. She writes, "Flannery O'Connor said, 'Fiction writing is about everything human and we are made out of dust, and if you scorn getting yourself dusty, then you shouldn't try to write fiction. It's not a good enough job for you.'" She adds, "I'd say the same thing applies to songwriting." As the youthful O'Connor felt called to write fiction, so Mary Gauthier says, "I write songs because I am called to." And she is not afraid to get disturbingly dusty doing so. Moreover, like O'Connor, she has been true to and truthful through her calling.

Chapter 4

KATE CAMPBELL

"Equal Parts Emmylou Harris and Flannery O'Connor"

Kate Campbell has said that her art and vision are very much inspired by the examples and works of southern women writers. "I think those who are familiar with Flannery O'Connor will see a bit of her in my songs, or Carson McCullers and Eudora Welty," she told an interviewer for a southern newspaper. In fact, she lists O'Connor among other writers and individuals she thanks for inspiration in the liner notes of *Moonpie Dreams* (1997), her second release on the independent roots music label Compass Records. As in O'Connor's stories, a strong sense of place informs Campbell's works; she writes about the South, its people, its geography, its fraught social history, its conflicted religiosity. Her songs about life in the desegregated South contain that "mix of believability and darkness" she finds intriguing in O'Connor's fiction.

Campbell started writing songs when she was in elementary school, but like Mary Gauthier—with whom she shares a birthplace a year earlier—she did not embark on a musical career until she was in her thirties. At that point she was pursuing an academic profession, enrolled in doctoral studies in southern history and teaching at Middle Tennessee State University. A performance at Nashville's famous Bluebird Café in 1991 introduced Campbell's songs to a country-music audience, but every record label in Nashville turned her down. After her self-made album *Songs from the Levee* was released by the upstart Compass Records in 1995, her music career blossomed: she appeared on *Live from Mountain Stage* and NPR's *All Things Considered* and was nominated singer-songwriter of the year by the National Association of Independent Record Distributors. She toured Europe with Emmylou Harris and Australia with the late Guy Clark. She has since released eighteen albums and played major venues including Merlefest and the prestigious Cambridge Folk Festival. Campbell is an accomplished songwriter, who, like Springsteen, often writes narrative songs in which a range of characters tell their stories, from a struggling cotton farmer ("Visions of Plenty") to a southern laborer working in the North and longing for home ("Red Clay after Rain"), and a convicted murderer doing time in Alabama ("Alabama Department of

Corrections Meditation Blues"). Her biography on the popular All Music website describes her as "Equal parts Emmylou Harris and Flannery O'Connor."

As in O'Connor's work, Campbell's stories in song weave together the South's concerns with place, race, and religion. The rich local texture and cultural depth of her songwriting makes for authentic southern art. "I used to worry about being too regional," she admits. "But I also realized that is what I know. You have to write what you know or else you'll be posing as something you are not.... I just decided to do what I do, and I realized that people are the same the world over."

Campbell's words on the value of knowing one's region and the imperative to "write what you know" could well be a paraphrase of O'Connor's creed as a southern writer. As O'Connor remarked in a talk to the Georgia Writers' Association, "The best American fiction has always been regional." When a writer comes from a place where there is "a shared past" and "a sense of alikeness," she said, there is "the possibility of reading a small history in a universal light." Such a "limitation" is for both O'Connor and Campbell "a gateway to reality." Campbell shares O'Connor's dictum, emphasized frequently in her talks to writers' groups, that a story writer's first consideration is to create believable characters and to set them down in a familiar and true space and time. And if that story world gives an honest picture of the South, it will be informed by the tensions and contradictions inherent in southern culture and society and will speak to larger human concerns. The longest and most besetting of these in the South is of course its history of racial oppression.

Campbell was born in 1961 in New Orleans and raised in the small town of Sledge, Mississippi. Though she was a child during the turbulent civil rights era, her early experiences have had a profound effect on her sensibilities and subjects as a songwriter. Her parents were intolerant of the racist culture of 1960s Mississippi, and her minister father actively supported desegregation and issues of racial equality, to the point of jeopardizing his preaching job by inviting Black civil rights leaders to visit his all-white Southern Baptist congregation. Like her preacher father, Campbell foregrounds matters of southern race relations in her work and deplores the deep social tensions and trauma that have resulted. "Because we've lived so closely together here, we have no excuse for what we have done," she has written. "I just cannot reconcile the proximity of the races in the South with the violence between them." "Crazy in Alabama," the fourth track on her *Visions of Plenty* album (1998), tells some stark tales of the times from a child's perspective, a point of view that O'Connor employs in several stories. In Campbell's song the white child narrator is aware of race privilege in her Alabama community. She has observed that when buying ice-cream cones at the corner Dairy Dip, "white people ordered from the front" while "the side was for the colored line." And she is aware that she numbers among "the privileged and the few" white children who play in the "cool blue" of the public swimming pool on hot summer afternoons, while "Brown children watched outside the fence." To the young narrator's mind, "it never made one lick of sense." Yet the "train of change" rolling through the racially charged social climate of Alabama during the civil rights era felt "crazy" and threatening. The song's chorus splices together news events of the times in a child-like way:

> It was crazy there were grown men fights
> Over segregation and civil rights
> Martin Luther King and the KKK
> George C. Wallace and LBJ
> And when the National Guard came in
> I thought the world was gonna end
> It was crazy in Alabama

The song's final verse alludes to the famous march from Selma, Alabama, to the capital in Jefferson in March 1965, led by Martin Luther King Jr. and members of the Southern Christian Leadership Council (SCLC), notably including the late John Lewis. In the song, the child's mother orders her inside the house, pulls the blinds, and locks the doors, as together they "felt the rumble heard the roar" of the freedom marchers passing by and saw that "they all held hands they sang and wept / And freedom rang in every step."

When desegregation became law, Campbell's socially progressive parents sent her to a largely Black junior high school, a story she tells in "Bus 109" on *Visions of Plenty*. A song on her *1000 Pound Machine* (2011) imagines racist Alabama governor George Wallace and civil rights icon Rosa Parks sitting together on a Greyhound bus from Montgomery to Mobile in the present day, both looking out the bus window "to see if the view has changed." O'Connor too chose to set inside a bus her one story focused on the historic racial divide in the South. She finished "Everything That Rises Must Converge" on 26 March 1961, just weeks before the original integrated group of Freedom Riders began their violence-wracked journey on a Greyhound bus from Washington, DC, to the Deep South—including a tense stop at the Hollywood Baptist Church, pastored by Campbell's father in the tiny town of Sledge, Mississippi.

Look Away

O'Connor's attitude toward the race issue in the South is a fraught subject. She refused to meet with Black American writer James Baldwin in 1959 at her Milledgeville home because, as she explained, "It would cause the greatest trouble and disturbance and disunion.... I observe the traditions of the society I feed on—it's only fair." She added brusquely, "Might as well expect a mule to fly as me to see James Baldwin in Georgia." Her own inherited attitudes toward Blacks—both personally and in her fictional representations—have been hotly debated by O'Connor scholars and today have somewhat stained her literary reputation. Her one "topical" story on the issue of desegregation, "Everything That Rises Must Converge," presents Mrs. Chestny, a woman whose values and social outlook are rooted in the class and race privilege of the Old South.

O'Connor's Mrs. Chestny does not want to ride on public transit alone since the buses have become integrated, so she compels her twenty-something son Julian to accompany her to her weekly "reducing class" at the local YWCA. Julian appears to hold progressive views on the race issue, but his gestures of solidarity with the few Blacks he interacts with on the buses are contrived and insincere, more a way to goad his mother than a reflection of his true beliefs in racial equality. Mrs. Chestny is given to fond recollections of her privileged white childhood, especially visits to her grandfather's stately mansion on a plantation with two hundred slaves. Her view of race relations in the new South is that Blacks should be allowed to rise socially "but on their own side of the fence," echoing Booker T. Washington's famous compromise. Where she has come from—a descendent of a prominent southern family that profited greatly from slavery—has determined who she is in the present, Mrs. Chestny maintains. To her son's insistence that "true culture is in the mind," she responds, "How you do things is because of who you *are*." She steps on to a city bus with a self-assured smile "as if she were going into a drawing room where everyone had been waiting for her." Observing that everyone on the bus is white, she remarks approvingly to her fellow passengers, "I see we have the bus to ourselves."

Though Mrs. Chestny is manifestly racist, O'Connor shows an uneasy sympathy for her. Like Miss Emily Grierson in William Faulkner's famous gothic story "A Rose for Emily," O'Connor's character embodies the values and manners of the Old South, and despite the blight of racism these things are not wholly to be despised, suggest both of these celebrated southern writers.

Though the world of the new South has changed so radically that it is possible for Mrs. Chestny to meet her "black double" and so shatter her sense of self, O'Connor indicates that the loss of her world and identity is a matter to mourn, not celebrate. Her spiteful and ultimately regretful son does just that when he realizes he has indirectly caused her death.

The song "Look Away" on Campbell's 1999 release *Rosaryville* admits a voice similar to Mrs. Chestny's in telling the South's story—a late-middle-aged woman who appears to share Mrs. Chestny's background and southern sensibility. The song's narrator recalls the night the mansion she lived in on "hallowed southern ground" burned down after being struck by lightning. The narrator reveals a state of social isolation and cultural innocence: "Never saw a cross on fire; / Never saw an angry mob." Rather, she has lived in a world of "sweet magnolia blossoms." Her version and vision of southern society prior to desegregation was oblivious to the fact that "others saw our way of life in black and white," an obvious allusion to the systematic racial oppression that defined the Old South. The complexity of that world, and a conflicted nostalgia for it, is captured in three parallel statements in the song's last verse: "Part of me hears voices crying / Part of me can feel their weight / Part of me believes that mansion / Stood for something more than hate." The song's refrain informs the listener that, not only in the South's past but in its ongoing story, the old tensions of race and privilege are still in play: "And it's a long and slow surrender retreating from the past. / It's important to remember to fly the flag half-mast and look away." The allusion here in the title and tag phrase "look away" is to the classic nineteenth-century minstrel show tune—and de facto Confederate anthem—"I Wish I Was in Dixie": "Look away! Look away! Look away! Dixie Land." While there are many versions (and parodies) of this controversial song, its original lyrics are implicitly proslavery. Thus, though the narrative voice is not hers, Campbell's use here of a signature phrase from "Dixie" might be considered problematic. The uneasy suggestion in the song perhaps connects with what O'Connor meant in commenting about the intent of her only story directly concerned with the race issue: "I say a plague on everybody's house as far as the race business goes."

Campbell reflected in a personal interview that she sees her music as a way "to have a conversation—with myself and with my people" about "the things the South is still having difficulty with: race, a sense of place, and religion." A writer whose major recordings *all* include one or more songs that reference matters of racial identity and tension in the South, Campbell was looking for a way to write about one of the most infamous and symptomatic events in the dark history of southern race relations: the 1964 bombing of a Black church in

Birmingham, Alabama. She reflected, "As soon as I read *The Violent Bear It Away*, I realized that was a way I could talk about, in a particular sense, the bombing of 16th Street Baptist Church." Her first gospel album, *Wandering Strange* (2001), includes a song that references the title of O'Connor's second novel. The folk gospel anthem "Bear It Away" briefly tells the story of the "Four little girls dressed up nice / Singing about Jesus, red and yellow, black and white" who were killed in this racially motivated bombing. While Campbell admits that her song has nothing to do with plot details in O'Connor's novel, she took its title, and the vexed theology in the verse from St. Matthew's gospel from which it is taken (11:12), recontextualized it in the context of a civil rights–era tragedy, and then brought it back to the dark spiritual truth that the phrase implies:

> One deadly blast shattered the peace
> Making for a dark Sunday morning on Sixteenth Street
> Who can explain such ignorant hate
> When the violent bear it away[?]

Though the "ignorant hate" and violence of a racist perpetrator might bear away four innocent young lives, there follows a divine bearing away of consequent human sorrow and suffering and of social memory that Campbell's chorus invokes: "Bear it away, bear it away / Merciful Jesus, lift up our sorrow / Upon your shoulder and bear it away." As O'Connor does in her novel, Campbell in her song addresses the paradoxical mystery at the heart of the dark truth registered in Matthew 11:12—that violence can bear with it the potential for redemption, and that there is a Redeemer who can take the aftermath of a violent, tragic event in the South and "bear it away." O'Connor remarked of the fraught record of modernity in her time, "Redemption is meaningless unless there is cause for it in the actual life we live." Both O'Connor's fiction and Campbell's songs underscore that the history of oppression in the American South has provided plenty of cause.

Signs Following

O'Connor had an eye for road signs and billboards in the South that might be seen to bear a double message or display a uniquely southern religiosity. Several such signs appear significantly in her fiction. A story set in the Bible Belt is surely authentic when a sign bearing a gospel message appears somewhere in the narrative. Photo essays of O'Connor's Georgia, as can be found in Barbara McKenzie's *Flannery O'Connor's Georgia* and Fickett and Gilbert's *Images of Grace*, include black-and-white photographs of such signs. On his first drive in his fifty-dollar "good car," *Wise Blood*'s Hazel Motes encounters a biblical message painted in white letters on a roadside boulder that seems particularly targeted: "WOE TO THE BLASPHEMER AND WHOREMONGER! WILL HELL SWALLOW YOU UP?" In smaller letters at the bottom of the sign is printed "Jesus Saves"—perhaps implying the measure of judgment to mercy in southern religion.

"Jesus and Tomatoes" on *Visions of Plenty* takes its refrain from a sign Campbell saw by a roadside vegetable stand in North Carolina, declaring in a glaring comic zeugma, "Jesus and tomatoes coming soon!" Like O'Connor in *Wise Blood*, Campbell satirizes the commercialization of religion in the South with a comic story about a tomato assisted by Miracle Grow that resembles the face of Jesus. The growers capitalize on this "vegetable from heaven," charging admission to see it, selling T-shirts with the "holy image," and even creating a website. The song ends with a knock at the door from a "lawyer for the Lord" with a cease-and-desist order, which is met with an invitation to dinner: "We'll have a BLT." A comic coup de grâce like this would have done the late John Prine proud—and he numbers among the A-list Nashville artists who have added vocals and instrumentals to various tracks on Campbell's albums. This stellar group includes Emmylou Harris, Buddy Miller, Rodney Crowell, and the late Nanci Griffith and Guy Clark—who once touted Campbell as "One of the finest singer-songwriters to emerge from Nashville."

Just as O'Connor took some delight in skewering southern manners and eccentricities, Campbell often has her folksinger's tongue firmly in cheek. She also shares a similar satirical sense of humor—or maybe that is just a quality of being a southerner. "Bud's Sea-Mint Boat" on *Moonpie Dreams*, about a retired Alabama civil servant who builds a boat out of cement in his front yard, parodies a southern accent in its title and gently lampoons a quirky southern character. Even the boatbuilder's previous career "Designing toilets for the space program" surely raises a chuckle if not an eyebrow, as does the punning punch line in the chorus: "A dream is anything that you want it to be / For some it's fame and fortune but for others concrete." "Funeral Food" on *Visions of Plenty* sends up a southern tradition of folks feeding well on potluck fare brought by family and friends to a funeral. The tables are set incongruously with "plastic cups and silverware" and ubiquitous "lime green Tupperware everywhere." A gothic humor runs through the song: "Pass the chicken pass the pie / We sure eat good when someone dies." But the song ends with a pointed social comment on the self-serving actions of supposed mourners comforting themselves more than they do the bereaved: "Everybody's here for the feast / But come next week where will they be[?]"

Campbell's *grave* humor here recalls O'Connor's irreverent gothic comedy at the outset of *The Violent Bear It Away* around old Tarwater's instructions to his nephew on how he wishes to be buried. The old man wants to ensure that he is given a Christian burial. As the corpulent old hillbilly climbs into his pine coffin to try it on for size, his nephew watching, his stomach protrudes over the top "like over-leavened bread." "It's too much of you for the box," young Tarwater says. "I'll have to sit on the lid to press you down or wait until you rot a little." Old Tarwater instructs the boy not to wait—to abandon the coffin if necessary. He will die "as close to the door as I can," he says, and his nephew can use two boards to roll him out the door—"I'll roll"—and to dig a grave where he stops rolling. "My Lord," the fourteen-year-old responds to these bizarre, comic funeral instructions. Conveniently, the old man dies at the breakfast table, his knife halfway to his mouth, and the boy, sitting across from the corpse, sullenly finishes his breakfast "as if he were in the presence of a new personality and couldn't think of anything to say." Young Tarwater begins to dig a grave under a fig tree "because the old man would be good for the figs." O'Connor admits in a letter that she took private pleasure in reading her darkly comic stories "over and over" and laughing uproariously at the ridiculous words and actions of her characters—then feeling embarrassed at the realization that she was the one who wrote them. Doubtless, Campbell too "can't help but smile" ("Bowl-A-Rama") when she performs her satirical songs about southerners. She remarked in an interview that southern audiences in particular enjoy the black humor in "Funeral Food," and she often closes her concerts with this song.

"God Bless You Arthur Blessitt"

Campbell's sympathy for the southern gospel of the grotesque that so captivated O'Connor is clearly evident in a paean to one of the modern South's most notable religious eccentrics. "God Bless You Arthur Blessitt," from *1000 Pound Machine*, begins with a piano intro, as one would hear before congregational singing of a hymn in a Baptist church—one time through to ensure that everyone knows the melody. And everyone in the South surely knows about Arthur Blessitt, a religious eccentric and Baptist minister from Greenville, Mississippi, who, following what he claimed as a divinely sent vision, set off on foot on Christmas Day 1969 from Hollywood's Sunset Strip to carry a large wooden cross across the continent and eventually around the world. In 2022, his fifty-fifth year of walking, Blessitt at age eighty-two boasts of having visited 324 countries on seven continents, traveled 43,340 miles on foot, and logged over 435,000 miles by automobile and an estimated 2,330,000 miles by air. As a blog on Blessitt's official website states, he has walked the world wheeling a cross leaning against one shoulder to restore its meaning—not as an ornament, an architectural decoration, or strictly a religious symbol but as an instrument of suffering. "People died [a] horrible bloody agonizing, tortured death on crosses. It was a symbol of the worst in man," his website declares. He accuses fellow Protestants of sanitizing the cross and chastens them for condemning Catholics for decorating churches and homes with crucifixes bearing the form of a dying Jesus. Though Blessitt acknowledges that an empty cross is meant to imply that Jesus has risen, Protestants have "made a grave error in cleaning up the cross." In the manner of O'Connor's Mason Tarwater, he exclaims, "A BLOODY MUTILATED Savior did hang on the cross." He praises Mel Gibson's graphic depiction of Jesus's suffering in his 2004 film *The Passion of the Christ* for restoring this fact to popular consciousness.

Campbell shares O'Connor's compassionate interest in religious eccentrics and in validating the extremism that manifests in some forms of southern Baptistry. Her hymn to the dogged pilgrim Arthur Blessitt tells his story respectfully and straightforwardly. The lyrics include Blessitt's claim to have been divinely called to carry the cross "around the world," to bring the gospel of Christ "to the common man" and to "keep it simple." While Campbell nods to Blessitt's worldwide celebrity status in the line "People know your name," a matter his website certainly underscores, his love for the people of the world he claims to have seen in his youthful vision on a hilltop in Nevada—"all colors, races, and religions . . . None of these faces I had ever seen before"—is genuine. He is praised for having "done [his] part / For peace in every land / And love in every heart." Campbell's song begins and ends with "God bless you Arthur Blessitt," and this blessing is meant sincerely.

Other extreme religious practices in southern Baptistry provide the background to the chilling "Signs Following," a song that recounts the case of an Alabama preacher in the Church of Jesus with Signs Following who attempted to kill his wife by twice forcing her to stick her arm into a box of rattlesnakes. Bitten both times, she survived. Campbell wrote the song after reading Dennis Covington's work of experiential journalism, *Salvation on Sand Mountain* (1995). His name follows O'Connor's in the liner-note list of people who inspired the songs on *Moonpie Dreams*. As a *New York Times* reporter, Covington became involved with this religious sect whose members practice snake-handling and drink poison in literal response to a prophesy of Jesus recorded in the Gospel of Mark (16:17–18): "And these signs shall follow them that believe; In my name shall they cast out devils; they shall speak with new tongues; They shall take up serpents; and if they drink any deadly thing, it shall not hurt them" (KJV). Campbell's "Signs Following" summarizes pastor Glenn Summerford's actions as "Domestic violence with a holy rage." Summerford, then forty-seven, was an alcoholic with a history of violent behavior, and his wife of eleven years, Darlene, was known for her infidelities. The song resolves with a court report: Summerford was convicted of attempted murder and, given his previous convictions, was sentenced by jury to ninety-nine years. But the song's chorus is not related to the criminal case; rather, in clipped phrases it summarizes the Signs Following doctrine that those of true faith will not be harmed when handling deadly serpents:

Reach down pick up
Have faith live right
If you believe signs following
The snake will not bite

Lucinda Williams once admitted to a fascination with southern snake-handlers and collected books on the Signs Following practitioners. She sings in the confessional "Get Right with God," her Grammy-winning song, "I would risk the serpent's bite / . . . I would kiss the diamondback / If I knew it would get me to heaven." Like Williams, Campbell is uncritical of the practices of religious extremists in the South: "I'm not putting people down who believe in snake handling," she has said, noting that "Signs Following" addresses a very "specific incident" of criminally mishandling poisonous snakes intended as murder weapons. "Faith will go where it needs to go," she concludes on the matter of holy-rolling snake-handlers and strychnine sippers. Yet Campbell would agree with Covington that those godly folk who handle deadly serpents move along a fine line between testing their faith and tempting self-termination.

My Word Is Coming

While there are no snake-handlers in O'Connor's fiction, she is sympathetic to religious eccentrics, such as Mrs. Greenleaf in "Greenleaf," whose practice of "prayer healing" finds her rolling on the ground over a hole bearing newspaper clippings of "morbid stories" of human suffering. "Jesus, stab me in the heart!" Mrs. Greenleaf cries, as she intercedes in prayer for the wounded of the world. But O'Connor is also wary of false prophets in the Protestant South, such as the farm help's wife, ignorant and bigoted Mrs. Shortley, in "The Displaced Person." Mrs. Shortley's apocalyptic inner vision that calls her to "Prophecy" that "the children of wicked nations will be butchered" is cast "in the opposite direction" of an outer celestial vision that appears once she has "opened her eyes." Mrs. Shortley's falseness is confirmed when she sights the gracious, patient priest who regularly visits Mrs. McIntyre, the farm owner, and mutters, "Come to destroy."

O'Connor's characterization of the Carmodys, the southern traveling evangelists in *The Violent Bear It Away*, provides further insight into how she regarded religious eccentrics in the Bible Belt. At fourteen pages, the scene with the Carmodys and their twelve-year-old preacher daughter, Lucette, is the longest dramatic passage in the novel, presented from the point of view of the virulent humanist Rayber, who observes them through a church window. Brief flashbacks to memories of Rayber's own religiously warped childhood intrude on the scene. As a world-traveling "hard-working team for Christ," the Carmodys open their evangelistic service with an appeal for money and attempt to manipulate their southern audience to give generously to support their ministry. But they are not charlatans like *Wise Blood*'s street preacher Asa Hawks. In the sermon of the child evangelist Lucette, O'Connor imparts the whole of the Christian salvation story—all the central doctrines and biblical accounts that she herself accepts as articles of her Catholic faith. Lucette's sermon runs the gamut from the doctrine of Original Sin ("God was angry with the world because it always wanted more") to Old Testament prophecies of a Messiah ("My Word is coming from the house of David") to a poetic reference to the Annunciation and Incarnation ("Is this the Word of God, this blue-cold child? Is this His will, this plain winter-woman?"), the flight to Egypt, Jesus's miraculous works ("Jesus grew up and raised the dead"), Christ's crucifixion ("they nailed him to a cross and run a spear through his side") and promised return ("Jesus is coming again!"). All this is loaded into the prophetic message of the child evangelist, who eventually targets her words at Rayber, peering through a window near the back of the church: "I see a damned soul before my eyes! I see a dead man Jesus hasn't raised . . . his ear is deaf to the Holy Word." At this, Rayber switches off his hearing aid to "cut off the voice" and drops his head below the window ledge. Here is the most protracted and potent expression in O'Connor's fiction of the Christian truths she believes: out of the mouth of a babe preaching southern style on a hot summer night at a gospel crusade. Maybe O'Connor "hadda hunch" that in the child evangelist Lucette she would find that peculiar "exaggeration" and "distortion . . . that reveals or should reveal" the big-R religious Reality that her fiction attempts to (re)present.

Even when O'Connor allows a jibe at her own religious traditions and practice, a religion "where minds are still chained in priestly darkness," as Lucette's mother declares, she is still on side with the fundamental truth the exploitative evangelists proclaim: that you got to get right with God, "to be ready so that on the last day you'll rise in the glory of the Lord." In fact, she puts the same words in the mouth of the child evangelist as she uses to describe the calling of her true backwoods prophet Mason Tarwater. "The word of God is a burning Word to burn you clean," Lucette declares to the congregation, echoing old Tarwater's revelations to his nephew and prophet-in-waiting of "the hard facts of serving the Lord," and his declaration that "he himself had been burned clean and burned clean again." Of her most eccentric and abrasive religious character, O'Connor once remarked in conversation, "I'm right behind him 100 per cent," adding in a letter, "It is the old man [Tarwater] who speaks for me."

Rosaryville

As O'Connor discusses at length in her essay "The Catholic Novelist in the Protestant South," the social life and religious practice in the Bible Belt "is both native and alien" to writers of Catholic faith. Christian scriptures inform the way southerners look at life, and southern history is linked to sacred history, its *mythos* tied to matters of eternity. But the South's traditions are Protestant, and its culture is largely resistant to change and outside influence. Reflecting on her nonetheless Catholic fiction set in the region, O'Connor comments, "The Catholic novelist in the South is forced to follow the spirit into strange places and to recognize it in many forms not totally congenial to him." And in those places she discovers the "underground religious affinities" between Catholics and Protestants in the South. Bred-in-the-bone Baptist songwriter Kate Campbell makes such a discovery in songs on *Rosaryville*, her fourth studio recording.

In the Catholic subjects and concerns that Campbell writes and sings about, *Rosaryville* inverts O'Connor's religious perspective on manners in the South. Likewise a writer with strong religious beliefs, Campbell peers into both the literal Rosaryville Spirit Life Center in Ponchatoula, Louisiana, operated by the Dominican Sisters, and a figurative though socially present *Rosaryville* in the lives and practices of the Bible Belt's Catholics. Not surprisingly, as does O'Connor with her fundamentalist Protestants, Campbell finds religious eccentrics among southern Catholics.

Nowhere in O'Connor's Catholic fiction does any character offer or exclaim an "Ave Maria," the familiar Catholic prayer to the Blessed Virgin Mary, yet Campbell does so twice in her *Rosaryville* songs. "Porcelain Blue" appears to be the observations and reflections of a woman on a spiritual retreat at the Rosaryville Center. Her view moves from observing a nun standing in a garden just before sunrise to looking at a porcelain blue vase bearing a sacred image of Mary. "Blessed Mary please don't slumber / Pray for us who need your care," the song's narrator pleads. The album ends with the beautifully voiced track "Ave Maria Grotto," which includes an aria that threads through the story of simple-minded Brother Joseph, an eccentric who builds miniature clay models of "the wonders of the world," embedded with seashells, bits of broken china, and rosary beads. His monastic life has confined him, but his imagination has not. And though he has not gone out into the world, he has "found peace within."

Rosaryville's "Heart of Hearts" tells the story of another Catholic eccentric who constructed a giant rosary made of bowling balls and displayed it in his front yard. Campbell's song registers the range of responses from non-Catholic southerners: "Some people laugh, some only frown, some shake their heads and wonder what it's about." Like O'Connor's representation of Protestant eccentrics (albeit of the more extreme sort), Campbell's portrayals of Brother Joseph and the devout oddball maker of the giant rosary sculpture are not satirical but highly sympathetic. The narrator of "Heart of Hearts" concludes by chastening her fellow Baptists for their implied anti-Catholic bias: "Some walk around counting prayers looking to find faith to spare / Some like to hear themselves talk but seldom say anything at all."

The bifold lyrics sheet accompanying the *Rosaryville* CD is printed in monochrome tones with edges stained to resemble parchment. Campbell's lyrics are typeset in paragraph form down the length of the sheet, without song titles separating the text or capitals to indicate line breaks. Here the mysteries and manners of southern Catholics are affirmed in four song stories: "Porcelain Blue," "Heart of Hearts," "Fade to Blue," and "Ave Maria Grotto." Track 3 tells the story of a devout Cuban woman who spends her days devotedly rolling Corona cigars, only abandoning her work to catch sight of Pope John Paul during his historic visit to Cuba on 21 January 1998. Other songs on the album contain elements of Campbell's biography and of southern history and society, including a sentimental song about a recently widowed, devout old woman caring for her mentally challenged adult son, who anxiously asks, "Who will pray for Junior when I'm gone?" The unbroken arrangement of lyrics on the page suggests a single story being told. The effect is like reading a sacred scroll.

The opening title song is presented as a kind of invocation to Campbell's presumably southern Protestant listeners: "Come on, let's go down the road to Rosaryville / Who knows what we will find?" Perhaps like O'Connor, Campbell has in these songs discovered and uncovered the "underground religious affinities" between southern Protestants and Catholics that O'Connor observed. Tellingly, Campbell has remarked that "Protestant southerners don't think the record is very Catholic."

As a southern Baptist, Campbell shows an exceptional affinity for Catholic belief and practice—the religious inverse of O'Connor. As a youth, Campbell attended Catholic mass with friends, as she remarked in a personal interview. She enjoyed the creedal liturgy, the rituals and statuary—words and symbols so absent from the beliefs and traditions of her Protestant faith. That Catholic influence has abiding resonances in her art. The listener who waits fifteen seconds after the misleadingly titled "The Last Song" on track 11 of 2001's *Wandering Strange* has concluded will hear at 5:00 Campbell's voice introducing a hidden final track: "This is a song Elvis recorded." To a simple strummed acoustic guitar and churchy piano accompaniment, Campbell sings a gospel hymn to the Virgin Mary, "Miracle of the Rosary," remarkably recorded by Presley and released in 1972 on an eclectic album of pop music covers, *Elvis Now!* The song's chorus is a setting of the Magnificat from St. Luke's gospel (1:46–55), and its concluding verse evokes a familiar Catholic prayer used with the rosary:

Oh Holy Mary, dear Mother of God
Please pray for us sinners
Now and at the hour of our death
And thanks once again for the miracle of your rosary

Two years after the *Rosaryville* recording, this may be Campbell's way of affirming—on her first album of southern gospel songs—that her own faith story includes the Baptist tradition she was raised in and embraces Catholic belief and practice. (This may have been Elvis's intent as well, though his brand of old-time southern religion had Pentecostal roots.) This reading is underscored by Spooner Oldham's extended piano outro to the song, which melds melodic elements from the classic "Tennessee Waltz" (memorably recorded by Elvis) with a mélange of chord progressions from almost-recognizable old hymn tunes. Elvis, the Baptist hymnal, southern Catholics, and all the

Christ-haunted South are caught in this single, halfway hidden song. The instructive ghost of Flannery O'Connor has surely cast her shadow here.

On the flipside of the printed lyrics included with the *Rosaryville* CD is a triptych of images. A drawing of a wrought-iron gate at the Rosaryville retreat fronts the CD case. The foldout panel inside features an image of the Virgin Mary painted on porcelain tiles and figured as in Hispanic Catholic iconography. In the center panel, a stylized photograph of Campbell's face looks earnestly and deeply at the viewer, her direct and penetrating gaze (as O'Connor herself appears in photographs) literally and literarily evidenced in this collection of songs. Underneath the photograph is a quotation from O'Connor that serves as a kind of credo for Campbell's calling as a songwriter: "Art is something that one experiences alone and for the purposes of realizing in a fresh way, through the senses, the mystery of existence."

Campbell concluded a personal interview by commenting on the O'Connor story that has affected her most deeply—"Parker's Back," from the posthumously published *Everything That Rises Must Converge*. This is the last story O'Connor worked on, scratching revisions in her manuscript on her deathbed. "I've been thinking about that story for a decade," Campbell said, and added that she has been "so intrigued" by O'Connor's narrative and vision in "Parker's Back" that she plans to write a song about it someday—a song that will surely be equal parts Kate Campbell and Flannery O'Connor.

Chapter 5

SUFJAN STEVENS

In Flannery's Territory

Sufjan Stevens is one of the most innovative, influential, and prolific songwriter/composers in the indie pop music scene of the new millennium. To date, he has released thirteen studio albums on his own Asthmatic Kitty label along with thirteen EPs, three compilations, and three soundtracks, including an avant-garde orchestral and multimedia work, *The BQE*. His song "Mystery of Love" from the coming-of-age film *Call Me by Your Name* was nominated for an Academy Award for Best Original Song in 2018 and received a Grammy nomination. Stevens has been active as a musician since the mid-1990s, in his early twenties playing in the Michigan folk-rock band Marzuki, named after his older brother. However, as he told an interviewer from the *Village Voice* in 2005, following the release of his fifth recording and third song cycle, *Illinois*, his first aspiration was to be a fiction writer like his "idol" Flannery O'Connor.

As a writer of songs, Stevens shares considerable common ground with O'Connor. Like O'Connor, he is a regional writer with a strong commitment to place and with a dedication to the craft of writing and to perfecting a form, in his case, cycles of song stories. His songs explore similar themes to those found in O'Connor's work: the subtle ways in which people are moved by the motions of grace, the redemptive possibilities in physical suffering, the effects of original sin, and the hope of salvation played out in the Devil's territory. These are all themes that trace through his full-length song collections to date. Stevens's artistic vision and work, like that of O'Connor, is also deeply informed by his Christian faith: "It's the most important thing in my life. It's unavoidable," he tells the *Village Voice*. And like O'Connor, Stevens's genius has gained him a solid following and accolades in the marketplace despite his orthodox Christian convictions in what he calls a "post-God society."

Sufjan (pronounced *Soof-yahn*) Stevens, like young Flannery O'Connor, initially set out to be a writer by enrolling in a writing program—for Stevens, at the New School for Social Research in New York City, where as a twenty-five-year-old in 2000 he completed an MFA thesis—a collection of short fiction. Before enrolling in the program, Stevens had written stories and vignettes and character sketches about a pair of fictional communities in his native Michigan that he named Pickerel Lake Town and Pickerel Lake City. He conceived of writing something akin to *Winesburg, Ohio*, a cycle of short stories by modernist American author Sherwood Anderson, whose own fictional places include a like-named Pickleville ("The Egg"). Stevens describes his stories as "about backwoods Midwestern kinsmen—Christian fundamentalists, Amway salesmen, crystal healers—all set in a small rural town in Michigan," in what might be considered Michigan's version of O'Connor's Bible Belt. Like O'Connor's, Stevens's short fiction conveys a strong sense of place and is inhabited by eccentric characters—his own regional grotesques. In the *Village Voice* review, Stevens is touted as "the Next Flannery." For the aspiring fiction/songwriter this might have had the same enervating effect as labeling an emerging singer-songwriter "the new Dylan."

The writing program at New School has chosen not to make its MFA theses available to the public, so there is no accessible copy of Stevens's short story cycle. Nonetheless, several stories extracted from his MFA thesis are available. One in particular resonates with O'Connor-like style and vision and bears the O'Connoresque title "We Are Shielded by the Holy Ghost." This story won an award as the best work of fiction in Stevens's graduating class and was published in 2003 in the New School Chapbook Series, an honor conferred on the top students in the program in both fiction and poetry. Two other shorter stories by Stevens were published in the New School literary journal *LIT* and were accessible at the time of publication on his Tumblr account. A fourth story was published in 2003 in *Image*, a faith-based journal. Stevens's chapbook story, in particular, confirms the comparison with O'Connor made by the *Village Voice* reviewer, though the bold bouquet to Stevens as "the Next Flannery" is so far an unfulfilled prophecy.

"We Are Shielded by the Holy Ghost" tells the story of a simple-minded religious extremist named Harriet John who comes home to her apartment one day to discover that she has had an intruder—not just any intruder but a "spiritual principality," a demon. Like Lucinda Williams, Stevens is at home with the idea of an incarnate evil being—a familiar agent in O'Connor's fictions. Harriet comes from the same mold as do a number of O'Connor's spiritual grotesques. She exists on an extreme edge of reality, her vision clouded and conflicted, her religiosity at once intense and questionable.

As a single mother (a stock O'Connor character), divorced for ten years from her unnamed husband, Harriet cares for the spiritual needs of her two teenage daughters by dragging them off to Sunday School at Harbor Life Holy Bible Church, introducing them to the pastor's sons "hoping one of them would fall in love." Her daughters, Gabby and Jan, are vacant headed and completely self-absorbed (somewhat like Mrs. Freeman's daughters Glynese and Carramae in the O'Connor story "Good Country People"). Harriet gives them books on Christian dating and how to succeed at selling Amway products, and generous allowances. She hopes to "build something intimate and profound" with her daughters but is not sure what. Her parenting strategy Stevens comically describes as "like letting bread sit to rise—you wait around while it happens." The girls soon draw away from their mother "like cockroaches scuttling from a kitchen light suddenly turned on." After they leave to attend college in "more liberal states" than Iowa, they stop going to church or believing in God. Forty-eight years old, overweight and alone, Harriet pushes through life with her "shopping cart of disappointments," praying that God will give her daughters "high regard" for the Almighty and for her as well. And she adds, "Help them to keep their high metabolisms."

Stevens's story is skillfully rendered, with the shading-to-black ironic comedy that characterizes O'Connor's fictional voice. He uses a method of layered flashbacks, a narrative structure O'Connor uses in some of her finest later stories, in particular "The Enduring Chill," "Parker's Back," and "Judgement Day." Stevens shares O'Connor's gift for the small, telling detail, as in Harriet's gesture when she thinks she is being followed by an evil spirit. She stomps her feet on the mat in front of the Montessori school where she works as a teacher's aide, "as if shaking off snow, but there was none." (That familiar O'Connoresque "as if" often signals "the added dimension" in the big-R Reality of O'Connor's fiction.) Another such detail is Stevens's description of Harriet "running her finger over each paragraph" as she reads the Old Testament Book of Esther, becoming frightened as she discovers that she cannot find the word *God* anywhere in the text.

O'Connor observed that her fiction is on the whole concerned with "the action of grace in territory held largely by the devil"; Stevens explores similar territory, and he figures in this story the Devil that O'Connor describes as "a real spirit who must be made to name himself . . . with his specific personality for every occasion." In "We Are Shielded," the Devil is an alleged house invader, someone whom Harriet believes has ransacked her apartment and rearranged her possessions. We are told that "Harriet believed in ghosts and demons, a supernatural plane above her own" and that "she believed in the Holy Spirit" and "she believed in the Devil." Harriet has a growing sense of the Devil's presence: the "quiet apparition" that haunts her apartment and rattles her window becomes a "phantom intruder" as she enters her place of work.

Stevens's "We Are Shielded by the Holy Ghost" also reflects the comic cosmic outlook that is a distinctive of O'Connor's works. His fiction appears attuned to O'Connor's observation in an occasional talk published as "Novelist and Believer," that "the maximum amount of seriousness admits the maximum amount of comedy. Only if we are secure in our beliefs can we see the comical side of the universe." Stevens's darkly comic tale resolves with a scene at the hypercheerful Montessori school—a setting that Stevens knows well from his own early education—deftly rendered in four short paragraphs. Harriet John is in the moment transformed into a kind of hysterical female old Tarwater as her religious paranoia comes to its moment of grotesque expression. She has been left in charge of the children while the teacher is absent for a dental appointment. Anxious and expectant, Harriet has a vision of a man's face looking in the window of the classroom, a face that is "all the faces of the world fused into one familiar face, showing itself with a terrible glow." Though the children see nothing, Harriet immediately recognizes the face as belonging to "the Devil." "Don't be afraid. We are shielded by the Holy Ghost," she tells the terrified children as she forcibly gathers them around her. "She prayed for the fire of the Lord to come upon them. She prayed for God's holy chariot to emerge from a seam in the sky. She prayed for the punishment of Satan's army, the fierce justice of the Holy Ghost, a legion of whips and guns and staffs with sharp edges"—while the children she presses to her begin to "whimper and squirm like newborn puppies." Stevens ends the story with Harriet screaming "an unpronounceable chatter" of glossolalia—words "that didn't exist, except in God's dictionary"—as in her near-psychotic state she sees "the hunched form of Satan, on all fours, creeping slowly towards [her]." The image is like a demonic inversion of the Holy Ghost that descends on Asbury Fox in the symbolic bird-shaped water stain at the end of O'Connor's story "The Enduring Chill."

"All the Nonsense of Suffering"

Although it is not included in the New School Chapbook, a further short short story, "All the Nonsense of Suffering" (available on Stevens's Tumblr account) is praised in a headnote to that publication by American novelist René Steinke (who has also published on O'Connor). Stevens's story, Steinke writes, "skillfully weaves incantatory speech" that "reveal[s] as much as it obscures" the inner workings of the fanatically religious and garrulous Bethany Peters. "All the Nonsense" is similar in tone and character type to "We Are Shielded" and has a kind of experimental structure, with details of the character's life and experience framed in sentences beginning with the phrase "Bethany Peters will tell you . . ." Like Harriet John, Bethany Peters has encountered the Devil—"disguised as a house painter in overalls, with a dirty clergy collar"—and managed to "[slug] him in the gut" before being left "flat on her back on the crabgrass by the P.O.," her groceries scattered in the street. The story reaches its apocalyptically charged climax in a final paragraph in which the tag phrase opening each sentence switches to "She won't tell you" or "She will never tell you." We learn then that Bethany Peters was sexually violated as a child, suffered domestic abuse, once had a miscarriage, has a gun hidden in the house, and keeps two vicious German shepherds in the cellar which she mistreats, "nourishing their tempers" so that "in the end times, when the world is one big riot, she will loose them on the antichrist, once and for all."

O'Connor's fiction is peopled with similarly hyper-religious figures whose maniacal beliefs and visionary experiences are figured as a form of madness that she nonetheless validates as authentically grounded in the divine. Her corn-whiskey-swilling, damnation-raging prophet figure Mason Tarwater in *The Violent Bear It Away*, who rants about the purifying "finger of fire" of "the Lord Himself," is a prime example; indeed, his nephew has had him committed to a mental institution for a time. The farmhand's wife in "Greenleaf" is similarly given to fits of religious frenzy in the act of "prayer healings," during which she sprawls over a hole she has dug in the ground and filled with "all the morbid stories out of the newspaper," writhing and moaning and crying out, "Oh Jesus, stab me in the heart." O'Connor presents neither of these religious fanatics unsympathetically, nor does she characterize their actions in language that is in any way derisory. Likewise, in Stevens's stories neither Harriet John nor Bethany Peters are, as Steinke observes, "satirical caricatures of fundamentalism." Stevens presents them in a way that makes plausible and real their near-psychotic religious behavior and their individual encounters with "the Devil." Their grotesque backwoods Michigan religious extremism is rendered as believably as anything in O'Connor's Bible Belt cast of misfits.

Stevens remarked in an interview that as an emerging writer he found the American market for short fiction "impenetrable." Despairing of a career as a writer of fiction, and already with some limited success in the music business, he moved on to "Plan B." He transmogrified his story ideas into a cycle of song narratives, which he released in 2003 as *Greetings from Michigan* on his own Asthmatic Kitty label. Pop music journalists paid it scant attention when it was first released: the album went unnoticed by *Rolling Stone* and *Billboard*, though *Pitchfork* gave it a "Best New Music" commendation. It would be a couple of years, following the release in 2005 of the well-reviewed *Illinois* (or *Come on Feel the Illinoise*), before Stevens was recognized as an innovative musical genius who has in effect become *the Boss* in the indie pop music scene. Indeed, the title of Stevens's first album with its *Greetings from* . . . tag echoes the title of Springsteen's 1973 debut album *Greetings from Asbury Park, N.J.* And this echo resounds to the extent that Stevens uses elements from a 1970s-era Michigan postcard in his album art, an imitation in effect of Springsteen's cover, which features a postcard of Asbury Park from the same period. The young aspiring pop artist thus announces himself in Springsteen fashion, though as someone "blinded by the light," Stevens would have more in common with Saul/Saint Paul than with Springsteen's Scooter and his friends.

Stevens's grand Whitmanesque project as a late twenty-something musician was to write cycles of songs that captured the distinctive culture, events, and personalities in the histories of each of the American states: the "50 States Project" he called it. This ambitious undertaking was set aside after the release of two eponymous song collections on the neighboring midwestern states of Michigan and Illinois. However pretentious and naïve, Stevens's impossible project—which he later dismissed as a publicity stunt—nonetheless situates him from the start as a songwriter with a grand vision who, like Woody Guthrie and Bruce Springsteen before him, announces his intention to sing his America. As much, or even more, a musician as a writer, Stevens is known for producing lengthy lyrical, symphonic pieces ("Impossible Soul" from 2010's *The Age of Adz* clocks over twenty-five minutes, for example). He offers his listeners generous recordings of his songs—fifteen tracks on *Michigan* and twenty-two on *Illinois,* and a collection of outtakes titled *Avalanche* with a further eighteen songs/song versions that did not make the cut for the *Illinois* recording. These collections have the thematic arcs and narrative continuities of works of fiction.

A Go(o)d Man Is Hard to Find

Double figures abound in O'Connor's fictions, as literary scholar Frederick Asals has shown in his landmark study of O'Connor's works, *Flannery O'Connor: The Imagination of Extremity* (1982). Asals observes that these double figures take one of two classic forms: "Either one character discovers that another is a 'replica' of himself, an almost identical reflection . . . or, much more often, one character is presented as the alter ego of another, the embodiment of qualities suppressed or ignored by the first, a mirror image, or inverse reflection." For O'Connor, possessed of a Poe-like imagination and a biblically informed sensibility, these double figures function sometimes as incarnations of a character's spiritual or moral state, or just as often as ironic mirror images that embody a larger social or existential condition that bears on the central character. Star Drake in "The Comforts of Home" is the symbolic twin of the emblematically named Thomas (his name, of Aramaic origin, actually means "the twin")— an example of the second type of double that Asals describes, an inverse reflection of the protagonist who embodies, ultimately, his true moral state. Star in Thomas's eyes is a "moral moron," a delinquent who has been in and out of jail and is sexually promiscuous, leering at him until he eventually explodes and threatens to have her locked up if she continues to bother his mother and his own comfortable existence. Thomas prides himself on his moral probity—he "wouldn't pass a bad check"—yet as his compassionate mother often reminds him, were it not for all the advantages he has had in his life, he "might be" no better than the girl. And, indeed, by the story's end, Thomas has hardened his heart to the point that he is capable of egregiously more than telling a lie or passing a bad check: he fires a gun with intent to murder, and ironically misses his intended target. In the final tableau in the story's concluding paragraph, Thomas and Star converge on each other, over the dead body of his mother, "about to collapse into each other's arms," their moral twinship signified in a suspended embrace.

Examples of the alter ego in O'Connor's fiction are numerous and often clearly indicated in the language of a given story. Julian's racist mother in "Everything That Rises Must Converge" unexpectedly meets her "black double" while riding on an integrated city bus in an unnamed city in the American South. And in a twist on a signal phrase in the story, she symbolically meets herself "coming and going." Likewise, the old southern redneck Tanner in "Judgement Day" has a Black companion, Coleman, whom upon first meeting he senses as an uncanny "negative image of himself," and in a later dreamlike vision imagines will be there in the hereafter to greet him on Judgment Day.

Stevens surely recognizes this double motif in "A Good Man Is Hard to Find," his musical homage to O'Connor's most famous story, from his 2004 recording *Seven Swans*. Like Bruce Springsteen, he has borrowed his song title from O'Connor's story, and in a form of postmodern appropriation borrowed as well O'Connor's character The Misfit as his narrator. In O'Connor's story, a family on a road trip to Florida has a car accident on a back road in Georgia. The grandmother on board—whose smuggled cat, sprung from a basket, is responsible for the accident—flags down an ominous-looking vehicle that is slowly approaching. It stops and after several minutes out step three armed men, all recently escaped convicts. O'Connor's grandmother immediately recognizes something "familiar" in the bespectacled, shirtless leader of the trio, who advances with a gun in his hand; she feels "as if she had known him all her life, but she could not recall who he was." Soon she identifies him as a notorious convicted killer who calls himself The Misfit, whom she has recently read about in the newspaper.

Stevens's simple, brief folk song comments on the meaning of O'Connor's story from The Misfit's point of view. Set in a minor key and played on an acoustic guitar, it is strummed in an off-balance time signature of 5/4, atypical for a folk song. The song narrative begins inversely with Stevens's Misfit narrator recognizing something about the grandmother: that "once in the backyard," during the innocent years of being, "she was once like me." This phrase is repeated three times in the first part of the song to underscore its truthfulness, a rhetorical strategy that O'Connor frequently employs in her fiction. Stevens's Misfit narrator offers his response to the moment of revelation in the story, in which the prattling grandmother recognizes her kinship with the man who is about to shoot her. The suggestion in the song is that The Misfit experiences a moment of insight similar to that of the grandmother—a conclusion that is at best obliquely implied in O'Connor's story.

Thus, Stevens's song both engages in an act of literary appropriation and offers a critical interpretation of O'Connor's complex short story. Even after Stevens's Misfit narrator has killed every member of the family including the grandmother, he continues to reflect that "someone's once like me"—and "once like me" is repeated six times in the eighteen printed lines of Stevens's lyrics. This conscious recognition of moral/spiritual likeness is one of the epiphanic devices in O'Connor's fiction: whether in "The Artificial Nigger," where the prideful Nelson and Mr. Head stare at the revelatory image of a lawn ornament in the form of a Black man "as if they were faced with some great mystery . . . that brought them together in their common defeat," or in "Revelation" as Ruby Turpin gazes miserably "as if through the very heart of mystery" at the hogs with which she shares a metaphoric likeness.

In O'Connor's story, the grandmother pleads for her life, appealing to The Misfit's sense of decency and supposed breeding: "You've got good blood! I know you wouldn't shoot a lady. I know you come from nice people." Failing at flattery, she offers him money. But The Misfit's life is not "off balance" on account of socioeconomic factors, but because he struggles to believe in the Bible Belt truth of the salvific act of Jesus Christ, a belief that would give his troubled life existential ground for being. The grandmother's words are of little help, and she is even willing to apostatize if to do so would save her life. In a gesture central to the meaning of O'Connor's story, she murmurs to the now distraught killer, "Why, you're one of my babies. You're one of my children!" and in an unexpected moment of compassion, reaches to touch his shoulder. Surprised, The Misfit recoils "as if a snake had bitten him" and shoots her three times point-blank in the chest. Her story is over; his is beginning a new chapter—or so, perhaps, O'Connor implies.

Stevens's lyrics conclude with reference to The Misfit's epiphanic insight at the grandmother's touch: "So I go to hell. I wait for it, / but someone's left me creased. / Someone's left me creased." The bullet that claims the grandmother, and in the face of which she ultimately lays claim to the gospel truth she has denied, has also "creased" The Misfit in Stevens's lyrical interpretation. Both are shot through with the same revelation of their common condition—that each is in need of grace. O'Connor comments in the hybrid piece titled "On Her Own Work" that at this point the grandmother recognizes that she is "joined to [The Misfit] by ties of kinship which have their roots deep in the mystery she has been merely prattling about." Indeed, as Stevens's song underscores, both characters are alike in their need of grace and their potential for evil.

This O'Connoresque double theme is also evident in a standout track on Stevens's acclaimed 2005 cycle of songs, *Illinois*. "John Wayne Gacy, Jr." briefly recounts the story of one of the most notorious serial killers in US history. Gacy was executed by lethal injection in 1994 for the horrific murders of thirty-three teenage boys and young men, whom he raped and strangled between 1972 and 1978, burying twenty-seven of their bodies in a crawl space beneath his home in Norwood Park, Illinois, near metropolitan Chicago. Gacy is known as "The Killer Clown" for his appearances in clown costume at local fundraising events and neighborhood birthday parties, and for reportedly donning a clown costume on several occasions when he sexually assaulted and killed his victims. Stevens read widely about Gacy, and some details in his lyrics derive from court documents—"the slight [sic] of his hand" referring to Gacy's tricking victims into wearing handcuffs, and "a cloth on their lips" denoting that he sometimes used a cloth soaked with chloroform to drug his victims or shoved rags in their mouths to stop their cries as he sodomized and slowly suffocated them. A clinically sane Gacy took no pleasure except in meanness and murder, committing unspeakable acts of evil on innocent boys, and to the day of his execution was unrepentant of his crimes. Yet Stevens ends his song with the following shocking lines:

> And in my best behavior
> I am really just like him
> Look beneath the floorboards
> For the secrets I have hid

The song's narrator comes to the same conclusion as does O'Connor's Mr. Head, "that no sin was too monstrous for him to claim as his own." Stevens emphasizes this idea in an illustration in one of many panels on the CD's multifold lyrics sheet: he is pictured in cartoon form wearing his signature ball cap, playing his banjo next to a clown figure with the unmistakable face of Gacy, holding three balloons bearing ghoulish skull images. The clown is dressed in red, and Stevens's caricature wears a red wristband, banjo strap, and cap; a red bird (a cardinal) is perched on the head of his instrument. The visual metaphors suggest that he and the killer have both been touched by the same potential for devilish evil.

Unlike O'Connor, a cradle Catholic and a privileged single child raised under the shadow of the steeple of St. Joseph's Church in Savannah, Georgia, Stevens grew up in the Midwest in an unstable family, his parents originally belonging to a religious cult known as Subud. A hybrid spiritual practice originating in Indonesia in the 1930s, Subud combines elements of Buddhism and Hinduism with monotheism and religious observances that align somewhat with Islam. Its focus is on finding the will of God for individual members. Sufjan and his brother and sisters were given Persian names by the cult's leader. *Sufjan* means "comes with a sword."

Stevens's mother, Carrie, who suffered from bipolar disorder and drug addiction, eventually abandoned her family of four children under ten when Sufjan was a year old. His father, Rajid, remarried, and the family moved around a lot. His father cooked at a Waldorf school so his children could have an alternative early education, Stevens reveals in an interview recorded at Calvin College in 2007, but there was never enough money to keep them well fed and well cared for.

Stevens's song "He Woke Me Up Again" recalls an occasion when his father roused all the children in the middle of the night to announce that the family had converted to Catholicism. After briefly attending the prestigious Interlochen Arts Academy as an aspiring oboist, Stevens concluded his public education in a Catholic high school before enrolling in a Christian postsecondary institution, Hope College in Holland, Michigan, where he studied literature and music.

Stevens's embrace of Christianity sometime in his late teens may well have been a reactive response to his nonconformist upbringing. Nonetheless, he holds strongly to the efficacy of the Christian doctrines of the Incarnation and the Crucifixion, and these beliefs inform several of his songs. For example, "Concerning the UFO Sighting near Highland, Illinois" figures the Incarnation; "To Be Alone with You" concerns the mystery of the Crucifixion. While early in his career he avoided discussing his faith in articles and interviews, in his late thirties and early forties he became more vocal about his beliefs. His denominational affiliation is unclear, but his beliefs and spiritual practice shade toward Catholic and Episcopalian. Whatever doctrines and practices he embraces, Stevens's art is thoroughly informed by his faith, and this is widely acknowledged by pop music journalists, who recognize him as "a spiritual songsmith."

In a 2010 interview in *The Quietus* in which he discusses his beliefs, Stevens exclaims, "What's the basis of Christianity? It's really a meal. It's communion. It's the Eucharist. It's the body and blood of Christ. Basically, God offering himself to you as nutrition." The latter image recalls young Tarwater's unstated physical-cum-spiritual hunger for "the bread of life" in O'Connor's *The Violent Bear It Away*, and O'Connor's own Eucharistic practices and beliefs. As she once famously remarked in a letter about the sacraments of bread and wine, "Well, if it's a symbol, to hell with it." And she added, "it is the center of existence for me; all the rest of life is expendable." Stevens has made similar statements about the importance of his sacramentally oriented Christian faith. As he tells a writer for *The Atlantic*, his faith informs the totality of his life, his "living and moving and being."

In the Devil's Territory

Stevens's *Seven Swans* album reflects his Christian spirituality more than anything he has since released. A second song on this twelve-track low-fi recording draws both its content and title from Stevens's reading of O'Connor's works. The title of track 3, "In the Devil's Territory," is an obvious echo of an O'Connor phrase and appears to have been borrowed from a subheading to a section in *Mystery and Manners* in which she memorably defines her "subject in fiction" as "the action of grace in territory held largely by the devil." Stevens's "In the Devil's Territory" combines multiple banjo tracks with pounding piano chords and pulsing rhythm, resolving eventually into a crescendoing, ascending, spooky riff on a theremin—the ethereal electronic instrument activated by hand motion and made famous on the Beach Boys' 1966 hit song "Good Vibrations."

Stevens's lyrics in this song are somewhat mystifying, evidently diabolic in subject matter, and possibly apocalyptic. But the song begins with a note of assurance—"Be still and know your sign / The Beast will arrive in time"—and concludes in a triumphalist way: "We stayed a long, long time / To see you, to beat you, / to see you, to meet you. / To see you at last." The assurance here in the face of cosmic evil is reminiscent of O'Connor's comment on the role of evil in our moral state: "To ensure our sense of mystery, we need a sense of evil which sees the devil as a real spirit who must be made to name himself." Like O'Connor in her fiction, Stevens ventures artistically into the Devil's territory in this song, names evil, gives it personality, and like O'Connor, in a phrase from a letter to John Hawkes, makes "certain that the Devil gets identified as the Devil and not simply taken for this or that psychological tendency." Given the multiple references to the Devil in his published short fiction and song narratives, Stevens too, in this respect, might also be considered one of Hawthorne's "descendents," as O'Connor referred to herself.

States of Being: *Michigan* and *Illinois*

Like O'Connor's fictions, Stevens's song narratives on his concept albums *Michigan* and *Illinois* present manners infused with mystery. Hardly a song is not threaded through with some sense of underlying redemptive or salvific possibility—an immanent grace that hovers over both geographical space and the travails of the human spirit, or a revelatory violence that results in a bleak epiphany for the song's narrator and for the listener as well. Stevens shares O'Connor's spiritual view of human experience: that our lives are lived under the shadow of the divine, and that the human drama is played out in territory held largely by the Devil. Stevens has moreover produced a body of often parabolic, sometimes biblically based song narratives that pursue themes similar to those found in O'Connor's fiction.

Stevens has stated in several interviews that the short stories he wrote for his MFA were transmuted into the lyric material on *Michigan*, an album of narrative songs set in his native state and composed while he was living in Brooklyn. On track 4, "Say Yes! to M!ch!gan!" the narrator reflects on how being "Made in Michigan" and growing up there has shaped his identity and consciousness. Though he "never meant to go away," he did. O'Connor was similarly absent from the South for a time, first while at the prestigious Iowa Writers' Workshop in 1947–1948, and later as she worked on her first novel on the Fitzgerald homestead in Connecticut, before the debilitating effects of lupus caused her to return to Milledgeville, Georgia, and to the social and geographical territory of her fictional worlds. Stevens's narrator too returns in memory at least "to the farms" and "Golden arms" of childhood and adolescent experience to transmute his fictional materials into song. He reminds himself three times in this short song "I was raised, I was raised / In the place, in the place" and concludes the last such refrain with "part to remind me."

Of what? Of the fact that these are the materials of his experience, the people and places and cultural realities that through his creative gifts he is fitted to write about—that he will be able to "demonstrate" imaginatively, as the first word of the lyrics announces. The song is a kind of artistic apology in which the sidelined writer of fiction says "Yes!" to his new vocation as a songwriter.

The short-story narratives that inform the *Michigan* songs are most evident in the tracks titled "The Upper Peninsula" and "Romulus." Like Springsteen's songs about the dispossessed and marginalized members of the American working class, "The Upper Peninsula" bears witness to the emptiness and bleakness of people's lives in economically repressed places and times. And as Springsteen often does, Stevens creates a narrator who tells his story in song. "I live in America," he states with an ironic undertone in the song's opening line, a variant on Springsteen's "Born in the USA" refrain. Stevens's unemployed workingman, separated from his wife and child and living in a broken-down trailer home just off an interstate, wears "Payless shoes," owns a snowmobile and a car, and sits around watching television news. Possibly his wife belongs to one of the hyper-fundamentalist religious groups in the region; she holds to "strange ideas" and is raising their boy child in such a way that "he's been reviled." The desperate first-person narrator is of the same cast as the existentially unraveling narrators of Springsteen's *Nebraska* songs. He concludes his story with a litany of confusion and loss: "I've no idea what's right sometimes / I lost my mind, I lost my life / I lost my job, I lost my wife."

The lyrics to "Romulus" include several descriptive details from Stevens's MFA story "My Mother, King Tut," one of the few stories he eventually published. The song and story share similar autobiographical content and point of view—particularly the child narrator's embarrassment over his addled and irresponsible mother, who has a penchant for garishly coloring her hair. The song is structured around a series of "once" moments, four vignettes that briefly recount the child's encounters with an absent mother of whom he is "ashamed." As Stevens underscores about his own art—and as O'Connor stresses regarding the art of storytelling in general—the essence of a story is caught in small details and observations: an awkward phone call, a broken-down Chevrolet, a new VCR given to the family by the mother's father in seeming compensation for her abandonment ("we grew up in spite of it"), and the moment of the grandfather's death, when his mother "didn't seem to care / She smoked in her room and colored her hair." "Romulus," titled with the name of the mythic Roman twin (and a Michigan place-name) is the lyric twin to Stevens's short story; both record the writer's long-abiding aggrievement over his birth mother, who abandoned him—in the lyrics, "her last child"—at a year old. Songs on his seventh studio album, *Carrie and Lowell* (2015), titled with the names of his mother and stepfather, express Stevens's sense of loss at being a motherless child and his efforts to reconcile with his mother before and after her death from stomach cancer in 2012.

* * *

O'Connor directs her readers to be on the lookout for "the almost imperceptible intrusions of grace" in her stories, often found in small details, in "the right gesture" or a subtle dramatic action, or by glimpsing "an experience of mystery itself" in the language of the text. In a short story, there is little room for the machinations of plot and the description of manners to set up the epiphanic moment in the narrative. So it is with Ruby Turpin's revelation in "Revelation" as she blindly hoses down the hogs with which she stands accused of having a likeness, and which in the "mysterious hue" of the evening sky are "suffused" with light and "[appear] to pant with a secret life." Or with the young girl at the end of "A Temple of the Holy Ghost," as a mental image of the hermaphrodite freak at the fair lifting their dress to show their genitals is overlaid with a vision of a priest "rais[ing] the monstrance with the Host ivory-colored in the center of it."

Such luminous moments in a work of short fiction are revelatory. Song lyrics, of course, afford even less narrative space in which to inform the song-story with subtle grace notes. One of Stevens's methods in both his abstract and vignette-like lyrics is to use a form of ecstatic exclamation that intrudes into the song narrative—a thrust of grace into the mundane and the profane subjects of his songs. His musical paean to Michigan places in "Sleeping Bear, Sault Saint Marie," for example, is in the form of four lyrical apostrophes of three lines each ("Oh Sleeping Bear!" / "Oh Sturgeon Bay!" / "Oh Saint Marie!") that describe a physical feature of each geographic location. The second verse is surprisingly set apart from the content of the rest and sounds like it might have come from *The Book of Common Prayer*: "Oh Lamb of God / Tell us your perfect design / and give us the rod." On *Illinois*, similar exclamations of the sacred are layered into the narrative song "Jacksonville": a verse celebrating its namesake American president Andrew Jackson and the virtues of capitalism makes reference to a "Colored Preacher," followed by the line "The spirit is here, and the spirit is fine." Track 7, "Decatur, or Round of Applause for Your Stepmother!" is a pastiche of childhood memories of a trip to this modest industrial city in the center of the state. Its rah-rah concluding verse fuses cheers for the city ("Go Decatur!") and for the largely despised stepmother ("Appreciate her!") with a four-fold antiphonal repetition of "It's the great I Am." The initial capital on "Am" in the phrase invokes a biblical reference to Yahweh's reply to the reluctant prophet Moses in Exodus 3:14: "I AM WHO I AM . . . Thus you shall say to the sons of Israel, I AM has sent me to you." The phrase "the great I Am," attributed to the poet Samuel Taylor Coleridge, has considerable currency in Christian theology and hymnology as a metonym for *God*. Punctuations of praise in Stevens's otherwise profane lyrics inform the listener that the mystery of God's grace and providence threads through space and history and the experience of the moment; it is there in the motions and manners of everyday existence, Stevens's songs suggest, for those with eyes to see and ears to hear.

The outstanding song in this respect on the two states recordings is *Illinois*'s "Casimir Pulaski Day," one of Stevens's most widely admired works. Its title refers to a local holiday throughout Illinois on the first Monday in March commemorating a Polish-born hero of the American Revolution, one of only eight honorary US citizens, known as the "Father of the American cavalry." Stevens told an interviewer for *The Guardian* in 2005 that the song recounts a real-life story of a teenage sweetheart who died of bone cancer. In a subsequent interview in *American Songwriter*, however, he says the story is a fiction, based on the lives of two friends, neither of whom succumbed to an illness, and that the event he writes about occurred "around" the Pulaski public holiday. His songwriting, says Stevens, is "a process of collage making" that combines "my memory and my experiences" with "my stories" to create something "new" in a narrative song. As one commentator has noted, Stevens, "like any great fiction writer," is "a master of making things that are fiction seem personal." Significantly, in *The Guardian* interview he ties his impulse to write about this youthful experience to his interest in O'Connor's fictions: "Flannery O'Connor said that anyone who survives a childhood has multitudes to write about, because really childhood is a succession of trauma and crisis over and over."

The ballad-like "Casimir Pulaski Day," with banjo accompaniment and bouncy, breathy vocal line, has an adolescent directness and innocence. Stevens maintains to *The Guardian* interviewer that the song registers his first experience as a teenager with the death of a loved one. A sense of an encounter with a mysterious unknown that is death pervades the lyrics. And the accumulation of details both underscores the reality of the narrator's adolescent experience while deflecting from the specter of having a girlfriend dying from "cancer of the bone." Threading through the song is the mystery of human mortality, the experience of loss, and the "complications" of death, even from a Christian perspective. Intimations of the speaker's romantic relationship with the dying girl in the second and fourth verses are punctuated with Psalm-like expressions: verse 2 resolves with "All the glory that the Lord has made / And the complications you could do without / When I kissed you on the mouth." The "All the glory" exclamation also unexpectedly intrudes into the narrative in verse 4, which appears to refer to a sexual tryst the young woman's father discovers the next morning. The penultimate verse tells of the moment of the young woman's death and includes a remarkable amount of story-like detail in six lines of lyrics: a "nurse runs in with her head hung low"; a "cardinal hits the window"; it is a "morning, in the winter . . . / On the first of March"—in Illinois the day of the Casimir Pulaski state holiday. The story of the young woman's illness includes a scene at a Tuesday-night Bible Study where "We lift our hands and pray over your body / But nothing ever happens." In the final verse, "All the glory that the Lord has made" does not prevent suffering and death and grieving. While the narrator affirms the Christian creedal truth of the Crucifixion that "He took our place," this offers little consolation and no remediation. In the end, in the last line of the song, "He takes and He takes and He takes," and there is little in the mystery of death that leaves us with any understanding or sense of its meaning. The assurances of Christian doctrine are not enough; yet there is nothing unchristian in questioning the silences and uncertainties in the life of faith, the song suggests. The "complications" of suffering and death will only resolve, the narrator implies in hymn-like discourse, "when I see His face."

Get Real, Get Right

The cover art for Stevens's 2010 release *The Age of Adz* features a crudely drawn bust of a robot-like creature. An accompanying booklet comprises twelve panels of fantasy-cartoonish drawings by eccentric and schizophrenic

Black American artist Royal Robertson (1936–1997). Robertson was a mentally unstable, self-proclaimed prophet figure from Baldwin, Louisiana, who claimed to communicate with angels and aliens. His comic-book-like drawings fuse bizarre and near-pornographic characters with prophetic passages from the Bible and apocalyptic pronouncements. Despite his illness, Robertson was capable of work that attracted the attention of serious art collectors. Indeed, a number of his works are held in major museum collections, including the Smithsonian American Art Museum. Something in Robertson's madly inspired vision appealed to Stevens at a critical point in his career.

Stevens's narrative songs typically fuse the factual with the fictional, often informed by the personal—as might well be said of O'Connor's short fiction. "Get Real, Get Right" from *The Age of Adz* is both Stevens's artistic response to Robertson—in the first half of the song—and his own confessional. Its title and dominant refrain combine hipster slang—"get real"—with a familiar imperative religious slogan found along the roadsides in the Bible Belt: "Get right with the Lord." Lucinda Williams's O'Connor-influenced "Get Right with God"—its title derived from a southern fundamentalist road sign—is a musical companion to Stevens's song.

Struggling with his own physical and mental health at the time, Stevens engages in a creative dialogue with Robertson in *The Age of Adz*. Robertson becomes a projection of the artist self that Stevens explores in his song cycle. In a revealing interview in *Under the Radar* in 2010, Stevens describes the sympathy he felt with Robertson during a period of personal and artistic crisis:

> I felt like I'd ventured into a state of madness because I had lost my bearings ... and was suffering a kind of creative psychosis or an aesthetic crisis because I had no boundaries, nothing to hold on to. And what I found inspiring with Royal was that within that state of madness, he created all this fantastic work. So, he became my companion. He became my reference point.

In some ways, Robertson might be considered a Mason Tarwater figure. Just as O'Connor took her mildly insane prophet figure seriously, so Stevens does the self-appointed prophet Robertson in *The Age of Adz* songs. The lyrics to "Get Real, Get Right" begin in an ambiguous narrative voice that could be Stevens's own or might be the Lord Himself speaking: "I know you really want to get it right / Have you forsaken, have you mistaken me for someone else?" Here is another instance of O'Connoresque doubling in Stevens's work. The imperative messaging in this song shifts from the second person—"You know you really got to get right with the Lord"—to a first-person voice that acknowledges a parallel condition to that of Robertson:

> I know I've lost my conscience
> I know I've lost all shame
> But I must do the right thing
> I must do myself a favour and get real
> Get right with the Lord

Expressions of personal piety and devotion to God inform the end of the "I" stanza ("I know I've always loved You"). The song concludes with the injunction to "Get real, get right with the Lord" directed at a "you" that may refer to the listener as much as to the songwriter. One of the many fan websites devoted to Stevens has as its banner phrase, "Between Hipsters and God There Is Sufjan Stevens." The discourse and *message* in "Get Real, Get Right" appears to be an effort to communicate in song the shocking truth of a familiar slogan of old-time southern religion in a way and with the hope that hipsters will take notice.

❧ ❧ ❧

Stevens's generous and somewhat disorderly song collection *Age of Adz* explores new territory both sonically and lyrically. In part, this is a result of his need as an artist to experiment and to create less pop-like compositions. (Reviewers compared songs on *Illinois* to compositions by the British pop group Coldplay, which did not sit well with Stevens.) In other part, the new direction of his music on *Adz* resulted from what Stevens acknowledged as his unbalanced personal life at the time, "a kind of creative psychosis" that manifested as both an artistic and an existential crisis. Stevens's artistic crisis might be understood as precipitated by what John Barth in his poststructuralist manifesto "The Literature of Exhaustion" refers to as the "exhausted possibility" of a given art form—"the used-upness of certain forms or the felt exhaustion of certain possibilities." Prior to the release of *The Age of Adz*, Stevens despaired that the album form in which he conceived his songwriting art had become both culturally and technologically outmoded, that he could no longer work in the conceptual framework that had guided his creative imagination. Thirty-five at the time, he had been playing music professionally since he was twenty. His comments in a widely read confessional interview in *Paste* in 2009 led to speculation that he was abandoning his craft as a songwriter. Stevens remarked that he felt the album as an art form had dissipated in a culture in which pop music was commodified one song at a time. "I no longer have faith in the album anymore," he stated, adding more surprisingly, "I no longer have faith in the song."

Other songwriters in this study who see themselves as *writers* in a literary sense—including Bruce Springsteen, Lucinda Williams, and Mary Gauthier—regard the decline of the concept album with a narrative unity between tracks as having had a marked effect on the art of the songwriter. Musicians and music critics alike have decried that the present mode of producing and marketing and engaging with contemporary pop music—song-by-downloaded-song on iTunes or Spotify—has led to the death of the album. Certainly, songwriters wishing to explore larger thematic concerns over a number of linked songs (Springsteen's *Darkness on the Edge of Town* or Mary Gauthier's *The Foundling*, for examples) will find a diminishing audience largely due to the ways in which contemporary music is presently marketed and consumed. It is, to use an outmoded image, as if the store of musical culture in postmodern America is stocked solely with A-sided 45s.

Interestingly, O'Connor seems to have had a similar artistic crisis, though under different conditions, at a similar stage in her career, which would tragically turn out to be the last year of her writing life. She writes a letter to Catholic Sister Mariella Gable in May 1963 asking for prayer and adding, "I've been writing eighteen years and I have reached the point where I can't do again what I know I can do well, and the larger things that I need to do now, I doubt my capacity for doing." At this crisis point in his career, Stevens could well have echoed O'Connor's words in relation to his own artistic expressions and calling.

It's the Same Fire

O'Connor's backwoods prophet Mason Tarwater in *The Violent Bear It Away* claims to have had his eyes "burned clean" when he was "touched" one day by "a finger of fire" out of the heavens and thus "torn by the Lord's eye." As a bona fide prophet, O'Connor tells us, Tarwater has "learned by fire," both by way of correction by the divine and as confirmation of his prophetic calling. One of the memorable bits of O'Connoresque doctrine in her second novel is found in the words of old Tarwater as he instructs his grandnephew "in the hard facts of serving the Lord." Grabbing him by the straps of his overalls, and shaking young Tarwater slowly, he would say, "Even the mercy of the Lord burns." Stevens too appears to acknowledge this harsh, paradoxical spiritual truth.

In "Vesuvius," from Stevens's *The Age of Adz*, the speaker invokes a revelatory "fire of fire" and in the song's refrain asks it to "Fall on me now / As I favor the ghost." The image here is of a Pentecostal fire that symbolizes the descent of the Holy Ghost, but it is equally a fire from an evil source that wreaks destruction. Dormant Mount Vesuvius in southern Italy, which famously erupted in AD 79 and destroyed the towns of Pompeii and Herculaneum, is still considered one of the most dangerous volcanoes in the world. It is indisputably an iconic symbol of destruction, of fire and brimstone that obliterates all in its path. Yet, in reference to his figurative Vesuvius, Stevens echoes a familiar phrase from Pentecostal hymnology, "fall on me," which is associated with "the holy fire from heaven," figuratively the Spirit of God, "the fire of Pentecost," still regularly invoked in Bible Belt churches and more broadly in hyper-fundamentalist faith communities. Stevens and O'Connor both allude to that fire in exploring a darksome divine mystery.

Though biblical sounding and seemingly resonant within the context of divinity, the phrase "fire of fire" is not found in canonical scripture and appears to have a single currency of meaning as a descriptor of Satan in both Talmudic and gnostic texts. In the apocryphal Gospel of Saint Bartholomew, the archangel Michael enjoins the fallen Lucifer to respond in worship to the image of God made manifest in humankind. To this Satan responds incredulously, "I am fire of fire; I was the first angel formed, and shall I worship clay and matter?" Stevens's use of this phrase is thus both complex and conflicted—and cryptically O'Connoresque. The spiritual nature of this song is further complicated by what appears to be an oracular voice directed at the singer-songwriter himself:

> Sufjan, follow your heart
> Follow the flame
> Or fall on the floor

The oracle continues in a similar vein:

> Sufjan, the panic inside
> The murdering ghost
> That you cannot ignore

The speaker is aware that the volcano has "destroyed" with "elegant smoke," but appeals to it to "be kind" for the moment, though he knows that "the path" he follows "leads to an article of imminent death." Purification and affirmation and annihilation are all conjoined here in a single flame that is both Vesuvian "fire of fire" *and* Sufjan's own fire—both "ghost" and "host," as indicated in the alternating word in the multiply repeated refrain that concludes the song:

Vesuvius
Fire of fire
Fall on me now
As I favor the ghost/host

The image here recalls the words of O'Connor's child evangelist Lucette in *The Violent Bear It Away*, who enjoins her congregation, "Be saved in the Lord's fire or perish in your own." This same idea is explored in the novel's protagonist, young Tarwater, after he has torched his backwoods home. Believing he has immolated the remains of his great-uncle, Francis Marion Tarwater confuses the flames of his homestead at Powderhead with "the glow from the city lights," where he is heading with the vacuous traveling salesman Meeks. "It's the same fire," he cries.

This image of conjoined fire, or divine and/or the devilish fire, is palpably illustrated in the demonic "grinning presence" that looks out of the flaming "forked tree" in the dramatic, symbolic concluding scene of O'Connor's second novel. The "red-gold tree of fire" Tarwater witnesses is both home to his "adversary" and a symbolic burning bush that signifies his calling to be a prophet. It is a fire that leads to "imminent death"—to self, as Saint Paul would have it, or to a discarded life on some personal Gehenna, to flames of self-extinction. Stevens's "fire of fire" in "Vesuvius" is the same fire that in O'Connor's sacramental symbology either/both destroys or/and purifies. As Tarwater must choose, so Stevens's narrator must discern whether the threatening Vesuvius is "The symbol of light / Or a fantasy host," and which fire he will "favor." This is the unresolved tension within this cryptic anthemic song, with its concluding imprecatory refrain intruded upon by discomfiting dissonant synthesizer sounds and a mix of seeming human cries of distress and exaltation beginning at 4:06 minutes and continuing to the song's end (5:27). The ontological center of both O'Connor's anagogical novel and Stevens's lyrically complex song aligns with an idea that poet T. S. Eliot formulates at the end of his Christian long poem, *Four Quartets*: that in matters of the spirit, "We only live, only suspire / Consumed by either fire or fire" ("Little Gidding")—that is, either consumed by the fire of our own longings and desires or refined by a divinely sourced fire of love that burns within our being.

The Habit of B-ing

Sufjan Stevens's canon in 2023 well exceeds one hundred original songs, but he has only just begun to tell his own stories in song—so far, a successful Plan B for the thwarted fiction writer, who is conflicted about his calling as an avant-garde pop composer and songwriter. While he is not the second coming of Flannery O'Connor, as he aspired to be, Stevens has, like all great artists, dedicated himself to making something new in his chosen medium. He melds a fiction writer's craft and consciousness of the mystery of the human condition with experimental instrumentation that often involves distortion, at times a raw simplicity, and more often a symphonic complexity. Spotify has defined his genre as "baroque pop." Reviewers have been quick to suggest that his song cycles have an affinity with the form of the postmodern novel, and Stevens himself has repeatedly commented that his talents as a fiction writer inform his songwriting: "I think they are very similar, writing fiction and writing music," he has remarked, echoing similar statements by Springsteen and Gauthier. "They require different skills and different ears, but there is a certain music to fiction, to the sentence—the rhythm of words put together. And I think it's the same in songwriting as well."

In his later compositions, Stevens pushes the aesthetic of pop music in songs frequently punctuated by orchestrated noise, dissonance, and staccato drumbeats, and quietly vocalizes his allusive yet often jarring lyrics. His art bears an aesthetic of "distortion . . . that reveals"—as O'Connor defined her own methods—more than it conceals "the deeper kinds of realism."

As is the case with Bruce Springsteen and Lucinda Williams in particular, O'Connor's art and vision has evidently had an abiding influence on Stevens. His early *Nebraska*-like work under O'Connor's influence, the 2004 low-fi album *Seven Swans*, as discussed above, offers two songs that directly reference her art and thought. Perhaps the title and very brief lyrics to "We Won't Need Legs to Stand" on that same album allude to Hulga Hopewell's condition at the conclusion of "Good Country People," a story Stevens invokes in a 2011 interview with German novelist Thomas Pletzinger. Further homage to and borrowing from O'Connor is likely registered in the opening line to the second verse of the song "Size Too Small": "Everything rises, going at it all." And the terms here gleaned from O'Connor's fiction inform the title and chorus and concept of track 4, "Everything That Rises," on his thirteenth studio album, *Javelin*, released in October 2023 when this book was in its final copyedit stage.

O'Connor discussed matters of her religious beliefs and practices in letters to fellow writers and friends, most notably to her lapsed Catholic correspondent Betty Hester, identified as "A" in O'Connor's collected letters, *The Habit of Being*. Epistolary relationships in this millennium are more often conducted through email or social media. Animated by the bigoted and racist policies of the early Trump administration, Stevens was active in 2017 on a *Tumblr* account and on his website sufjan.com. Casting himself in a role like that of O'Connor's inflamed prophet Mason Tarwater, Stevens urges his online community to read and heed the Ten Commandments, posting them with a comment that they are not a particularly religious prescription but "basic rules for being a human." He calls for compassion in the wake of new anti-immigration and antirefugee laws and bigoted public opinion, reminding his readers that "Jesus Christ was a refugee baby." Under a slogan like those on Bible Belt road signs—"AMERICA YOU WILL PAY FOR YOUR SINS"—Stevens cites Christ's words from the Gospel of Matthew, "Ask and it will be given you; seek and you will find; knock and the door will be opened to you," and points to Christ's hard sayings about money: "The love of money is the root of all evil" and "Again I tell you, it is easier for a camel to pass through the eye of a needle than for a rich man to enter the kingdom of God."

Like other songwriters under O'Connor's good spell (Lucinda Williams and Nick Cave, for examples), Stevens could be a character in one of her fictions, to the extent that he casts himself in the role of a postmodern prophet. His fundamentalist-like sign postings along the Internet highway, like the injunction to young Tarwater in the closing lines of O'Connor's second novel, are intended to "WARN THE CHILDREN OF GOD OF THE TERRIBLE SPEED OF MERCY," as O'Connor writes. And like the children of God in the dark city toward which young Tarwater ultimately slouches—as described in the last word of O'Connor's novel—Sufjan Stevens's community of listeners and readers also appear to lie "sleeping."

From the initial evidence in the *Seven Swans* songs, the arc of O'Connor's influence on Stevens's work and creative life is well documented and acknowledged. In a 2007 PEN interview, Stevens mentions O'Connor's influence on his MFA thesis cycle of stories about a fictional Michigan town, adding, "I have a slight southern fetish mixed with fear." He has been compared to O'Connor in numerous critical assessments of his art in pop music trade and fan magazines and in online journals and blogs. A posting on sufjan.com in 2014 shortly after the publication of Flannery O'Connor's *A Prayer Journal* makes a solid argument for her abiding influence on his sense of himself as a writer and artist within her religious tradition. There he presents eighteen numbered phrases and sentences extracted from O'Connor's penned prayers that resonate with his own statements in interviews and blogs, including, "I don't want to have invented my faith to satisfy my weakness"; "Hell is our only hope. Without it we are a wasteland"; "The only way to live right is to give up everything"; and, lastly, the final two sentences in O'Connor's published journal: "Today I have proved myself a glutton—for Scotch oatmeal cookies and erotic thought. There is nothing left to say of me." The coup de grâce in Stevens's post is his closing parenthetical comment on the eighteen excerpts: "These could also work as potential chapter titles for my autobiography, *There Is Nothing Left to Say of Me*, by Sufjan Stevens."

That Stevens inserts himself in this way into O'Connor's self-expression as a young writer struggling with the relation between faith and a desire to write enduring fiction—"to be the best artist it is possible for me to be, under God," she writes in her published journal—speaks to the directness and the degree to which he continues to carry a sense of O'Connor's influence: not only through evident elements in his art but in self-confessed parallels in his life as an artist both trafficking in and in tension with his Christian faith.

Chapter 6

NICK CAVE

"In the Bleeding Stinking Mad Shadow of Jesus"

Nick Cave might have stepped out of the pages of Flannery O'Connor's fiction. Christ-haunted, self-possessed, and with a sense of his prophetic mission, Cave has carried on an argument with God and exposed his troubles in love in songs and essays and novels over his more than forty-five-year career. Born and raised as a nominal Anglican in small-town Australia, with native pluck and gallows humor, Cave has been described as "a modern man of letters fed on Iggy Pop, Elvis, and the Bible." In his late teens he emerged as the front man of the notorious Australian punk band the Birthday Party, forerunners in the cacophonous gothic rock scene during the band's rough ride from 1978 to 1983. One critic described the group as "heroes of literate oblivion," and Cave has remarked that as the band's songwriter and lead singer, his screeched lyrics were based on his reading at the time. The band's often violence-wracked concerts featuring young Cave's convulsive vocal performances are the stuff of postmodern music legend. In 1983, Cave and other survivors of the Australian punk era formed the alternative rock band the Bad Seeds and moved from Melbourne to London. From 1985 to 1989 they were a fixture in the goth scene in West Berlin. To date, Cave and various incarnations of the Bad Seeds have released eighteen studio albums and are regarded as one of the most innovative and acclaimed post-punk/alternative rock groups of the 1980s onward.

Songwriter, novelist, essayist, scriptwriter, actor, composer of soundtracks, biblical commentator, blogger, and, to some, a secular saint: Nick Cave is all of these. He has been and continues to be a prolific and innovative creator of products of popular culture. His murder ballad "Red Right Hand" haunts the soundtracks of the first three installments in the horror comedy franchise *Scream* (1996, 1997, 2000), and songs by Nick Cave and the Bad Seeds have been featured in numerous films, notably *Batman Forever* (1995) and *Harry Potter and the Deathly Hallows—Part 1* (2010). With Bad Seeds bandmate Warren Ellis, Cave composed standout soundtracks for the film version of Cormac McCarthy's novel *The Road* (2009), along with the celebrated indie films *Hell or High Water* (2016) and *Wind River* (2017). Now in his midsixties, he is an accomplished, complex, and often conflicted artist. And during an intense productive period early in his long and diverse career, Cave became obsessed with Flannery O'Connor's fiction, especially her first novel *Wise Blood* and its profane protagonist, Hazel Motes.

The literary quality in Cave's art began in his early teens and was nurtured by his father, an English teacher and aspiring fiction writer. Cave describes in his 1996 BBC broadcast "The Flesh Made Word" how his father would usher him into his study and excitedly recite to him "great bloody slabs" from Shakespeare and Dostoevsky and particularly Nabokov's *Lolita*. It is possible he even encountered Flannery O'Connor's stories at this time. Cave saw in his father the way that literature "elevated him" and moved him "closer to the divine essence of things." His own love of literature and language he attributes, in an O'Connoresque way, to "the blood of my father in me." His father's death in a car accident when Cave was nineteen left "a great gaping hole" in his world and, as he understands, compelled him to become a writer of songs and stories—to be about his father's unfinished business. His choirboy days in an Anglican church in Australia filled him with the language and stories of the Bible and a disaffection for organized religion. He read the Holy Scriptures voraciously in his fatherless late teens and early twenties and found in the Old Testament "a cruel and rancorous God" with whom he has long contended in his songwriting and essays. O'Connor and the Bible were his literary guides as, alongside his musical career, Cave set himself the task of becoming a novelist.

According to Cave biographer Ian Johnston, between musical projects with the Bad Seeds during his West Berlin years, Cave holed up in a cheap apartment, often high on heroin or meta-amphetamines, working feverishly and spottily on his first novel *And the Ass Saw the Angel*. (Published in 1989 by Black Spring Press, it has been available "extensively revised by the author" in a popular Penguin paperback since 2009.)

A photograph by Australian photographer Bleddyn Butcher shows Cave at the time he was writing the novel, in his small cave-like apartment, its walls plastered with images and taped-on manuscript and torn-out book pages. An early photograph of Elvis is tucked beside a Sunday school image of cherub-like girls representing the Three Graces: Faith, Hope, and Charity. Three locks of black hair dangle from an electrical conduit, and other fetishes adorn the room—items that Cave, "an avid collector of curios," picked up in frequent visits to a local flea market. Cave is pictured squatting, eyes looking upward and right, like a saint in a gothic painting in a moment of divine ecstasy. His bandaged right hand rests on an open Bible with a thumb index. Among the many books stacked and propped around the tiny room, the Faber edition of

"In the Bleeding Stinking Mad Shadow of Jesus"

Pound's *Selected Cantos* is half visible as is C. S. Lewis's autobiographical *A Grief Observed* and a pulp novel edition of *Cyrano de Bergerac*.

Bleddyn Butcher, who has photographed Cave for more than thirty years, remarks in an interview that in 1985 Cave and the Bad Seeds were "smacked out, for one thing, and full of themselves and what they were doing." He emphasizes Cave's literary aspirations, which were shared by the band: "They were interested in American literature, in the southern gothic, mostly Mary Flannery O'Connor." Butcher staged what has become his best-known photograph to signify the parallels between Cave as writer and the mad mute narrator of *And the Ass Saw the Angel*, both of whom squat in a squalid bower packed with collectibles. This womb-like ground zero of Cave's literary imagination was reconstructed in exacting detail for the extended North American premiere of *Stranger Than Kindness* at Montreal's Galerie de la Maison du Festival (8 April–25 September 2022), billed as "a multi-media journey into the complex works, creative life, and artistic legacy of musician, songwriter, storyteller and cultural icon Nick Cave."

And the Ass Saw the Angel

The subtitle of Carol Hart's study of Cave's first novel, "*And the Ass Saw the Angel*: A Novel of Fragments and Excess," well describes this flawed work of faux southern gothic fiction. The novel concerns the life and "divine" mission of Euchrid Eucrow, who is whelped into a family of violently grotesque inbred hillbillies in the fictional Ukulore Valley. Euchrid, who though mute nonetheless narrates most of the story, is subject to visions and inner voices. He is attracted to the town prostitute, Cosey Mo, who becomes a kind of Madonna figure in the novel. Cosey is blamed for a three-year-long deluge that has turned the valley into swampland and devastated the sugarcane fields from which Ukulites earn their living. Cosey ends up severely beaten and driven out by the hypocritical townspeople, among them many of her clients. Euchrid alone witnesses her placing a swaddled infant at the foot of a memorial statue nine months after her banishment, and later discovers Cosey's drowned body. The townspeople name the abandoned baby Beth. As her arrival coincides with an end to the insufferable years of rain, the superstitious Ukulites regard the child as a kind of saint.

Into the valley rides a charlatan preacher, Abie Poe, released from prison where he has spent seven years on charges of fraud and extortion. The sickly Poe finds lodging as the sole boarder in the house of an older woman. Poe, of course, bears the surname of one of O'Connor's literary progenitors, and Cave's character has the frenzied, maniacal intensity of O'Connor's blaspheming preacher Hazel Motes from her first novel. Cave has described *And the Ass Saw the Angel* as "a comic novel in the manner of Flannery O'Connor's *Wise Blood*," explaining that along with its themes of alienation, obsession, and voyeurism, the book is largely, as is O'Connor's first novel "an exposition on the subject of faith." While Cave acknowledges the influence of *Wise Blood*, his story also has strong resonances of plot details relating to young Francis Marion Tarwater, the reluctant backwoods prophet who is the focus of O'Connor's second novel, *The Violent Bear It Away*. Cave appears to draw literary inspiration from O'Connor's artistic method in both novels and from her Christ-haunted central characters. Borrowings and fragments from her two novels can be found scattered throughout Cave's profane, often gruesome, and in every way disturbing tale.

Like Hazel Motes, Abie Poe takes on the persona of a street evangelist, dressed in "a severe black suit and tall wide-brimmed hat . . . also black"—not unlike the garb of Motes, who wears a cheap suit and a "stiff black broad-brimmed hat." Unlike Motes, Poe becomes a Bible-thumping, sin-sniffing preacher who eventually takes up the abandoned pulpit in the town church from where he excoriates the townsfolk: "Not a soul among you is clean. You are all steeped in filth." John the Baptist–like, Poe offers to baptize them. In what Cave renders as a parodic scene of religious fervor, one of the gathered women cries out, "I want to be clean. Renew my spirit, Baptist!" The charlatan Poe, a parody of so many televangelists, claims to be inhabited by "the spirit of Elijah" and has come to offer the people "a little cleansing, a little healing, a little crying in the wilderness."

Cave invokes O'Connor's *Wise Blood* through the repeated use of the signal word *clean*—a lexical marker in O'Connor's text associated with the person and words of her blaspheming preacher Hazel Motes. (Similarly, Springsteen locates his "Nebraska" song in O'Connor's story "A Good Man Is Hard to Find" by borrowing a signal word in her story—*meanness*—to link his tortured serial killer narrator to a key word in O'Connor's text associated with her likewise murderous and nihilistic character, The Misfit.) In one scene in O'Connor's novel, Motes is repeatedly referred to as "a clean boy." In his unrepentant state he twice insists "I AM clean," and while preaching his gospel of the Church without Christ, he tells his street congregation that salvation through Jesus is unnecessary because "Every one of you people are clean." In the novel's concluding pages, the self-blinded Haze mortifies his own sinful flesh by filling his shoes with gravel and bits of glass and wrapping his chest with barbed wire, explaining to his landlady, "I'm not clean."

For Cave as for O'Connor, *clean* denotes the state of being of a righteous, repentant individual—not surprisingly, a character type absent from both novels. Cave's Euchrid responds to Poe's efforts to cleanse him in the waters of baptism by gobbing spit at him. And despite Poe's having supposedly "cleansed [their] souls in the sacred waters," incited by their crusading preacher, his congregation proceeds savagely to assault the town whore, Cosey Mo, beating her near to death and destroying her pink caravan of pleasure. In the absence of true cleanness, there is meanness in the fictional worlds of O'Connor and Cave. And Cave appears to be aware, even in parody, that in O'Connor's lexicon, *clean* invokes the divine refining fire meant "to burn you clean."

Several parallels between Cave's novel and O'Connor's *The Violent Bear It Away* are also worth noting to underscore the extent to which his first work of fiction owes some of its content and intent to her two odd novels. Euchrid Eucrow, Cave's protagonist-cum-part-time narrator, comes tumbling into the world when his caterwauling, liquor-addled mother gives birth to twins "in the back seat of [an] old burnt-out Chevy." Like O'Connor's protagonist Francis Marion Tarwater, Euchrid is physically "born in a wreck" and symbolically as well: into the moral and spiritual wasteland of Ukulore and his degenerate family. His twin brother dies within hours, and in his infant mind he is conscious of the loss.

AND THE ASS SAW THE ANGEL

NICK CAVE

Like Tarwater, Euchrid is subject to voices in his head, in his case, directly resulting from the stupefying effects of his father's corn liquor, known as "White Jesus." After many slugs, Euchrid has a sense that he is on a "celestial mission" and hears "His voice" instructing him as to his diabolical prophetic task. O'Connor's young Tarwater, reluctantly digging a grave for his dead great-uncle, a raving backwoods prophet figure, is distracted by a Black man who comes to fill a jug with the great-uncle's moonshine. Tarwater eventually becomes stone drunk on it. The voice of "the stranger" informs him that his intoxicated state is the effect of "the Hand of God laying a blessing on you."

Tarwater returns to his charred homestead, Powderhead; Euchrid, having caused the death of his father, who has brutally slain his mother, converts his parents' hovel into a ramshackle fortress he calls Doghead, imagining himself its deranged king. Voices in Euchrid's head lead him to an encounter with the mysterious Beth at the town monument where she was left as a swaddled babe by her mother, Cosey Mo. In her own childish delusion, Beth sees Euchrid as a savior figure come to redeem her. Instead, like the Grim Reaper, he slays her with a sickle, and his demon deed is done. But Beth does not die before a final revelation in the novel's two-page epilogue: she gives birth to a boy child, "as the prophet predicted," presumably conceived with Euchrid (though this plot detail in Cave's narrative is hard to follow). Euchrid's obsession with the miraculous child Beth, whom he spies on and feels divinely called to destroy, bears echoes of young Tarwater's singular prophetic purpose and obsession with the idiot child Bishop. Both unlikely prophet figures fulfill similar destinies that paradoxically involve murder and the realization of a divine mystery (Tarwater both baptizes and drowns Bishop). All that remains to bring an end to Cave's tortuous narrative and tortured central figure is for the townsfolk to torch the abominable Doghead (Tarwater torches his hillbilly home Powderhead) and hunt down Euchrid, who flees into a swamp where he lies down in a bog in fetal position and is eventually swallowed into the earth.

Gruesome scenes of animal cruelty, of wanton physical violence, and degradation of the human body in Cave's narrative (including cannibalism), rendered in a fragmented, profanity-riddled text written largely in faux southern dialect have little in common with O'Connor's subjects and narrative style. Yet Cave shares with his literary mentor an interest in the extremes of human experience, particularly of a religious kind—in the perceived madness of the prophet figure, whether self-appointed, or a seemingly divinely chosen "prophet gone wrong"; in the visionary life of grotesque characters, however self-unaware, for and through whom daily human reality appears warped and empty of meaning; and in the possibility of redemptive actions in the world, where "almost imperceptible intrusions of grace" are possible and transformative. Cave himself recognizes parallels between his art and vision in his first novel and O'Connor's. He once gave a reading from *And the Ass Saw the Angel* in Sydney, Australia, while John Huston's film adaptation of *Wise Blood* was projected on a screen behind him—a kind of performative palimpsest and public acknowledgment of O'Connor's influence on his odd, flawed work of southern gothic fiction.

From Her to Eternity

Nick Cave and the Bad Seeds appear in a crucial scene near the end of Wim Wenders's Cannes award-winning art film *Wings of Desire* (1987). In the film, a guardian angel—one of many assigned to watch over citizens in the grim urban landscape of 1980s West Berlin—is tempted to forsake his ethereal state and take on human form for the pleasures of everyday sensual experience. He is enamored with a woman, a beautiful tragic trapeze artist who performs with desperate grace in a tawdry traveling carny show. The conceit of a supernatural or angelic being forsaking the divine state for mortal love is well traveled, of course, from Greek and Roman mythology to popular movies. In Wenders's film, there is a biblical resonance. The English captioning of the trapeze artist's monologue at a moment of communion with the angel-man states that theirs "will be a story of giants, invisible, transferable. A story of new ancestors"—surely an allusion to the mythic Nephilim referenced in Genesis 6:4: "There were giants in the earth . . . when the sons of God came in unto the daughters of men, and they bare children to them" [KJV].

The angel-man is seen munching an Edenic apple as he wanders in the night. Eventually he is drawn into a Berlin dance club attached to a stylish bar, where the now out-of-work trapeze artist, in an alluring scarlet dress, is seen swaying with longing on the dance floor. On stage, Nick Cave, looking like "an irate drenched crow" (as O'Connor describes her delinquent prophet figure Rufus Johnson), growls out his punk ballad "From Her to Eternity" to a roomful of head-nodding, black-clad clubbers, while the angel-man and scarlet woman look on and sway to the Bad Seeds' thrashing sound. The camera soon takes the point of view of the woman as she leaves the dance floor to walk to the bar; there, in a stylized scene of earthly and spiritual communion, she sips from a glass of wine offered by the angel-man as Cave's song plays on the soundtrack. Wenders's scene is a kind of artistic mise-en-abyme (representation in miniature) for Cave's larger concern as a post-punk writer of what he idiosyncratically defines as "the Love Song." Like the scarlet trapeze artist (Cave's shirt as he performs is the same color as her dress), he is looking for transcendence through human love, to move "From her to eternity," and like the trapeze artist, he is serious in his quest.

A union of the physical with the divine, the profane with the sacred, the sexual with the spiritual: these are themes that trace through Cave's considerable body of work and that characterize his own sensualized incarnational theology, part Dionysian and part Beatrician. These themes are particularly pronounced in the songs on Cave's 1997 *The Boatman's Call*, written following the emotionally devastating end of an intense romance with alt rock artist PJ Harvey. Here are songs of unrequited love, both earthly and divine—the one anticipating, reflecting, and perhaps even to some extent enacting the other. As the Australian literary scholar Lyn McCredden observes, "Cave's sacred is deeply enmeshed in the human dimensions of flesh, erotics, and violence" that are in "dynamic and conflicting conjunction" in his work. Cave adds an element mostly absent in O'Connor's art—the erotic. His idiosyncratic theology embraces "the fleshed or carnal sacred," and his songs often express a spiritual hunger for the divine, often mediated through the erotic and largely experienced as a regretful absence.

Cave has expressed this ideational tension within his art elsewhere graphically, in both the major senses of this word. In a Dutch-made biopic *Stranger in a Strange Land*, filmed in March 1987 while Cave was living in West Berlin, he displays for the camera a black scrapbook he has created by juxtaposing pictures cut from a children's book of saints with pornographic postcards from the 1950s (both discovered in stalls at a Berlin flea market). "I found that an extremely pleasing relationship existed between these two things," he writes. "I nailed a brass Christ onto the cover for good measure." He acknowledges this particular scrapbook, "the Sacred and Profane notebook," as a favorite among the many he has compiled. A portion of it is reproduced in a book titled *Nick Cave Stories*, whose inside cover is crammed with handwritten names of literary figures who have informed Cave's imagination, including Flannery O'Connor (misspelled *O'Conner*). Several of these small scrapbooks were displayed at the *Stranger Than Kindness* installation in Montreal and their pages reproduced more extensively in the 275-page exhibition catalog designed by Nick Cave and Christina Back and published in hardcover by HarperOne in 2021.

The Boatman's Call, Cave's tenth studio album and his most acclaimed recording, presents his conflicted credo, his own catechism for the kind of God that he *does* believe in and the sacramental encounters in which that God *might be* felt and known—often momentarily displaced by or transfused with sensual desire, the "her" that intimates "eternity." The six songs on the A-side of the 2011 remastered vinyl reissue of the album form a narrative unit, presenting a story like a profane *The Pilgrim's Progress*; indeed, some movement from this world into a spiritual world to come, either intimated or anticipated, fairly describes the arc of meaning in this suite of songs. The A-side songs begin with a conflicted notion of the possibility of divine intervention and progress to songs that describe erotically charged encounters with the sacred. They resolve with what might be understood as a confession of a kind of dark faith, and conclude with a song that poses the question that was on the lips of the imprisoned John the Baptist: "(Are You) The One That I've Been Waiting For?"

Into My Arms

Cave's existential tension between belief and unbelief is expressed in the opening track of *The Boatman's Call*, the melodic piano ballad "Into My Arms," his most commercially successful recording to date, which one critic describes as Cave's "most theologically brilliant song." Credo-like, however invertedly, it begins with one of the oddest and most provocative statements in pop music: "I don't believe in an interventionist God / But I know, darling, that you do."

This declaration stands in stark contradiction to O'Connor's belief and art, wherein in myriad ways some form of divine intervention is subtly active alongside and in opposition to willful human actions. But for Cave's narrator, this disbelief appears to be an ironic ploy, since everything in the song is focused on the narrator's willingness to importune God and the angels to intervene to grant his desire for the affections of a woman. Fully aware of the irony—the *aporia*, as literary critics would label it—the speaker engages in a seriously playful dialogue with an imagined self, appealing to the interventionist God he does not believe in to guide the beloved "Into my arms, O Lord / Into my arms." The pilgrim at this point might be described in O'Connor's term as an "unbelieving searcher," someone who desires to believe yet is stifled in an age of unbelief, and still hasn't found what he's looking for. O'Connor writes, "We have to look in much of the fiction of our time for a kind of sub-religion which expresses its ultimate concern in images that have not yet broken through to show any recognition of a God who has revealed himself." Her words may well apply to artists like Cave. McCredden echoes this idea when she argues that Cave's lyrics often engage in "confrontational dialogue with divine forces which may or may not be 'there.'" She concludes, "What we find stamped across his songs, over and over, is the dark, lonely figure of a man caught up in desire for a divine source or balm."

O'Connor understands the internal struggle of the artist "who can neither believe nor contain himself in unbelief and who searches desperately, feeling about in all experience for the lost God." Arguably, this is a central theme of her fictions, which explains in part the considerable continuing appeal of her work, and perhaps Cave's interest in her art and vision. This is the condition of The Misfit in her most celebrated story, "A Good Man Is Hard to Find." Struggling to believe in a Jesus who is "the only One that ever raised the dead," The Misfit cries out in anguish moments before he shoots the grandmother, "'If I had of been there I would of known and I wouldn't be like I am now.'" This tension between belief and unbelief is also compellingly embodied in O'Connor's reluctant teen-age backwoods prophet, Francis Marion Tarwater. Jonah-like, Tarwater runs from his calling, hell-bent on thwarting the prophetic injunctions of his God-crazed great-uncle Mason Tarwater. In his efforts to lose God, young Tarwater finds, as O'Connor writes elsewhere, "the devil we are possessed by" and comes to discover and experience another of O'Connor's axiomatic truths, "that the devil accomplishes a good deal of groundwork that seems to be necessary before grace is effective." In the spiritual economy of O'Connor's novel, that groundwork is Tarwater's necessary violation through homosexual rape. As harsh and shocking as this muted event is in the novel, O'Connor insists that it is absolutely necessary and remarks that "Tarwater's final [prophetic] vision could not have been brought off" without this dirty deed.

O'Connor defends the violent means by which the sacral truths at the core of her fictions are revealed, explaining that in her stories "violence is strangely capable of returning my characters to reality and preparing them to accept their moment of grace. Their heads are so hard that almost nothing else will do the work." Likewise, a strain of revelatory violence threads through the corpus of Cave's song narratives, complemented and sometimes combined with the erotic—elements in Cave's works that, as McCredden observes, he sees "as intimately entwined with any access to the sacred."

Lime-Tree Arbour

Understandably, given Cave's considerable biblical knowledge and reading, and the libidinal elements in his songwriting, he is attracted to the erotic spirituality in the Old Testament long poem Song of Solomon, as he acknowledges in a version of his 1999 lecture "The Secret Life of the Love Song." It is tempting in this respect to read the second track on *The Boatman's Call*, "Lime-Tree Arbour," as a kind of sensual psalm that intimates the actions of the divine in the life of the speaker. Here the beloved is physically and affectionately present: "She puts her hand over mine." A gentle eroticism is evident in the lyrics, which at the same time evoke the world of the spirit. The sacred and the sensual conjoined in the lyrics are underscored by Cave's invoking a trope from medieval English and German lyric tradition: the lime tree or linden as a trysting place for lovers (as in the twelfth-century erotic lyric "Under the Linden Tree"). According to scholars, the lime tree has sacred associations as well, particularly in middle European folk tradition and literature. And so the hand of the beloved offered in the lime-tree arbor is both erotically immanent and spiritually transcendent:

> Through every breath that I breathe
> And every place I go
> There is a hand that protects me
> And I do love her so

The omnipresent hand of the beloved begs a metaphorical reading as a kind of spiritual presence. But beyond merely a romantic theology that might abstract the beloved to an ethereal presence or force, Cave adds a God-like omniscience in the language of the closing stanza:

Through every word that I speak
And every thing I know
There is a hand that protects me
And I do love her so

The physically present hand of the woman has transformed into a divine hand that holds knowledge and offers protection. The two are connected: her hand is linked to an eternal hand.

Flesh and spirit, the sacred and/in the profane—Cave's song cycle on the A-side of *The Boatman's Call* explores this tension and fusion in ways that parallel what O'Connor does in her profound story "Parker's Back." O. E. Parker is a man who can't get no satisfaction, though he has tried—through a succession of tattoos. His skin is covered in an assortment of designs he acquired while in the US Navy traveling the world: serpents, hawks, an eagle perched on a cannon, a spread hand of cards, hearts with arrows, and obscene words. Yet as he examines himself in a mirror, Parker sees that his intent to replicate the "intricate arabesque" of color and design that inspired him at fifteen after seeing a tattooed man at a fair has resulted in a fleshly exhibit that appears only "haphazard and botched." His efforts to make sense of himself, to follow whatever impulse compels him and to find purpose and meaning, have confounded him and left him hugely dissatisfied. All the self-examinable space on his body is patterned; the only area without a tattoo is on his back, a location where the mirror gives him no satisfaction. And so, metaphorically, from Parker's perspective, he has come to the end of himself—or to the end of his disaffecting efforts to define and design that self.

In hopes that marriage will cure his disaffection, Parker impulsively weds to bed a shy fundamentalist backwoods plain-Jane daughter of a Straight Gospel preacher. But Sarah Ruth is forever sniffing out sin and haranguing her husband: "Parker did nothing much when he was at home but listen to what the judgement seat of God would be like for him if he didn't change his ways." He conceives the idea that he will appease his shrewish wife by getting a religious tattoo on the unmarked space on his back. Distracted by this thought and ruminating on what kind of religious image should go there, he crashes a tractor into a large tree in the center of a field he is tilling. As he is catapulted into the air, Parker yells out "GOD ABOVE!" and watches tractor and tree—and the shoes he has been vaulted out of—burst into flame. This encounter with both a literal and figurative burning bush propels him to a tattoo parlor convinced he must have a picture of God tattooed on his back (where figuratively God has been all along!). After deliberating over kindly images of Jesus as "The Good Shepherd, Forbid Them Not, The Smiling Jesus, Jesus the Physician's Friend," Parker feels compelled to choose an image of a "a flat stern Byzantine Christ with all-demanding eyes."

Here in the trope of a tattoo, an image incarnated through the piercing of the body, O'Connor presents an instance of the enfleshed sacred. The Christ tattoo with "all-demanding eyes" on Parker's back has a transformative effect on his whole being: as he examines his soul, "he observed that his dissatisfaction was gone." Moreover, upon confessing his true identity, concealed in the initials O.E. that he goes by (*O* is for Obadiah, a Hebrew name meaning "worshipper of the Lord"; *E* is for Elihue, meaning "my God is He"), Parker senses "light pouring through him, turning his spider web soul into a perfect arabesque of colors, a garden of trees and birds and beasts"—the Adamic image of human wholeness that he caught sight of as a youth and has been haphazardly trying to replicate in and by himself. Parker's achievement of a Christ-like state, now that the spirit of Christ has entered into him—as the Pauline doctrines would have it—is clearly indicated in the story's concluding scene. Here we find Parker being thrashed across the back with a broom by his righteously irate wife for having in her view committed "Idolatry!" by tattooing himself with the face of Christ. Suffering and bleeding like Christ at his scourging, Parker is last seen leaning against a pecan tree (its graphemic cousin, Latin *peccans*, means *sinful*) and in the story's last words, "crying like a baby." His now sacredly enfleshed self has been—to invoke a common lexical marker of Christian conversion—*born again* in spirit.

People Ain't No Good

Alongside the latent theology in O'Connor's title phrase and story "A Good Man Is Hard to Find," Cave offers his own more absolute statement on the presence of sin and evil in the world: "People just ain't no good," proclaims the narrator of the third track on *The Boatman's Call*. O'Connor would wholeheartedly agree. In story after story, her singular intent is to dramatize this same truth about fallen human nature. To the grandmother's desperate self-saving assertion, "I just know you're a good man," The Misfit replies after a moment of consideration, "Nome, I ain't a good man." Outside of any possibility of a saving grace, he knows in his heart that he has a bent for "meanness." Ruby Turpin in "Revelation" considers herself "a good woman" in her imagination. Yet O'Connor suggests that the pride and bigotry Ruby displays in thought and eventually word, and her tendency to peg everyone on a scale of social value, are of a kind with the Nazi ideologies that sent Jews "in a box car . . . to be put in a gas oven." The trope of "good country people" is debunked in the seemingly guileless Bible salesman Manley Pointer, in a story that takes its title from the cliché. In the aborted hayloft seduction of the disabled and humiliated Hulga Hopewell, Pointer eventually confesses to being a liar and thief who believes in none of the religious "crap" he has been spouting to his advantage. The juvenile delinquent Rufus Johnson who has been welcomed into the home of the do-gooder Sheppard in "The Lame Shall Enter First" says of the social worker, "He thinks he's Jesus Christ!" The narrative confirms this view in a passage of indirect discourse that reveals Sheppard's thoughts: "He knew without conceit that he was a good man, that he had nothing to reproach himself with." As so often in O'Connor's short fiction, this story ends with a moment of revelation, a personal epiphany for Sheppard that nonetheless fails to avert the suicide of the young son whom he has neglected emotionally and spiritually: "He had stuffed his own emptiness with good works like a glutton. He had ignored his own child to feed his vision of himself. . . . His image of himself shrivelled until everything was black before him." Sheppard's belief in his own goodness is shattered. Here and throughout her fiction, O'Connor aims to shock the reader out of believing that true goodness is an innate human quality. Her people just ain't no good at being good.

For both O'Connor and Cave, human nature is fallen and bound to sin. Cave's sense of human total depravity leads him to pen a song whose refrain repeats over and over "People they ain't no good." In the last verse, the lyrics attempt some redemptive content, suggesting momentarily "It ain't that in their hearts they're bad": people offer comfort and compassion on occasion, the song's narrator notes. But, ultimately, any contrary assertion is "just bullshit / People just ain't no good" intrinsically, the song concludes.

For Cave, a good man is impossible to find, and in this he is morally and doctrinally alongside O'Connor. Both writers espouse the Calvinist belief that we are all marked by evil, literalized in the E.V.I.L. tattooed across the knuckles on the left hand of Cave's narrator in his O'Connoresque song-story "The Mercy Seat," an earlier work from *Tender Prey* (1988), a song cycle composed as he was finishing *And the Ass Saw the Angel*. This dramatic and powerful song is a first-person narrative by a convicted murderer facing execution by the electric chair, similar to the scene in Springsteen's O'Connor-influenced "Nebraska," where his Starkweather narrator is unfazed by his imminent death by electrocution. The evil "kill-hand" of the "Mercy Seat" narrator nonetheless has added Good-ness, figured as "a wedding band" with the letters G.O.O.D. engraved on it. A metaphoric marriage is suggested here—perhaps a reference to the parable of the bridegroom coming for the bride recorded in St. Matthew's Gospel (25:1–13). Whatever Good we have in us is the gift of grace, Cave suggests, and comes at a great price, as O'Connor's fiction dramatizes. "'Tis a long-suffering shackle," remarks Cave's narrator of the G.O.O.D. wedding band. And as O'Connor has remarked in her preface to *A Memoir of Mary Ann*, "in us the good is always something under construction."

Brompton Oratory

A further O'Connor-like fusion of the sacred with the profane, centered symbolically on the sacred elements of the Eucharist, is expressed in "Brompton Oratory," the fourth track on *The Boatman's Call*. The setting is the well-known Roman Catholic cathedral in London, founded by Cardinal Newman, where the narrator has gone on the first Sunday of Pentecost to attend mass and to reflect, in a detached way, on the mysteries of the Christian faith. Light melodic organ accompaniment announces the hymn-likeness of Cave's song, and its first stanza intersperses narrative describing the speaker's entrance into the church with the opening lines from a fourth-century Christian hymn celebrating the events of Pentecost—the gift of the Holy Spirit and the advent of a spiritual language described in Acts 2:1–13: "Hail this joyful day's return / . . . Hail the Pentecostal morn."

Cave's narrator notes in these very prosaic lyrics that "The reading is from Luke 24 / Where Christ returns to his loved ones." The New Testament account underscores the theme of the embodied sacred, the Word made flesh, that haunts Cave's imagination and is central to Christian theology. The risen Christ enjoins his disciples to confirm that He is still of human form and substance though resurrected: "Behold . . . it is I myself: handle me, and see, for a spirit hath not flesh and bones, as ye see me have" (Luke 24:39 KJV). Matter and spirit are still joined even in the transcended Christ and indeed appear essential to defining both his earthly *and* otherworldly divinity.

The theological stumbling block for O'Connor's The Misfit, who staggers in unbelief because he "wasn't there," likewise trips up Cave's narrator. The revelation and redemption of Christ is "all right for some" he reflects, and then muses,

> And I wish I was made of stone
> So that I would not have to see
> A beauty impossible to define
> A beauty impossible to believe
> A beauty impossible to endure

O'Connor remarks in a letter on the "awful" tension at the heart of her writing: that for an artist who is a Christian, "the ultimate reality is the Incarnation, the present reality is the Incarnation, and nobody believes in the Incarnation." The impossibility of such a belief plagues Cave's narrator, who wishes he were "made of stone" so that he would not have to reconcile himself to a glimpse of divine "beauty" that demands his response. Though having partaken of the bread and wine of the Presence, he is still left feeling "Forlorn and exhausted, baby / By the absence of you." This "absence" and the pronoun "you" surely relate to both the earthly and the divine lovers referenced in this song.

"Brompton Oratory," comments music critic Seán O'Hagen, "has that collision of the sacred and profane that is pure Nick Cave." As Cave's narrator is administered the sacraments, and raises the communion cup to his lips, he thinks of another recent union, with the flesh of his lover, whose "smell" he remarks is "still on my hands." The convergence of the sacred with the sexual here in the narrator's thoughts while partaking of the Eucharist bears an uncanny similarity to the epiphanic moment at the end of O'Connor's early short story "A Temple of the Holy Ghost."

"A Temple of the Holy Ghost"

The precocious twelve-year-old girl in this story, untypically unnamed and identified only as "the child," appears to have similar sensibilities to those of the (somewhat older) Sally Virginia Cope in "A Circle in the Fire," a companion story in O'Connor's first collection. O'Connor critics have remarked that both young female characters bear a strong resemblance in personality and outlook to a youthful version of the author: "I was a very ancient twelve," O'Connor writes in a letter. The child's sexually aware fourteen-year-old cousins have arrived for a weekend visit to the farm where the girl lives with her mother. Once out of their convent-school uniforms, Joanne and Susan don garish blouses and red skirts, lipstick and high heels, and spend much of their time admiring their figures in the hallway mirror. The girls jokingly refer to themselves as "Temple One and Temple Two" in response to a lecture on preserving their sexual purity, presented by the oldest nun at the convent, the comically named Sister Perpetua. The good Sister has instructed them how to react if a young man should "'behave in an ungentlemanly way with them in the back of an automobile.'" They are to exclaim, "'Stop sir! I am a Temple of the Holy Ghost!'"—a response sure to forestall any sexual advances.

In an effort to entertain the girls, the mother invites two Church of God boys named Wendell and Cory to accompany them to a fair that has come to town. To the satisfaction of the increasingly mean-spirited child, the cousins go with their bumpkinish beaus and leave her at home, with the sights and sounds of the fair in the distance, to imagine what goes on in the circus tents. She knows that some are closed to children, "because they contained things that would be known only to grown people," matters she innocently imagines "concerned medicine." The older girls have gone into one of these tents and seen something freakish and perplexing. When they return near midnight and are readying for bed, the child, wakened by their giggling, asks for a report. Joanne tells her they saw "all kinds of freaks" but did not like one in particular—"the you-know-what," she remarks codedly to Susan. Cajoled by the child, the girls recount that they visited a tent divided by a black curtain into two sides, one for men and the other for women, in which "a freak with a particular name" they could not remember was on display. "God made me thisaway and if you laugh He may strike you the same way," the "freak" said in a flat nasal southern voice. And added, "I'm making the best of it." The child is puzzled. One of the girls eventually reveals the mystery: "It was a man and woman both. It pulled up its dress and showed us." The child wonders "how it could be a man and woman both without two heads" but does not ask her more worldly cousins that question.

As she drifts off to sleep, the child imagines the country men and women in the tent acting "more solemn than they were in church." In her half-dreaming state, the hermaphrodite's reported patter and the spectators' reactions are transformed into a southern gospel service, a call-and-response exchange, with the people's Amens punctuating the freak's declarations of their double-natured sexuality. The freak's language in this dream-vision is translated into sermon rhetoric and informed with the Pauline doctrine of the human body as God's "temple" [1 Corinthians 6:19]:

"God done this to me and I praise Him."
  "Amen. Amen."
"He could strike you thisaway."
  "Amen. Amen."
  "Amen."
"Raise yourself up. A temple of the Holy Ghost. You! You are God's temple, don't you know? Don't you know? God's Spirit has a dwelling in you, don't you know?"
  "Amen. Amen."

The next day the cousins are returned to Mount St. Scholastica, arriving as a chapel service is in session. A "big moon-faced nun" bustles them into the sanctuary as the benediction begins. As the child enters the chapel, she sees a priest bowed low in front of the monstrance containing the consecrated wafers; behind him a boy in a dress-like surplice is swinging a censor. The moment the priest raises the lid of the monstrance to reveal the "Host shining ivory-colored in the center of it," the child's imagination overlays the scene with an image of "the tent at the fair that had the freak in it," wherein the hermaphrodite pulls up their dress to reveal a bisexed identity saying, "I don't dispute hit. This is the way He wanted me to be."

This juxtaposition of the hermaphrodite and the Host in O'Connor's story on one level images the Catholic doctrine of transubstantiation—the two-natures of the hermaphrodite standing metonymically against the Eucharistic mystery manifest in the consecrated ivory-colored wafer. But this juxtaposition also broaches the territory of the sexual as mediating the sacred—indeed, in O'Connor's Catholic beliefs, a sacred Presence. For O'Connor in this story, as with Cave's narrator in "Brompton Oratory," the sacred and carnal are conjoined: moreover, a divine mystery is comprehended through the metaphoric agency of a deviant sexuality. On another level, here is imaged the scandalous doctrine of the Incarnation—for those who "don't dispute hit."

The choice of sacramental element in each work presents the writers' respective theological positions: the solid particulars through which the divine is mediated in O'Connor's "concrete" fiction, and the intoxicating fluidity of Cave's often oblique lyrical lines. Yet both writers embrace what Lyn McCredden, in reference to Cave, calls a "contemporary theology of the fleshed or carnal sacred." Flesh and spirit converge in the "incarnational art" of both artists, a mystery "impossible to define" but present nonetheless.

There Is a Kingdom

A listener to the tracks as arranged on *The Boatman's Call* is confronted with the contradiction between the mediated transcendence of the beloved in "Lime-Tree Arbour" and the sensual immanence that transcends the "impossible" truth of the gospel story that has left the narrator of "Brompton Oratory" feeling "forlorn and exhausted" with a felt sense of "absence." This evident tension is surprisingly resolved in the next song on the album, the fifth track, "There Is a Kingdom." It begins like many of Cave's piano-based love ballads, lightly musical, with the singer expressing a powerful faith and love of which "all the world's darkness / Can't swallow up / One single spark." These exalted notions are of a kind with the sentiments and ideas expressed in "Into My Arms" and "Lime-Tree Arbour." But the transcendent truth expressed in the lyrics is even more pronounced here as the narrator contemplates the cosmic nature of his existence—"So the world appears"—invokes "the starry heavens above," and speaks of "the moral law within."

These verities are enforced by Cave's triumphalist, hymn-like delivery of the chorus, to instrumentation on piano, Hammond organ, and classical guitar, with added backing vocals. The effect is like that of a church choir, the context in which Cave, like many rock 'n' roll artists, began as a child to develop his musical abilities. The lyrics draw their theological substance from Christ's words as recorded in St. Luke's Gospel 17:21. Asked by the Pharisees, the religious leaders in Jerusalem, when the kingdom of God will be established, Jesus replies, "Behold, the kingdom of God is within you" (KJV). God immanent, present, and (femininely) embodied is a tropic doctrine of the gospel of Saint Nick. But the truth-claims in "There Is a Kingdom" go beyond this creed to suggest a decidedly Pauline sense of the mystery of God omnipresent in body, spirit, and created matter:

> There is a kingdom
> There is a king
> And He lives without
> And He lives within
> And He is everything

As McCredden observes, this song "draws on a thoroughgoing kind of incarnationalism" and is not simply another expression of Cave's roving desire to move "from her to eternity." The "He" in the lyric with its initial capital, the King Jamesian masculine proper pronoun for God or Christ, has being both "without" (incarnationally) and "within" (spiritually). Cave's lyrics recall Saint Paul's similar claim in one of his epistles that Christ is "before all things and by Him all things consist" (Colossians 1:17). The all-encompassing nature of the "king" here joins with the protecting hand that in "Lime-Tree Arbour" is over "every thing."

The faith-in-the-dark affirmed in "There Is a Kingdom" stands against the agnostic response in "Brompton Oratory" that the gospel message of the resurrected Christ recorded in Luke 24 is "all right for some." In "Kingdom," a kind of visionary experience "so sweet / It will never come again" appears to affirm an Absolute "He" in whom and by whom and through whom "is everything." Or, as the singer concludes penitently, "So the world appears / Through this mist of tears." As McCredden notes, in many of his songs "Redemption is imagined by Cave, but rarely without the accompanying shadows of uncertainty." "There Is a Kingdom" is one of the rare exceptions to this observation. It is important to note, in this respect, that even amid evident gnostic uncertainty, on the first Sunday of Pentecost the speaker in "Brompton Oratory" queues up to celebrate the Eucharist.

(Are You) The One?

The dialectic between sensual and spiritual desire that threads through the narrative of the six A-side songs of *The Boatman's Call* finds its fullest and finest expression in the last song in this cycle, "(Are You) The One That I've Been Waiting For?" Indeed, the narrative tension between knowing and unknowing is caught grammatically in the title: the parenthetical "(Are You)" supports the interrogative, while its separation from the rest of the title pairs it with the declaiming tone of "There Is a Kingdom." Here as elsewhere, as McCredden observes, we find the familiar Cave persona, "the same unbeliever hovering between belief and unbelief." The question in the title, repeated in the refrain, echoes the query of the imprisoned John the Baptist, sent to the Christ through his disciples: "Are you the one who is to come, or are we to wait for another?" (St. Matthew 11:3 RSVA). Like O'Connor, Cave is particularly intrigued by the liminal prophet figure John the Baptist, who bridges between the old and new dispensations in the biblical narrative. Cave's song "Mercy" and his short, salacious play *Salomé* also reference the imprisoned prophet. The epigraph to O'Connor's second novel that gives her its title, *The Violent Bear It Away*, is likewise taken from a verse in the eleventh chapter of Matthew's gospel that references John the Baptist (11:12 Douay-Rheims).

Flesh and spirit, the sensual and the sacred, are here again conjoined in alternate verses of "(Are You) The One?" that move from an approaching "girl" to the approach of some anticipated revelation, a moment when "all will be revealed." Cave's rhetoric reaches beyond describing an anticipated sensual encounter to suggest some longed-for and long-time-coming "destiny" that is manifesting itself. "My soul has comforted and assured me," remarks the narrator with biblical overtones, "That in time my heart it will reward me." A notion of theophany—a manifestation of the divine in human form—is suggested in the narrator's questions to an approaching female figure: "Is this how you'll appear? / Wrapped in a coat with tears in your eyes?"

Cave's notion here invokes O'Connor's singular foray into a kind of erotic sacramentalism in the figure of Sarah Ham / Star Drake in "The Comforts of Home," a critically marginalized work in her canon. This short story is focused on a middle-aged historian, Thomas (emblematically both doubter and twin), who lives with his indiscriminately charitable mother. She has brought home a promiscuous juvenile delinquent who calls herself Star Drake. Star makes flirtatious schoolgirl comments and gestures toward Thomas, until one night she appears naked in his bedroom. His mother explains that the girl is a "Nimpermaniac" and that her condition is "something she can't help. Something she was born with." To Thomas, Star is "a moral moron" who has upset his comfortable home. Bedeviled by the inner voicings of his deceased father, who, toad-like, takes up "a squatting position in his mind," Thomas follows the suggested thought of "the old man" in an effort to get rid of the girl. Eventually, "guided by his father," Thomas finds himself holding a gun he has planted in Star's purse to frame her. ("Freud is dogging my tracks all the way," O'Connor once wrote in a letter, and here she gives him plenty of scent.) At the command of "the old man," Thomas pulls the trigger, unintentionally killing his mother instead of "the dirty criminal slut."

Star is a symbolic character in O'Connor's short-story-as-morality-play for the nature of divine love, the "pure idiot mystery" that Thomas senses around him—"forces, invisible currents entirely out of his control." This mystery manifests itself both in the ministrations of his "sybil-like" mother and in the amorous, "possessive" advances of Star. Thomas's resistance to Star's presence is a dramatic analog for his resistance to the invading presence into his comfortable self-centered existence of divine *caritas*, practiced by his do-gooding mother and symbolically embodied in the oversexed Star Drake. In the closing scene of the story, a bedeviled Thomas "damn[s] not only the girl but the entire order of the universe that made her possible." Love would have Thomas, but he will have none of it. In the freeze-frame scene that concludes the story, Thomas and Star are pictured in a suspended near embrace—however ironically, through the local sheriff's point of view—"about to collapse into each other's arms." The story evidences O'Connor's own embracing of the possibility of an erotically charged image of the sacred.

"The Comforts of Home" has received mixed critical reviews, mostly unfavorable. Perhaps, as Rick Asals comments, the plot lacks plausibility and the story is more of a "psychic drama" than a believable exploration of how a sexually repressed middle-aged man might respond to the disturbing advances of a highly sexed teenage girl. But this is not an anti-*Lolita* tale. Asals's Jungian reading of the story notwithstanding, as O'Connor remarked on several occasions, particularly in a talk titled "Some Aspects of the Grotesque in Southern Fiction," her stories are concerned with "an experience of mystery"—a word that in noun and adverb forms appears three times in "Comforts." For O'Connor, "the meaning of a story does not begin except at a depth where adequate motivation and adequate psychology and the various determinations have been exhausted." In "Comforts," O'Connor's propensity toward the dramatized morality tale is perhaps more foregrounded than in her finer stories. The theme of irresistible grace in stories such as "Parker's Back" and "The Enduring Chill" here becomes intensified in a tale of *irrepressible* grace, of divine love that "can't help" but pursue the doubting and devilishly directed Thomas until it both dispossesses and repossesses him. Thomas finds himself face to face with a naked, sighing, discomforting love that will not let him go. If Cave's erotic, theological, and violence-charged lyric works are all expressions of what he calls "the Love Song," then O'Connor's "Comforts" in kind might be considered an offering of the Love Story. Of the many convergings dramatized in O'Connor's last story collection, here in Sarah/Star the sacred is conjoined with the erotic.

A similar convergence occurs within the lyric lines of the concluding song on the A-side of *The Boatman's Call*. Counter to the indirection in the sensual and spiritual metaphors at play in "Into My Arms" and the theological doubt evident in "Brompton Oratory," there is an assured, psalm-like quality to the expressions of longing and searching in "(Are You) The One That I've Been Waiting For?" The beloved here is neither hesitant nor absent, but "surely" in motion toward the lover:

> As you've been moving surely toward me
> My soul has comforted and assured me
> That in time my heart will reward me
> And that all will be revealed

That revelation, as the song concludes, is found in a reference to the apotheosis of the enfleshed sacred—the god-man "who spoke wonders," as He is described by the speaker in the final verse (though he nonetheless claims to have "never met him"). The song's final verse paraphrases the words of Christ recorded in St. Matthew 7:7, part of the familiar Sermon on the Mount: "Ask, and it shall be given you; seek, and ye shall find; knock, and it shall be opened unto you" (KJV). The effect of the allusion here ("He who seeks finds / And who knocks will be let in") is either a blasphemous seduction lyric or further expression of Cave's carnal incarnational theology. Like the cup of wine sipped at the Eucharist in "Brompton Oratory" that combines with the smell of the girl on the speaker's hands, so the words of Christ here are aligned with the approaching presence of the girl: "I think of you in motion and just how close you are getting / And how every little thing anticipates you."

The tension in McCredden's phrase "carnal sacred" conveys Cave's idiosyncratic theology. Its ultimate expression in his art can be found in one of the outtakes from the recording sessions for *From Her to Eternity* (1984), with a title appropriated from the old Methodist hymn, "Just a Closer Walk with Thee." The lyrics are included in *Nick Cave: The Complete Lyrics, 1978–2022*. Cave's sacral-sexual theology is all here in the four lines of the song's mildly blasphemous opening verse:

> Just a closer walk with thee
> Come back, honey, to me
> Then I'll be moving up close to thee
> O let it be, O Lord, let it be

In *Wise Blood*, O'Connor explores the substitutionary appeal of sex as a way to fill "a God-shaped hole," as Cave suggestively describes it, echoing Pascal. Believing that he does not believe in anything, Hazel Motes finds himself in the bedroom of the prostitute Leora Watts. He means to commit a sin—fornication—in order to prove that the notion of sin is invalid, that "there was no Fall because there was nothing to fall from and no Redemption because there was no Fall and no Judgment because there wasn't the first two. Nothing matters but that Jesus was a liar." Despite his rejection of the Christ of the Gospels, Haze is a man wearing a "Jesus-seeing hat." When he first meets the nymphet Sabbath Lily, he exclaims, "My Jesus." Then O'Connor writes, "He sat down by the girl's leg and set his hand on the step next to her foot." The scene recalls his awkward encounter with the prostitute, where his first physical contact prior to his first sexual experience is to pick up her foot. A further reference to the girl is also punctuated by Haze's epithet "My Jesus." This motif in the novel is also evidenced in Enoch Emery's salacious response to a sunbathing woman who unexpectedly pulls down the shoulder straps of her bathing suit: "King Jesus!" he whispers, both an epithet and signifying an instance of sacral-sexual association. Indeed, the repeated juxtapositions of "Jesus" with a sexualized figure of a woman underscore this motif in the novel.

O'Connor validates even as she parodies an erotic theology in *Wise Blood*. Hazel Motes's liaison with Leora Watts illustrates this on several levels. That he is unable to convince either the taxi driver or Leora that he is not a "preacher" associates his desire for sex with the call of the divine. Leora even puts on his "Jesus-seeing hat" as prelude to their second sexual encounter, signifying her own sacral symbolic agency. Yet the baseness of Haze's erotic adventure is signaled from the outset: he finds Leora's name and phone number scrawled on a wall in a bathroom stall, notionally a site for expressing vulgarity and obscenity and soliciting illicit sex. His performance with the prostitute is described in an unseemly metaphor—"he was like something washed ashore on her"—and this encounter is further diminished by recurring thoughts that, post-coitus, Leora "had made obscene comments about him." Haze's sexual experiences leave him far from realizing the desire for transcendence through sex that Cave's songs explore.

While O'Connor is thickly ironic in Hazel's comic exclamation, "What do I need with Jesus? I got Leora Watts," this same notion unironically resonates across Cave's lyric art, nonetheless with the same sense of unfulfillment. The narrator of "Brompton Oratory" partakes of the Eucharist and his thoughts turn not to the Presence in the sacraments but to the "absence of you"—in one sense of the woman with whom he has recently had sex. Songs on *Let Love In* (1994), produced two years before *The Boatman's Call*, well illustrate the idea of the fraught pursuit of the "carnal sacred." The narrator of "Do You Love Me?" hears "the bells from the chapel [go] jingle-jangle" as he makes love to a woman he names "My Lady of the Various Sorrows." While he tries to hold on to this female figure "So completely filled with light," he soon acknowledges, "Our love-lines grew hopelessly tangled." Like Christ to Peter, he questions her three times—"Do you love me?"—and discovers he already knows the answer: "I knew before I met her that I would lose her." The narrator of "Nobody's Baby Now" has "searched the holy books / Tried to unravel the mystery of Jesus Christ the Saviour" and not found an answer to his questions and longings. He has loved a woman and admits, "I guess I love her still," but comes to understand that "there are some things even love won't allow." He concedes, "I held her hand but I don't hold it now." A darker revelation comes to the lustful lover in "Hard On for Love," from *Your Funeral, My Trial* (1986), in a lyric monologue that parodies Psalm 23:

> The Lord is my shepherd I shall not want
> But he leadeth me like a lamb to the lips
> Of the mouth of the valley of the shadow of death
> I am his rod and his staff
> I am his sceptre and shaft
> And she is Heaven and Hell
> At whose gates I ain't been delivered

Like O'Connor's blaspheming yet spiritually searching Hazel Motes before he blinds himself, the narrators of Cave's songs move feelingly but unseeingly, their ultimate longings unfulfilled, their stumbling transcendent desires unrealized. As one critic observes, "Cave's wretched protagonists seek salvation in the arms of women but simply find more pain."

The Church of Cave without Christ

Cave himself embodies many of the traits and obsessions of O'Connor's Hazel Motes. Indeed, Cave can be seen as a kind of living O'Connor character, one of her tortured prophet figures: Christ-haunted, Christ obsessed, running Jonah-like from his calling as pop prophet. He acknowledges melding "stolen" images from O'Connor in a line in "I Had a Dream, Joe" from his 1992 album *Henry's Dream*: "A shadowy Jesus flitted from tree to tree." The image combines references in both of O'Connor's novels to her Jesus-stalked prophet figures: the wayward young Tarwater in *The Violent Bear It Away* resisting his destiny to follow his great-uncle "in the bleeding stinking mad shadow of Jesus" and *Wise Blood*'s Hazel Motes sensing "a wild ragged figure" of Jesus "mov[ing] from tree to tree in the back of his mind." Cave's lyrical blaspheming, like Haze's, appears to mask an underlying urge to believe the very doctrines he decries.

Just as Haze challenges passersby on the streets of Taulkinham to question if not deny their nominal religious beliefs, so Cave preaches in the public space of alternative pop music his own gospel of a Church without Christ, or at least without the resurrected Christ of the Christian creeds. As O'Connor did on the art of story and on her theology of fiction, Cave has lectured to students on the art of writing songs and presented a radio broadcast on his personal religious views. His theology is highly protean, but the dogma he expounded in his 1996 lecture "The Flesh Made Word" on BBC Radio lays out his notably gnostic beliefs in a Motes-like screed and as well reveals insightful biographical details. O'Connor's Haze believes in a "new kind of jesus . . . one that can't waste his blood redeeming people with it, because he's all man and ain't got any God in him." Likewise, Cave's Christ "called himself both the Son of Man and the Son of God" and is "exactly that—a man of flesh and blood." Rather than God in the flesh, Cave's "new jesus" is the apotheosis of the artist, "so in touch with the creative forces inside himself . . . that he became the physical embodiment of that force." The potently imaginative word made flesh defines Cave's notion of all that might be incarnate in the Christ: "Christ is the imagination, at times terrible, irrational, incendiary, and beautiful; in short, Godlike." Thus, Cave's sanctified aestheticism allows him to claim that as a writer he is "actualizing God through the medium of the Love Song," an objective, he says, that "remains my prime motivation as an artist."

Sounding very much like an evangelical, Cave has sung "There is a Kingdom, there is a King / He lives without and He lives within/ And He is everything," but his religious beliefs appear to be far from O'Connor's Christian orthodoxy. O'Connor believed in "an unlimited God and one who has revealed himself specifically. It is one who became man and rose from the dead. It is one who confounds the senses and the sensibilities, one known early on as a stumbling block." As a writer holding to a Catholic vision of human purpose and earthly reality, O'Connor expresses her credo clearly in a manifesto-like essay written in 1957 shortly after the release of *A Good Man Is Hard to Find*: "I see from the standpoint of Christian orthodoxy. This means that for me the meaning of life is centered in our Redemption by Christ and what I see in the world I see in its relation to that."

Cave's songs and other writings are deeply informed by his religious sensibility and resound with the rhetoric of Judeo-Christian doctrine and references to biblical characters and narratives. His youthful experiences in Australia in the Anglican Church, where from ages eight to twelve he was a choirboy, deeply imprinted him with what Bruce Springsteen calls an "internal landscape" shaped by the doctrines of the Church (though Cave views the form of Anglicanism he was raised in as "the decaf of worship"). Indeed, Cave's profane religiosity thoroughly directs his artistic vision, determines his whole view of the world, and manifests itself throughout his sizable corpus of songs and writings. In the essay "God Is in the House" included in the catalog to the Cave retrospective *Stranger Than Kindness*, Darcey Steinke observes that Cave's songs "confront us with lush, far-reaching theological questions." Cave is an oxymoron: an irreligious religious writer.

O'Connor too gives a nod to the notion of the sanctified imagination and links her gifts as a writer to her theological beliefs. Early in her literary life she explains in a letter to a young writer, "I write the way I do because I am a Catholic. I feel that if I were not a Catholic, I would have no reason to write, no reason to see, no reason ever to feel horrified or even to enjoy anything." Reflecting on the vision and moral sense that her religion has given her, she adds hyperbolically, "I feel myself that being a Catholic has saved me a couple of thousand years in learning to write." While Cave believes that as a writer he is a "conduit" for the divine, that "through us God finds his voice," O'Connor offers up her religiously informed art free of "obnoxious pieties" in the hope that it might be used for some holy purpose. As ground for her view of divinely intended/attended art, she cites French novelist and poet Francois Mauriac, a devout Catholic and Nobel laureate: "Mauriac says God does not care anything about what we write. He uses it. So much the more reason I think that we have to give Him the best we've got for His use and leave the uses to Him."

✒ ✒ ✒

"I can hear the urge for Jesus in his voice," O'Connor's charlatan street preacher Asa Hawks says of Hazel Motes. Those closely attending may well find that this statement applies to Cave's writing voice, whether in his songs, his dizzying fiction, or his self-aggrandizing essays. His art speaks another language than does the man being interviewed. Indeed, Cave observers have commented on a perceived change of heart in the characteristically irascible artist; the older Nick Cave has become more like the self-mortifying Hazel Motes in the latter scenes of *Wise Blood*. A contributing factor may be the blinding grief Cave experienced over the tragic loss of his fifteen-year-old son Arthur, one of twin boys with wife Susie Bick. In July 2015, Arthur died from a sixty-foot fall off a cliff near his home in Brighton, England, while under the influence of LSD. Cave grieves his son's death publicly throughout the songs on *Skeleton Tree* (2016), an album that was largely completed prior to this numbing personal tragedy, and this deep loss is the long-sustained subtext and eventually the subject in the biopic *One More Time with Feeling*, also released in 2016. The *cri de coeur* in the refrain of the prescient song "I Need You," track 6 on *Skeleton Tree*, addresses in its multiplicity of meanings the loss of a beloved child, the desire for human comfort (a woman in a "red dress"), and a longing for an indwelling divine presence: "I need you / In my heart I need you." The song ends with a prayer-like repetition of the "I need you" phrase, which Cave performs both painfully and piously in the *One More Time* biopic.

Its companion song on the *Skeleton Tree* recording is titled "Jesus Alone." This powerful work of invocation, with its haunting, growling synthesized bass sounds and eerie, tweaked high tones, accented by piano and strings, is *Skeleton Tree*'s opening track and the biopic's major focus. The process of arranging, performing, recording, and ruminating on this song occupies the opening 29:40 minutes of the 112-minute film. This segment might be understood best as grief observed and translated into sonic and lyric art. As Cave is seen listening to the song in a recording studio control room, he fingers rosary beads interspersed with small white crosses. In one scene, he enters the studio to add overdub vocals wearing a white T-shirt with the words "I Believe" in black letters across the chest, clearly visible under his bespoke suit jacket. These are surely intentional signals to the viewer. While "Jesus Alone" makes no direct reference to the Christ, its sorrowful, insistent refrain echoes the lamentations (particularly Psalm 142) of the Hebrew psalmist David, also bereft of a son:

> With my voice
> I am calling you
> With my voice
> I am calling you

Cave defines all of his musical compositions as forms of "the Love Song." Whether "songs of exaltation and praise, songs of rage and of despair, erotic songs, songs of abandonment and loss," for Cave "they all address God, for it is the haunted premise of longing that the true Love Song inhabits." His compiled songs make up the profanely sacred hymnbook of the Church of Cave and reveal a deeply religious sensibility at work, however conflicted. The blurb on the slipcase of the *One More Time with Feeling* two-disc set DVD describes the biopic as "a true testament to an artist trying to find his way through the darkness." The phrasing unwittingly echoes O'Connor's response to a correspondent regarding the nature of the Christian spiritual journey: "You arrive at enough certainty to be able to make your way, but it is making it in darkness." As Cave himself reflects in the lyrics to "Waiting for You" from his grief-ridden 2019 album *Ghosteen*, "Well, sometimes a little bit of faith / Can go a long, long way." It may well be, as O'Connor says of her Christ-haunted character Hazel Motes, that Nick Cave too is "a Christian *malgre lui*"—in spite of himself. The last words on his 2022 spoken word recording *Seven Psalms* are "I have nowhere left to go / But to you Lord / Breathless, but to you."

Chapter 7

PJ HARVEY

Uh Huh, O'Connor

While other songwriters examined in these chapters may allude to an O'Connor novel or short story or borrow a story title from her for use as a song title—as do Bruce Springsteen, Sufjan Stevens, and Tom Waits—and even quote an occasional word or phrase from her fictions—as do Springsteen, Bono, Stevens, Cave, and a host of other artists—PJ Harvey owes a unique debt to O'Connor. In three narrative songs on her 1998 song cycle *Is This Desire?* Harvey effectively produces *found* lyrics, formed largely through a bricolage of sentences, phrases, bits of dialogue, and paraphrase from three of O'Connor's stories from her first collection, *A Good Man Is Hard to Find*. Harvey is a visual artist as well as a musician, and by her own admission enjoys making art from found objects—pictures, photographs, things she has collected in walks along the beach. As a lyricist, she has done something similar with O'Connor's texts. No other songwriter has so directly informed his or her lyrics with O'Connor's words.

Newcomers to Harvey's recordings and to their grinding alternative rock and minimalist synth-pop sound might be unsurprised to learn that the PJ Harvey band was once paid to *stop* playing at a musical venue. Certainly, Harvey's music is directed at an audience outside of mainstream popular tastes, more at home in the musical underground with punk and alternative subcultures. Nonetheless, and perhaps fittingly, Harvey and her band were the opening act for U2's visually enhanced Elevation tour in 2001. In 1999 the *Times* (London) declared PJ Harvey "without doubt one of the most important British female artists of the decade" for her contributions to popular culture. Two years later, she was awarded the prestigious Mercury Music Prize (the UK version of a Grammy), and again in 2011—the only performer to be twice so honored. To date, Harvey has also been nominated three times for a Grammy Award. Moreover, in December of 2013, the late Queen Elizabeth II, in person, appointed Polly Jean Harvey a member of the Most Excellent Order of the British Empire (MBE) "for services to music."

Like other major songwriters/performers discussed in this study, Harvey has acknowledged O'Connor's direct influence on her songcraft, though belatedly and perhaps misleadingly. Her personal life is "terra incognita" according to one critic, and she seldom gives interviews and rarely talks about the contexts and experiences that inform her songs. She did, however, tell a BBC interviewer in 2007 that a shift in her songwriting style on one of her albums owed much to her reading of Flannery O'Connor. In Harvey's words, "reading a lot of Flannery O'Connor's stories . . . probably was . . . shaping the way my third-person narrative was becoming—in the whole record actually." Harvey appears here to have misremembered twelve years after the fact and references her 1995 recording *To Bring You My Love* as being O'Connor-influenced. However, *none* of the songs on this recording is a third-person narrative; *all* are written in the first person. Surprisingly, Harvey posted on Instagram in September 2020 a photograph of herself lying beside an open copy of *Wise Blood*, with a message reiterating her statement twenty-five years earlier that O'Connor influenced *To Bring You My Love* and singling out the novel as "a huge influence on my writing as I began to explore storytelling through song." Perhaps the post is in response to multiple blogs in recent years by fans and others who have identified references to and quotations from O'Connor's works in Harvey's songs.

While several songs on *To Bring You My Love* have narrative elements—including the opening title track, and track 8, "I Think I'm a Mother," and the closing track "The Dancer"— this is not a collection of narrative songs written in the third person. Further, any direct influence of *Wise Blood* in Harvey's lyrics on this recording is difficult to discern, though it may be implied by her first-person narrator's similar states and conditions to the novel's main character Hazel Motes. Like the reprobate Haze, the narrator of "To Bring You My Love" has "Forsaken heaven / Cursed god above," although, unlike Haze, all for the sake of love. The narrator of "Working for the Man" would be in accord with Haze's credo that "Nobody with a good car needs to be justified." The "steel machine" Harvey's narrator drives is both temple and gas-powered deity, a "God of piston, god of steel," with the narrator in the driver's seat proclaiming, "God is here behind the wheel." A Christ-hauntedness evidently shadows these ten songs, six of which make specific reference to God or Jesus or Lord, resolving in an existential plea in the closing lines of the album's final track: "Oh, Lord, be near me tonight / . . . Bring peace to my black and empty heart."

Seven of the twelve songs on Harvey's next album, *Is This Desire?* are third-person narratives, and three of them draw significant lyric substance from O'Connor's stories. In the BBC interview, Harvey adds, reiteratively, "I often find that I might suddenly become very excited by a particular writer or a painter or a filmmaker even, and the way that they present their work will somehow make me think differently about how I present mine. And I think I was reading a lot of Flannery O'Connor at the time." Her comment echoes one made by Bruce Springsteen—"I was deep into O'Connor"—who similarly acknowledges O'Connor's transforming influence on his songwriting style, particularly a shift to third-person narrative in his first solo recording of story-songs, *Nebraska*.

Harvey's interest in O'Connor may possibly have come about in the course of a short-lived romance in 1995–96 with alt-rocker Nick Cave. Cave lays open his side of the affair in *The Boatman's Call* (1997), a collection of love songs to and about Harvey. During the time they were romantically involved, Harvey reportedly read a proof copy of Ian Johnston's 1996 Cave biography, *Bad Seed*. In it, Johnston acknowledges Cave's well-known obsession with O'Connor's work, particularly *Wise Blood* and its blaspheming preacher-gone-wrong, Hazel Motes. Harvey's O'Connor-influenced album *Is This Desire?* was released a year after Cave's *Boatman*, following much personal and artistic torment in her life, particularly during three months of recording for the album when she confessed to having "reached a stumbling block" both personally and artistically. "I knew I needed to get help," she later remarked to an interviewer. "Tired of seeing only darkness in [her] art," Harvey nearly quit the music business with the rash and romantic idea of becoming a nurse in Africa.

Not surprisingly, then, *Is This Desire?* presents a collection of songs about oppressed and distressed female characters. Anyone familiar with the art of both Cave and Harvey would confirm that they explore the dark regions of the human spirit; both have written songs that describe the grotesque actions and deeds some people are capable of (murder ballads for Cave; songs about self-harm for Harvey). Harvey's biographer notes that both artists are "interested in investigating similar things." So, it may well be that just as Springsteen introduced Bono to O'Connor's art, Cave did the same with Harvey. Both Cave and Harvey are also given to quoting or borrowing—accidently *and* deliberately, admits Cave—from authors whose works have been impressed upon their artistic imaginations.

Like O'Connor's, Harvey's art and vision are directed toward some of the extremes of human being and doing. O'Connor has remarked that her fictional form of divine comedy explores the darkness of faith, the stumblings of human striving, and our blind, stubborn selves. And she was resigned to her own observation that as a writer with a Catholic religious view, "instead of reflecting the image at the heart of things," perhaps all her art had accomplished was to have "reflected our broken condition and, through it, the face of the devil we are possessed by." Harvey told an interviewer for the *London Times*, "I've always examined the dark side of one's psyche . . . It is a large part of my character and one that I don't understand, so naturally I want to explore it."

As an artist, Harvey discovered her own territory, and, as with O'Connor, that discovery has been as much a shock to her as it is to some of her listeners. O'Connor writes that she makes her religious vision apparent in her fiction "by shock." As a young artist, Harvey too undertook to shock. Her disturbingly dark and emotionally naked second album, *Rid of Me*, released in 1993, sounds like a sex tape recorded in Bluebeard's chamber. Harvey has said that even she was shocked by it. Her songs often feature grinding, distorted guitar and bass sounds punctuated by her raunchy vocals, orgasmic groans, or sinister *sotto voce*. While Harvey is far from O'Connor in subject matter and sensibilities (though she evidently identifies with O'Connor's conflicted intellectual Joy/Hulga), like O'Connor, she nonetheless chooses to shock her audience out of necessity to get her vision across. A *London Times* reviewer describes her as "a tortured artist, renowned for songs of morbid intensity"; *SPIN* magazine describes the *Is This Desire?* songs as "monologues of longing and dialogues of despair." Harvey herself describes her work as "depressing, slash-your-wrists music."

Critics on both sides of the Atlantic failed to see any allusion to O'Connor's works in songs on *Is This Desire?* when the recording was released. Nonetheless, some sensed literary influences. Of Harvey's song "Joy," a *Los Angeles Times* critic suggests the title may allude to something in the poetry of Wordsworth or Blake. *SPIN* magazine judged the album as "unapologetically Brontë goth in theme." Harvey biographer James Blandford in *Siren Rising* (2004) echoes a number of reviewers who regard the narrative songs on *Is This Desire?* as highly autobiographical. He singles out the thirty-year-old protagonist of "Joy" as having parallels to Harvey—then a twenty-nine-year-old living a life unwed. Blandford suggests the intimations of sexual predation in "No Girl So Sweet" have biographical resonance, and he understands her song "The River" as "possibly a throwback to the river Harvey played in as a child, become a place where pain could be washed away." And though at the time of the album's release, Harvey remarked in a BBC interview that the songs had been influenced in part by the stories of Flannery O'Connor and J. D. Salinger, neither her reviewers at the time nor her biographer followed up on this revelation.

In a 2011 *Guardian* interview, Harvey comments on the extensive reading that informs her lyric craft and her efforts to hone her skills as a writer: "I feel that I am getting somewhere I want to get as a writer of words . . . I wanted [in my writing] a greater strength and depth emotionally, and all these things require work." She adds, "I'm inspired by . . . great writers I go back to and read again and again, and think How did they do that?" At the time *Is This Desire?* was released, Harvey was quoted as saying, "I think for the first time in my life, I can say that I am singing with a voice that is my own . . . which isn't wearing a mask or playing a part, but it's me, and it's entirely different to anything I've done." In light of a close examination of Harvey's lyrics on the album, the statement is ironic.

The O'Connor-haunted *Is This Desire?* is one of Harvey's strangest and darkest albums and takes her in a new musical direction. Its story-songs focus on several distressed, disappointed, and possibly confused female characters: a prostitute named Angelene, the tortured Catholic Saint Catherine, a haunted beauty named Leah, and the sexually desirable women Elise and Dawn. And then there is Joy, who is undoubtedly one and the same with Joy/Hulga Hopewell, the main character in O'Connor's short story "Good Country People."

Harvey's song "Joy" draws attention to one of the crucial details in the O'Connor story it distils in the lyrics' opening line, "Joy *was* her name" (emphasis added). O'Connor's character, having lost a leg in a hunting accident when she was ten, develops a self-loathing at her disabled condition. Later, with a PhD in philosophy, she disdains the commonness of the "good country people" with whom she was raised and despises their mindless piety. On turning twenty-one, Joy legally changes her Christian name to the ugliest name she can conceive of: Hulga. She barely tolerates country life and her divorced mother's cliché-riddled conversation and listens with amused outrage to the inane chatter of the nosey farmhand's wife. O'Connor's narrative explains that "Joy had made it plain that if it had not been for this [heart] condition, she would be far from these red hills and good country people," teaching at a distant university. Her mother laments her daughter's hopeless condition, seeing her as a "poor stout girl in her thirties who had never danced a step." Harvey incorporates these details in the first verse of her song. (Underlined words and phrases in Harvey's lyrics below are taken directly and proximately from O'Connor's texts):

> Thirty years old
> Never danced a step
> She would have left these red hills far behind if not for her condition

As a philosopher, O'Connor's Joy/Hulga has adopted a nihilistic outlook and wishes "to know nothing" of the "Nothing" she sees at the center of existence. Into this atheistic nothing of her life comes an apparently guileless, simple-minded Bible salesman, the suggestively named Manley Pointer. Pointer charms his way into the Hopewell house and eventually into Joy/Hulga's inexperienced amorous imagination. She pursues a sexual tryst with him in a barn loft, imagining that she can easily seduce him and, given her intellectual superiority, give him "a deeper understanding of life." The encounter does not go the way she imagines it. Harvey's lyrics summarize Joy/Hulga's humiliated state as she sits helpless and hopeless in a hayloft, spurned by her would-be lover:

> She looked away
> Into a hollow sky
> Came face to face
> With her own innocence surrounding her

As the underlined words and phrases indicate, Harvey's lyrics are evidently a pastiche of phrases and dramatic details drawn from O'Connor's narrative (pages 287 and 289, respectively, in *The Complete Stories*), in effect a compressed lyric summary of O'Connor's tale. In an example of what might be called song-as-criticism, Harvey offers a reading of Joy/Hulga's moment of revelation in the hayloft after the aborted seduction. Hulga believes that in her tryst with the young Pointer she is "face to face with real innocence." But Harvey turns this perspective around in her lyrics, and in doing so offers a key critical insight on the story. Hulga has to this point innocently believed in "Nothing"—neither faith, nor hope, nor love. She reiterates this belief to Pointer when he insists that she say she loves him before they have sex. "I'm one of those people who see through to nothing," she responds, though after his kisses and insistent question, "do you love me or don'tcher?" she eventually relents and replies "Yes, yes." Her belief that she seduced Pointer "without even making up her mind to try" is quickly unhinged when he asks permission to remove her wooden leg and eventually sets it out of her reach. Like other of O'Connor's spiritual misfits, Joy/Hulga discovers that she is not in the presence of a good man. While she looks "into the hollow sky" of her disbelief and disinterested sexual desire, Pointer reaches into a "hollow" Bible he has brought along and takes out a small flask of whiskey, a deck of pornographic playing cards, and a condom. Hulga's shocked and "almost pleading" response is to ask, using one of her mother's banal clichés, "Aren't you just good country people?"

In the unconsummated encounter, Joy/Hulga has been parted from her innocence in a way other than what she expected, a way that Harvey's lyrics suggest has called into question her nihilistic beliefs. Immobilized and abandoned in the hayloft, bereft of her false leg and, symbolically, of her false philosophy, Joy/Hulga is brought "face to face with *her own* innocence" [emphasis added], as Harvey revises O'Connor's phrase applying to Hulga's perspective on Pointer. In Harvey's reading, this is an "innocence so suffocating / Now she cannot move, no question." Pointer has taken her false leg, symbolic of Hulga's false beliefs, which can carry her no further. She is left to face the innocence of her questionable belief in "Nothing."

On a dramatic level in the narrative, Joy/Hulga is shocked by the discovery that, to cite her mother's observation, she and Pointer "had the same condition," which Harvey interprets as "No hope or faith." Moreover, as she looks out from the barn loft at Pointer's retreating figure, symbolically Joy/Hulga watches as her false beliefs vanish. She finds herself with altered vision (Pointer has taken her glasses as well) "sitting on the straw in the dusty sunlight," in the Bethlehem of her potential spiritual rebirth. In her lyrics, Harvey appears to understand the true state of Joy's conflicted soul at the end of O'Connor's story, both the existential innocence of her willful desire "to go blind" (as the narrative notes is Hulga's desire in the story's opening pages) and of an inner unconscious need that her encounter with Pointer has pointed out: as Harvey expresses it, Hulga also "wanted hope to stay." Harvey's lyrics conclude by quoting, with some liberty but with quotation marks, Manley Pointer's shocking parting line as, diabolically, he leaves with Hulga's false leg and a mocking retort: "[I've] been believing in nothing [ever] since I was born!" To this nearly direct quotation from O'Connor's story, still in quotation marks, Harvey adds, "it never was a question." Harvey's words in the mouth of Manley Pointer further, and ironically, implicate Joy/Hulga's questionable nihilism. He has asked her, biblically, three times, "Do you love me or don'tcher?" She has said "Yes . . . in a sense" but is unwilling to consummate her desire when Pointer shows himself an imposter. Harvey's lyrical coda on Pointer's parting words underscores the central epiphany of O'Connor's story: that Hulga and Pointer share "the same condition" of nihilistic disbelief, no question.

The tenth track on *Is This Desire?* "The River," is a piano ballad with a see-saw melody that Harvey sings with quietly crescendoing conviction. The song shares more than a title and a similar dramatic event with O'Connor's story. Like found poetry, Harvey's text is again in large part *found* lyrics. Words and phrases from O'Connor's "The River" have been extracted and reformed in a pastiche composed of bits from her fictional text and summaries of actions in her story, along with original but similarly contextualized verse lines. The song begins *in medias res* at a scene in O'Connor's story where five-year-old Harry Ashfield is walking with his caregiver for the day, Mrs. Connin, being taken to see a young preacher named Bevel Summers baptizing and healing at a nearby river. Harvey's direct borrowings in the song are largely simple narrative description from the story; other details describe the actions of O'Connor's characters and elements of the setting, including "the slow circles of two silent birds revolving high in the air" over the river in which the preacher stands. Harvey's chorus borrows, with a variant word, the preacher's exhortation to the people who have come down to the river. The underlined words and phrases in Harvey's lyrics below are directly quoted from O'Connor's text, *The Complete Stories*, pages 164–65 and 168. The lyrics begin with descriptive details quoted and paraphrased from O'Connor:

> and they came to the river
> . . . .
> and he wanted the sun
> just to call it his own
> and they walked on the dirt

The voice of O'Connor's baptizing preacher enters the lyrics here:

> Throw/Leave your pain in the river
> To be washed away slow

O'Connor's preacher calls out to the people gathered on the riverbank to "leave your pain in the river" and "lay your pain in that River," which he defines as "a River full of pain itself, pain itself, moving toward the Kingdom of Christ, to be washed away, slow." On the recording, Harvey repeats the preacher's invitation three times, replacing the verb with "Throw" in the first two, but quoting O'Connor directly for the third repeat: "Leave your pain in the river."

Further descriptive details drawn directly from this scene in O'Connor's story also inform the lyrics:

<u>two silent birds</u>
<u>circled</u> by

and <u>the white [light] scatter[s]</u>
[<u>to be washed away, slow</u>]

The lyrics sheet accompanying the CD does not contain all of the lines for Harvey's "The River" as recorded: the final bracketed line cited above, sung in the first chorus—a direct quotation from O'Connor—does not appear. A further image and phrase also drawn directly from O'Connor's text complements the second chorus, which begins with repetition of the phrase "Like a pain in the river" and follows with a varied line that repeats a striking image from a crucial scene in O'Connor's story: "And the/Like a white light scatters." Just as young Harry, now renamed Bevel, is about to be baptized, as he is held in the preacher's arms, he looks over his shoulder "at the pieces of the white sun scattered in the river," and then the preacher pushes him under the water while speaking the words of baptism.

One side of the seven-fold CD insert provides lyrics to all of the songs, the first of Harvey's recordings to do so. Across all of the printed lyrics, and the song credits as well, Harvey has overwritten in colored pen draft lyric lines and recording notes, at times obscuring and revising the printed words. Tellingly, on two of the eight panels she has handwritten lines with words and narrative details taken from O'Connor's "The River" and "The Life You Save May Be Your Own." The printed lyrics to "Joy" and "The River"—largely pastiches of O'Connor's words—have been overlaid with tidily penned lines from "No Girl So Sweet," notably, the borrowed phrase "Took her from heaven and gave her to [me]"—with the last word cut off. This strategic artistic expression could be read as both an attempt by Harvey to make the words her own *and* a way to signal that some of her lyrics are at once pastiche and palimpsest.

Joy

Joy was her name
A life untried
Thirty years old
Never danced a step
She would have left these red hills far
behind if not for her condition
"Would have left these red hills far
behind if not for my condition"
Pitiful Joy.
She looked away
Into a hollow sky
Came face to face
With her own innocence surrounding her
until it never was a question
Innocence so suffocating
No one cannot move, no question
No hope for Joy
No hope or faith
She wanted to go blind
Wanted hope to stay
"I've been believing in nothing since I was born
It never was a question."

The River

And they came to the river
and they came from the road
and he wanted the sun
just to reach us
and they walked on the dirt
and they walked from the road
'til they came to the river
'til they came up close
Throw your pain in the river
To be washed away slow
and we walked without words
and we walked with our lives
Two silent birds
circled by
like our pain in the river
and we followed the river
and we followed the road
and we walked through this land
and we called it a home
but he wanted the sun
and I wanted the whole
and for the light to douse
and the sun sets low
like the pain in the river

On the backside of the insert is a series of images: Harvey in a tube top, a neck-to-waist composite image of her in a push-up bra, a doctored page from a children's Bible storybook (like the one O'Connor's Harry/Bevel Ashfield steals from Mrs. Connin) showing Mary and Joseph on the way to Bethlehem, a picture of a headless bird on sand, and other images from England's Dorset coast where Harvey makes her home. A Post-it Note is set against a purple-tinted image of foaming water meeting a sandy shore—a shore of art and imagination and reading where Harvey figuratively likes to walk and collect things. The sticky note, with a scratched-out patch, bears in sloppy penciled block letters the words "LYRICS TO SONGS PRINTED OR WRITTEN."

Harvey's graphemic overwriting here is symbolically suggestive of her method of composition for the three songs with lyrical substance extracted from O'Connor's stories. Harvey has found in O'Connor's PRINTED stories the essential materials for the LYRICS she has WRITTEN. The result is two songs that in the texts of their lyrics are more O'Connor than Harvey, and a third song, "No Girl So Sweet," in which the last verse references characters from O'Connor's "The Life You Save May Be Your Own," a story that appears just before "The River" in her *The Complete Stories* collection. The song's final verse is largely a pastiche of words and phrases snipped from O'Connor's text (underlined in the cited lyrics below, with slight variants indicated in square brackets), and the song's title is a composite from a clip of dialogue in the story. The raucous refrain, which appears in quotation marks in the lyrics sheet, is taken from a speech by O'Connor's Mr. Shiftlet character, a devious one-armed tramp who attempts to con an old backwoods woman, Lucynell Crater, comically described by O'Connor as "about the size of a cedar fence post" with "a man's gray hat pulled down low over her head." As the story comes to an end, Mr. Shiftlet has driven off with the old woman's car after repairing it. In the bargain, he has taken his new bride, the old woman's simple-minded, deaf and dumb daughter, also named Lucynell—described by a hitchhiker he has picked up as "an angel of Gawd"—whom Shiftlet intends to abandon at the first opportunity:

> He <u>drove</u> it <u>fast to make</u> the <u>night</u>
> and <u>look[ed] at</u> his <u>angel</u>, where <u>she</u> lay
> <u>rest[ing] her head, and [closed] her eyes</u>

Mr. Shiftlet's revelation in the story forms the concluding lines in Harvey's lyrics, the last line vociferously repeated as the song concludes:

> <u>Deep in the sky, a storm</u> he'd seen
> <u>["There ain't] nothing</u>, no girl <u>so sweet"</u>
> <u>"Took her from Heaven and [gave her] to me"</u>

Harvey's lyrical bricolage in this song and in "Joy" and "The River" raises interesting issues regarding artistic inspiration and influence. In these songs, Harvey grants O'Connor's literary voice and vision a preeminent place over her own lyric craft through quotation, paraphrase, and summary from O'Connor's stories. One critic has commented of Harvey's *Is This Desire?* songs, "She tells her tales in the third person, but the stories are unmistakably hers." While as James Blandford conjectures, there may be some biographical truth to this statement, the stories in three songs on the recording are unmistakably O'Connor's. Harvey's borrowings might be considered both testament and homage to O'Connor's informing and transforming influence on the art and vision of this celebrated singer-songwriter and emerging poet.

Chapter 8

WISE BLOOD, PUNK, AND HEAVY METAL

In her published letters, Flannery O'Connor mentions occasionally receiving disturbing correspondence from readers of her first novel, *Wise Blood*, and remarks, "I seem to attract the lunatic fringe." The same label might be extended to some of the musicians attracted to O'Connor's characters and vision in this novel. In contemporary popular music, *Wise Blood* is the most widely referenced—and misread—of O'Connor's works and has had particular appeal to artists working in the extreme genres of punk and heavy/industrial metal and in what is widely defined as alternative rock. A single explanation is likely impossible to construe for the interest that songwriters in these marginal genres have shown for O'Connor's odd, flawed story and its tormented central character, Hazel Motes. In some respects, punk and heavy metal readings of *Wise Blood* are of a kind with the responses of early reviewers of O'Connor's first novel who missed its irony and satire. Thus, references to key scenes and passages in the novel and to O'Connor's prophet-gone-wrong Hazel Motes in the works of these songwriters are often in line with literalist misreadings of the novel that marred its early reception and, it appears, continue to this day.

Current fans of O'Connor's fiction may not be aware of the scathing critical reception her first novel received, including when it was reissued in 1962. A reviewer in the *Savannah Morning News* describes *Wise Blood* as "a shocking book, with lust flaunted and blasphemy rampant," a book that claimed attention "for its very obscurity and obscenity." Replace *book* here with *musical recording*, and this statement could blurb the album covers of half a dozen heavy-metal releases that have some connection with O'Connor's *Wise Blood* and its central character Hazel Motes. Veteran book critic John W. Simon, reviewing the novel in *Commonweal*, sees satanic ritual in the obsessive and perverse behavior of Enoch Emery, a minor character in the novel, and extrapolates Enoch's claim to have "wise blood" as akin to witch-likeness, seeing him as "a demoniac" and an emissary of "an unnamed evil." Even with O'Connor's literary reputation well established and her Catholic beliefs and redemptive themes well known, a *Chicago Sun-Times* reviewer of the novel after its 1962 reissue writes that *Wise Blood* is primarily "a study of evil" and finds the evil in the story "so complete" that it "form[s] a monolith of satanic darkness." No wonder, then, that this novel offers fertile imaginative ground for nihilistic, often anti-Christian, and suggestively satanic heavy metal songwriters.

Even the great movie director John Huston misread the novel he adapted into film in 1979. Or perhaps he had been subtly duped by the screenplay by Benedict and Michael Fitzgerald, who took great pains to be true to O'Connor's language and tone. Huston, an adamant atheist, thought he was making a film that satirized Bible-thumping southern religion, only to come to the surprising revelation near the end of filming that, in his words, "Jesus wins."

One O'Connor scholar has ventured explanations for why *Wise Blood* has had a marked influence in the more extreme, aggressive contemporary music genres. Monica Miller's solidly researched article in the *Flannery O'Connor Review*, "Preaching Rock and Roll Salvation from O'Connor's *Wise Blood* to Ministry's 'Jesus Built My Hotrod,'" argues that the "aggressive masculine rock and roll ethos" and "celebration of masculinist nihilism" and its association with car culture in both punk and metal music explains the "particular sway" that *Wise Blood* and Hazel Motes have for those subcultures. Lyricist Al Jourgensen of the Chicago-based industrial metal band Ministry evidences this influence in the band's hard-driving anthem "Jesus Built My Hotrod"; released in 1991 as a maxi-single, it sold 1.5 million copies. An extended mix of this recording, the "Redline, Whiteline Version," includes forty seconds of quoted dialogue from Huston's film adaptation of *Wise Blood* in the opening ninety seconds of the 8:15-minute track. The back of a promotional T-shirt for this recording bears one of Hazel Motes's memorable lines, slightly misquoted (as so in the movie dialogue), printed in large black block letters: "NO MAN WITH A GOOD CAR NEEDS TO BE JUSTIFIED."

It's a stretch to think that anyone who reads O'Connor's novel carefully or has viewed Huston's film adaptation (likely the inspiration for Ministry's songwriter Jourgensen) would equate Hazel Motes's spluttering "high rat-colored" Essex with a hot rod. His murmured declaration in O'Connor's text that "Nobody with a good car needs to be justified"—sampled in clips of more emphatic dialogue from Huston's film at the beginning of "Jesus Built My Hotrod"—is, of course, laughably ironic given the $40 rattletrap Haze is referring to, with a leaking radiator and gas tank and a plank for a back seat. And there is nothing celebratory about Haze's car as a symbol of his blasphemous, careening self-determinism. O'Connor scholars have discussed her symbolic use of automobiles to signify modernist humanist values of autonomy and

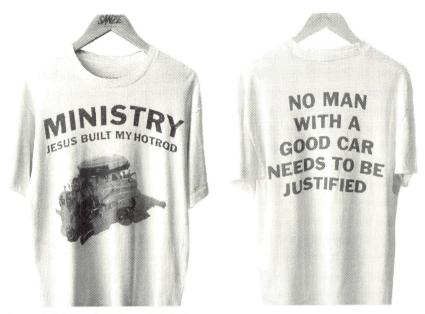

Photo credits Chris Miner. T-shirt from author's closet.

individual agency—most notably and extensively Brian Abel Ragen in his monograph *A Wreck on the Road to Damascus* (1989). That most American notion of the rugged and revving individual who, pedal to the metal, heads out for the territories is a conceit that O'Connor is well aware of and exploits to her own purposes. But the belching, stalling Essex that Haze drives does not take him far without breaking down or running out of gas. Thus Haze's "good car" statement can hardly be read as *affirming* the American tradition of the car as symbol of aggressive, masculine self-assertion and rebellious freedom. Haze and his Essex are manifestly, in every way, ironic and ultimately powerless against the implacable force of grace to which he ultimately and violently surrenders. Read the book or watch the film adaptation until the titles roll and the notion that either work might grease the imaginations of proponents of a hypermasculinized hopped-up car culture is patently an egregious misreading.

Alongside Miller's argument that *Wise Blood*'s themes appeal to "a particularly masculine, aggressive form of rebellion central to the ethos of rock and roll," it might be strongly argued that Hazel Motes's anti-Christian, blasphemous, and self-aggrandizing rhetoric and his devil-may-care licentiousness are what give the novel topical appeal for heavy metal music—a genre, according to cultural sociologist Jonathan Cordero, that is characterized by an essential overt anti-Christian, nihilistic, and hedonistic ideology. Cordero has published a study based on nearly one hundred CD reviews and exactly

one hundred prepublished interviews with members of bands in the extreme subgenres of heavy metal, labeled black metal and death metal. He observes in their song lyrics and band branding pervasive anti-Christian sentiments largely communicated by "indicating alliances with ideologies and themes conventionally understood as antithetical to Christianity." He cites in particular use of the inverted pentagram, an iconographic symbol used in satanic ritual—visibly tattooed on the right shoulder of Ministry's front man Jourgensen in his mocking pose as a thorn-crowned Christ in the image above. Gothic paraphernalia of skulls, skeletons, and gravestones also decorate the covers of recordings by heavy metal bands as well as their stage settings—including Ministry and Corrosion of Conformity discussed below—all intended to communicate an association with darkness and death-dealing.

Sacrilegious images on album and CD cover art that profane or invert/subvert Christian symbols also constitute what Cordero identifies as a further type of anti-Christian expression in the marketing of heavy metal music. According to Cordero, this form of music explicitly targets Christianity as a religion that imposes "social and moral constraints" while its adherents are hypocritical in "not practicing what they preach." An antiauthoritarian "self-as-god" philosophy emphasizing freedom from constraints defines heavy metal ideology and, according to Cordero, echoes a dictum in the Satanic Bible, "Do what thou wilt." Nonetheless, Cordero states that only a few of the members of metal bands he researched were official practicing members of the Church of Satan, though he contends that most "tend to agree with its principles" and engage in what he refers to as "popular Satanism." Deena Weinstein, the leading authority in heavy metal studies, argues that the themes found in heavy metal songs are "acts of metaphysical rebellion against the pieties and platitudes of normal society." She affirms with Cordero that what she calls "the discourse on chaos" in the genre, with its manifold references to various forms of paganism and occult practice, is directed against Judeo-Christian tradition and culture.

Of further interest from a cultural studies perspective is that heavy metal lyrics are also heavily influenced by literary sources, particularly works of science fiction (*Dune, Brave New World*) and fantasy that contains magic and a sense of cosmic evil (*Lord of the Rings*), mythology (Ragnarök and other Old Norse mythology), or works that exhibit gothic romanticism. (Coleridge's *Rime of the Ancient Mariner* and the stories and poems of Edgar Allan Poe are retold in a number of heavy metal ballads.) Indeed, according to pop culture critic Heather Lusty, a penchant for the gothic and the grotesque—terms often applied to O'Connor's art—largely informs the subject matter of heavy metal music compositions and album art. Lusty, along with Deena Weinstein, singles out the stories of Edgar Allan Poe, one of O'Connor's literary progenitors, as having the widest currency in heavy metal lyrics. Perhaps the Poesque qualities of O'Connor's *Wise Blood*—with its half-crazed Hazel Motes, who murders his doppelganger Solace Layfield, has sex with a prostitute and then a fifteen-year-old girl, and eventually engages in acts of self-harm and mutilation—provide ample grotesque subject matter to explain the novel's appeal to a particular set of heavy metal sensibilities.

The pervasive ideology in metal music culture is well articulated in Hazel Motes's Christ-denying remarks in Huston's film, sampled at the beginning of an extended mix of Ministry's "Jesus Built My Hotrod [Redline/Whiteline Version]": "I come a long way since I believed in anything" (only slightly misquoted from the novel). The selective use of quotations from the film in a song marked by vulgarity, inanity, and blasphemy ("Jesus was an architect previous to his career as a prophet") attests to O'Connor's influence on the darker products of popular culture. A further sample from Haze's street preaching is presented as a kind of nihilistic rallying cry before the blistering music begins: "Where you come from is gone, where you thought you were going to weren't never there, and where you are ain't no good unless you can get away from it." This quotation is from a scene that opens chapter 10 of O'Connor's novel, preceding Haze's haranguing theatergoers from the hood of his car about the impossibility of Jesus redeeming anybody. Yet the words in Ministry's hard-driven and arguably obscene song have little if anything to do with O'Connor's novel, or with car racing for that matter, and largely express the singer's urgent desire to "ding a ding dang [his] dang a long ling long"—to quote a distinctive line in the largely unintelligible lyrics.

Ministry's association with an explicitly anti-Christian ideology, and indeed with the dark arts, is expressed in images on their album covers and in their promotional materials. The iconography is virulently sacrilegious. The band's brand includes the occult image of a broken cross and a doubling of the anarchist symbol, as if to underscore the anarchist axiom "No gods, no masters." Al Jourgensen is often photographed in Christ-like poses that are darkly mocking. While the photograph of a car engine on the CD cover for the maxi-single containing the *Wise Blood*-influenced preamble to "Jesus Built My Hotrod" seems innocuous—and likely prompted Miller's argument that the song celebrates American hotrod car culture—the album on which the song appears has a main title, *Psalm 69*, that is sexually suggestive and so somewhat blasphemous. The album's subtitle, "The Way to Succeed and the Way to Suck Eggs"—also sexually suggestive—is a phrase taken from the writings of famed occultist Aleister Crowley. "The only way to the truth is through blasphemy," Haze reiterates ironically in O'Connor's novel. Ministry's songs and branding appear to indicate that the band has embraced blasphemy as an end in itself.

Corrosion of Conformity: *Wiseblood*

An album titled *Wiseblood* (1996) by the heavy metal band Corrosion of Conformity, from Raleigh, North Carolina, contains a number of songs that allude to themes in O'Connor's novel and to the words and actions of her false preacher protagonist. One reviewer has written, "The myth surrounding the album is that a handful of the songs are loosely based around the Flannery O'Connor novel *Wise Blood*," although band members have made no statements confirming O'Connor's influence on the album and have in fact suggested other sources for the title phrase. Yet a blogger has encouraged fans of the band, "Go read Flannery O'Connor's *Wise Blood* and then go listen to that same album again. It adds whole new strata of meaning!"

Corrosion of Conformity's sound is composed of raw power chords with bursts of lightning-fast guitar pyrotechnics, backed by steady rock drumming. Lead vocalist Pepper Keenan growls and shout-sings his lyrics, though with clear articulation and a Robert Plant–like care for hitting his notes precisely.

The narrator of the *Wiseblood* album's title song declares, "I did what I could when I was able / to keep the truth away from our table," a sentiment that echoes Hazel Motes's claim from the hood of his Essex about his vision to form the Church without Christ: "There's only one truth and that is that there is no truth." As sole member of his self-made church, Motes aligns himself with the sentiment expressed in the Corrosion of Conformity song lyrics: "I've seen them devils pound our bible / you saints and sinners are both my rival." The song concludes with a statement closely paralleling Motes's solipsistic doctrines: "I walk alone but at least I walk for free." The song's refrain nonetheless evokes the concept of grace found in many of O'Connor's stories—here related to Motes in particular: "You need wise blood / shake 'em down to his knees."

"Freedom," writes O'Connor in reference to her character Motes, "cannot be conceived simply," for, as she explains, "free will does not mean one will, but many wills conflicting in one man." The truth of O'Connor's observation here is borne out in the conflicted, evidently Christ-haunted state of the narrator/singer of the songs on the Corrosion of Conformity album. "Wiseblood" is followed by track 4, "Goodbye Windows," with a refrain that alludes to an image in O'Connor's novel: "I'd rather have holes in my eyes / than to watch your soul paralyzed." Hazel Motes is described as having eyes "like two clean bullet holes"; his final act of self-blinding leaves "dark tunnel" holes where his eyes once were. Track 5, "Born Again for the Last Time" is a song of spiritual anguish and its refrain repeats a telling adjective that may refer to Hazel Motes—both his condition and character: "My life is hazy hazy hazy / So I'm born again for the last time." The narrator of track 11, "Wishbone (Some Tomorrow)," begins by describing himself as "torn from within, disciple till the end" and refers to himself as "losing sight losing sight / without a fight": again, all possible references to the anguished state and actions of Motes, whose encounter with the fraudulent street evangelist Asa Hawks might be figured in a closing line of the song, "feel the kick from the heartless heretic / that once made you shine."

Track 10, the slow-rocking anthem "Redemption City," stands out on this collection of songs that, to invoke an image in the lyrics, are largely "baptize[d] with gasoline." Here Pepper Keenan's vocals and the power-chord-driven walking beat appear to be moving toward some potential grace that is figured as regrettably inaccessible. Like O'Connor's character The Misfit—and like other artists in this study, notably Nick Cave—the narrator of this song is "stuck in between" unbelief and belief, and yearning, like Springsteen's *Nebraska* characters, to be delivered from "nowhere." Following a short lyric bridge and a melodic note-bending instrumental, the tone of the song briefly

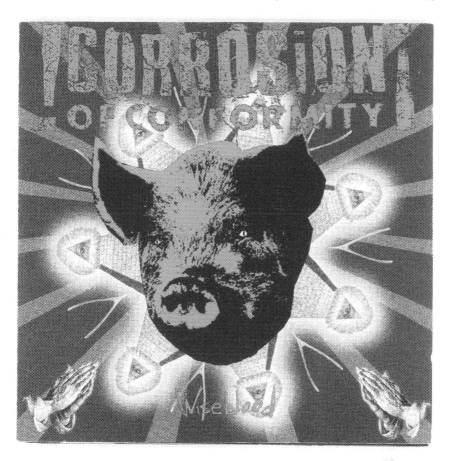

changes at the outset of the final verse and the music softens to express an unfulfilled longing of a tired "soul" desiring to "go home,"

> And close the curtain on everything you've known
> But the curtain is high, wide, and long
> ....
> Stuck in between, and I know you know what I mean
> What a pity, redemption city

Despite the notes of spiritual yearning in the album's collected songs, any straightforward reading of *Wiseblood*'s cover art would regard it as sacrilegious. Albrecht Dürer's praying hands are shown lifted up to a fire-red pig-headed god inset over a seven-pointed star comprised of the Kabbalist and later Masonic symbol of the All-Seeing Eye in a triangle atop a pyramid. Seven is the most sacred and beloved number in Jewish and Christian biblical interpretation, according to Talmudic scholars. Of course, the eye in the triangle is a familiar symbol from the American dollar bill. Some believe it to be symbolic of the eye of God or Providence, but in occult lore it is considered the "All-Seeing Eye of Lucifer," and its association with occult practice is undisputed. Clearly, the iconography of the *Wiseblood* CD cover art, like the rhetoric of *Wise Blood*'s blaspheming street preacher, mocks the sacred.

JG Thirlwell / Wiseblood

Wiseblood is, on the one hand, the name of an industrial/noise rock band known for its violent, explicit songs, and on the other, the moniker for the man behind the musical mayhem, JG Thirlwell. A note on Thirlwell's website, foetus.org, offers this description of the band's songs: "Thematically, Wiseblood's lyrics center around the misanthropic exertion of power, typically via murder, sex, or assault." Musically the group's styles range from Led Zeppelin–like blues rock to cacophonous hardcore punk to a snappy big-band sound—what one critic has hybridly called "demented-electro-avant-jazz." Wiseblood the band was active in various collectives from 1984 until the mid-1990s, sometimes as a duo featuring Thirlwell and percussionist Roli Mosimann, releasing four albums—*Motorslug* (1985), *Stumbo* (1986), *Dirtdish* (1987), and *PTTM* (1991)—comprising a total of fourteen compositions, mostly concerned with depraved or obscene subject matter. A reviewer of *PTTM* offers that the "seething" and "eerie" guitar work on the album, along with Thirlwell's "growl to screech" vocal stylings, evoke "an oppressive atmosphere Hazel Motes would feel at home in."

Wiseblood is one of numerous musical ensembles and personas Thirlwell has embraced over a long career as a composer on the margins of musical culture with a megalomaniac's penchant for extremes and excess. Thirlwell likes to think of himself as unclassifiable. His early influences were minimalist music experimenters Steve Reich, John Cage, and Phillip Glass. In his various personas from the 1980s to early 2000s, particularly in his most enduring and offensive incarnations as Clint Ruin and Foetus, Thirlwell's lyrics exalt explicit sexual violence, murder, blasphemy, and various forms of self-degradation, aimed at offending just about everyone regardless of race, religion, or sexual persuasion.

While some of the Thirlwell's lyrics hint at occultish activity, the popular satanism of Ministry and Corrosion of Conformity is largely absent. Most interestingly, like his Australian copatriot and companion in the dissolute British punk-rock scene of the 1980s, Nick Cave, Thirlwell has cast himself as

Wise Blood, Punk, and Heavy Metal 175

a kind of Hazel Motes figure—both the sin-seeking Haze at the beginning of *Wise Blood* and the self-tortured specter at the end. His website is glutted with images of himself. A darkly stylized image used on an album cover shows him fornicating with Lydia Lunch, his muse and partner for several shocking and disturbing musical and performance collaborations. In a Pieta-like tableau after the manner of Michelangelo's famous sculpture, Lunch poses as the Blessed Virgin Mary while Thirlwell plays the crucified Christ. An image on his website, taken in Berlin in 1988 when Thirlwell was associating with Cave, appears to be a deliberate mirroring of a frame from the *Wise Blood* film, with Brad Dourif as Hazel Motes after he has blinded himself and begun mortifying his flesh with various forms of self-torture. The pigs' heads on stakes in Wiseblood's photo invoke the themes of sacrilege and blasphemy associated with the pig's head image on the Corrosion of Conformity cover.

Wisebloody Awful

Thirlwell's Wiseblood persona, he acknowledges in an interview, comes from the nickname given him by Lydia Lunch, Nick Cave's paramour while he was in Berlin obsessively working on his drug-fueled and *Wise Blood*–inspired novel *And the Ass Saw the Angel*. Around this time, according to his online biography, Thirlwell was briefly a member of Cave's band the Bad Seeds and involved in a short-lived musical side project with Cave in 1983 known as the Immaculate Consumptive. As Bruce Springsteen is credited with introducing U2's Bono to O'Connor's writings, it was likely Cave who introduced Thirlwell to O'Connor's *Wise Blood* with its gothic themes, mock biblical symbolism, and images of self-torture. Like O'Connor's wise-blooded character Enoch Emery, who was forced to attend the Rodemill Boys Bible Academy where "it was Jesus all day long," Thirlwell was educated for twelve years at an all-boys Baptist school in Melbourne, Australia—and hated every moment of it. So, like the young Motes, whose mother in a brief flashback scene acts to beat the be-Jesus into him, Thirlwell's anti-Christian outlook also needs little psychologizing.

While several song lyrics by Cave cite phrases from O'Connor's fictions and owe some of their vision to her influence, the highly offensive lyrics to songs on Thirlwell's four *Wiseblood* recordings bear no discernible direct references to O'Connor's first novel or to her other fictions. But, as has been written of Cave, Thirlwell as artist and performer inside his Wiseblood persona appears to have cast himself as an exaggerated Hazel Motes figure in his pursuit of all manner of sexual gratification and degradation. "Fornication and blasphemy and what else?" asks the faux-blind street preacher Asa Hawks when he first encounters Motes. That "what else?" in the Wiseblood recordings includes songs that glorify rape and sodomy and other forms of sexual violence against women, and "grisly sacrificial slaughter," to quote a line from "O-O (Where Evil Dwells)," a song based on an actual case of occult-motivated murder. Collectively, the songs reveal their narrator's disturbing and blasphemous Christ complex. Indeed, the growly, chanted closing refrain in the excruciating song "Godbrain" on the 1987 LP *Dirtdish* repeats, "Well, I'm God! God! God! . . ." If there is such a thing as *evil* music, Wiseblood's *Dirtdish* and *Motorslug* recordings might be so cataloged.

For the unclassifiable musical artist known as Wiseblood, the title terms of O'Connor's novel, and perhaps her Hazel Motes character as well, are associated with the ideas of sacrilege, blasphemy, and immorality present in the novel—with added vileness and violence and a flirting with the demonic. Unlike the O'Connor-influenced albums of Ministry and Corrosion of

Conformity, however, Wiseblood recordings are not packaged with covers adorned with sacrilegious imagery. In a nod to Monica Miller's thesis, cover images on albums released by the band relate to hot-rod and car-racing culture—the checkered flag design used at racetracks (*Motorslug*, *Dirtdish*, and *Stumbo*) and a stylized drawing of a car engine (*PTTM*).

Yet, only two songs ("Motorslug" and "PTTM") out of the fourteen on the four Wiseblood albums have the automobile as subject matter. And there are no images on Thirlwell's website showing himself or other band members behind the wheel of a fast car. The cover art appears to be a cover for the records' less acceptable subject matter of transgressive sex, raw violence, and anti-Christian polemics. A host of images on Thirlwell's website present him in the period of his Wiseblood persona imitating a self-inflicted Christ-like suffering. One image shows Thirlwell/Wiseblood as Christ nailing himself to a cross, as if staging a dramatic literalization of Hazel Motes's claim to all who will listen that the crucifixion of Jesus "wasn't for you," since ultimately some form of self-crucifixion must be endured. Though Thirlwell as Wiseblood does not engage in the kind of popular satanism found on the O'Connor-influenced Ministry and Corrosion of Conformity recordings, it is worth remarking that among the dark, disturbing images on his website are several of a diabolical nature, including one taken with leading Satanist Anton LaVey and evidently in a place of occult practice given the Baphomet symbol—the official insignia of the Church of Satan—visible in the background.

Over a lengthy musical career that began in his late teens, JG Thirlwell has released more than thirty recordings under nineteen pseudonyms. He has performed commissioned works at UCLA and Yale, and one of his works was performed by the famed Kronos Quartet at Carnegie Hall in 2010. That year he was also awarded a fellowship in music by the New York Foundation of the Arts. He has scored soundtracks for seasons 7 to 9 of the adult animated spy spoof series *Archer*, which won an Emmy Award in 2016 for outstanding animation in its season 7. An online review article on his extensive and diverse catalog of musical recordings, projects, and personas concludes tellingly, "Where JG Thirlwell is concerned, there is no rest for the wicked."

Gang of Four: "A Man with a Good Car"

A song titled "A Man with a Good Car" on the album *Hard* (1983) by the 1980s post-punk band Gang of Four makes strong textual and thematic reference to O'Connor's first novel. The song's chorus appears, without irony, to promote Hazel Motes's gospel of self-determination and self-reliance: "A man with a good car needs no justification / Fate is in my hands and in the transmission." The first line of the chorus closely paraphrases Haze's assertion "Nobody with a good car needs to be justified." The second line of the chorus conveys the same idea as Haze's boast to the one-armed roadside mechanic who assists him a few pages further on in the novel: "This car'll get me anywhere I want to go." This statement, repeated three times over a page and a half at the end of chapter 7, underscores O'Connor's symbolic use of the hapless vehicle as an objective correlative for Haze's Christ-less existence and vacuous beliefs. The Gang of Four song appears to side with Haze's Christ-denying doctrines and thus be another example in pop music of an unironic (mis)reading of O'Connor's character and novel.

But just as O'Connor's novel was initially misunderstood by critics as a satire on Bible Belt religiosity, so "A Man with a Good Car" lyrically turns back on itself to confront listeners with the possibility that they have misheard the message in the song. The resulting conflicted content is signaled in lines from the bridge: "I know that you think that you know what I said . . . / But do you realize that what I said's not what I meant?" The lyrics appear directly to address the *problem* of misreading the sense of the song's key phrase/idea borrowed from O'Connor's novel.

O'Connor does not state such an explicit caveat in her author's note to the 1962 reissue of *Wise Blood*, but she does offer some direction to the tired, spiritually alienated reader who might miss the novel's irony. What the words and actions of her blaspheming, sin-seeking protagonist literally say is not what she meant, she explains: "That belief in Christ is to some a matter of life and death has been a stumbling block to readers who would prefer to think

it a matter of no great consequence. For them, Hazel Motes's integrity lies in his trying with such vigor to get rid of the ragged figure that moves from tree to tree in the back of his mind. For the author, Hazel's integrity lies in his not being able to do so."

The novel's paradoxical message is underscored in the cryptic opening lines of the second verse of the Gang of Four song as the narrator confesses, "I don't have wise blood / I'm deep in the mystery." O'Connor explains her concept of "wise blood," as what people who do not practice a formal religion have as a "means of grace." And the doctrine of grace is one of the deep Christian mysteries. The spiritual truth conveyed by this song is thus difficult to discern; its ironic, conflicting overtones echo the irony in O'Connor's novel. And the existential tension in the lyrics between the declarative refrain borrowed from the novel ("A man with a good car needs no justification") and the contradictory statement in the bridge is matched by the overstated

1980s synth-pop sound and pulsing staccato rhythms of this danceable tune. What this song on the *Hard* album is about is hard to discover through casual listening; its meaning is there only for those who have ears to hear.

King Swamp: *Wiseblood*

The short-lived British rock band King Swamp (1988–1990) is hard to classify musically: their sound has been described as post-punk, new wave, and Britpop. As one online reviewer of their 1990 album *Wiseblood* comments, "There is a little bit of everything going on here." The title song was released in several mixes as a promotional CD and vinyl twelve-inch with a misspelled parenthetical subtitle, "Wiseblood (Mote's Rave 12")." There are a number of possible thematic connections between the songs on King Swamp's *Wiseblood* recording and O'Connor's first novel, its central character Hazel Motes, and his sidekick Enoch Emery; as well, the lyrics to the title song appear to allude directly to several elements in her text.

Heavy metal and punk misinterpretations of *Wise Blood* the novel, it has been argued, accord with O'Connor's tongue-in-cheek view of Hazel Motes as "an admirable nihilist," as she describes him in a letter. Certainly, the songs collected on King Swamp's *Wiseblood* are of a dark, apocalyptic tone. And the powerful, emotive voice of lead singer Walter Wray, described as "the most gothic Southern rock singer to be found anywhere in England," delivers the songs with high angst and existential resignation. The lyrics to the title song refer to humans "crushed beneath the weight of their own history" and "Puppets of chemistry, / God's own toys"—phrases that well describe how critics have read Enoch's character as controlled by unconscious forces. Far from O'Connor's do-it-yourself sacramentalism in *her* wise-blooded characters, however, the characters in these songs are faithless, dissatisfied, and edging toward violence. The narrator of "One Step over the Line" prowls cautiously "through the jungle of confusion one more day." He fears for his life in a world marred by what O'Connor identified as "meanness": "There's a wind a-blowing, fit to blow me clean away / And the night's so wounded keeps bleeding into the day." A nihilistic doctrine informs track 3, "Floating World," a song about a desperate character like one of the narrators in Springsteen's *Nebraska* songs, who buys a gun, writes a suicide note, and is found drunk on his bed with the gun barrel in his mouth, unable to pull the trigger. "We are nothing / Nothing more than shadows," the song's refrain concludes. The track titles "Walk the Knife" and "Can't Be Satisfied" are thematically self-explanatory and speak to the "bitterness of [the] empty cup" that is life as portrayed in these songs. Hazel Motes is asked by the sheriff who destroys his rattletrap car by pushing it over an embankment, "Was you going anywheres?" "No," answers Haze. The narrator of "Can't Be Satisfied" concludes his song story similarly: "I'm just heading down the backroads / I'm only in it for the ride." The biblically informed "Nightfall over Eden" takes a cosmic view of fallen humanity, as does O'Connor throughout her fictions. But there is no means of redemption offered, no Promised Land to make one's way back to in this song, only resignation that Eden is lost. As the narrator stands with a lover on "the rock of ages" and looks "down on the country wide," only desolation and devastation can be seen, and the only consolation is in what little love can be found: "Nightfall over Eden, take my hand." The bleakness of King Swamp's *Wiseblood* appears thematically similar to what some critics have found in O'Connor's *Wise Blood*: a *New York Times* reviewer describes the novel as a work of Kafkaesque surreality that presents "a world of darkness" in which "there has been no light to take away."

Allusions to Motes's character and existential condition in the *Wiseblood* songs are complemented with lyrical content that might apply as well to Enoch Emery, a simple-minded, obsessive-compulsive teenager from the backwoods with a father who "looks just like Jesus" and a mother he has never known. His daddy runs off with a woman and tells Enoch he must fend for himself in the city. Enoch meets Hazel Motes when he first arrives in the fictitious southern town of Taulkinham and tags along with him, desperate for a friend. O'Connor's narrator states that Enoch has "wise blood like his daddy" that operates in him like a mode of mystical intuition, guiding him and informing him about what he is supposed to do and what is going to happen.

One of the shortcomings of O'Connor's novel is her treatment of Enoch, whom she abandons two chapters before the end. He is last seen wearing a gorilla suit, stolen violently from a film promotion crew, and acting friendly to strangers, who naturally are frightened and run from him. In comments collected with other oddments in a section of *Mystery and Manners*, O'Connor dismisses Enoch as "a moron and chiefly a comic character." But his desire for human connection and a meaningful existence, as scholarly readers of the novel have argued, is of a kind with Hazel Motes's manic pursuit of truth outside of the Christian creeds, though certainly not as intentional nor as deep. Enoch's religion is a naturalistic humanism that is self-sacralized and self-satisfying, "sort of what we have instead of God," as Hemingway once wrote. Enoch's actions and person are evidently comic, as O'Connor describes her novel as a whole, but his story, along with that of her "Christian *malgre lui*" Hazel Motes, as she asserts in her author's note, is "very serious"; she adds emphatically, "all comic novels that are any good must be about matters of life and death." The same longing for transcendence amid the absence of conditions or forms through which to find it that is dramatized in O'Connor's *Wise Blood* is evidenced in the songs on the King Swamp album that share her novel's title words.

O'Connor explains her wise blood symbol in a letter to experimental novelist John Hawkes, one of her regular correspondents. Referring doubly to her fictional characters and to the religious character of the South, she remarks, "Wise blood has to be these people's means of grace—they have no sacraments. The religion of the South is a do-it-yourself religion, something which I as a Catholic find painful and touching and grimly comic. It's full of unconscious pride that lands them in all sorts of ridiculous religious predicaments. They have nothing to correct their practical heresies and so they work them out dramatically."

O'Connor's idea is illustrated in chapter 8 of her novel, which is wholly concerned with dramatizing the effect on Enoch of having "wise blood." His ritual daily visits to the Frosty Bottle for a chocolate malted milkshake, then to the zoo to mock the monkeys, and on to the "muvseevum" to gaze reverently at a mummified shrunken man are a form of religious observance, a lived liturgy. In the absence of other sacred practices, Enoch's wise blood compels him to make up his own, however misdirected. This reading is signaled in Enoch's references to receiving a "sign" that something is about to happen and waiting for confirmation, and the narrator noting that his visits to the animals at the zoo "were only a form he had to get through." When he arrives with Hazel Motes in tow to a dark room in the museum with "three coffin-like" glass cases in the middle of the floor, Enoch speaks "in a church whisper." He is in a self-determined sacred space. As the reader soon discovers, both Enoch and Haze are looking for "a new jesus" in the absence of belief in the old one, and Enoch eventually comes to believe that he has found him.

As Enoch's blood is described as "rushing around" in him and behaving "in secret conference with itself," so the King Swamp song lyrics state, "There's a ripple in the silence / It's Wiseblood / Pumping in the whispering night." What the curiously capitalized "Wiseblood" in the lyrics to this song refers to is uncertain, just as Enoch's "wise blood" is a mystery both to himself and to readers of O'Connor's novel. Further, the "whispering night" in the lyrics does not correspond with any similar symbolic atmospheric setting in *Wise Blood*. Nonetheless, Enoch's claim to have inherited his "wise blood" is perhaps referenced in the outro to King Swamp's song. This synthesizer-heavy recording, with attacking drumbeats, suddenly shifts at the end to a southern gospel-like coda, with vocal harmonies interweaving in a doo-wop rhythm and repeating,

Tell me what your mama give you
Tell me what your daddy give you
Meet me on down by the river
With your Wiseblood

King Swamp released only two albums, an eponymous first release in 1988 and *Wiseblood* in 1990. The band had a major label, Virgin Records, a top-flight recording studio at The Manor in Oxford, England, and sound engineering by Bob Clearmountain, celebrated for his work with O'Connor devotees U2 and Bruce Springsteen. Despite some initial success with their first album, the band disbanded after *Wiseblood* was panned by critics and failed to make the record charts in either the UK or the US. It's a dark and despairing album, and "Wiseblood" is the *only* one of the nine songs about original sin on this recording that offers even a "ripple" of hope. Of her novel's protagonist, O'Connor writes, "Haze is saved by virtue of having wise blood; it's too wise for him ultimately to deny Christ." Enoch Emery's "wise blood," so the novel demonstrates and critical readers surmise, is not as wise, and thus it betrays him. What or whose wise blood/Wiseblood is pumping in songs on this album is left for the listener to imagine.

Coda: Converging

One of the founding members of King Swamp and cowriter of its "Wiseblood" song, bassist David Allen, was an original member of Gang of Four. Allen's apparent interest in O'Connor has led him to write lyrics for a number of songs that reference her works. Before forming King Swamp in 1988, Allen joined the "intellectual dance band" Shriekback and cowrote a song that quotes Flannery O'Connor and borrows one of her story titles based on a cosmic concept, "Everything That Rises (Must Converge)." In this anthemic song with a jungle beat, sung by male voices, the phrase appears to relate both to elements of the concrete world and to a further emotional and physical connection with a woman. The mantra-like refrain in the stream-of-consciousness lyrics repeats,

Everything that rises must converge
She says one day soon
You and I will merge
Everything that rises must converge

The phrase "Everything that rises must converge" is taken from the writings of the controversial French Jesuit anthropologist and mystic Pierre Teilhard de Chardin. O'Connor's deep interest in Teilhard's thought and eschatological theology is evidenced in comments she makes throughout her collected letters. His notion of the ultimate converging of biological, social, and spiritual forces to what he called "Omega Point" appealed to O'Connor's visionary sensibilities. "Teilhard believes the Church fulfills a continuing evolutionary purpose that will be completed at the end of time in Christ," she writes approvingly. Her own comprehension of the phenomenological world was greatly influenced by his thought. O'Connor writes in 1962 to a correspondent, "I have got, over the years, a sense of the immense sweep of creation, of the evolutionary process in everything, of how incomprehensible God must necessarily be to be the God of heaven and earth." Despite the Vatican's condemning Teilhard's work for "serious errors, as to offend Catholic doctrine" in a monitum issued 30 June 1962, O'Connor continued to recommend to several correspondents that they read his works. Teilhard's theo-evolutionary thought in his masterwork *The Phenomenon of Man*, translated into English in 1959, both informs and arcs across her posthumous second collection of short stories, *Everything That Rises Must Converge* (1965).

Thee Mighty Caesars: *Wise Blood*

Yet another *Wise Blood* album was produced in the mid- to late 1980s by Thee Mighty Caesars, three working-class lads from Chatham, England. The group was instrumental in reviving the 1970s-style punk music of the Clash and the Ramones in a district in southeast England known as the Medway. By the time their *Wise Blood* album was produced, true punk was a distant memory as a new wave of more complex and studio-produced alternative music entered the mainstream. The website of their record company, Damaged Goods, defines the music of Thee Mighty Caesars as "primitive garage punk," a fusion of R & B chord structures played thrashingly with added lead guitar colorings that sound like jangling hooks lifted from California surfer songs. The band's lyrics are repetitive but sensible, offering misogynistic reflections on love and mildly angry and angsty confessional outbursts. Typical of punk, most of the songs clock in at around two minutes. And in keeping with the musically unsophisticated, anticommercial ideals of punk, the liner notes to the *Wise Blood* CD boast that the band took under two days and spent under £300 to record the album's twelve songs. It shows.

How O'Connor's novel came to be known to Thee Mighty Caesars is difficult to trace. At the height of the band's brief recording career, 1985 to 1989, the irrepressible Nick Cave was writing his *Wise Blood*–influenced novel and, according to reports, extolling O'Connor to anyone who would listen. JG Thirlwell's Wiseblood persona was also alive and unwell in the British alternative music subculture. The Caesars' founder and primary songwriter, Billy Childish, had little formal education but read widely in Beat poetry in his twenties and cites Dostoevsky as an influence. In his post-punk career, Childish has published more than twenty books of fiction, poetry, and memoir, produced several experimental films, and become a fixture in the British visual art scene. In his formative years, he obviously encountered O'Connor's *Wise Blood* somewhere along the way. Songwriter fans of O'Connor's story art and spiritual vision, it is important to observe, have passed along their enthusiasm, as previous chapters have noted is true for Bruce Springsteen, Lucinda Williams, Sufjan Stevens, and Nick Cave. Perhaps these factors explain in part how *Wise Blood* came to influence a late punk song titled "The Wise Blood."

Connections between the content of Thee Mighty Caesars' song and details of O'Connor's novel are tenuous and distorted at best, yet the lyrics bear some evidence of the novel's influence. However, the argument for misreadings of the novel by artists on the alternative, extreme edges of popular music here finds its apotheosis, beginning with the added definite article in the song title. "The Wise Blood" appears to be voiced by Hazel Motes and directed toward someone addressed as "child." While *child* has currency in rhythm and blues lyrics in reference to an unnamed auditor of indeterminate age, interestingly, this is the word O'Connor uses most frequently throughout the first half of her novel to identify Sabbath Lily, the fifteen-year-old daughter of charlatan preacher Asa Hawks. The premise of the story in Thee Mighty Caesars' song is that Sabbath, or someone like her, has claimed to have "the wise blood" but shows no sign that she does. This detail in the song is at variance with details in the novel, in which Sabbath is more focused on responding to her hormones than to any mysterious religious impulses determined by her blood. O'Connor's character does not claim to have *wise blood* (nor, for that matter, does Hazel Motes). Nonetheless, the song connects most closely with details in O'Connor's novel in its second verse:

> You say you've got the wise blood
> Nothing's hidden from view
> But your eyes are like mud
> An old man's using you

O'Connor's Sabbath Lily is indeed being used, knowingly, by an "old man," her father, in his con scheme as a poor, blind street preacher. As Motes discovers, and Sabbath eventually elaborates, Asa Hawks is "just a crook . . . and when he gets tired of that he begs on the street."

> When your world is over
> Finally you'll be through
> Well then you'll realize, blood
> What I gave to you

In the novel, Haze gives nothing to Sabbath other than an alternative living arrangement after her father has run off; she gives him plenty, night after night, as O'Connor indicates in the sexually suggestive scenes that end chapters 10 and 11. But like the narrator in this progressive punk song who repeats to the unnamed female auditor, "I'm sick and tired of you, child," Haze tries repeatedly to get rid of the girl. Sabbath soon leaves after Haze blinds himself, but eventually returns like a "harpy" to pester and scream at him. An unhappy fate awaits the girl in the song, or so says the narrator: "When your world is over / Finally you'll be through." Likewise, O'Connor and Haze are through with Sabbath when Haze's landlady calls "the Welfare people" and has this female minor sent to a detention home.

In the short author's note reluctantly written as a preface to the reissue of *Wise Blood* ten years after its initial publication, O'Connor marvels and is grateful that the novel "is still alive." Given the novel's poor sales in her lifetime and the often unfavorable and sometimes dreadful critical reviews, she had considered it, and her Hazel Motes character in particular, more or less "a failure." That her novel has inspired contemporary lyricists in the extreme musical genres of punk and heavy metal, in which nihilistic expressions and anti-Christian sentiments abound, indicates the surprising staying power and the reach of her art and vision—however much she continues to be misread. But while she was happy to have the cash for permissions payments, O'Connor had little good to say about the commercialization of her work. She was appalled by the adaptation for television of her story "The Life You Save May Be Your Own" and mildly aghast at the sensational covers used to market dime-store editions of her first novel and first collection of short stories. That her *Wise Blood* story could inform the lewd, nihilistic content of a million-selling heavy metal single or a post-punk dance tune would likely have disturbed O'Connor. And given the chance to listen to the high-wattage songs her novel has inspired, probably she would have been grateful for that professed affliction of a tin ear.

Chapter 9

EVERYTHING THAT RISES

If the songwriter is a southerner, tells stories in song with a gothic edge, perhaps has a song about a violent murder or a hillbilly moonshiner, or one that describes a scene of Bible Belt fanaticism, then a music critic somewhere will make a comparison with Flannery O'Connor. In many cases the common ground is "only southernness," as R.E.M.'s bassist Mike Mills has remarked somewhat disingenuously about the connections between O'Connor's art and vision and the song catalog and concerns of the Athens, Georgia-based pioneers of indie rock. Pop music journalists are wont to drop O'Connor's name in an album review or band biography in a way that suggests influence where none is directly evident or acknowledged.

Elements found in O'Connor's stories do appear in popular song lyrics by major artists. But without direct reference to distinctive plot details or a quoted key phrase or image lifted from her fictions, such as Bono's quoting her title terms "enduring chill" in "One Tree Hill," influence is hard to prove. Critics have suggested an allusion to O'Connor's Hazel Motes in Bob Dylan's "High Water (For Charlie Patton)," which includes the lines, "I'm preachin' the word of God / I'm puttin' out your eyes." But Dylan is characteristically silent about any possible influence. And to be precise, Hazel Motes does not go about puttin' out anyone's eyes but his own. Patty Griffin recorded a song on *American Kid* (2013) in which the southern-born narrator asks to have his body shipped out by train rather than be buried in Florida ("Don't Let Me Die in Florida"). This detail in the song narrative bears some similarity to old T. C. Tanner's request in O'Connor's story "Judgement Day": captive by infirmity in his daughter's apartment in New York City, Tanner, a virulent southern redneck, insists that when he dies his body is to be crated and sent by train back to his hometown in Georgia. But if Griffin, who describes herself as "a lapsed Catholic," is familiar with O'Connor's short fiction and has been inspired by it, she has not revealed it in published interviews or album liner notes.

The short commentaries that follow, arranged alphabetically by performer/artist, discuss individual contemporary songs that directly reference O'Connor or her fictions, along with artists who acknowledge O'Connor's shaping influence on particular songs or to some small degree on their artistic sensibilities. O'Connor claimed she had no ear for music, but many songwriters have ears to hear what she had to say in her remarkable stories and novels and in her *wisdom* writings—her published essays and letters. Her prophetic voice continues to resonate in popular songs sixty years after her death.

Frank Brannon: "Flannery's Waltz"

Frank Brannon's musical tribute to his "famous cousin" waltzes along in country gospel style with lyrics that offer a prosaic biography of O'Connor. Brannon's voice and musical style on this recording recall the songs of the late Guy Clark. In notes on CD Baby, where—prior to closing its online store in 2020—tracks from Brannon's albums *Dance on the Wind* (2014) and *For the Love of It All* (2017) were available for download, he recounted reading O'Connor's stories in high school and becoming interested in "what made her tick." A listener unfamiliar with O'Connor's life and art will find a helpful précis in "Flannery's Waltz," track 3 on *Dance on the Wind*. The lyrics relate that she was "a writer from Georgia / She lived near [the] town of Milledgeville," that "Her family farm was named Andalusia," and that "She wrote her stories in a little front bedroom." After that brief biographical opening, the song notes O'Connor's concerns as a writer—"She wrote to understand the mystery of God's plan"—and, in the lyrics' standout line, her often violent fictional methods of doing so—"She delivered God's grace at the end of ropes, rivers, and guns."

Brannon shares his cousin Flannery's sense that religiously focused art is divinely inspired. His own works, he claims in notes to the album, "come from a spiritual place" and are a "gift from God." This is the theme of the concluding tenth song on *Dance on the Wind*, "When Heaven Speaks," whose songwriter narrator pleads at the last, "Please dear God just have those angels keep sending [songs] down." Whether deliberately or not, Brannon's sentiment here echoes O'Connor's strained confession in a letter to a Catholic sister a year before her death: "I appreciate and need your prayers. I've been writing eighteen years and I've reached the point where I can't do again what I know I do well, and the larger things that I need to do now, I doubt my capacity for doing." In her correspondence she would occasionally ask Catholic friends to pray that she would be able to write what she was meant to say and appears to have been aware when they did so.

While the gospel message that arcs through Brannon's collected songs is gentler, more heartfelt, and more transparent than it appears in O'Connor's story art, like her, Brannon looks at life "from the standpoint of Christian orthodoxy." His themes in songs on *Dance on the Wind* indicate that he would echo her credo "For me the meaning of life is centered in our redemption by Christ and what I see in the world I see in its relation to that."

John Campbell: *Howlin Mercy*

Songwriter and blues guitarist John Campbell died young and at the height of his powers, as is said of Flannery O'Connor. Hailed as the premier contemporary Delta bluesman following the death in 1990 of Stevie Ray Vaughan, Campbell suffered a heart attack in his sleep and died at age forty-one in 1993, shortly after the release of his third studio album, *Howlin Mercy*. Campbell's songs explore themes of death, fragile love, and black magic. One commentator describes his music as "full of mystery, pathos, and dark energy, and plenty of rock & roll strut 'n' growl." Campbell plays the "spooky side of the blues" and his electric slide guitar work is highly expressive and often frenetic. His song "Wiseblood," track 9 on *Howlin Mercy*, is addressed to O'Connor's character Hazel Motes and draws considerable lyrical content from O'Connor's first novel.

"You blasphemed in the church of no religion / You told a great big lie," sings Campbell as the song opens. Indeed, O'Connor's Haze preaches to a gathering outside a movie theater that "The only way to the truth is through blasphemy." And he repeatedly denies the central tenet of the Christian faith, declaring that "Jesus was a liar" and even that "Jesus don't exist." Haze intends to found a new religion, the Church without Christ, a "church that the blood of Jesus don't foul with redemption." Campbell's song summarizes Haze's doctrines, "Ain't no salvation / Ain't nobody bein' saved," and refers directly to the text of one of the sermons he delivers from the hood of his car: "Well the blind still can't see / And the dumb still can't talk / The lame are still crippled / And they can't walk."

Campbell's reading of O'Connor's blaspheming preacher supports the author's own understanding of what "wise blood" means for Haze. In a letter to novelist John Hawkes, O'Connor declares, "Haze is saved by virtue of having wise blood; it's too wise for him ultimately to deny Christ." Campbell's song concludes on a similar note: "Now you've got wiseblood / You can't turn away / You can't wash it off / Wiseblood's there to stay." The lyrics to this Delta blues song offer a kind of supporting critical commentary on O'Connor's themes and central character in *Wise Blood* and underscore the meaning of her sanguinary symbol.

Samantha Crain: "The River"

Daughter of a southern Baptist evangelist (and powerlifter!) who traveled his circuit with a twelve-string guitar, Samantha Crain grew up in a small town near Shawnee, Oklahoma, and has a strong Choctaw heritage. Crain studied English literature at Oklahoma Baptist University where she took an interest in the southern gothic works of Flannery O'Connor, Eudora Welty, and William Faulkner—literary influences that seeped into her writing and influenced the stories and images in her songs. A semester-long songwriting seminar transformed her and gave Crain her calling as a singer-songwriter. Over the course of her career so far, she has won three Native American Music Awards (Nammys) and been honored with an Indigenous Music Award for the Best Rock Album in 2019. Her sizable suite of recordings to date—eight studio albums and two EPs—and her energetic stage performances have been praised in mainstream popular music media, including *Rolling Stone*, *SPIN*, *Mojo*, *No Depression*, *NME*, and *Uncut*. Samantha Crain has toured extensively in the US and internationally with headliners Brandi Carlile, the Avett Brothers, First Aid Kit, and others.

Crain's first collection of songs, a five-track EP titled *The Confiscation*, was recorded when she was nineteen and released on independent label Ramseur Records in 2008. It is subtitled "A Musical Novella," and its somewhat abstract, narrative-style songs Crain describes as being "about different people's stories of loss." Track 1 is titled "The River," and she remarks in an interview that the song "was written in direct response to Flannery O'Connor's story of the same name."

In a YouTube video, Crain introduces "The River" from the stage as being "about a preacher who drowns a man he's baptizing." This bouncy folk murder ballad tells the gothic story of a man who preys on young girls and then drowns them in a river. A preacher tracks him down, and after hearing the murderer's guilty confession and desire to repent of his crimes, tells the man he must be baptized in order to purge his sins. The preacher then takes justice into his own hands and drowns him in a river. Here is the song's last verse as it appears in lyrics that, incidentally, are printed on the CD's label:

> "Well my son you must be baptized
> If you want to see the Christ."
> The preacher holds him down when his feet won't touch the ground
> And he waits for judgement to come

While Crain's song title and the dramatic occasion that ends the song bear similarities with the river baptism of young Harry/Bevel Ashfield and his eventual self-drowning in O'Connor's like-titled short story, more so the scene invokes the converged baptism and drowning of the mentally disabled boy Bishop, a central event near the end of O'Connor's second novel, *The Violent Bear It Away*. Crain remarks to an interviewer that before she started writing songs, she wrote short stories. Her O'Connor-inspired narrative song "The River" is also based on one of her own stories and presents a gothic tale well told and well sung.

Annie Crane: *Jump with a Child's Heart*

Annie Crane is a classically trained musician and songwriter from Rochester, New York, with a sensibility and sound that would be right at home in Chattanooga, Tennessee. Her website states that she has toured extensively, "from Copenhagen to Kentucky and from Berlin to Albany," played at the "essential" clubs in New York and once shared a Nashville stage with Emmylou Harris, one of her musical idols. Crane released two collections of songs, *Through the Farmlands & the Cities* (2009) and *Jump with a Child's Heart* (2011) before transitioning from a music career to raise a family. "Ghost Body," track 7 in the collection of nine songs on *Jump with a Child's Heart*, is described on Crane's website as a "Flannery O'Connor-influenced literary piece; dark and painfully truthful." The song bears striking parallels with one of O'Connor's lesser-known and grimmer stories, "A Late Encounter with the Enemy."

Though brief, "Ghost Body" is a complex, disturbing, and brilliantly crafted narrative song that in a mere eleven lines offers three points of view on the life and death of Jim, an old man who was once a mail carrier. When he does not respond to his wife's morning call, she discovers him dead "in their once warm bed" and in that moment addresses him in a revealing and damning eulogy:

> Dear Jim, you're dead.
> I should've seen it coming. Your soul left you long ago.
> It's been a long time since your words kept me warm.
> Instead, they've only come with scorn.
> Dear Lord, forgive me, but I'm glad he's dead.

In O'Connor's "A Late Encounter with the Enemy," we witness through her stream-of-consciousness narrative the conscious descent into death and damnation of irascible Civil War veteran General Tennessee Flintrock Sash. Though "dead," Crane's character Jim similarly abides in some netherworld state in which he can hear his wife's words as his soul is departing: "As he heard her words, he felt his ghost body move downwards." General Sash also hears "words . . . coming at him like musket fire," and O'Connor describes him as experiencing sensations as his bodily life is receding into death: "He *felt* his body riddled in a hundred places with sharp stabs of pain"; "he *saw* his wife's narrow face looking at him critically" (emphasis added).

O'Connor's General Sash has in his life and words damned "every goddam thing to hell" and appears to recognize the final resting place of his falsehood-riddled soul, the "black procession" that "all his days" he has been party to. In his death throes, his hand clenches the blade of a ceremonial sword across his lap "until the blade touched bone." Given O'Connor's spiritual economy, the phrase is an obvious allusion to a metaphor in Hebrews 4:12: "For the word of God is quick, and powerful, and sharper than any two-edged sword, piercing even to the dividing asunder of soul and spirit, and of the joints and marrow, and is a discerner of the thoughts and intents of the heart" [KJV]. The General's heart has been discerned in O'Connor's story; he has been judged and departs his life into a place of damnation—of his own choosing, so she would have the reader understand. This story appears to be a dramatization of one of O'Connor's axioms: "[H]ell is what God's love becomes to those who reject it."

Crane's story of the soulless postman is likewise a tale of damnation. Like O'Connor's General Sash, Jim both feels and sees his "ghost body" make its journey into the afterlife. In the last line of the song, "With a fright, he noticed not a light, but his eternal night." The parallels in Crane's song lyrics with O'Connor's plot and character and language in "A Late Encounter with the Enemy" are strikingly evident.

Colin Cutler: *Peacock Feathers*

An up-and-coming Americana musician, Colin Cutler has the singular distinction of writing and producing, with the help of a Kickstarter campaign, a full album of songs based on O'Connor's short stories. *Tarwater* was released in November 2023, after this book had gone to final edit. Its sampler and forerunner, *Peacock Feathers* (2018), is an EP that features songs based on four of O'Connor's stories, each with a narrator appropriated from one of the central characters in each story.

Image courtesy of Colin Cutler, *Peacock Feathers* cover art by Kelley Wills of Brain Flower Designs+.

Cutler comes to O'Connor from a literary background—he teaches college English when he is not on tour—with southern roots and old-time Pentecostal religion informing his artistic sensibilities. He is also an Iraq War veteran. He describes O'Connor's fictions as "human stories, with sparks of the divine burning through." A skilled musician and songwriter, he has an eclectic style that ranges across the spectrum of Americana, from honky-tonk country to folk and gospel, acoustic blues, and front-porch banjo picking. An NPR commentator has remarked that Cutler's songs "do justice to the great American traditions of both wry lyricism and fiery sermons."

The standout track on the *Peacock Feathers* EP is "Mamma, Don't Know Where Heaven Is," based on O'Connor's long story "The Lame Shall Enter First." This 1950s country-style duet featuring Stacey Rinaldi is back picked on acoustic guitar with added Telecaster stylings and an underlying fiddle line running through. Its rolling rhythm carries the song along much the way O'Connor's story progresses to its unsurprising shocking conclusion. The song's narrator is ten-year-old Norton Sheppard, who is grieving his recently deceased mother, and his words are addressed to her. In O'Connor's story, Norton's insufferable father espouses strong humanist doctrines and denies that Norton's dead mother has any existence in an afterlife. "Your mother isn't anywhere . . . She just isn't," he tells his distraught and emotionally neglected child. The juvenile delinquent Rufus Johnson, one of O'Connor's rough-cut reluctant prophet figures, whom Sheppard, a social worker, is attempting to "save" from his own worst tendencies, informs Norton that "The Bible has give the evidence" that there is indeed a heaven and a hell, and that his mother is in one place or the other. He asks Norton, "Did she believe in Jesus?" Over the protestations of his father, Norton replies, "She did all the time."

"She's saved," Johnson said.

The child still looked puzzled. "Where?" he said. "Where is she at?"

"On high," Johnson said.

"Where's that?" Norton gasped.

"It's in the sky somewhere," Johnson said, "but you got to be dead to get there."

And so, following on Johnson's catechism, O'Connor's story moves toward its inevitable tragically redemptive end in Norton's suicide by hanging, as Cutler's opening chorus anticipates:

Momma, I don't know where heaven is,
But I hear that's where you've gone.
Momma, I don't know where heaven is, Oh Lord,
But I'll be there with you before too long.

As does Sufjan Stevens, Cutler appropriates O'Connor's familiar character The Misfit as narrator for a song based on her well-known short story "A Good Man Is Hard to Find." Only, he reverses the axiomatic truth of O'Connor's borrowed title with a counter claim, "But a bad man's easy." Cutler's The Misfit narrator is anguished and introspective as is O'Connor's The Misfit. But details in his song "Bad Man's Easy" diverge from the story somewhat. O'Connor's character remarks that his daddy said he was "a different breed of dog" and would "be into everything." Cutler adds dialogue in which The Misfit refers to his mama as well, who told him, "there's two kinds of people: / You're going to heaven, or you're going to hell." This cuts to the quick with O'Connor's spiritually distraught escaped killer, who is desperate to know for certain whether or not the Christian salvation story is true—whether Jesus really "raised the dead": "I wasn't there so I can't say he didn't," The Misfit exclaims in the affirmative. After he shoots the grandmother, Cutler's The Misfit narrator does not come to clarity about his condition as some commentators on O'Connor's story suggest. What his narrator has encountered in the grandmother's touch "Might be the Devil, might be God, might be both / Might be grace, might be the law, I don't know," he exclaims in the song's concluding verse.

A song that draws on O'Connor's "The Enduring Chill" is somewhat lamely given the paraphrastic title "The Cold That's Forever"; her story title based on a slogan for a safe driving program in the 1960s, "The Life You Save May Be Your Own," becomes "Save Your Life and Drive" for the longest song on the sixteen-minute recording, which makes extensive reference by way of paraphrase to details in O'Connor's story.

The *Tarwater* album features rerecordings of some of the *Peacock Feathers* songs and further songs based on O'Connor's stories: "The River," "A Temple of the Holy Ghost," and three tracks that treat arguably O'Connor's finest story, "Parker's Back," including an outstanding acoustic blues number titled "Parker's Reprise."

There are details in Cutler's lyrics that are at variance with or that embellish the content in the selected stories behind his songs. O'Connor's Norton, for example, does not have a deceased baby sister "up in heaven, too," nor does her Asbury Fox, who "had never been a sniveler after the ineffable," have any consciousness that he is "Like the prodigal son," as Cutler's lyrics state. None of the dialogue in any of the *Peacock Feathers* songs is directly extracted from O'Connor's texts, as other songwriters in this study have done. Though there are a few phrases that closely echo from the stories, such as Asbury's chorus lines "What's wrong with me / It is far beyond you," mostly Cutler engages in a form of liberal paraphrase of narrative details and dialogue. And there is something refreshing in this artistic license that adds inventive glosses to O'Connor's tales, as in the modified retort of the hitchhiking boy in the lyrics to "Save Your Life and Drive," who responds to Mr. Shiftlet's homely comment on his mother, "My ma's the meanest bitch that ever cut a switch." Cutler makes O'Connor's stories somewhat his own, interprets them in his lyrics, and gives new focus to the characters that speak from her fictions into his songs.

Faggot: *A Good Man Is Hard to Find*

A badass British synth punk duo named Faggot recorded a song titled "Flannery O'Connor" on a digital album with eight tracks that borrows its title from O'Connor's first collection of short fiction, *A Good Man Is Hard to Find*. In this narrative song about a breakup, the partner is packing his books in a crate while, to a driving distorted guitar and drumbeat, the narrator-singer laments the dissolution of their relationship with punning references to O'Connor's story titles:

> when the heat was there between us
> well, I thought you were the comfort of my home
> but now the chill endures and though I've tried
> it seems the life I saved was not my own

In the fourth of five verses, the narrator retrieves books by O'Connor from the packing crate and declares to the departing partner, "if you want to get your Flannery O'Connor back / you'll have to stay in touch." As this fast-paced (two minutes, twenty-three seconds) punk ballad concludes, the narrator admits to being "in a state" after reading O'Connor's works concurrent with the revelation that his lover is leaving. The song ends with the narrator's consoling thought, "It could be worse; you could be Flannery O'Connor / and be dead at 39."

Father John Misty: "Pure Comedy"

Folk-rock performer Joshua Tillman (sometimes just J. Tillman) has a near cult-like following for his musical alter ego, a profane, blaspheming preacher-like persona named Father John Misty. Tillman/Misty has informed interviewers that he is "a voracious reader of Flannery O'Connor's work," and his bio on Spotify notes that O'Connor's writings are one of the "key influences" on his artistic sensibilities. He disclaims, however, that his songwriting has been directly influenced by her. Rather, like Nick Cave and JG Thirlwell, Tillman could have stepped out of the pages of one of O'Connor's fictions. A fan of O'Connor's *Wise Blood*, he has adopted a Hazel Motes–like stage persona. Like Haze, the quasi-biblical, atmospherically named performer espouses a blasphemous anti-Gospel, and, similarly, Father John Misty usually performs wearing a dark blue suit—or blue suit jacket—not the "glaring blue" suit worn by O'Connor's character, but a garment much like the dark, dark blue suit worn by Brad Dourif's Hazel Motes in John Huston's film adaptation of the novel.

Tillman/Misty grew up in a strict evangelical Christian household in Maryland and was raised in a Baptist church in the 1990s era of pop-inflected contemporary Christian worship music, which he used to perform with members of his family. After losing his religion in his late teens, he began to define himself by his "fierce opposition to God." In a 2017 interview article in the *Los Angeles Times*, Tillman/Misty reveals that reading O'Connor's novel *Wise Blood* about an obsessed preacher's grandson who rails against the Christian religion "opened his eyes to what was happening to him." Perched on his rat-colored Essex outside the Odeon Theater, Hazel Motes harangues theatergoers with his nihilistic message that there is no such thing as sin and therefore no need for redemption by Christ in the modern world. Rather, he preaches a liberating gospel of self-redemption and declares, "In yourself right now is all the place you've got." In his blasphemous magnum opus "Pure Comedy," as if channeling Haze, the Christ-haunted Father John Misty decries as ridiculous a belief in "some all-powerful being" who "[e]ndowed this horror show with meaning." In the song's concluding line, he tells any listeners longing for transcendence, "I hate to say it, but each other's all we got."

Headphones: "Wise Blood"

Reviewers of indie songwriter David Bazan's various projects frequently invoke Flannery O'Connor, both to draw comparisons between their similar ironic and satiric artistic responses to religious hypocrisy in contemporary America, and to align the eventually apostate Bazan with O'Connor's notion of being Christ-haunted. As the front man and creative force behind the immensely popular indie band Pedro the Lion, Bazan, raised an evangelical Christian, enjoyed crossover success in both the mainstream and contemporary religious music business for a ten-year run, beginning in the late 1990s in the burgeoning Seattle music scene, until in 2005, as he puts it, he "stopped being a Christian."

Like Nick Cave, David Bazan has since carried on a public conversation in his song art about his disagreements with Christian doctrine and disdain for institutionalized religion, both as a solo artist under his own name playing largely house concerts and, since 2017, with the revived Pedro the Lion persona (sometimes with a band), playing what one critic labels his brand of "Christ-haunted indie rock." While Bazan acknowledges that, like O'Connor, his sensibilities and concerns as an artist have been "formed by the Church," he has moved from being a communicant to a curious yet deeply doubtful observer. Ironically, as a Christian expatriate, as one reviewer observes, "Bazan seems to have ended up talking about God a lot more since he stopped believing in Him." It may be that fans of Bazan's post-Christian self and songs will infer something similar to the charlatan street preacher Asa Hawks in *Wise Blood*, who remarks of the blaspheming Hazel Motes, "I can hear the urge for Jesus in his voice."

Following the disbanding of Pedro the Lion, Bazan and drummer Tim Walsh formed a duo named Headphones and released a single eponymous album in 2005 on Suicide Squeeze Records. Its ten tracks of synthesizer-based, narrative-driven "mope-rock balladry" feature Bazan's "emo-tinged vocals," as a reviewer in *Pitchfork* describes the duo's sound. Track 9, "Wise Blood," is a minimalist composition both musically and lyrically, with strong rock cymbal and bass drum underlay to a few distorted sustained notes on a Moog, with Bazan's hollowed-out vocals well back in the mix. Half of the lyrics derive from a clip of dialogue found in the opening scenes of O'Connor's *Wise Blood*. Her protagonist Hazel Motes is en route via train to the fictional big city of Taulkinham, as he explains to the talkative Mrs. Wally Bee Hitchcock, to "do some things I never have done before." In the dining car, he sits in forced company with three young women "dressed like parrots," one of whom blows smoke in his face and observes him bemusedly. Not one for casual conversation, and already rehearsing his reprobate street preacher persona, Haze remarks to her face, "If you've been redeemed . . . I wouldn't want to be." Headphones's song ends with threefold repetition of a variation of this quotation from the novel: "If you think you've been redeemed / Then I wouldn't want to be." The song's closing refrain Bazan fittingly sings in falsetto.

Simon Joyner: *Beautiful Losers*

Jagjaguwar recording artist Simon Joyner has written a song ostensibly in tribute to O'Connor which appears on a compilation disc that cribs its title phrase from the late Canadian poet and songwriter Leonard Cohen, *Beautiful Losers: Singles and Compilation Tracks 1994–1999*. Joyner's acoustic folk song "Flannery O'Connor" is track 18 on an offering of twenty-one ragged low-fi recordings of modest musical merit. The lyrics in this song randomly reference several deaths, among them those of actor Yul Brynner, politician (and now Broadway legend) Alexander Hamilton, the best friend of the narrator's father, and someone named Phil who has died by suicide. But nowhere in this piece is there any direct or even indirect reference to O'Connor's person or story art that would support the song's title. Perhaps O'Connor is somehow invoked by/for the songwriter in his heartfelt concern "For the faithful and the blind."

Killdozer: "Lupus"

A trio from Madison, Wisconsin, Killdozer made its nasty, comic brand of noise rock / posthardcore music from 1983 until the band's last waltz on their Fuck You, We Quit! tour in 1996. Their sound has been compared to the Birthday Party, Nick Cave's first foray into primal rock as musical catharsis. A blogger writes that Killdozer's music is for "lovers of loudness" and remarks on the "moronically offensive lyrics" on the nine albums the band released. Track 3, "Lupus," on *Twelve Point Buck* (1989) is about Flannery O'Connor. Like other lyrics on the album, such as those of a song that summarizes the plots of several 1970s disaster movies, the narrative in "Lupus" is written in the style of a grade-school book report. "Lupus took the life of Flannery O'Connor / She wrote many books before death came upon her," the song begins and ends, with lines delivered in the trademark growly vocals of bassist and lead singer Michael Gerald. The medical information is correct, but O'Connor's literary output is overstated. The middle verses of the song summarize plot details from O'Connor's story "Judgement Day," with some editorializing on the encounter in his daughter's New York apartment building between Tanner and the Black actor, said to resemble the late Sidney Poitier.

Killdozer's hard-rock biographical commentary on O'Connor's struggle with lupus is exceptional not only for its unusual mix of grating heavy metal sound and guttural vocals with melodic horn parts tootling on top, but for its attention to the life of the author as well as to one of her works. Why O'Connor's death resulting from her long battle with lupus was chosen as a topic is curious given other subjects addressed on the album, which include a song about sex touring in Amsterdam and lyrics that extol one of William Blake's contrarian *Proverbs of Hell*: "The road of excess leads to the palace of wisdom." What is certain is that the song does not eulogize O'Connor but appears to express perverse satisfaction in emphasizing her death from a debilitating disease.

The Legendary Shack Shakers: *Tent Show Trilogy*

Colonel J. D. Wilkes, frenetic front man for the Nashville-based band the Legendary Shack Shakers, has been described as "a true Southern Renaissance man": songwriter, folklorist, visual artist/cartoonist, filmmaker, cultural historian, novelist, Wilkes's creative energy and vision has taken many forms. Raised in Paducah, Kentucky, Wilkes describes himself as "a God-fearing Southern boy," and with the Shack Shakers he has to date written and produced nine studio albums, including a trilogy with songs satirizing southern Bible Belt religion and paying homage to the gothic storytelling identified with the region: *Believe* (2004), *Pandelerium* (2006), and *Swampblood* (2007)—collectively the *Tent Show Trilogy*. In his song art, Wilkes comments that he pays homage to Flannery O'Connor, both musically and lyrically, and in an animated music video, graphically acknowledges her as among his major artistic influences.

The Legendary Shack Shakers' brand of rockabilly music is generally labeled southern gothic—a blend of traditional hillbilly music with, in their case, a mash-up of punk-paced rock and polka and fast-step barn dance melodies. The original group was formed in 1995 by Wilkes and three of his friends at Kentucky's Murray State University as a kind of stunt act. Imagine a band with a stage show and sound as if the Sex Pistols teamed up with a klezmer group and recruited a singer with vocal stylings like Tom Waits—a sound like what might result when Bad Religion meets old-time religion. Wilkes's stage antics have been compared to those of Iggy Pop, David Byrne, and Jerry Lee Lewis, and hearing and seeing his frenzied blues harmonica-playing is worth the price of admission. The band has opened for Robert Plant and Hank Williams III, and its fans include the late legendary guitarist Jeff Beck, horror novelist Stephen King, and actor/musician Billy Bob Thornton, who contributed to a cut on the band's 2015 album *The Southern Surreal*. Legendary Shack Shakers songs have been featured in several HBO series and a long-running TV commercial for the insurance giant Geico.

Unlike fellow southerner Jim White or the erudite Nick Cave—both also contemporary Renaissance men in their own right—Wilkes is not so much like a character in one of O'Connor's fictions as he is an artist who appears to be cut from some of the same cloth. Wilkes's first passion, like O'Connor's, was (and perhaps still is) cartooning, and like her, he has a gift for storytelling and considers the songs he writes to be miniature short stories. Moreover, he shares O'Connor's satiric method and focus—exposing the hypocrisies in southern religion and manners in his songs through what O'Connor called "the kind of distortion . . . that reveals, or should reveal." Wilkes reflects insightfully that the Shack Shakers have created a musical language that matches O'Connor's rhetoric in fiction. What he describes as "rickety, rustic sounds" on the band's recordings—using cowbells, the bones, and Wilkes's own haunting harmonica playing—he sees as the instrumental equivalents of O'Connor's often jarring fictional style. As Jewly Hight has commented, a kind of "musical violence—like the violence in O'Connor's stories" is intrinsic to the band's signature style and sound. Neither gratuitous nor intended to be cathartic—like the violence at a punk show—it is, as Wilkes explains,

Art by Zach Bellissimo.

intended to shock the listener/audience member into "read[ing] a little further into" their songs and performance art. In a PBS interview in 2018, Wilkes remarks on the "over-the-top dynamic" of the Shack Shakers' music and live performances, which he says is influenced not as one might expect by punk artists, but by what he calls "the southern surreal"—that is, "charismatic religion, Pentecostalism, vaudeville, sideshow, circuses, things like that." He ends his self-reflexive remarks by channeling O'Connor's own words: "Large, startling figures—that's what I'm trying to draw."

O'Connor's influence on Wilkes's artistic sensibilities is, moreover, graphically signaled in the official music video for Shack Shakers' vaudeville-styled "Sing a Worried Song," from their 2017 album *After You've Gone*. Drawn by Zach Bellissimo, this animated cartoon featurette presents a Betty Boop–like character named Posey found by the Devil taking selfies in a graveyard and summarily cast down to the netherworld through a hole in the ground. There she is eventually rescued by the ghost of Colonel JD (Wilkes). But before that, the entombed head of J. D. Wilkes, in photographic detail, is seen sprouting branches that create a tree of influences on which hang cartoon cameos of contributors to Wilkes's maniacal imagination, among them entertainers Cab Calloway and Buster Keaton, blues masters Dock Boggs and Junior Wells, and authors Flannery O'Connor, William Faulkner, and Edgar Allan Poe. O'Connor is singled out in the video as the only author whose name appears on a series of cartoon headstones pulled underground and translated into the multibranched tree that sprouts from the opened top of Colonel JD's head.

Swampblood

Like O'Connor's, Wilkes's brand of humor and cultural critique takes the form of folksy though biting satire. Track 8 on the *Swampblood* album, "Born Again Again" satirizes the superficial religiosity of southern baptistery, addressing the moral distance between Saturday night and Sunday morning, as the expression goes. The narrator of this honky-tonk, polka-beat song confesses to "Talkin' the walk but not walkin' the talk." He takes refuge in the belief that "Faith can cover up a sea of iniquity" and describes himself as "In and out of the world of sin and back in / Guess I'm a little noncommittal / Born again again." Like Wilkes in this song, O'Connor takes aim at all manner of religious hypocrisy in her story art and in particular that of born-again southerners, such as Ruby Turpin in "Revelation" or nominal believers like Mrs. McIntyre in "The Displaced Person," one of O'Connor's good Christian women who, in a frozen moment, becomes complicit in the murder of a Polish refugee working on her farm. O'Connor would no doubt be in bemused accord with Wilkes's metaphysical image in "Jumblyleg Man," of humankind as like the musical entertainer's jointed wooden figure dancing on the end of a stick. In Wilkes's song, "At the end of the stick is a big, black hand / The Devil is the master of the Jumblyleg Man." The darkly redemptive themes on *Swampblood* are played out in a gothic fictional world that like O'Connor's ethos is "territory held largely by the devil."

"Preachin' at Traffic," track 14 on this album, a talking-blues song recorded using a shotgun mic, is a lyrical pastiche with sexual overtones, a dash of rock 'n' roll rebellion, and some Pentecostal apocalyptic references, resolving with a fundamentalist southern preacher cliché, "And if it ain't King James, it ain't Bible, y'all." Included in the comical romp of the song's abstruse lyrics is the narrator's statement, "String a buncha bob-wire 'round my birthday suit / There's nothing indecent about the naked truth," surely a direct reference to Hazel Motes's act of extreme penance at the end of *Wise Blood*. After blinding himself with quick lime, Haze lines his shoes with "gravel and broken glass and pieces of small stone" in an effort "[t]o pay" for something undisclosed. His landlady eventually discovers him with "three strands of barbed wire, wrapped around his chest," an act of self-torture committed because Haze has judged himself "not clean." "You must believe in Jesus or you wouldn't do these foolish things," his landlady tells him, in a line that must surely be read as the author's interpretive gloss on Haze's own slipped crown of thorns. For O'Connor cognoscenti, there is perhaps a further nod to her here in the use of "bob-wire" in the printed lyrics in *Swampblood*'s cardboard CD case.

O'Connor, an admitted "very innocent speller" and with a thick southern accent when she spoke, remarks in a letter that she had always thought that *bob*-wire was the correct spelling!

A hypocritical southern preacher "with an Amplified Bible cranked up to 10" starts "cussin' in tongues" in the title phrase to a song on the first of the Tent Show Trilogy recordings, *Believe*. Like Onnie Jay Holy and Asa Hawks in Wilkes's favorite of O'Connor's works, *Wise Blood*, his character in this song is a charlatan given to "False propheteerin' off the hopes of the damned." He is kin to O'Connor's false prophets, whether religious or secular, like Sheppard in "The Lame Shall Enter First," and like them "He ain't *right!*"—a key expression in O'Connor's story that is also title and refrain to a song on *Swampblood*. The point of both songs is to warn the listener to "run on along" and to avoid religious and *ir*religious phonies, "Before the cock crows three times tonite." With full satiric force, J. D. Wilkes and the Legendary Shack Shakers have borrowed O'Connor's method of truth-telling for a postmodern, Christ-haunted audience, translating into their shocking southern sound and fury her artistic credo (at one time posted on the band's website): "To the hard of hearing you shout, and for the almost-blind you draw large and startling figures."

A Love Song for Bobby Long: Original Motion Picture Soundtrack

In the 2004 film *A Love Song for Bobby Long*, featuring John Travolta and Scarlett Johansson, works of southern literature, including a collection of O'Connor's short fiction, form a variety of subtexts. Johansson's character, Purslane Hominy Will, described on the cover of the DVD as "a jaded teenage loner," is seen at the opening of the film sitting in a bus station obsessively reading Carson McCullers's *The Heart Is a Lonely Hunter*—a beloved book of her recently deceased drug-addicted mother, Lorraine. Her mother's personal effects consist solely of a small suitcase filled with paperbacks of modern American literature. Later in the film, Purslane pursues an education, encouraged by a dissolute and disgraced former English professor, Bobby Long, played brilliantly by Travolta, and his drunken misfit teaching assistant, Lawson Pines, played by Gabriel Macht. Both are squatting in a house in New Orleans Pursy has unknowingly inherited. In a scene that lasts nearly three minutes, she is seen curled on a couch reading O'Connor's *Everything That Rises Must Converge* (its FS&G first edition cover clearly visible). A collection of stories about misfits roughed up by grace is here significantly referenced in a film featuring a collection of misfits likewise in the rough and tumble of the

struggle between flesh and spirit—"thankful for a God who has not given up on [them]," as Bobby Long confesses in the film's concluding minutes. As the titles roll, the movie's theme song plays, written and performed by Americana artist Grayson Capps. Though not the whole of it: the last track on the CD of the *Original Motion Picture Soundtrack*, released by Hyena Records in 2005, includes in its lyrical character sketch of Bobby Long a third verse omitted in the movie. The narrator-singer's love song sums up the Christ-haunted, Prufrockian Long in the opening two lines of its final verse: "He was a friend of my papa's, he used to drink and tell lies / Praise Flannery O'Connor, smoke cigarettes and philosophize."

The Moaners: *Dark Snack*

The Moaners are a female guitar and drum duo from Chapel Hill, North Carolina, whose minimalist nihilistic punk sound one reviewer labels "Southern trash rock." Their 2005 debut album *Dark Snack* treats the ears to distorted electric guitar over steady rock drumming, with an occasional second guitar part, harmonica riff, or percussive embellishment overdubbed. The solo vocals are not wholly unappealing. Two tracks reference the band's roots in southern culture. The simple bluesy harmonica-centered "Elizabeth Cotten's Song" on track 4, perhaps the best piece on the recording, pays homage to an American folk music icon. It is followed by the song "Flannery Said," which slightly misquotes—and in effect misattributes—a standout bit of dialogue from O'Connor's second novel, *The Violent Bear It Away*. The original quotation is an ironic response from "the stranger," a diabolical presence who speaks within the consciousness of the novel's protagonist—another of O'Connor's backwoods, reluctant prophet figures, young Tarwater. As he makes a half-hearted effort to bury his recently deceased and corpulent great-uncle "in a decent and Christian way," "the stranger" in his head remarks, "You can't be any poorer than dead." O'Connor thought the sentence resonant enough to use it as the title for a version of the first chapter from her novel-in-progress, published in *New World Writing* in 1955 and collected in *The Complete Stories*.

The Moaners' "Flannery Said" is a joyful punk anthem played with heavily distorted power chords. The nihilistic overtone of the retort by O'Connor's "the stranger" is employed to further the song's hedonistic ideology, in a fairly straightforward statement in its first verse:

"You can't get any poorer than dead"
Yeah, that's what Flannery said
Thank God I'm not that poor yet
So, come on honey, let's just go to bed

The CD cover image shows an electric guitar leaning against a snare drum, both engulfed in flames and smoke, like objects on a gothic sacrificial pyre. A photograph of a house destroyed by a hurricane, as seen through what appear to be rose-colored glasses, spreads across the inside of the bifold insert. Perhaps it is a warning to the listener not to crank up the stereo too loud.

Unexpectedly, *Dark Snack* concludes with a 1:40-minute instrumental titled "Chasing the Moon," featuring a rhythmically strummed reverberating electric guitar over top of primitive ethereal tones from a bowed saw. The Theremin-like quaverings form a faint hymn-like melody. Lead singer and guitarist Melissa Swingle has a cameo near the end of Jim White's film *Searching for the Wrong-Eyed Jesus* playing "Amazing Grace" on a bowed saw while perched on the cluttered trunk of a derelict car. In this film, as on the *Dark Snack* recording, the haunting sound is a reminder, as in O'Connor's stories and novels, that the spirit of old-time southern religion lies beneath it all.

Pierce Pettis: "Flannery's Georgia"

Pierce Pettis, an accomplished singer-songwriter and virtuosic guitar player, and a Catholic southerner, has commented in an interview, "I'm a Christian and a Catholic and there's no doubt that has impact on the way I think about everything." His remark echoes similar statements by O'Connor. Indeed, Pettis states in an interview with the *Mars Hill Review* that he is familiar with her writings, including her collected letters, and was a personal friend of the late scholar Bill Sessions, O'Connor's friend and correspondent. Pettis, now in his late sixties, has toured extensively as a solo act and as a double bill with his daughter Grace. Since 2013, he has performed with label-mate Kate Campbell and southern singer-songwriter Tom Kimmel as the New Agrarians. Pettis has to date released eleven studio albums since his first independent release in 1984, *Moments*, including three critically acclaimed recordings on the Windham Hill / High Street label, among them *Tinseltown* (1991), which features a track with a solo guitar instrumental titled "Flannery's Georgia." The album is produced by the late, faith-based musician Mark Heard, and the instrumental is in the style of Windham Hill's William Ackerman, acknowledged in the liner notes as overseeing the project. Track 5, "Flannery's Georgia" is a strongly themed, fingerpicked guitar piece in a minor key, with an abundance of pulled and hammered notes. Running two minutes and twenty-five seconds, this instrumental begins with a light progression of arpeggio-style jazz chords and moves to what sounds like a gentle, traditional folk melody, phrased as though unspoken lyrics were in mind. This melody repeats twice until at 1:25 the music changes key, repeats a variation on the melody, then features a sequence of harshly plucked chords before descending to a strongly picked reprise of the melodic theme phrase. Flannery's Georgia is all that.

R.E.M.: *Document*

In R.E.M.'s long run from its formation in 1980 to an amicable disbanding in 2011, the Athens, Georgia-based alternative rock innovators vied with U2 in some critics' ears and minds as the greatest pop band in the world. R.E.M. recorded fifteen studio albums, sold over eighty-five million records, and won three Grammys and numerous other awards. The band's post-punk-styled anthems "It's the End of the World as We Know It (And I Feel Fine)" (1987) and "Losing My Religion" (1990), and teen ballad "Everybody Hurts" (1992) are as iconic to 1980s and '90s pop music culture as the Beatles' hits were to the '60s. *Document* (1987), the band's fifth recording, gave them their first Top 10 radio hit, "The One I Love," and was the first of six albums to reach platinum status. Two songs on *Document* make both indirect and direct references to Flannery O'Connor's works.

R.E.M.'s artistic ethos, like O'Connor's, is the South, its traditions, its haunted history, its distinctive and often oddball cultural terrain. And like O'Connor's fiction, R.E.M.'s songs are peopled with southern eccentrics and exude a latter-day gothic southernness of both place and sensibility. Critics and band members themselves allude to O'Connor's art and vision when referring to R.E.M.'s musical fables about the South. Guitarist Peter Buck declared in an early interview that O'Connor was his favorite writer and referenced "A Good Man Is Hard to Find," noting to the Canadian interviewer for MuchMusic, "Everyone reads that [story] in high school in America." In that same interview, front man Michael Stipe refers to *Wise Blood* as a favorite book.

"King of Birds," *Document*'s penultimate track, echoes the title of O'Connor's biographical essay "The King of the Birds," the first item in the collection *Mystery and Manners* published in 1969, five years after O'Connor's untimely death. This essay, the only one O'Connor published in a commercial magazine, appeared in *Holiday* in September 1961 as "Living with a Peacock." (An editorial note in *Mystery and Manners* indicates that "The King of the Birds" was O'Connor's title choice.) In the essay, O'Connor muses on her fascination with the mysterious peacock and recounts stories of her steadily multiplying flock (once as many as forty) at Andalusia, the family farm outside Milledgeville, Georgia. O'Connor scholar Monica Miller, describing R.E.M.'s song as "a pensive reflection on the passage of time," observes that it "echoes similar themes" to O'Connor's essay, referencing its description of a spread peacock's tail as an "unfurled map of the universe."

With its marching beat and layered dulcimer overdubs "King of Birds" is musically a small song of the South. In what might be understood as an assertion of self-identity and artistic individuality, singer Michael Stipe declares with Shakespearean overtones, "I am the king of all I see / My kingdom for a voice." The singer wants "A *mean* idea to call my own" (emphasis added), claiming, "Standing on the shoulders of giants leaves me cold." Stipe's "foggy lyricism," as a reviewer in *The Atlantic* describes his writing, may leave the critical listener cold, but that "voice" desires to speak to something beyond the southern stereotypes the band was accused of appropriating and exploiting. Perhaps one of those "giants" the song refers to is O'Connor, whom Miller notes was "a significant influence on the band" in its formative years. O'Connor had her own ideas about the source and meaning of modern "meanness," a word germane to a theme in her most familiar short story, "A Good Man Is Hard to Find." "King of Birds" thus seems both to reference and then reject the influence of her art and vision on the postmodern "New South orientation" that became associated with R.E.M. Miller cites guitarist Peter Buck from a 1987 interview, the year *Document* was released: "When you compare our songs to writers like Flannery O'Connor... I'm flattered but don't quite make the connection. Flannery's characters are all struggling to reconcile their faith to a modern world where faith doesn't play any apparent part. In our case, I'd say none of us have got any faith anyway. I don't believe in God."

"Oddfellows Local 151" concludes the album, a song that Buck describes as being about some derelicts and alcoholics who lived next door to Michael Stipe in Athens, including, apparently, a character named Pee Wee. It is one of many songs in R.E.M.'s canon inspired by Stipe's interest in real-life southern outsiders and eccentrics, such as the tree-obsessed mystic character in "Wendell Gee" and the religious visionary and painter of sacred art, Howard Finster, referenced in "Maps and Legends." Craig Rosen's *R.E.M.: Inside Out: The Stories behind Every Song* promises to reveal "the mysteries and inspirations" behind every one of the band's songs, but says nothing about references to O'Connor in any R.E.M. lyrics. "Oddfellows" contains a reference to the title of O'Connor's fiction fragment "Why Do the Heathen Rage?" included in *The Complete Stories* and initially published in *Esquire* magazine in July 1963 as the opening sections of a third novel in progress.

The 378 manuscript pages of O'Connor's unfinished novel contain fictional elements that echo her stories "The Enduring Chill" and "Judgement Day," and a highly biographical projection of herself in Walter Tilman, a practically incompetent young man who spends his time reading and writing and avidly corresponding while his mother runs a dairy farm. The stalled novel also includes an atypical female character for O'Connor, a social activist involved in a racially integrated Christian commune—likely modeled on O'Connor's Milledgeville friend and correspondent Maryat Lee. O'Connor scholar Virginia Wray suggests that the author began the novel as a satire on 1950s–1960s liberalism and social activism and may have abandoned her disjointed manuscript as she came to perceive the gospel truths behind certain forms of social liberalism and the civil rights movement. As in all of O'Connor's fictions, the novel—should it have been completed—would have entailed revelatory violence, as indicated in the concluding sentence of the published fragment, and ultimately would have had something to do with Jesus—its last word.

R.E.M.'s "Oddfellows Local 151" perhaps both images the latter-day effects of that liberalism and underscores the failure of a culture of social activism to ameliorate entrenched conditions of exclusion and poverty in the South. The song presents a dissipated, Christ-haunted contemporary South writ small. Stipe's Pee Wee character is like a diminutive Hazel Motes, a raging heathen who "sits upon the wall to preach" in back of the local firehouse, where an emblematic Oddfellows hall is located. (Stipe, however, slightly alters O'Connor's biblically derived title phrase [Psalms 2:1 KJV], singing, "Why do the heathens rage behind the firehouse.") The drunken preacher Pee Wee falls to the ground but regains himself and makes an effort "to prove a sage, to teach." But the words "Falling from his mouth" are heard only by a "boy and girl," who vainly listen in hope that they will "gather pearls of wisdom" by the "firehouse"—surely a metonym for the hell-fire-and-brimstone religion of the South. Instead of being "washed *in* the blood" as the familiar southern evangelistic hymn would have it, the boy and girl "Wash *off* the blood" as the song concludes. That's the next generation of southerners behind the firehouse, losing their religion.

South: "Flannery"

South, a collective of musicians from Richmond, Virginia, made a single recording in 1998 on the Jagjaguwar label. The six tracks of ambient music feature repetitive guitar, vibraphone, and synthesizer sounds with a bit of down-home hammered dulcimer in the mix. Minimalist composers Philip Glass and Steve Reich are acknowledged influences, as is O'Connor, named in the last track, "Flannery." Guitarist and singer Patrick Phelan remarks on the brief vocals added to four of the six tracks, "The idea is to shape the verse from a feeling. We're trying to convert our life experiences to music. To that end, the song 'Flannery' is a highly personal tribute to Flannery O'Connor." This is the only track that begins with sung lyrics, breathy and low in the mix, for the opening minute and forty seconds of a piece that clocks at five minutes and nine seconds. The music is a sequence of pulsing and ringing electronica, with added chiming notes on the vibraphone. The opening lyric phrases "long arms / surround, pull me down" invoke the concluding scene in O'Connor's story "The River," where, in the river in which young Harry Ashfield was baptized, "the waiting current caught him like a long gentle hand and pulled him swiftly forward and down." A further image in the scant opaque lyrics, "clear ice eyes dyed with sky" also bears O'Connoresque overtones. Eyes are everywhere in her fiction and often strikingly described. *Wise Blood*'s Hazel Motes has eyes "the color of pecan shells and set in deep sockets." His teenage lover Sabbath Lily Hawks has eyes that "glittered . . . like two chips of green bottle glass." Nowhere in her fiction does O'Connor describe a character as having eyes "dyed with sky," but the image in Phelan's lyric line might have been suggested by the description of the patrolman who pushes Haze's decrepit car over an embankment in chapter 13 of *Wise Blood* as having "eyes the color of clear fresh ice."

U2: An Enduring Chill

As U2's charismatic front man and lyricist Bono tells it, he was introduced to Flannery O'Connor's works by Bruce Springsteen backstage at the Hammersmith Palais theater in London after a U2 performance in June 1981. According to an insider in the U2 organization, the moment of that exchange was fortuitously captured on camera in the photograph below. Bono recalls that in a conversation about books they were reading, he asked Springsteen whether, given the economically depressed, Dustbowl imagery in some of his recent songs, he had read John Steinbeck's works. Springsteen answered that he had but said Flannery O'Connor had been a far more important influence on his work. Considering the spiritually informed music that U2 was then making, Springsteen felt that Bono, an alienated Irish boy with both Catholic (father) and Protestant (mother) upbringing, might find something of interest in O'Connor's fiction. Bono later reflected, "I don't think [Springsteen] knew what he was saying because I've never felt such sympathy with a writer in America before."

U2's collaborative method of songwriting is unique in the world of pop music. Unlike Lennon and McCartney, for example, who tended to present well-formed or finished songs to the other band members to learn and develop, and unlike Springsteen himself with the legendary E Street Band, U2 has typically produced its songs through a more organic, intuitive, and collective process, often improvising in the studio in the process of recording an album. As rock critic Robert Hilburn describes the process, often Bono may simply mutter a kind of glossolalia that fits with a musical groove his bandmates are playing. The band jokes that they engage in a process of "songwriting by accident." Sounds evolve into words that express feelings evoked by the improvised music. And the words form into expressionistic lyrics fed by experiences, beliefs, and Bono's extensive reading. According to Hilburn, Bono reads widely—fiction, poetry, the Bible, and essays and newspapers—and his reading feeds his songwriting. The few references to O'Connor's fiction in U2 songs are thus part of a matrix of meaning, of images meant to evoke an emotional response in the listener—a method of composition similar to that of Bob Dylan and Nick Cave, and acknowledged by Canadian songwriter Bruce Cockburn.

Photo credit to Adrian Boot. Bono and Bruce.

In 1986, U2 was working on an album that would catapult them to international attention and prove to be one of the band's most successful and enduring recordings, *The Joshua Tree*. Bono was at the time "reading a lot by a writer called Flannery O'Connor," according to an insider publication. In his autobiography *Surrender* (2022), he writes that he bought copies of O'Connor's works at San Francisco's famed City Lights Bookstore while recording the album and has remarked that his favorite book of hers is *Wise Blood*. At the Grammy awards ceremony in 1988, *The Joshua Tree* was acclaimed as both Album of the Year and Best Rock Performance by a Group. In an acceptance speech for the second Grammy that evening, U2's guitarist the Edge offered some thank-yous and then read from a list of individuals who had inspired the band and influenced songs on the album. Fourth on the list, after former South African bishop Desmond Tutu, Martin Luther King Jr., and Bob Dylan, was Flannery O'Connor.

An image from an O'Connor story appears in the lyrics to the elegiac "One Tree Hill," written as a memorial for U2 staffer Greg Carroll, a Māori New Zealander who had moved to Ireland to work as a personal assistant for the band members. Carroll died in Dublin in 1986 while on an errand for Bono, losing control of Bono's motorcycle on a rain-soaked street and colliding with a car. Carroll's death haunted the band as U2 were recording songs for *The Joshua Tree*. Bono told a *Rolling Stone* interviewer that Carroll was "like a brother." The album is dedicated to his memory.

The opening line of the song references the title of one of O'Connor's stories, as Bono pictures the mourners at Carroll's funeral—himself especially—who "turn away to face the cold, enduring chill" of their collective grief and loss. Bono has stated that his favorite O'Connor story is "The Enduring Chill," for its "sad and pathetic portrait" of the young, failed artist Asbury Fox. In Bono's reading of this story, the "enduring chill" that Asbury experiences in the final scene is "his death . . . that begins slowly." Perhaps John Donne's elegiac observation that "any man's death diminishes me" also underlies Bono's use of O'Connor's phrase. "One Tree Hill" ends with a haunting lament, a post-chorus that repeats the line "raining in your heart," preceded by a confessional statement by Bono that suggests his abiding feelings of guilt and sorrow over Carroll's death: "When it's raining raining hard / That's when the rain will break my heart."

The song's title refers to a famous dormant volcano that overlooks the New Zealand capital, Auckland, a historically conflicted site sacred to the Māori people. The lone tree atop it for which the hill was named was damaged by Māori activists and removed in 2001. An obelisk remains, intended as a memorial to the achievements and character of the Māori people. In Bono's biblically informed imagination, "One Tree Hill" also resonates with a religious significance as a place of sacrifice and redemption, the Golgotha of a friend and valued employee.

"One Tree Hill" is followed on *The Joshua Tree* album by "Exit," which U2 critic Steve Stockman suggests is also influenced by O'Connor. Stockman alludes to a thematic sympathy with O'Connor in the song's "twist and tragic end to religious experience and deepest darkness related to light." But the influence here may go further than theme and theology. The "he" in the song appears to be struggling against a love that is trying to reach out to him—the "hands of love" with "healing" in them. The final verse of the song presents a scene that would be familiar to a reader of the O'Connor story that follows "The Enduring Chill" in her second collection, "The Comforts of Home":

He put his hands in the pocket
His finger on the steel
The pistol weighed heavy
His heart he could feel
Was beating, beating
Beating, beating oh my love . . .

In O'Connor's story we meet Thomas, a thirty-five-year-old repressed intellectual who lives with his loving mother, a woman given to spontaneous acts of charity, true *caritas*. Into Thomas's comfortable existence comes Star Drake, a seductive nineteen-year-old his mother has paroled from the local jail and invited to live in their home. Thomas resists Star's advances when she comes naked into his bedroom one night. To Thomas, Star is a "moral moron," a psychopathic personality with nymphomaniac and suicidal tendencies. His loathing for the girl and her indiscriminate desire is, however, countered by a "pure idiot mystery" in his awareness of his mother's capacity to love him and others. She bears the familiar "hands of love" for Thomas; any "shine" of love from Star/"stars" is for him "like nails in the night" ("Exit"). In the story's emblematic symbolism, the nymphomaniac Star embodies a divine love that just can't help itself as it pursues the disturbed and doubting Thomas. Star too "moves in mysterious ways," though as an adolescent female "breathing small tragic spearmint-flavored sighs."

As O'Connor's story progresses, Thomas moves "deeper into black" ("Exit"), heeding the diabolical urgings of his father, whose presence in his consciousness doubles as both his reprehensible, deceased parent and the "father of lies" (John 8:44 ESV). In a wincingly Freudian action in the narrative, Thomas plants his pistol in Star's purse, intending to frame her for stealing it. In the story's final scene, Thomas is confronted with his deed and grapples with Star for the gun. The devilish presence of his "father" in his consciousness commands his hand to pull the trigger. Thomas fires, but the bullet misses Star and kills his mother, who has leaped to protect the girl. Like Thomas, Bono's character too discovers in the end the darkness he is capable of—that his own hands "could also pull down . . . / The hands of love" ("Exit").

❧ ❧ ❧

As do Bruce Springsteen and Lucinda Williams, Bono also acknowledges the influence on his sensibilities of O'Connor's *Wise Blood*. A scene from this novel is suggested in a line in the song "Please" from the 1997 album *POP*. As critics have noted, *POP* presents the most Christian set of songs that U2 has released, or, to use O'Connor's term, the most "Christ-haunted" of their recordings. The name "Jesus" occurs seven times in its twelve songs, most memorably in the Nick Cave–like opening lines of the haunting final track, "Wake Up Dead Man":

> Jesus, Jesus help me
> I'm alone in this world
> And a fucked up world it is too

In "Please," Bono's reference to "your sermon on the mount / from the boot of your car" is possibly an allusion to O'Connor's protagonist Hazel Motes, who preaches his new gospel of the Church without Christ while standing on his rat-colored Essex. While he still may not have found what he's looking for, Bono has found inspiration in O'Connor's fiction and translated it into compelling pop music.

Velma and the Happy Campers: *Lo-Fi Therapy*

An artist-produced collection of songs on the CD *Lo-Fi Therapy No. 1: Songs about Flannery O'Connor* by Velma and the Happy Campers is only marginally connected to O'Connor's story art or person. The seven short tracks, with a total playing time of 16:16, feature a slightly out-of-tune strummed acoustic guitar, drums, and occasional harmonica. Track 2, "Wooden Leg" comes closest of any of the songs to having content related to O'Connor's fictions. Its narrator is evidently Manley Pointer, the devilish Bible salesman in "Good Country People," who in the song's verses asks successively for Hulga/Joy's love, glass eye (mistakenly), and wooden leg. Background ambient noise on a number of tracks, punctuated by snaps and creaks and cracking sounds—and occasionally indecipherable vocals well back in the mix—makes listening a challenge. As the title to this DIY CD indicates, this collection of songs purportedly about Flannery O'Connor may have more value as therapy for the singular singer-musician than it has aesthetic pleasure or interest for the listener.

Tom Waits: "Murder in the Red Barn"

One of Tom Waits's unauthorized biographers has noted similarities between Waits and Nick Cave: both are from middle-class families with a schoolteacher father; both had a religious upbringing and later became "obsessed by the Bible and the Southern Gothic strain in American Literature." Like O'Connor's young O. E. Parker, Waits was dragged off by his mother to Sunday morning services at her Quaker church in Whittier, a suburb of Los Angeles. Her attempts to evangelize her son continued after he dropped out of school to become a hipster troubadour, fed on Kerouac and Ginsberg and an unhealthy amount of alcohol. Waits's rebel side, he says, came from his father, Jesse Frank Waits, named for the nineteenth-century outlaw brothers Jesse and Frank James. "On my father's side we had all the psychopaths and alcoholics," he once told an interviewer, "and on my mother's side we had all the evangelists."

After his parents divorced when he was ten, Waits took refuge in reading. In his early persona as a down-and-out bohemian singer-songwriter, he was often seen with a book under his arm or on the bar counter in front of him. And like Bono, Springsteen, and Cave, his reading often informs his songwriting. While Beat writing, especially Kerouac's *On the Road* and the well-crafted prose of the dissolute Charles Bukowski, had the greatest influence on Waits's sensibilities, he also "devoured" southern fiction—the works of William Faulkner, Carson McCullers, and Flannery O'Connor.

Waits references O'Connor when discussing his song "Murder in the Red Barn" from 1992's *Bone Machine*, the first of his albums to win a Grammy and, according to some critics, his most accomplished collection of songs. He tells biographer Barney Hoskyns, "I buy the local papers every day. They're full of car wrecks . . . I'm always drawn to these terrible stories, I don't know why. 'Murder in the Red Barn' is just one of those stories. Like an old Flannery O'Connor story." Corinne Kessel, in a critical monograph analyzing Waits's lyrics, describes the songs on *Bone Machine* as "dark narrative vignettes gathered from biblical allegories and newspaper clippings." This is not a stretch from describing the source materials for several of O'Connor's short stories.

"Murder in the Red Barn," however, shares little with O'Connor's fictions other than violence in a rural setting, such as the murder by tractor of the Polish Guizac in "The Displaced Person" or the impaling of Mrs. May by a rogue bull in "Greenleaf" as she stands in a pasture honking the horn of her car. Waits's song is an example of what he refers to as his "sururalist" compositions: "a surreal aesthetic melded with rural sounds, themes, and images." A murder mystery in miniature, Waits's ballad hints at attempts to cover up a brutal crime: "Someone's crying in the woods / Someone's burying all his clothes." An axe with bloodstains is found in a barn, but is not considered suspicious because "There's always some killin' / You got to do around the farm." And a character named Cal on a nearby farm has a "scar upon his face" that "no one's asking" about. Instead, the murder is pinned on a drifter who sleeps under a bridge and is eventually apprehended and hauled off in chains. Waits's description of the weather following this injustice has an O'Connoresque quality mixed with a bit of Nick Cave: "The sky turned black and bruised / And we had months of heavy rains." (O'Connor describes the sky as "a bruised violet color" in "A Temple of the Holy Ghost.") Nothing redemptive follows on the violent event the song recounts. There is a suggestion that it might have been motivated by jealousy, a desperate act to acquire a lover and her property, as is hinted at in the bridge:

> Now thou shalt not covet thy neighbor's house
> Or covet thy neighbor's wife
> But for some
> Murder is the only door through which they enter life

The lady of the manor is seen "Drinking alone in her room" in the song's last lines, and we are reminded in closing that "there was a murder in the red barn"—a murder somebody got away with that still haunts the place.

Like Bruce Springsteen and Sufjan Stevens, Waits has written a song titled "A Good Man Is Hard to Find," which pop music commentators have suggested borrows its title and themes from O'Connor's story more than it alludes to the Eddie Green song made famous by Bessie Smith. Indeed, Waits's song is included in a compilation, *Songs Inspired by Literature: Chapter Two*, with album notes that state the song was "Inspired by Flannery O'Conner's [sic] short story 'A Good Man Is Hard to Find.'" The original version of Waits's song was performed in the art musical *Woyzeck* produced in 2000 by Waits and his wife, Kathleen Brennan, based on a play fragment by nineteenth-century German playwright Georg Büchner. *Woyzeck* is about a soldier who suffers from delusions and eventually kills his unfaithful wife. The first verse of the theater version, sung by Woyzeck's wife, Marie, could well be voiced by O'Connor's The Misfit:

> I lit a wooden match; I let it burn down
> I've broken every rule; I've wrecked it all down
> There are no words in the wind, the trees are all bare
> Life's mean as a needle, but why should I care?

While O'Connor's The Misfit's denies the wrongdoings that sent him to prison and cannot reconcile himself to the punishment he has received for his putative crimes, Waits's narrator here confesses to multiple transgressions. But like The Misfit, who ultimately finds "No pleasure but [in] meanness" and casually murders a family of six for no reason except perhaps to steal their car, Waits's narrator comes to a similar conclusion about the meanness of life and expresses a similar callous response. The recorded version of the song on *Blood Money* (2002) omits the first verse and thus reads like a story of a reckless woman trying to forget about serial lovers in her past and longing for "a good man" to come into her life:

> A good man is hard to find
> Only strangers sleep in my bed
> My favorite words are good-bye
> And my favorite color is red

Just as O'Connor's fiction often parodies a soft-pedaled, self-satisfying, undemanding perversion of the Christian gospel in contemporary society, so Waits in "Chocolate Jesus" on *Mule Variations* (1999) mocks an insipid religiosity through a narrator who "Don't go to church on Sunday / Don't get on [his] knees to pray" but prefers to go to the "candy store" for "a chocolate Jesus" that makes him "feel good inside." The Jesus who is "gonna be here soon," as chorused in track 7 of *Bone Machine* ("Jesus Gonna Be Here"), is as mummified by materialism and as commercialized as the "new jesus" in O'Connor's satirical novel *Wise Blood*. Sings Waits,

> I got to keep my eyes open
> So I can see my Lord
> I'm gonna watch the horizon
> For a brand new Ford

The coup de *ungrâce* in this lisped gospel song is found in an altered second line of the Lord's Prayer: "I said Hollywood be thy name."

Gospel truth, nonetheless, often resonates in Waits's songs, revealing the same rough and unrelenting grace that O'Connor presents in her fiction. In describing this grace, former Archbishop of Canterbury, Rowan Williams, has observed in O'Connor's fiction that "the actuality of grace is uncovered in the moment of excess—which may be in a deliberately intensified gracelessness." As one Christian theologian has observed, a "deliberately intensified gracelessness" informs Waits's "lyrical theology," the kind of grace that O'Connor saw that interrupts and disrupts human affairs, that "shatters and strips things bare to the bone" and that is "often shockingly" revealed. Waits presents his own gospel of the grotesque in his art, most compellingly in the blues spiritual-cum-sermon "Way Down in the Hole," which he performs like a decadent southern evangelist warning of the Devil's wiles. The rolling piano hymn "Never Let Go" contains the eminently Waitsian lines, "I'll fall from your grace / But I'll never let go of your hand." And "Down There by the Train," a song covered by the elder Johnny Cash, shares the track with Springsteen's "Land of Hope and Dreams"—about a train that carries "saints and sinners" alike (Springsteen) and those who "never asked forgiveness" and "never said a prayer" (Waits), all rolling along as a single community under grace. Waits describes the destination of his hapless travelers as the canonical hymn-writers would express it—a place "where the sinners can be washed / in the blood of the lamb."

A rough grace often comes riding in Waits's songs on *Mule Variations*, which appeared seven years after *Bone Machine* and is his only other recording to date to be awarded a Grammy. In the ragged piano gospel song "Come on Up to the House" that ends this record, Waits delivers an altar call, according to Kessel, "to all the wanderers, strangers, and misfits who inhabit [his] lyrics and narratives":

> Does life seem nasty, brutish and short
> Come on up to the house
> The seas are stormy, and you can't find no port
> Come on up to the house

This song ends insistently, implying the intense spiritual struggle of those who might finally make their way "up to the house." Waits adopts his Preacher Tom voice, inimitably growling out this Bible Belt blues hymn:

> Well, you're high on top
> Of your mountain of woe
> Come on up to the house
> Well, you know you should surrender
> But you can't let go
> You gotta come on up to the house

Like Nick Cave and Lucinda Williams, Tom Waits could be seen as a living O'Connor character, aware that "Jesus [has] thrown everything off balance," and in the carnivalesque world of his song art, trying to keep himself from falling as he steps along the wire of his own balancing act.

Jim White: *Wrong-Eyed Jesus*

Jim White is our guide "into the soulful, sacred, and profane South" in the 2003 BBC documentary *Searching for the Wrong-Eyed Jesus*, directed by British filmmaker Andrew Douglas. The film traverses the South's backroads and kudzu-covered landscape, sampling its concrete block juke joints, its prisons and diners, its scrapyards and trailer parks, its hyper-Pentecostal churches, and mostly its impoverished and pained religious grotesques. Everywhere "Jesus Saves" or "Jesus Is Lord," and everywhere people are broken yet believing.

As he reflects on the religious culture of the South, White tells the viewer, "Here you feel the presence of the Spirit. You might not like it. It might be wearing the costume of crazy religious people or wild hillbillies or whatever. But it's real, and it's alive, and it's awake." His comment recalls O'Connor's purview of Bible Belt religion from her Catholic perspective as a writer: "Religious enthusiasm is accepted as one of the South's more grotesque features . . . When you write about backwoods prophets, it is very difficult to get across to the modern reader that you take these people seriously, that you are not making fun of them, but that their concerns are your own and, in your judgment, central to human life."

Following scenes of frenzied worshippers shaking and speaking in tongues, lying prone on a church floor "slain in the Spirit," and ecstatically emerging from the waters of baptism, White offers this thought by way of explanation: "I guess they have what Flannery O'Connor called 'the wise blood'; the blood rules them, they don't rule the blood. You wanna know the secrets of the South, you gotta get it in your blood."

White himself has southern religion in his blood. Raised in a Pentecostal family in Pensacola, Florida, with an abusive father, Michael Davis Pratt (his birth name) lived in a home where, like Enoch Emery's upbringing, "it was Jesus all day long." He "got saved" when he was fifteen, but it didn't take. He's been a professional surfer, boxer, fashion model in Europe, wannabe filmmaker, preacher, and New York City cabby for a fifteen-year ride. He has also suffered severely from a near-fatal drug addiction and from years of mental illness—like Springsteen, his family has a history of bipolar and personality disorders. He took the stage name Jim White from the first and last names of two friends, one of whom, Steven White, provides the photography for his debut album, *(The Mysterious Tale of How I Shouted) Wrong-Eyed Jesus*, released on David Byrne's Luaka Bop label in 1997, when White was forty. But while Jesus is frequently name-dropped in White's songs, and cross images and signs with God references appear in the liner notes of his CDs, the now Athens, Georgia-based artist is not a gospel singer. White's quietly voiced songs are largely about losing his religion.

In an interview in *The Believer* magazine, White recalls that he first encountered O'Connor's fiction at a time when he was suffering from a nervous breakdown and a friend thought to bring him a copy of O'Connor's collected stories. "My brain burned as I read those stories," White says. He was particularly affected by "The River," which he read as a story about a young boy "taken to a serious Deep South religious realm" who "sees salvation and it's utterly dark." The story helped to ground his own experiences with southern Pentecostalism: "It was like all those thoughts I'd been having for so many years, they finally had a place in the world."

As does Springsteen, White credits O'Connor's storytelling art with giving him the necessary insight to revise the songs he recorded on his debut album, helping him to root his initially abstract lyrics in southern time and place. (A story with "no sense of place," writes O'Connor, "cannot say much that is significant" about the mystery of human experience.) White's hypnotic Sufjan Stevens–like tune "Still Waters" thus illustratively begins in a specific place and time: "Well I was shacked up down in Mobile / With a girl from New York City / She woke me up one night to tell me / That we weren't alone." O'Connor's fiction became "sort of a model" for White's own songwriting, he says. He admired the way her stories would shift from the mundane to the darkly cosmic, how they would "start in one world and go to another world," as happens to the unfortunate family in O'Connor's terrifying story "A Good Man Is Hard to Find." White's meditative ballad "Borrowed Wings" and exotically musical anthem "Counting Numbers in the Air," in particular, have this kind of O'Connoresque twist and arc.

Accompanied by Mary Gauthier, White once made a pilgrimage to Andalusia, the O'Connor farm south of Milledgeville, Georgia, when both musicians were touring in the area in 2008. He and Gauthier made a field recording of his song of the South, "Fruit of the Vine," on the front porch of the O'Connor farmhouse, a rare opportunity and an act of homage. (Gauthier is also listed in the album credits for 2004's *Drill a Hole in That Substrate and Tell Me What You See*, singing background vocals on "Phone Booth in Heaven.") The chorus to "Fruit of the Vine," with a subtext signaled in an echo

Photo courtesy of Jim White. Taken on the O'Connor family farm, Andalusia.

of a line from Springsteen's "Badlands," gives a sense of White's sensibilities about the Bible Belt badlands with which his art contends:

> It ain't no crime in being alive
> Ain't no sin—we're just trying to get by
> Lead our lives one day at a time
> Hand to mouth—low down in the dirty old South
> Living on the fruit of the vine

White's *Wrong-Eyed Jesus* CD comes with booklet-sized liner notes containing a lengthy, complex short story titled "The Mysterious Tale of How I Shouted 'Wrong-Eyed Jesus!' A True Story by Jim White"—the "handshake" to his first album, as White describes the tale. This almost surreal story, he acknowledges, was influenced by his reading of O'Connor's fiction. The protagonist, a fifteen-year-old boy, is picked up by a predatory homosexual while hitchhiking, like O'Connor's young Tarwater. As he realizes the driver intends to rape him, White's character falls into a maniacal state in which he recalls an experience at a tent revival meeting where a missionary couple revealed a five-foot-high velvet painting of Jesus's face with "pretty blue eyes." The boy was incredulous that the missionary artist would have gotten Jesus's eyes so wrong. While the congregation excitedly chants "Jesus, Jesus, Jesus," he shouts along, adding the words "wrong-eyed" in front of "Jesus." Now in the car, rocking back and forth, the boy in the story starts to howl the same phrase. The O'Connoresque elements of the narrative are evident when the enraged sexual predator pulls off the remote country road and releases the boy in a place "so dark with that wall of pines pressing down on us and the crickets mad with their singing"—two images that appear in O'Connor's fiction. (The descriptive phrase "black wall of woods" appears in *The Violent Bear It Away*, and the affronting though affirming revelation that comes to Ruby Turpin in "Revelation" is accompanied by "invisible cricket choruses.")

White's young character is next picked up by a remorseful Christ-haunted hippie who shortly compels him to pray; together they "[open their] hearts to Jesus" and repent of their individual wrongdoings. When the boy eventually arrives home, he attempts to remedy the "wrong-eyed Jesus" with his own drawing of Jesus's face but finds that he cannot get the eyes right. After his many attempts and multiple erasures, the drawing becomes worn and torn, and he is left with "two ragged holes in the paper where the eyes should have been."

White's search for something beyond the "wrong-eyed Jesus" recalls the revelatory moment for O'Connor's character O. E. Parker as he searches through a book of designs looking for an appropriate religious subject to have tattooed on his back, ostensibly to placate his fundamentalist wife. But his intent is as much to relieve his own growing dissatisfaction with himself, and partly in response to a vague premonition after he survives crashing a tractor into a tree. As Parker flips through the tattooist's book of religious images, he rejects the "up-to-date" representations of the Christ—The Good Shepherd, The Smiling Jesus, The Physician's Friend. A voice seems to speak to him out of the silence, telling him "GO BACK." This is both manual instruction to revisit an image he has thumbed past, and sylleptically an indication to ground his vague religious understanding in the historical image of "a flat stern Byzantine Christ with all-demanding eyes." No "wrong-eyed," kind Aryan face of Christ for Parker. He has found what he wants and what he needs, and is willing to pay the price for it, even though, as the tattooist doubly remarks, "That'll cost you plenty."

After the first session, Parker's Jesus tattoo is unfinished, without the eyes; only after the "all-demanding eyes" have been drawn on his flesh does the tattoo of Christ make its claim on his life: "The eyes that were forever on his back were eyes to be obeyed." It is telling that the pencil-drawn picture of Christ in the booklet accompanying the *Wrong-Eyed Jesus* CD has holes where His

eyes should be. This is both a literal illustration to White's story and possibly a metaphor for his own metaphysics.

White's third album, *Drill a Hole in That Substrate and Tell Me What You See*, also on the Luaka Bop label, is an apologia contra the Christian doctrines he no longer believes in. Its opening track, "Static on the Radio," a jazzy prosaic pop song with backing vocals from alt-folk artist Aimee Mann, dismisses all doctrines and ideologies as empty of meaning: "Everything I think I know is just static on the radio." In its final verse, the narrator is parked outside a church on Sunday morning listening to his neighbors singing hymns. He muses confusedly, "Ten years ago I might have joined in, but don't time change those inclined to think less of what is written than what's wrote between the lines?" The mildly irreverent "If Jesus Drove a Motorhome" imagines a world without the strictures of religion, where for the truth seeker there is only one highway, "Ain't no yours or my way." The lyrics allude to the opening idea in John Lennon's "Imagine" with the phrase "No country to die for," as if to underscore a like theme of conceiving "One world" in which people all live peacefully without the impositions of religion. "Phone Booth in Heaven" is the concluding track-plus-one. (On the CD cover, it is listed as the tenth and last song on the album; however, the recording includes an eleventh track titled "Land Called Home," the only song for which the attractively illustrated insert does not supply lyrics.) An atmospheric, finger-picked song with shades of Townes Van Zandt, "Phone Booth" makes the point that there ain't no mainline to Jesus by which you can tell him what you want. Rather, White subverts a Black gospel and bluegrass cliché: "there's a phone booth in heaven that no one is calling" because "the Good Lord designed [it] to be broken." White clearly articulates here his position as a nonbeliever: "Though the ghosts of redemption might whisper odd promises / I for one don't put much faith in them specters."

Jim White is a true "hillbilly nihilist," a label at one time applied to O'Connor, and one she adamantly refuted. As he recounts in a Dutch TV interviewer in 2017 his almost unbelievable journey into a musical career, White uses an image that evokes the blaspheming Hazel Motes in O'Connor's novel *Wise Blood*: "I jumped around with the Jesus hat on. After a while, I realized this Jesus hat doesn't fit, but it sure felt good jumping around. Maybe I should take it off and jump around anyway? That's what I did." White has his own gospel, as expressed in the John Prine–like song "Jim 3:16," with a singalong refrain, from the live EP *A Funny Little Cross to Bear* (2008). With a bar stool as his "pew" and a pretzel as "communion," the singer ponders "the demons I fought / And all the crap I've been taught" and observes, "Half my life I lived in fear / I'd burn in Hell, but now it's clear / That a bar is just a church where they serve beer." In a blog, White has described himself as "worse than backslidden, more like an apostate on the slippery slope toward true heresy."

✒ ✒ ✒

In the closing scene of *Searching for the Wrong-Eyed Jesus*, White removes the statue of Jesus-of-the-Sacred-Heart that he has been hauling around the South in the trunk of a beat-up 1970s Chevrolet, stands it on the side of a busy highway at night, climbs back into his car, does an about-turn, and drives off into the dark. His search is over, and he has found nothing worth keeping in the southern Pentecostalism in which he was raised. Still, the film ends with a slow, slow zoom of almost eighty seconds—a film technique favored by Stanley Kubrick—toward the face of the statuesque Christ. White's song "Christmas Day" plays on the soundtrack, reminding the viewer that "the Devil is in the details." The closing close-up image is a reminder too, in O'Connor's words, that "while the South is hardly Christ-centered, it is most certainly Christ-haunted." As a careful listening to his corpus of inimitable songs readily reveals, so is Jim White.

Wild Strawberries: "Everything That Rises"

Wild Strawberries is a Canadian pop group that gained recognition and some international success in the first half of the 1990s. The group is composed of songwriter-keyboardist Ken Harrison and Roberta Carter-Harrison on vocals. Ken is a practicing psychiatrist and Roberta is a physiotherapist. They live in a restored old church in the Ontario rural community of New Hamburg, north of Toronto, where they have raised four children and continue to record their brand of ethereal synth-pop music in their home studio. In homage to their favorite writer, the couple wanted to name their first child Flannery, but family and friends "gave us quizzical looks," Roberta wrote in an email. Instead, they named their daughter Georgia, a more subtle association with O'Connor.

Flannery O'Connor has been an inspiring presence since the beginning of Wild Strawberries' music-making. Their first recording, released on cassette in 1989, was titled *Carving Wooden Spectacles*, an overt allusion to an image in O'Connor's story "Judgement Day." Songwriter Ken Harrison has said in a personal interview that he understood the image as a challenge to the artist "to methodically craft something that would alter the way we see the world around us." He was a bit disappointed, he said, that in interviews with college radio stations at the time no one picked up on the O'Connor reference. Wild Strawberries' song "Postcard from a Volcano" makes reference to her image of constructed social vision in the wooden spectacles that her redneck character T. C. Tanner carves:

> Carving wooden spectacles
> Is nothing more than wishful thinking
> Read it on the line below
> Some things never change

Harrison's interpretation of O'Connor's symbol in the second line of the verse suggests a reading that concurs with that of most critics of the story. The spectacles that Tanner carves and presents to the Black character Coleman in "Judgement Day" are meant symbolically to enforce the dominant social vision of white racial superiority that has so deeply tarnished southern history and society. "What you see through those glasses?" Tanner asks the Black man:

> "See a man."
> "What kind of a man?"
> "See the man make theseyer glasses."
> "Is he white or black?"
> "He white!" the negro said as if only at that moment was his vision sufficiently improved to detect it. . . .
> "Well, you treat him like he was white," Tanner said.

Coleman's comic response to a potentially violent encounter with the white mill boss Tanner explodes the specious nature of southern racism and the construction of any social hierarchy based on race. The false eyeglasses that Tanner has carved as though his hands were "directed solely by some intruding intelligence" reveal him to be no more than "a man" like Coleman. To think otherwise is to engage in "wishful thinking," and, gravely, of the kind that continues to spawn racial prejudice across world cultures: "Some things never change."

Harrison remarked in an interview that "the juxtaposition of darkness and light" that he finds in O'Connor's fiction resonates with the human realities he encounters in his work in psychiatry. This juxtaposition, he says, is what attracted him as a songwriter to O'Connor: "I think it always brings more meaning to something when there is a contrast between what the words are saying and the form that presents them. It takes people off guard. I see that in Flannery all the time; it's what draws me to her. That is the way life is: everything is mingled. There is a mixing of all these elements. Our ability to maneuver through the world is dependent on our ability to see the humor and the absurdity in things."

From their 1989 recording to the present, Wild Strawberries has continued to be drawn to O'Connor in their song art, releasing a song in 2019 that borrows the title of O'Connor's most celebrated story, "A Good Man Is Hard to Find." While the song makes no direct reference to details in O'Connor's story, Ken Harrison has written that "Our 'Good Man' came out of the ever increasing *#metoo* reports but with an echo of The Misfit's 'She would have been a good woman' insight." The song's chorus addresses the topical by addressing the typical male: "I don't wanna know what I oughta know / What I oughta know."

The duo's second recording, *Grace*, released independently in 1991, features a song titled "Everything That Rises," directly referencing in both its title and lyrics O'Connor's story "Everything That Rises Must Converge." Unhappy with the initial recording of this song, they rerecorded a more danceable pop version on their 1995 release *Heroine*. Canadian pop diva Sarah McLachlan plays and sings on this recording, released on the Canadian Nettwerk label. Wild Strawberries later toured for three seasons with McLachlan's *Lilith Fair* franchise. *Heroine* reached sales of over fifty thousand, warranting a gold record by Canadian standards.

Heroine's "Everything That Rises" begins with a descriptive list of symbols and characters in O'Connor's story. Harrison has said that the song's lyrics are the most direct he has been in referencing an influence on his songwriting by "sticking close to the author." He wrote the song "as a way of pointing to a writer I loved and wanted to get other people excited about." The phrase O'Connor took from Teilhard de Chardin also made a "catchy chorus." Here is the first verse and chorus, followed by the opening couplet to the song's second verse:

> There's a penny poised on a whitewashed fence
> There's a little black boy praying for his government
> There's a nervous lady reaching for her place
> There's a red-faced son running from his race
> Everything that rises
> Everything that rises
> Everything that rises must converge
>
> This is my country—this is your sign—
> We are painting fences, drawing lines

O'Connor's one "topical" story presents a drama centered on social tensions around the racial integration of public buses during the civil rights era in the American South, a historical moment infamously familiar to most North Americans through the story of heroine Rosa Parks. As a Canadian songwriter, Harrison's choice of this O'Connor story is telling. As his lyrics make plain, the allusion to systemic racial tensions that inform O'Connor's story is directed at his compatriots: "This is my country," where racial lines are also being drawn. While writing the song, Harrison said, he was thinking about the ways in which O'Connor's "themes are broader than America, and that we as Canadians can also take meaning from them."

Indeed, in recent decades, Canada has had to account for its own legacy of racist government policies toward its Indigenous peoples, Ukrainian and Japanese immigrants, and Black Canadian community. This pop song speaks to the cultural translatability of O'Connor's art and vision and to issues of racism that continue to raise social fences in North America and increasingly in the global community. The image of a "whitewashed fence" is an apt metaphor through which to view the inherited racist attitudes of mother and son in O'Connor's story and to address racism in contemporary society, where a culture of white privilege and a whitewashing of implicitly racist government and social policies are similar, and damning, on both sides of the US-Canada border.

In the outro to the song, Roberta Carter-Harrison performs a spirited jazz scat that includes the syllables "fla-fla-fla." At this point on the *Heroine* recording, those who have ears to hear may discover deep in the mix the name "Flannery" sung by a male voice—a bit of "mischief," as Ken Harrison calls it. Perhaps it subtly encodes this song with the "mischievous hope" that Wild Strawberries finds in O'Connor's stories and that is present in their own song art.

Coda

"GONTER ROCK, RATTLE AND ROLL"

Within her small corpus of short fiction, Flannery O'Connor created one rock 'n' roll rebel: a juvenile delinquent named Rufus Florida Johnson, the antagonist of her late story "The Lame Shall Enter First." Her second-longest story next to her novella "The Displaced Person," it is a kind of small-scale recasting of characters and themes developed in her second novel *The Violent Bear It Away*. The do-gooder social worker Sheppard in the story is a version of her virulent secular humanist George Rayber in the novel, a self-described "good man" who is not so. Sheppard's intellectually vacant ten-year-old son Norton is a higher-functioning "dim-witted child" than is Rayber's evidently mentally disabled boy Bishop. Her roustabout and reluctant prophet character Rufus Johnson, writes O'Connor in a letter to novelist John Hawkes, is "one of Tarwater's terrible cousins." And like Tarwater, Rufus appears to be running Jonah-like from his prophetic calling. The emblematic surname *Johnson* signifies his pedigree as a prophet-in-the-making—Rufus is a *son* of *John*, O'Connor's prophet of choice, The Baptist.

Unintentionally, surely, but fortuitous for the argument at hand, his family name and initial also link Rufus to one of the progenitors of American rock, 1930s Mississippi bluesman Robert Johnson, about whom O'Connor likely knew nothing. Yet even the description of Rufus's hair—"his thin dark hair hung in a flat forelock across the side of his forehead"—identifies him with the coifed rock 'n' roll teen idols of the late 1950s to early 1960s. Moreover, and evidently, Rufus is identified with Elvis Presley. Her caveats aside, O'Connor was not completely oblivious to the popular culture and early rock 'n' roll music of her day. She likely saw Elvis's first appearance on the *Ed Sullivan Show* in September 1956, a performance that surely informs Rufus's hip-swiveling Elvis imitation shortly after he enters Sheppard's house. Rummaging through the dresser drawers in the bedroom of Norton's recently deceased mother, Rufus retrieves a "faded corset," and straps it on like a campy androgynous rock performer. He begins "to snap his fingers and turn his hips from side to side" as he sings an imitative version of "Shake, Rattle and Roll," the million-selling rock 'n' roll hit of 1954 by the curly forelocked Bill Haley and His Comets—also recorded by Elvis: "Gonter rock, rattle and roll. Can't please that woman, to save my doggone soul." In Rufus Johnson, O'Connor appears to understand the sensibilities, familial and social forces, and often conflicted soul of the rock 'n' roller. Johnson uncannily shares many characteristics with the O'Connor-influenced contemporary music figures examined in the foregoing pages.

Many of the contemporary bands and songwriters who bear evidence of O'Connor's influence, as has been argued, are Christ-haunted. Sometime in their formative years they have been subject to a strident strain of religion, as in Springsteen's constraining Catholic childhood or Jim White's dysfunctional hyper-Pentecostal upbringing; or somewhere in their genes runs a propensity for religious extremism: Lucinda Williams's fire-and-brimstone preacher grandfather or Sufjan Stevens's cult-following family. O'Connor's wise-blooded characters are all offspring or descendants of religious extremists, and Rufus Johnson is especially so. We read that he was raised in a shack without water and electricity by a physically abusive grandfather, who has retreated to the hills with other extremists to form a survivalist cult intended to outlast the approaching Apocalypse. The biographies of many accomplished contemporary songwriters and rock performers—including a number in this study—reveal that in their formative years they were abandoned emotionally and/or physically by a parent—most often a father (as is true of O'Connor). In a 2012 article in the *New Yorker*, Bruce Springsteen acknowledges T Bone Burnett's pained observation that rock 'n' roll is, more often than not, "one embarrassing scream of 'Daaaaddy!'" Rufus's father died before he was born, and his mother is serving time in a state penitentiary. His upbringing, combined with his "fanatic intelligence" and transgressive tendencies, gives Rufus the bona fides of a rock 'n' roll rebel.

As might be observed particularly of the O'Connor-influenced punk and heavy metal artists explored in this study, Rufus is both Christ-haunted and somewhat bedeviled. The fourteen-year-old explains his criminal inclinations and behavior by declaring to Sheppard, "Satan . . . He has me in his power." Later in the story, Sheppard's confident declaration (three times), "I'm going to save you" is met with Rufus's hissed confessional retort, "nobody can save me but Jesus." Rock 'n' roll can be a highway to hell or a stairway to heaven—and songwriters and bands in this study appear to have taken O'Connor along for the ride on both journeys. It's "Jesus or the devil," as young Tarwater acknowledges his options in *The Violent Bear It Away*. Or, more often, as Mary Gauthier sings in "Mercy Now," "We dangle between hell and hallowed ground." O'Connor's tale of Rufus Johnson's encounter with grace and his coming to consciousness of his prophetic calling is emblematically a rock 'n' roll salvation story.

Bruce Springsteen has remarked that the Catholic doctrines and sacramental practices that informed his upbringing created in him what he calls an "internal landscape," a religious sensibility and underlying redemptive narrative that has shaped his songwriting and directed the lives of the characters in his many first-person narrative songs. O'Connor literalizes the metaphor of an inwardly informing and nourishing gospel truth by having Rufus Johnson eat pages of the Bible in a remarkable scene of defiant spiritual transformation. To confirm to the God-denying Sheppard that he truly believes the biblical doctrine of salvation that, like the evangelist after whom he is named, he has been explaining to Sheppard's son, Johnson takes the Bible he has been reading at the dinner table, tears out several pages and swallows them, exclaiming three times, "I believe it!" Like the religiously tattooed O. E. Parker, Rufus too becomes an emblem of the Word made flesh—a Christ-one—his transformation symbolically transacted as he literally devours the scriptures, his prophetic destiny accepted and perhaps complete.

Just as O'Connor's reluctant young prophet Francis Marion Tarwater has one divinely appointed task to perform in baptizing the child Bishop, so Rufus Johnson, her rock 'n' roll rebel prophet, may have only a limited engagement. As a *son* of John the Baptizer, who prepared the way for the Christ, Rufus has come to shake up Sheppard's life and, *sub specie aeternitatis*, nefariously to save the child Norton's. He is what Mary Gauthier calls a "truth-teller," come to speak truth to the Devil's lies. He has come, as O'Connor writes, as "the sounder of hearts," preparing the way for Sheppard's self-revelation and ultimate repentance at the end of the story. That may be the sum of it, and that is a calling worthy enough for a prophet in O'Connor country. We are left with the impression that Rufus Johnson, like so many teen idols of the 1950s and 1960s, will be a one-hit wonder.

That O'Connor crafted a story in the early 1960s featuring a young prophet rock 'n' roller belies her professed ignorance of the popular culture of her day. While claiming to have no ear for music, O'Connor had enough familiarity with the pop songs of the early 1960s to remark in a letter written 15 February 1964, "all classical music sounds alike to me and all the rest of it sounds like the Beatles." Less than a week earlier, on 9 February, the Beatles made their celebrated American debut on the *Ed Sullivan Show*, a culturally transforming media event watched by more than seventy million Americans—among them, presumably, O'Connor. As the contemporary folk and rock 'n' roll generation begins its long play in the late 1950s and early 1960s, O'Connor appears to lend a sympathetic though literally tone-deaf ear to what the counterculture is saying. An outsider in many ways as a cultural observer, O'Connor is perhaps attractive to the musician-songwriters in this study because they sense a kinship as artists who in their own ways are each a "sounder of hearts."

O'Connor's comic exclamation that she was possessed of "the Original Tin Ear" and had no appreciation whatsoever for music of any kind appears to be somewhat overstated. In possession of a cast-off record player sometime after Christmas 1963, a gift from a group of Dominican Sisters in Atlanta, O'Connor resolved to "educate [herself] if possible" in the meaningful pleasures of music. Over what would prove to be the final months of her life, she made her way through a box of apparently both classical and pop records sent by her friend and correspondent Thomas Stritch. In a letter to Stritch dated 11 February 1964, she asks him to send some music reviews that he had written, explaining, "I would like to see how knowledgeable folks talk about it." And she confesses remarkably, "This is the first time I've listened to music except when I was at Yaddo"—the writers' colony in upstate New York that she left fifteen years before in February 1949! In one of her last letters, written just weeks before her death shortly after midnight on 3 August 1964, O'Connor confides to Stritch, "The records are a real boon and when I'm not working, I'm listening to them." She remarks somewhat knowingly on enjoying a classical record with a "4-hand piano Chopin thing" and adds, "there is a point in it where the peafowls join in."

Would O'Connor, like her fellow southern novelist, Catholic, and friend Walker Percy, have written a fan letter to Bruce Springsteen? Or agree with Father Andrew Greeley, who labeled Springsteen "a Catholic Meistersinger"? She had no qualms about letting young Lucinda Williams chase her peacocks. Would she have finally purchased that new record player she once considered buying rather than the pair of swans she ordered instead, and listened over and over to Williams's Grammy Award–winning rockabilly song "Get Right with God," with its imagery influenced by *Wise Blood*? Would she have nodded approvingly on hearing Mary Gauthier's "Wheel within the Wheel," with its motley parade of freaks and outsiders, as in Ruby Turpin's vision, winding their way heavenward along "Eternity Street"? Had she lived a fuller life in years, until the turn of the century, as might have been expected for an American woman born in 1925, she would have discovered in the works of contemporary bands and songwriters whose art she has influenced that, like the music she came late to appreciate, there are places in their songs where again the peafowls might join in. As Flannery O'Connor concludes in her published reflection on her beloved peacocks, "I am sure that, in the end, the last word will be theirs."

BONUS TRACK

Stage Names from O'Connor's *Wise Blood* and Characters

Along with the iconoclast post-punk performer and composer JG Thirlwell, who in the late 1980s adopted a persona named Wiseblood, a number of contemporary bands and singer-songwriters have taken their stage names from the compelling title of O'Connor's first novel or from one of her characters. These O'Connor-derived names, however, do not appear to signify any significant or lasting O'Connor-derived content or vision in the works or performance art of these pop and folk musicians. As rising chamber pop artist Natalie Mering confesses, she read *Wise Blood* as a teenager, picked a phonetically modified artist's handle that echoed the novel's title, Weyes Blood, "and then never thought about it again."

Wise Blood, a.k.a. Christopher Laufman, is a Pittsburgh-based artist who, as described in a *Pitchfork* review, "makes woozy, inward pop songs out of other people's music." Wise Blood released his debut five-song digital EP + on Bandcamp in 2010 and has since released four other collections of his "dreamlike, melodic sound collages." Raised a Catholic, Laufman was a youngster when his grandfather noted that he was different from other children and told him "you have wise blood." He later discovered the novel *Wise Blood* and claims to have "read everything by Flannery O'Connor" and to have a religious temperament. He feels destined to have the nickname Wise Blood. It's not clear whether O'Connor's art and vision have had a direct influence on this "noise-pop artist." His several music videos posted on YouTube show him, like Hazel Motes, engaged in various transgressive activities. Laufman's falsetto vocals—the only original element in his songs—are usually buried deep in the mix and barely audible. His lyrics are mostly hard to discern on his recordings; one of his most well-crafted lyrics, to 2011's "Penthouse Suites," contains the boasting aspirations of the artist, expressed in several interviews available online and in the title of his debut song "B.I.G. E.G.O." Along with declaring "I'm shooting for the moon," Laufman offers this telling *cri de coeur*, an apparent appeal to something outside of himself: "So calm my nerves, and send your word /

Just let me know this life is what I deserve." O'Connor's characters, it might be observed, never get what they deserve, only what they need.

A southern acoustic blues band from Birmingham, Alabama, recorded in 2008 an EP of eight largely expressionistic songs with biblical and apocalyptic overtones under the name **Wiseblood**. Behind the plastic CD holder in the packaging is a photo of a left hand, palm up, on which is printed in fine block script the prophetic words of Saint John from the closing chapter of the *Book of the Revelation* (KJV). The hand-printed lyrics for each of the eight songs on the CD liner contain echoes of phrases and images from Saint John's vision, and a line from T. S. Eliot's "The Love Song of J. Alfred Prufrock," but bear no evidence of citations from or allusions to any of O'Connor's works. On the band's website is a review/interview published in the *Birmingham News* on the day of the EP's release in which songwriter/producer Ashby Pate remarks that the band takes its name from the title of his favorite novel. The review concludes, "O'Connor's influence has helped Pate to craft lyrics that are rich in Gothic imagery, laden with apocalyptic themes, and laced with a love-hate relationship to religion."

In an interview with the *Baltimore Sun* in 2015, indie singer-songwriter Natalie Mering states that the influence of O'Connor's fiction and vision on her as an artist is limited to her appropriating and adapting her stage name, **Weyes Blood**, from the title of the author's first novel, and the fact that she identifies with the isolated outcast characters in the novel. Mering's musical roots are in the traditional and contemporary worship hymns and songs she heard while growing up in Pennsylvania in a deeply religious Pentecostal family. Her rich, pure voice, often amply layered on her five studio albums to date and soaring over sustained synth sounds, invites comparisons to the Celtic diva Enya and at times sounds uncannily like the late Karen Carpenter. Mering's unclassifiable sound has been variously labeled psychedelic folk, chamber pop, experimental rock, and adult alternative.

Inclined to an esoteric spirituality, Mering is like a millennial Hazel Motes—the evolved character we meet near the end of O'Connor's novel—heading out for new territory in his not-so "good car" leaking gas and water, not going "anywheres." As Weyes Blood describes her journey, "there is a little bit of a wanderer in my music who is just wandering and seeking and waving goodbye as I continue on my journey to nowhere." *Vice*'s Charlotte Gush observes that Weyes Blood's lyrics reflect the "existential anxiety" of her generation. On the track "Something to Believe" from her 2019 release *Titanic Rising*, for example, the narrator confesses to having "a case of the empties," the wisdom of how to live in this world for her "a lost forgotten pearl." She asks existentially, echoing O'Connor's The Misfit, "Give me something I can see / Something bigger and louder than the voices in me / Something to believe." As a millennial artist negotiating and interrogating a world that is off balance interpersonally, environmentally, spiritually, and socio-politically, Weyes Blood is searching the galaxy beyond her feelings and experiences for "something" she thinks she "may never find." Like other Christ-haunted pop artists featured in this study, Mering may well encounter through the truth-telling of her song art "a great crow-filled tree" of O'Connoresque grace that may transform her into the potential pop prophet she might be.

Mason Tarwater was the name of a cover band from Murfreesboro, Tennessee, a town thirty-five miles south of Nashville that was home to an accomplished O'Connor scholar, the late R. Neil Scott. The five-member band took a "jukebox approach" when performing in bars and clubs and played everything from jazz to country. A band out of Texas called **Tarwater** played "hard country music" in the 1970s, led by the late legendary Pinto Bennett, who over his long musical career shared the stage with Waylon Jennings and Willie Nelson. "Now why the hell would anyone want to name a band Tarwater?" was the opening question on the band's former website, but none of Tarwater's promotional materials made any attempt to answer this question or to provide the source for the band's name. American novelist and musician Clyde Edgerton, author of five *New York Times* Notable Books, produced an album of original and traditional folk under the name **Tarwater Band**. Released in 1992 on cassette on the Flying Fish label, the recording is titled after one of Edgerton's most successful novels, *Walking across Egypt*.

But not all Tarwaters alluded to in the names of pop music groups have a fictional pedigree. A German duo who play post-rock instrumental music go by the name **Tarwater**. Their website states that the band name was taken from guitarist Craig Tarwater, who for a time in the early 1970s played in the American psychedelic rock band Love. Searches in 2020 on www.whitepages.com in Tennessee retrieved 219 records of folks named Tarwater, and a similar search for Georgia found forty-eight people with that family name. The surname has considerable currency in the South, and includes Tennessee-born Davis Tarwater, a gold medalist in swimming at the 2012 Olympics. And, yes, there is a Mason Tarwater in Missouri and a Francis M. Tarwater in Indiana. Added to the not-from-Flannery side is a horror punk band from New Jersey that existed from 1977 to 1983 called the **Misfits**, reportedly named after the title of Marilyn Monroe's final film *The Misfits* (1961), not from the O'Connor character of the same name and possibly similar inclinations.

Courtesy of Kele Fleming

Red Sammy is the stage name of Adam Trice, an American singer-songwriter from Baltimore who began performing at small folk festivals in 2007 and to date has released nine studio albums. His website notes that he takes his moniker from Red Sammy Butts, a minor character in O'Connor's most familiar story, "A Good Man Is Hard to Find"—a "FAT BOY WITH [A] HAPPY LAUGH" who operates a "FAMOUS BARBEQUE" along with a combination gas station and dance hall. O'Connor's Red Sammy is distinguished, ironically, as the only self-declared "good man" in her fiction and the character who utters the story's title phrase. Red Sammy the performer is likewise a hybridized musical enterprise specializing in "Lyric-driven Americana Folk Rock 'n' Roll," sometimes performing in a duo or with a backing band. Listed on his website among the songwriters who have inspired him are O'Connor-influenced artists Lucinda Williams and Tom Waits.

An active Canadian folk performer with a day job, Kele Fleming founded and fronted a Vancouver-based "haunting indie band," **Hazel Motes**, which in the early 1990s toured Canada three times, charted on college radio on both sides of the border, and released four self-produced short-play collections of original songs on cassette. Two of these, *Eponymous* (1991) and *Ragnarok* (1992), have been reissued as free digital downloads on Bandcamp. Fleming encountered O'Connor's fiction while studying as an English major at the University of British Columbia, where she currently works as an administrator. "I was so inspired by Flannery O'Connor's writing—especially her grasp of the undercurrents of religion and spirituality—that I named my first band after Hazel Motes from *Wise Blood*," she writes in an email. Kele Fleming currently performs solo or with a backing band under her own name. "Inescapable Jesus" from her 2010 album *World in Reverse* draws imagery from *Wise Blood* in a song that codedly addresses the tragedy of missing and murdered women from Vancouver's Downtown Eastside. This song is available for download on Spotify.

ACKNOWLEDGMENTS

This book has been many years in the making and began with a casual remark. O'Connor scholar and biographer Jean Cash, who in the 2010s had heard several of my conference papers exploring O'Connor's influence on popular musicians, approached me after a session at the American Literature Association conference in Boston in May 2017 and suggested that I might have the makings of a book. Not something I had considered until our conversation. So, after that nudge, I followed through, taking the book title from a paper I had presented at the *Startling Figures: A Celebration of the Legacy of Flannery O'Connor* symposium in Milledgeville, Georgia, in April 2011.

Materials to prime and support my discoveries of O'Connor's influence on popular musicians were obtained in two funded research trips to the Center for Popular Music in Murfreesboro, Tennessee, in 2011 and 2017. My thanks for invaluable assistance to the center's staff: Directors Grover Baker and Greg Reish, archivist Rachel Morris, librarian Lindsay Million, and Yvonne Elliott. Mona Okada assisted in securing licenses to reprint Springsteen's lyrics and Karen at Karen Schauben Publishing offered advice and generous licensing agreements. Big thank-yous to Tim Kosel at Easy Song for his persistence in obtaining print licenses from lethargic publishers; Brian Lipsin, anarchist owner of Brian's Record Option, for the CDs and LPs that provided my primary sonic sources; Oscar Milan at Novel Idea for timely arrival of books needed in my research; Chris Miner, photographer, for several images in the book; and Don Sleeth (owner) and Randy deKleine-Stimpson (technician) at Camera Kingston for resolution of my photo engineering needs. My daughter Flannery Evangeline (Evie) drew the concept drawing that influenced the cover design for the book.

Work on the book began in a private study room on the fourth floor of the Stauffer Library at Queen's University, Kingston, which served as a research space for many years through the generosity of the late chief librarian Paul Wiens and his successor Martha Whitehead. Sister Pat and Sister Kathy provided on several occasions an inspiring apartment at Stillpoint House of Prayer on the mighty Madawaska River, and a sunny compartment at Sanctuary Coworking in Kingston was a welcoming place to write one COVID-plagued summer.

Several friends offered places to retreat and write over the years of the book's becoming. My thanks to Steve and Ann Lukits for a month at The Ranch on Opinicon Road, filling birdfeeders along with many pages; Doug Babington and Susanne Fortier for a weeklong writing retreat at their former chalet at Mount Tremblant; Eric Prost and Mary Rowland for timely use of their Devil's Lake cottage on several occasions; and Daniel Shipp and Theresa Brouwer for knowingly harboring a B & E suspect at their lakeside cabin.

The many fine coffee shops in my hometown of Kingston, Ontario, provided "a sip of community" (as Bruce Cockburn describes it) and a clean and well-lit spot to sit and write, notably the former Coffeeco and Common Market, Balzac's, Common Ground Coffeehouse, and Coffee and Company. Toronto's famed L'Espresso Mercurio provided me with a corner table at which to write and sip my favorite beverage during several long days over getaway weekends.

I am grateful for the ongoing encouragement from my colleagues in the Department of English, Culture, and Communication at the Royal Military College of Canada: Chantel Lavoie, Steve Lukits, Michael Hurley, Huw Osborne, along with former dean Jim Denford and historian and Springsteen aficionado Jim Kenny. Friends who have inquired about the book's progress over the years and listened patiently to my overly detailed responses include Elizabeth and Kim Alexander-Cook, Sue and Doug Caldwell, David and Jacqui Grier, Val Hamilton, Bruce Kauffman, Faye Koshel and Bob Hood, Murray and Gloria Martin, Damaris Martin, Vince Ramsay, and Ray Vos.

Tim Drake carefully read a near final draft of the manuscript and offered detailed suggestions and corrected errors, as did the inimitable Gary Rasberry. And Bruce Gentry, editor of the *Flannery O'Connor Review*, noted errors in the draft and offered encouragement over the course of the book's long gestation. Thanks goes as well to my *BOSS* coeditors Jonathan D. Cohen and Roxanne Harde, and to my friend and authority on Springsteen, writer and editor June Skinner Sawyers, who also created the book's index.

Nancy Davis Bray, associate director for Special Collections at Georgia College & State University offered emailed assistance with details about O'Connor's manuscripts and matters of O'Connor scholarship, and former executive director of the O'Connor-Andalusia Foundation, Craig Amason, answered my questions regarding O'Connor's engagement with popular culture and her life on the family farm at Andalusia. Irene Burgess kindly invited me to present a talk in March 2022 on the book in progress at one of the virtual events she curated, sponsored by the Andalusia Institute.

I am deeply indebted to Maureen Garvie, editor extraordinaire, whose writerly and readerly skills helped to straighten my prose and clarify my reasoning.

Thank-yous to Katie Keene, then acquisitions editor at University Press of Mississippi, for encouraging me to submit a book manuscript, and to Mary Heath for ongoing editorial oversight. The book and notes have greatly benefited from exacting copyediting by Deborah Upton and the press's Corley Longmire. For patient and persistent help in obtaining hard to find research materials and for sleuthing out needed bibliographic details, I am especially grateful for the efforts and encouragement of librarians at RMC's Massey Library, Suzanne Burt and Suzanne Côté, and especially for the dedicated persistence of Margaret Janaway in Interlibrary Loan Services.

Funding for this research began with an Insight Development Grant in 2011–2013 from the Social Sciences and Humanities Research Council (SSHRC), a federal agency in Canada, shared with Professor Roxanne Harde (University of Alberta-Augustana) for a joint book project that went another way south. Further substantial funding over the years from the Canadian Defense Academic Research Program (CDARP) made a book of this kind possible. Two generous grants from RMC's Research Bursary Fund enabled payment of the last sets of print license agreements for song lyrics liberally quoted to support the critical commentary in the book.

Finally, I owe more than I can say to my late friend and mentor and coeditor R. Neil Scott, and offer this monograph to honor his memory and as a promise fulfilled to his widow Sheila and son David.

And to Susan and our five now grown children: for the many times when a good husband and father was hard to find.

NOTES

Abbreviations of Flannery O'Connor's primary works, in the order in which they were published:

- WB   *Wise Blood* (1952). 2nd ed. Farrar, Straus and Giroux, 1962.
- VBA   *The Violent Bear It Away*. Farrar, Straus and Giroux, 1960.
- MM   *Mystery and Manners: Occasional Prose*. Ed. Sally Fitzgerald and Robert Fitzgerald. Farrar, Straus and Giroux, 1969.
- CS   *The Complete Stories*. Farrar, Straus and Giroux, 1971.
- HB   *The Habit of Being: Letters of Flannery O'Connor*. Ed. Sally Fitzgerald. Farrar, Straus and Giroux, 1979.
- Con   *Conversations with Flannery O'Connor*. Ed. Rosemary M. Magee. University Press of Mississippi, 1987.
- CW   *Flannery O'Connor: Collected Works*. Ed. Sally Fitzgerald. Library of America, 1988.

The author has been initialized as FOC when citing her published fiction, occasional pieces collected in *Mystery and Manners*, and correspondence collected in *The Habit of Being*. Quotations from O'Connor's stories are from *The Complete Stories*, the most popular and widely available collection of her short fiction.

Introduction

- 3   "sounds like the Beatles": FOC to Betty Hester, 15 February 1964, *HB*, 566.
- 3   "finding out for myself": FOC to Betty Hester, 25 January 1964, *HB*, 563.
- 3   "fourth from the top": Recording Academy / GRAMMYs, "Watch U2 Accept Their First-Ever GRAMMY in 1988 | GRAMMY Rewind," YouTube Video, 2:33, 7 August 2020, https://www.youtube.com/watch?v=nypK7pzGAnI.
- 4   "the cold, enduring chill": U2, "One Tree Hill," track 9 on *The Joshua Tree*, Island Records, 1997, CD.
- 4   "startling figures": FOC, "The Fiction Writer & His Country," *MM*, 34.
- 5   "relation to that": FOC, "The Fiction Writer & His Country," *MM*, 32.
- 5   "no great consequence": FOC, "Author's Note to the Second Edition," *WB*, 5.
- 6   "terrible predicament": FOC, "A Good Man Is Hard to Find," *CS*, 128.
- 6   "the best way you can": FOC, "A Good Man Is Hard to Find," *CS*, 132.
- 6   "any of it was true": FOC, "Greenleaf," *CS*, 316.
- 6   "O'Connor's core beliefs": FOC to Betty Hester, 2 August 1955, *HB*, 92. ["One of the awful things about writing when you are a Christian is that for you the ultimate reality is the Incarnation, the present reality is the Incarnation, and nobody believes in the Incarnation; that is nobody in your audience."]
- 6   "pagan babies": "Bruce Springsteen," *VH1 Storytellers*. Filmed at Two River Theatre, Red Bank, NJ, 4 April 2005, DVD.

6	"godly power": Bruce Springsteen, *Born to Run* (Simon & Schuster, 2016), 17.
7	"It really does": Lucinda Williams, intro to live recording of "Bus to Baton Rouge," track 17 on *The West East North South Tour*, El Rey Theatre, 6 September 2007, Lost Highway, 2007, CD.
7	"tells her audience": On the limited-edition live recording of her album *World without Tears*, track 11 on *The West East North South Tour*, El Rey Theatre, 5 September 2007 (Lost Highway, 2007), Williams tells her audience that her song "Atonement" is "influenced by the books I read by Flannery O'Connor."
7	"from the stage": *Bruce Springsteen: Van Andel Arena, Grand Rapids, Michigan August 3, 2005*, disc 2, track 4, Nugs.Net Enterprises, 2018, CD: "There's that great line in *Wise Blood*, Flannery O'Connor—what was it? Guy starts a church of Jesus Christ, dead, buried, and remaining that way [*laughs*]. It's an idea!" [5:12–31].
7	"Without Christ": FOC, *WB*, 157.
7	"favorite book": Barbara Hoffman, "In My Library: Lucinda Williams," *New York Post*, 20 June 2015, https://nypost.com/2015/06/20/in-my-library-lucinda-williams/.
7	"Twelve Steps program": Jewly Hight, *Right by Her Roots: Americana Women and Their Songs* (Baylor University Press, 2011), 121.
7	"does not know it": FOC, "Parker's Back," *CS*, 513.
8	"in like manner to": FOC, "A Temple of the Holy Ghost," *CS*, 248.
8	"action of mercy": FOC, "The Artificial Nigger," *CS*, 269.
8	"a secret life": FOC, "Revelation," *CS*, 508.
8	"a character's 'soul'": FOC, "Good Country People," *CS*, 288.
8	"the stuff of": FOC, "The Catholic Novelist in the Protestant South," *MM*, 196–97.
8	"winds its way": Gauthier, "Wheel inside the Wheel," track 3 on *Mercy Now*, Lost Highway, 2005, CD.
9	"O Lord, let it be": Cave, "Just a Closer Walk with Thee." *The Complete Lyrics: 1978–2013* (Penguin Books, 2013), 95.
9	"the world of things": FOC, "Novelist and Believer," *MM*, 157.
9	Quotation from Thomas Merton, cited by Robert Giroux in "Introduction" to *Flannery O'Connor: The Complete Stories*, xv.
9	"instrument of Your story": FOC, *A Prayer Journal* (Farrar, Straus and Giroux, 2013), 11.
9	"prophetic vision": FOC, "Some Aspects of the Grotesque in Southern Fiction," *MM*, 44.
9	"ultimate reality": See for example O'Connor's use of this phrase in her occasional talk "Catholic Novelists and Their Readers," *MM*, 179; and in her letter to Betty Hester, 2 August 1955, *HB*, 92.
9	"what God gives you": FOC to John Lynch, 6 November 1955, *HB*, 115.
9	"realm of the impossible": FOC to Betty Hester, 22 September 1956, *HB*, 177.
10	"the habit of art": FOC, "The Nature and Aim of Fiction," *MM*, 65.
10	"wrote to discover": FOC to Elizabeth McKee, 21 July 1948, *HB*, 5.
10	"not conscious of": FOC to Betty Hester, 17 November 1956, *HB*, 180.
10	"preternatural power": Harold Bloom, "Introduction," *Bloom's Modern Critical Views: Flannery O'Connor*, New edition (Infobase, 2009), 2.
10	"best artist she can be": FOC, *A Prayer Journal*, 29, 38.
10	"She's just incredible": *Rolling Stone* staff, "The *Rolling Stone* Interview: Bruce Springsteen," *Bruce Springsteen, the Rolling Stone Files: The Ultimate Compendium of Interviews, Articles, Facts, and Opinions from the Files of* Rolling Stone (Hyperion, 1996), 156.
10	"influence of her Catholicism": FOC to Betty Hester, 2 August 1955, *HB*, 92. ["I won't ever be able entirely to understand my own work or even my own motivations. It is first of all a gift, but the direction it has taken is because of the Church in me or the effect of the Church's teaching ..."]

10	"confesses not to hold": Bruce Springsteen, *Born to Run*, 17.
10	"internal landscape": Springsteen quoted in Jon Pareles, "Bruce Almighty: The Boss Turns to God," *New York Times*, 24 April 2005, late ed., sec.2: 1+.
10	"knew original sin": Will Percy, "Rock and Read: Will Percy Interviews Bruce Springsteen," *DoubleTake* 4, no. 2 (1998), 37.
10	"bedrock of original sin . . . mystery of incompleteness": FOC, "Novelist and Believer," *MM*, 167.
11	"about original sin": FOC to Sally Fitzgerald, 26 December 1954, *HB*, 74.
11	"but it is making it in darkness": FOC to Louise Abbot, [undated] Sat. 1959, *HB*, 354.
11	"then find my way": "Bruce Springsteen and Martin Scorsese Talk Influences and Inspirations," *Variety* (6 May 2019), https://variety.com/2019/music/news/bruce-springsteen-martin-scorsese-talk-netflix-1203206046/.
11	"a 'something' or a 'more'": [One or the other of these terms appears in significant lines in lyrics to "Straight Time" and "Highway 25" on *The Ghost of Tom Joad*, in "Leah" on *Devils & Dust*, and in "Johnny 99" on *Nebraska*.]
11	"pin point of light": FOC, the last words in *WB*, 232.
11	"remembers waiting": Benjamin Hendin, "Lucinda Williams: Where the Spirit Meets the Bone," *Radio Silence* 2 (March 2014), https://longreads.com/2014/08/19/where-the-spirit-meets-the-bone-a-memoir-by-lucinda-williams/?.
11	"ducks and peacocks": Miller Williams, "Remembering Flannery O'Connor," *Flannery O'Connor: In Celebration of Genius*, edited by Sarah Gordon (Hill Street Press, 2000), 2.
11	"read everything": Barbara Hoffman, "In My Library: Lucinda Williams."
11	"her favorite book . . . her favorite movie": Silas House, "Happy Woman Blues," *No Depression* (May–June 2001), 86.
12	"a major influence": *Rolling Stone Encyclopedia of Rock and Roll*, 3rd edition (Fireside, 2001), 1068.
12	"two grandfathers": Hight, *Right by Her Roots*, 17.
12	"like a stinger": FOC, *WB*, 20.
12	"southern religious fanaticism": Bill Buford, "Delta Nights: A Singer's Love Affair with Loss," *New Yorker* (5 June 2000), 53.
12	"she has compared": "Lucinda Williams," https://reggieslive.com/band/lucinda-williams/ (reposted from www.myspace.com/lucindawilliams).
12	"of the roses": Williams, "Words Fell," track 13 on *World without Tears*, 2003, CD.
12	"broken butterflies": Williams, "Broken Butterflies," track 11 on *Essence*, 2001, CD.
12	"get right with God": Williams, "Get Right with God," track 9 on *Essence*, 2001, CD.
12	"read everything": personal interview, 25 April 2009.
12	"does not identify": Hight, *Right by Her Roots*, 122.
12	"talks and essays": FOC, see in particular her comments on "the cost of" redemption in "Some Aspects of the Grotesque in Southern Fiction," *MM*, 48.
12	"Mississippi-raised daughter": Mark Woodworth, editor, *Solo: Women Singer-Songwriters in Their Own Words* (Delta, 1998), 321.
13	"liner notes": See Kate Campbell, lyrics booklet, *Moonpie Dreams*, Compass Records, 1997, CD; *Rosaryville*, Compass Records, 1999, CD.
13	"late-comer status": Robert K. Oermann, "Songs of the South: Kate Campbell's Music Tells It Like It Is," *Tennessean*, 29 January 1997, D3.
13	"believability and darkness": Chris Flisher, "Country Charm: Kate Campbell Writes What She Knows," http://worcesterphoenix.com/archive/music/97/04/25/CAMPBELL.html.
13	"his idol": Nick Sylvester, "Without a Prayer," *Village Voice*, 2 August 2005, https://www.villagevoice.com/2005/08/02/without-a-prayer/.

- 13   "impenetrable": Stevens's interview with Rick Moody and Wesley Stace, "PENultimate Lit: An Evening on Music & Literature," 16 October 2006, https://soundcloud.com/penamerican/penultimate-lit-an-evening-on [Stevens cites a *Harpers* editor's comment at 1:02:58].
- 13   "Plan B": Jason Crock, "Interview: Sufjan Stevens," *Pitchfork* (15 May 2006), https://pitchfork.com/features/interview/6335-sufjan-stevens/.
- 13   "by the devil": FOC, "On Her Own Work," *MM*, 118.
- 14   "one hundred thousand": Chris Maume, "Nick Cave: Devil's Advocate," *Independent*, 11 March 2006, https://www.independent.co.uk/news/people/profiles/nick-cave-devils-advocate-350562.html.
- 14   "interventionist God": Nick Cave and the Bad Seeds, "Into My Arms," side A, track 1 on *The Boatman's Call*, Reprise Records, 1997, Remastered ed., 2011, LP.
- 14   "I've been waiting for": Nick Cave and the Bad Seeds, "(Are You) The One that I've Been Waiting For?" side A, track 6 on *The Boatman's Call*.
- 14   "unbelieving searchers": FOC, "Novelist and Believer," *MM*, 160.
- 14   "lacking category": FOC to Betty Hester, 25 November 1955, *HB*, 117.
- 14   "sex potential": FOC to Betty Hester, 25 November 1955, *HB*, 118–19.
- 14   "romantic relationship": James Blandford, *PJ Harvey: Siren Rising* (Omnibus Press, 2004), 99.
- 15   "Protestant saint:" FOC to Ben Griffith, 3 March 1954, *HB*, 69.
- 15   "only southernness": quoted in Monica Miller, "Only Southernness: Flannery O'Connor and R.E.M.," *Flannery O'Connor Review* 17 (2019), 116.

Chapter 1: Bruce Springsteen: "The Flannery O'Connor of American Rock"

- 16   "Flannery O'Connor of American Rock": Australian alt-country artist Toby Burke quoted in "Big Boss Grooves," *Uncut Legends #4: Springsteen*, Special ed. of *Uncut* [London, UK] 1, no. 4 (2004), 24. [Roseanne Cash has similarly remarked about Springsteen's songwriting on *Nebraska*: "He's into really well-drawn third-person writing, as if he were Flannery O'Connor." Quoted in Warren Zanes, *Deliver Me from Nowhere: The Making of Bruce Springsteen's* Nebraska (Crown, 2023), 238.]
- 16   "writers we love": Terry Gross, "Ed Norton Interviews Bruce Springsteen on 'Darkness,'" NPR, *Fresh Air*, 15 November 2010, https://www.npr.org/transcripts/131272103.
- 16   "*Complete Stories* given to him": Zanes, *Deliver Me from Nowhere*, 138.
- 16   "Huston's film adaptation": Dave Marsh, *Glory Days: Bruce Springsteen in the 1980s* (Pantheon, 1987), 97.
- 16   "in himself": Marsh, *Glory Days*, 97.
- 17   "deep into O'Connor": Will Percy, "Rock and Read: Will Percy Interviews Bruce Springsteen," *DoubleTake* 4, no. 2 (1998), 38.
- 17   "unknowability of God": "Bruce Springsteen: By the Book," *New York Times Sunday Book Review*, 2 November 2014, 8.
- 17   "culture at large": Bruce Springsteen, *Born to Run* (Simon & Schuster, 2016), 431.
- 17   "best records": Broken Record Podcast, "Rick Rubin & Malcolm Gladwell Interview Bruce Springsteen," YouTube Video, 59:59, 27 October 2020, https://www.youtube.com/watch?v=6HZcuw2mznA&ab_channel=BrokenRecordPodcast.
- 17   "writing kind of *smaller*": Rolling Stone staff, "The *Rolling Stone* Interview: Bruce Springsteen," *Bruce Springsteen, the Rolling Stone Files: The Ultimate Compendium of Interviews, Articles, Facts, and Opinions from the Files of* Rolling Stone (Hyperion, 1996), 156.
- 18   "She's just incredible": "The Rolling Stone Interview: Bruce Springsteen," 156.

18	"confronting the questions": Percy, "Rock and Read: Will Percy Interviews Bruce Springsteen," 38.
18	"telling good stories": Percy, "Rock and Read: Will Percy Interviews Bruce Springsteen," 40.
18	"narrative impressionism": Larry David Smith, *Bob Dylan, Bruce Springsteen, and American Song* (Praeger, 2002), 130.
18	"happen to rhyme": Smith, *Bob Dylan, Bruce Springsteen, and American Song*, 161.
18	"already reeling": "Bruce Springsteen," *VH1 Storytellers*, filmed at Two River Theatre, Red Bank, NJ, 4 April 2005, DVD.
19	"folk-related style": quoted in Marsh, *Glory Days*, 104.
19	"my own vision": quoted in Smith, *Bob Dylan, Bruce Springsteen, and American Song*, 152.
19	"very influenced": "Bruce Springsteen and Martin Scorsese Talk Influences and Inspirations," *Variety*, 6 May 2019, https://variety.com/2019/music/news/bruce-springsteen-martin-scorsese-talk-netflix-1203206046/.
19	"original sin": FOC to Sally Fitzgerald, 26 December 1954, *HB*, 74.
19	"biography entitled *Caril*": Marsh, *Glory Days*, 97–98.
20	"deep into O'Connor": Percy, "Rock and Read," 38.
20	"some fun": Bruce Springsteen, "Nebraska," track 1 on *Nebraska*, Columbia, 1982, CD.
20	"no sign": Ninette Beaver, *Caril* (Lippincott, 1974), 199.
21	"no real pleasure": FOC, "A Good Man Is Hard to Find," *CS*, 133.
21	"feels 'unfit'": Springsteen, "Nebraska."
21	"No pleasure but meanness": FOC, "A Good Man Is Hard to Find," *CS*, 132.
21	"in this world": Springsteen, "Nebraska."
21	"of my own": Percy, "Rock and Read," 37.
21	"don't stop me": Springsteen, "State Trooper," track 6 on *Nebraska*.
22	"ain't got one": FOC, *WB*, 208.
22	"from nowhere": Springsteen, "State Trooper."
22	"Haze replies": FOC, *WB*, 208.
22	"destined and fateful": Bruce Springsteen, *Bruce Springsteen: Songs* (HarperEntertainment, 2003), 138–39.
22	"as bizarre as": Marsh, *Glory Days*, 137.
22	"nothing at all": Marsh, *Glory Days*, 138.
23	"reason to believe": Springsteen, "Reason to Believe," track 10 on *Nebraska*, Columbia, 1982, CD.
23	"collected songs": Marsh, *Glory Days*, 141.
23	"one of the darkest songs": Zanes, *Deliver Me from Nowhere*, 141.
23	"of light": FOC, *WB*, 232.
24	"of a saint": Jim Cullen, *Born in the U.S.A.: Bruce Springsteen and the American Tradition* (Wesleyan University Press, 2005), 165.
24	"salvation history": George Yamin Jr., "The Theology of Bruce Springsteen," *Journal of Religious Studies* 16, no. 1–2 (1990), 6.
24	"a Catholic Meistersinger": Andrew Greeley, "The Catholic Imagination of Bruce Springsteen," *America* (6 February 1998), 110.
24	"the Sacraments": Greeley, "The Catholic Imagination of Bruce Springsteen," 111.
24	"shinin' on through": Springsteen, "Valentine's Day," track 12 on *Tunnel of Love*, Columbia 1987, CD.
24	"liturgist": Greeley, "The Catholic Imagination of Bruce Springsteen," 111.
24	"Catholic perspective": Greeley, "The Catholic Imagination of Bruce Springsteen," 114.
25	"the Church": FOC to John Lynch, 6 November 1955, *HB*, 114–15.
25	"defensive about it": quoted in Jon Pareles, "Bruce Almighty: The Boss Turns to God," *New York Times*, 24 April 2005, late ed., sec.2: 1+.

25	"21st-century albums": Pareles, "Bruce Almighty: The Boss Turns to God," *New York Times*, 24 April 2005, late ed., sec.2: 1+.
25	"spiritual songwriter": Broken Record Podcast, "Rick Rubin & Malcolm Gladwell Interview Bruce Springsteen."
25	"heroic Catholic": Percy's letter is reproduced in Percy, "Rock and Read: Will Percy Interviews Bruce Springsteen," *DoubleTake* 4, no. 2 (1998), 42.
26	"search for faith": Springsteen's letter is reproduced in part in Percy, "Rock and Read," 42.
26	"incompleteness": FOC, "Novelist and Believer," *MM*, 167.
26	"Kyle's sin": Springsteen, "Reason to Believe," track 10 on *Nebraska*.
26	"inherit the sins": Springsteen, "Adam Raised a Cain," track 2 on *Darkness on the Edge of Town*, Columbia, 1978, CD.
26	"'unatoned' sins": Springsteen, "My Father's House," track 9 on *Nebraska*.
26	"the bedrock of": FOC, "Novelist and Believer," *MM*, 167.
26	"life of denials": Springsteen, "The Price You Pay," disc 2, track 7 on *The River*, Columbia, 1980, CD.
27	"carried him home": Springsteen, "Spare Parts," track 4 on *Tunnel of Love*.
27	"chief characteristics": FOC to Shirley Abbott, 17 March 1956, *HB*, 147–48.
27	"a holy life": FOC to Betty Hester, 2 August 1955, *HB*, 92.
28	"very quietly": Percy, "Rock and Read," 38.
28	"moment of grace": FOC, "On Her Own Work," *MM*, 112.
28	"into the world": Percy, "Rock and Read," 38.
28	"(his word)": in Springsteen's title and lyrics to his song "Devils & Dust," track 1 on *Devils & Dust*, Columbia, 2005, CD.
28	"favor for him": Springsteen, "Atlantic City," track 2 on *Nebraska*.
28	"more 'n all this": Springsteen, "Johnny 99," track 4 on *Nebraska*.
29	"psychological tendency": FOC to John Hawkes, 20 November 1959, *HB*, 360.
29	"rational explanation": Cullen, *Born in the U.S.A.: Bruce Springsteen and the American Tradition*, 173.
29	"their choices": Bruce Springsteen, *Bruce Springsteen: Songs* (HarperEntertainment, 2003), 138.
29	"write about": Springsteen, *Songs*, 274.
30	"from my hands": Springsteen, "Straight Time," track 2 on *The Ghost of Tom Joad*, Columbia, 1995, CD.
30	"it was something": Springsteen, "Highway 29," track 3 on *The Ghost of Tom Joad*.
30	"off balance": FOC, "A Good Man Is Hard to Find," *CS*, 132.
30	"carnival artiste": FOC, "Parker's Back," *CS*, 513.
30	"angel of Gawd": FOC, "The Life You Save May Be Your Own," *CS*, 154.
31	"foreign lands": Springsteen, "Straight Time."
31	"Sierra Madres": Springsteen, "Highway 29."
31	"anything goes": *Rolling Stone* staff, "The *Rolling Stone* Interview: Bruce Springsteen," 156.
31	"extreme situation": FOC, "On Her Own Work," *MM*, 113.
32	"sporadically believable": Frederick Asals, *Flannery O'Connor: The Imagination of Extremity* (University of Georgia Press, 1982), 108–9.
32	"worried about": FOC to Cecil Dawkins, 28 January 1960, *HB*, 371–72.
32	"dissatisfied with": FOC to John Hawkes, 6 November 1960, *HB*, 416.
32	"mystery": FOC, "The Comforts of Home," *CS*, 384 ("mysteriously"), 385, 388 ("mystery").
32	"invisible currents": FOC, "The Comforts of Home," *CS*, 385.
32	"born without": FOC, "The Comforts of Home," *CS*, 385.
32	"unendurable form": FOC, "The Comforts of Home," *CS*, 390.
32	"the better": FOC, "The Comforts of Home," *CS*, 397.

32	"guided by": FOC, "The Comforts of Home," *CS*, 403.
32	"end to evil": FOC, "The Comforts of Home," *CS*, 403.
33	"made her possible": FOC, "The Comforts of Home," *CS*, 403.
33	"anything goes": *Rolling Stone* staff, "The *Rolling Stone* Interview: Bruce Springsteen," 156.
33	"moment of grace": FOC, "On Her Own Work," *MM*, 112.
33	"off balance": FOC, "A Good Man Is Hard to Find," *CS*, 132.
33	"meanness": FOC, "A Good Man Is Hard to Find," *CS*, 132.
33	"prefer to think": FOC, "On Her Own Work," *MM*, 112.
33	"the others": FOC, "A Good Man Is Hard to Find," *CS*, 133.
33	"my own children": FOC, "A Good Man Is Hard to Find," *CS*, 133.
33	"real heart": FOC, "On Her Own Work," *MM*, 111.
33	"grandmother's soul": FOC, "On Her Own Work," *MM*, 113.
33	"makes the story 'work'": FOC, "On Her Own Work," *MM*, 118.
33	"every minute": FOC, "A Good Man Is Hard to Find," *CS*, 133.
33	"Bandy": Stephen C. Bandy, "'One of my babies': The Misfit and the Grandmother," *Studies in Short Fiction* 33, no. 1 (Winter 1996), 107–18.
33	"pleasure": FOC, "A Good Man Is Hard to Find," *CS*, 133.
34	"the devil": FOC, "On Her Own Work," *MM*, 112.
34	"specific personality": FOC, "On Her Own Work," *MM*, 117.
34	"devil to frenzy": FOC to Andrew Lytle, 4 February 1960, *HB*, 373.
34	"bitten him": FOC, "A Good Man Is Hard to Find," *CS*, 132.
34	"hard to find": Springsteen, "A Good Man is Hard to Find (Pittsburgh)," disc 3, track 2 on *Tracks*, Columbia, 1998, CD.
34	"the video": Springsteen, *Devils & Dust* [Incl. "Bonus DVD," dir. Danny Clinch], Columbia, 2005, CD.
35	"making of *Nebraska*": Springsteen, *Songs*, 135.
35	"TEAC Tascam 144": [The TEAC Tascam 144 4-Track Cassette Recorder that Springsteen used to record the *Nebraska* songs resides in the Rock and Roll Hall of Fame museum in Cleveland, Ohio. (See photo insert between pages 146–47 in Zanes, *Deliver Me from Nowhere*.)]
35	"composing material for": Pareles, "Bruce Almighty: The Boss Turns to God," *New York Times*, 24 April 2005, late ed., sec.2: 1+ (24).
35	"at risk": Pareles, "Bruce Almighty: The Boss Turns to God," *New York Times*, 24 April 2005, late ed., sec.2: 1+ (2).
35	"commentator": Pareles, "Bruce Almighty: The Boss Turns to God," *New York Times*, 24 April 2005, late ed., sec.2: 1+.
36	"devils and dust": Springsteen, "Devils & Dust," track 1 on *Devils & Dust*, Columbia, 2005, CD.
36	"it appeared": Springsteen, "Jesus Was an Only Son," track 8 on *Devils & Dust*.
36	"no getting out": "Bruce Springsteen," *VH1 Storytellers*, filmed at Two River Theatre, Red Bank, NJ, 4 April 2005, DVD.
36	"sweet salvation": Springsteen, "Maria's Bed," track 6 on *Devils & Dust*.
36	"the only sound": Springsteen, "Leah," track 9 on *Devils & Dust*.
37	"Matamoros banks": Springsteen, "Matamoros Banks," track 12 on *Devils & Dust*.
37	"good storyteller": quoted in Chris Willman, "Bruce Springsteen and Martin Scorsese Talk About 'Are You Talkin' to Me?' and How 'Last Waltz' Influenced 'Broadway,'" https://variety.com/2019/music/news/bruce-springsteen-martin-scorsese-talk-netflix-1203206046/.
37	"ongoing novel": quoted in Smith, *Bob Dylan, Bruce Springsteen, and American Song* (Praeger, 2002), 155.

37 "pen to paper": Bruce Springsteen, "Bruce Springsteen – Letter To You (Official Video)," YouTube Video, 3:59, 10 September 2020, https://www.youtube.com/watch?v=AQyLEzoqy-g&ab_channel=BruceSpringsteenVEVO.
37 "incarnational art": FOC, "The Nature and Aim of Fiction," *MM*, 68.
38 "beautiful reward": Springsteen, "My Beautiful Reward," track 10 on *Lucky Town*, Columbia, 1992, CD.
38 "of any depth": FOC, "The Church and the Fiction Writer," *MM*, 152.

Chapter 2: Lucinda Williams: Chasing Flannery's Peacocks

39 "want her to": Miller Williams, "Remembering Flannery O'Connor." In Sarah Gordon ed., *Flannery O'Connor: In Celebration of Genius* (Hill Street Press, 2000), 2.
39 "greatest songwriter": Chris Mundy, "Lucinda Williams: Home-Grown Masterpiece," 6 August 1998, https://www.rollingstone.com/music/music-news/lucinda-williams-home-grown-masterpiece-79686/.
39 "best songwriter": Emmylou Harris, "Lucinda Williams: Songwriter," *Time*, 9 July 2001, 41.
39 "real love": Lucinda Williams, "Real Love," track 1 on *Little Honey*, Lost Highway Records, 2008, CD.
39 "out playing ball": Lucinda Williams in *Solo: Women Singer-Songwriters in Their Own Words*, edited by Mark Woodworth (Delta, 1998), 292.
40 "a reference": Miller Williams, "Remembering Flannery O'Connor," 2.
40 "commented on them": Lucinda Williams in *Solo*, 292.
40 "a hundred great books": Buford, "Delta Nights," 54.
40 "novels and story collections": Steve Huey, "Lucinda Williams Biography," https://www.allmusic.com/artist/lucinda-williams-mn0000837215/biography.
40 "a lot of my songs": David Browne, "The Last Word: Lucinda Williams," interview, *Rolling Stone* 1254 (11 February 2016), 66.
40 "lies very deep": FOC, "The Regional Writer," *MM*, 58.
40 "Pentecostal weirdos": Buford, "Delta Nights," 63.
40 "O'Connor as Loretta Lynn": Bob Ruggiero, "Lucinda Williams," *Dallas Observer*, 22 February 2007, https://www.dallasobserver.com/music/lucinda-williams-6376833.
40 "a major influence": *The Rolling Stone Encyclopedia of Rock & Roll* (3rd ed.), edited by Holly George-Warren and Patricia Romanowski (Fireside, 2001), 1068.
40 "favorite novel . . . favorite movie": Silas House, "Happy Woman Blues," *No Depression* (May–June 2001), 86.
41 "Carolina Theatre": "Film: Acoustic, Lucinda Williams and Wise Blood," *No Depression*, 1 February 2015, https://www.nodepression.com/film-acoustic-lucinda-williams-and-wise-blood/.
41 "shaping and abiding influence: See Williams's comments in *Don't Tell Anybody the Secrets I Told You: A Memoir* (Crown, 2023), 35.
41 "more out there": From "Where the Spirit Meets the Bone," *Radio Silence*, March 2014, quoted in *Literature: An Introduction to Fiction, Poetry, Drama, and Writing*, edited by X. J. Kennedy and Dan Gioia, 450.
41 "bed of nails": From "Where the Spirit Meets the Bone," *Radio Silence*, March 2014, quoted in *Literature: An Introduction*, 450.
41 "keep herself fed": Buford, "Delta Nights," 59.
41 "difficult to work with": Bill Friskics-Warren, "Setting the Record Straight," *No Depression* (July–August 1998), 66.

Notes

42 "to do otherwise": FOC to John Selby, 18 February 1949, *HB*, 10.
42 "uncooperative, and unethical": FOC to Robert Giroux, 3 December 1951, *HB*, 29.
42 "prematurely arrogant": FOC to Paul Engle, 7 April 1949, *HB*, 14.
42 "Dixie white ass": David Fricke, "Q&A: Lucinda Williams," *Rolling Stone*, 19 July 2001, 25.
42 "legendary perfectionism": Ian Gittins, "Review: Lucinda Williams," 16 November 2006, https://www.theguardian.com/music/2006/nov/16/popandrock.
42 "such musical luminaries": Bob Bradley, "Lucinda Williams: Passionate Wishes," *Journal of Country Music* 18, no. 2 (1996), 31.
42 "music gumbo": Buford, "Delta Nights," 52.
42 "executives at Columbia": Williams, *Don't Tell Anybody*, 141.
42 "three Grammy awards": "Recording Academy Grammy Awards," https://www.grammy.com/artists/lucinda-williams/7914.
42 "a class of her own": Steve Huey, "Lucinda Williams Biography," https://www.allmusic/com/artist/lucinda-williams-mn420837215/biography.
43 "country and blues flavors": Huey, "Lucinda Williams Biography."
43 "get right with God": Scott Simon, "Profile: Lucinda Williams Discusses Her New CD *Essence*," NPR: Weekend Edition, 26 May 2001, https://www.npr.org/2001/05/26/1123535/Lucinda-williams.
43 "some folks would do": FOC, "Writing Short Stories," *MM*, 90.
44 "one of your daughters": Lucinda Williams, "Get Right with God," track 9 on *Essence*, Lost Highway, 2001, CD.
44 "to pay": FOC, *WB*, 222.
45 "barbed wire": FOC, *WB*, 224.
45 "kind of borrowed": Erin Williams, "Q&A: A Conversation with Lucinda Williams," *St Louis Magazine*, 20 April 2017, https://www.stlmag.com/culture/music/a-conversation-with-lucinda-williams/.
45 "deeply interested": Williams, *Don't Tell Anybody*, 174.
46 "Holy Spirit preachers": Buford, "Delta Nights: A Singer's Love Affair with Loss," *New Yorker*, 5 June 246, 53.
46 "the southern grotesque": Alanna Nash, "Lucinda Williams Talks Renewed 'Spirit' on Double Album," *Rolling Stone*, 6 October 2014, https://www.rollingstone.com/music/music-country/Lucinda-williams-talks-renewed-spirit-on-double-album-183596.
46 "Jesus of the Sacred Heart": Buford, "Delta Nights," 53.
46 "loves the symbolism": Hight, *Right by Her Roots*, 18.
46 "one instant longer": FOC, *VBA*, 45.
46 "backlash to that": Dan Ouellette, "Fruits of Her Labor," *Acoustic Guitar* 14, no. 2 (August 2003), 59.
46 "reading of Flannery O'Connor": [On the limited-edition live recording of her album *World without Tears*, track 11, *The West East North South Tour*, El Rey Theatre, 5 September 2007 (Lost Highway, 2007), Williams tells her audience that her song "Atonement" is "influenced by the books I read by Flannery O'Connor."]
46 "Hell fire scorched lungs": Lucinda Williams, "Atonement," track 7 on *World without Tears*, Lost Highway, 2003, CD.
46 "burn you clean": FOC, *VBA*, 135.
47 "killed the beast": Williams, "Atonement."
47 "Unsuffer me": Lucinda Williams, "Unsuffer Me," track 5 on *West*, Lost Highway, 2007, CD.
47 "song of redemption": "Lucinda Williams," https://www.reggieslive.com/band/lucinda-williams/ (reposted from www.myspace.com/lucindawilliams).
48 "O'Connor's short stories": https://www.billboard.com/articles/news/56485/lucinda-williams-looks-west-on-new-album.

48	"been lifted up": FOC, "Some Aspects of the Grotesque in Southern Fiction," *MM*, 47–48.
48	"dark and disturbing": "Lucinda Williams," https://www.reggieslive.com/band/lucinda-williams/ (reposted from https://www.myspace.com/lucindawilliams).
48	"ancient twelve": FOC to Betty Hester, 11 February 1956, *HB*, 137.
48	"through a child's eyes": Lucinda Williams, stage patter during live recording of "Bus to Baton Rouge," track 18 on *The West East North South Tour*, El Rey Theatre, 6 September 2007, Lost Highway, 2007, CD.
49	"admired James's novels": FOC to Betty Hester, 28 August 1955, *HB*, 99.
49	"innocent victim": Howard Burkle, "The Child in Flannery O'Connor," *Flannery O'Connor Bulletin* 18 (1989), 59.
49	"vision of himself": FOC, "The Lame Shall Enter First," *CS*, 481.
49	"Fortune, Georgia": FOC, "A View of the Woods," *CS*, 337–38.
49	"line of woods": FOC, "A View of the Woods," *CS*, 342.
49	"both die violently": FOC, "A View of the Woods," *CS*, 356.
49	"given her a present": FOC, "A Temple of the Holy Ghost," *CS*, 238.
49	"inwardly to comprehend": FOC, "A Temple of the Holy Ghost," *CS*, 248.
50	"side of her face": FOC, "A Temple of the Holy Ghost," *CS*, 248.
50	"not a symbol": FOC to Betty Hester, 16 December 1955, *HB*, 124.
50	"about four or five years": Lucinda Williams, "Car Wheels on a Gravel Road," track 2 on *Car Wheels on a Gravel Road*, Lost Highway, 1998, CD.
50	"approximate age": FOC, "The River," *CS*, 158.
50	"scene at breakfast time": see FOC, "The River," *CS*, 158–59; FOC, "The Lame Shall Enter First," *CS*, 445–46.
50	"do what you're told": Williams, "Car Wheels on a Gravel Road."
50	"suffering from a hangover": FOC, "The River," *CS*, 168.
50	"dead cigarette butts": FOC, "The River," *CS*, 157.
51	"old man": FOC, "The River," *CS*, 169.
51	"gradually seeing": FOC, "The River," *CS*, 172.
51	"my heart would know": Williams, "Car Wheels on a Gravel Road."
51	"old before their time": Burkle, "The Child in Flannery O'Connor."
51	"on a gravel road": Williams, "Car Wheels on a Gravel Road."
51	"apologized to her": Buford, "Delta Nights," 60.
51	"difference it makes": Holly Crenshaw, "Lucinda Williams: An Eye for Detail," *Performing Songwriter* (May/June 1996), 59.
51	"a song's naked truth": R. J. Smith, "Lost in America," *SPIN* (July 1998), 80.
51	"principles of good writing": Miller Williams with Marshall Bruce Gentry and Alice Friman, "'Our conversations were in script': Miller Williams on Visiting Flannery O'Connor at Andalusia," *Flannery O'Connor Review* 7 (2009), 12.
52	"dirt mixed with tears": Williams, "Car Wheels on a Gravel Road."
52	"it's all true": Lucinda Williams, intro to live recording of "Bus to Baton Rouge," track 18 on *The West East North South Tour*, El Rey Theatre, 6 September 2007, Lost Highway, 2007, CD.
52	"her debut single": Syd Fablo, "Honky Tonk Girl: The Loretta Lynn Collection," rocksalted.com/2015/11/loretta-lynn-honky-tonk-girl-the-loretta-lynn-collection.
52	"buy 'em anywhere": Loretta Lynn, "You Ain't Woman Enough (To Take My Man)," side A, track 1 on *You Ain't Woman Enough*, Decca Records, 1966, LP.
52	"man-stealing hussies": Fort Meyers News-Press, "No dancing for Loretta Lynn, but she can still sing," https://www.wtsp.com/article/entertainment/no-dancing-for-loretta-lynn-but-she-can-still-sing/67-376685901.
52	"sat down for a drink": Jackson Meazle, "The Kinship is Real," *Oxford American*, 5 March 2013, https://www.oxfordamerican.org/item/1527-the-kinship-is-real.

52	"Hank's voice on the radio": Williams, "Car Wheels on a Gravel Road."
52	"mental illness and alcoholism": Hight, *Right by Her Roots*, 25.
52	"electroshock therapy": Williams, *Don't Tell Anybody*, 5.
53	"caregiver and housekeeper": Buford, "Delta Nights," 59–60.
53	"not necessarily what happened": Miller Williams, "Remembering Flannery O'Connor," 3.
53	"It really does": Lucinda Williams, intro to live recording of "Bus to Baton Rouge," track 18 on *The West East North South Tour*.
53	"uncomfortable talking about": Buford, "Delta Nights," 59.
53	"to get things out": Williams, intro to live recording of "Bus to Baton Rouge," track 18 on *The West East North South Tour*.
54	"piano nobody played": Lucinda Williams, "Bus to Baton Rouge," track 10 on *Essence*, Lost Highway, 2001, CD.
54	"supposed to talk about": Lucinda Williams, stage patter during live recording of "Bus to Baton Rouge," track 18 on *The West East North South Tour*.
55	"too hard . . . Ghosts . . . Follow me": Lucinda Williams, "Bus to Baton Rouge," track 10 on *Essence*, Lost Highway, 2001, CD.
55	"down in my soul": Williams, "Bus to Baton Rouge."
55	"childhood traumas": Williams, *Don't Tell Anybody*, 134.
55	"a map of my life": Alexis Coleman, "Lucinda Williams—*The Ghosts of Highway 20* (Album Review)," https://crypticrock.com/?nonce=68bda5cc7e&search_count=3&s=ghosts+of+highway.
56	"back into the present": Tom Overby, #Hwy20InsideJobBlog, 5 February 2016, **(site discontinued)**. [Author has a transcript of Overby's blogs in his files.]
56	"Looking back on the rough": Lucinda Williams, "Louisiana Story," disc 1, track 7 on *The Ghosts of Highway 20*, Highway 20 Records, 2016, CD.
56	"head like a stinger": FOC, *WB*, 20.
56	"tell 'em you fell": Lucinda Williams, "Louisiana Story."
57	"The weight of centuries": FOC to Betty Hester, 11 February 1956, *HB*, 137.
57	"a difficult childhood": Hight, *Right by Her Roots*, 25.
57	"wasn't brought up right": Lucinda Williams, "He Never Got Enough Love," track 3 on *Sweet Old World*, Chrysalis Records, 1992, CD.
57	"beat you black and blue": Lucinda Williams, "Sweet Side," track 8 on *World without Tears*, Lost Highway, 2003, CD.
57	"he goes to his Maker": FOC, *Con*, 58.
58	"its foreshadowings": FOC, *Con*, 107.
58	"no other reason than 'meanness'": FOC, "A Good Man Is Hard to Find," *CS*, 132.
58	"not for the dead bodies": FOC, *MM*, 113.
58	"meditation on death": Huey, "Lucinda Williams Biography," allmusic.com/artist/lucinda-williams-mn580837215/biography.
58	"tumultuous affair": Williams, *Don't Tell Anybody*, 99, 103.
58	"of another friend": Williams, *Don't Tell Anybody*, 103–4.
58	"*Wrecking Ball*": Emmylou Harris, "Sweet Old World," track 8 on *Wrecking Ball*, Elektra, 1995, CD.
59	"tender kiss": Lucinda Williams, "Sweet Old World," track 4 on *Sweet Old World*, Chrysalis Records, 1992, CD.
59	"for thirteen years": Buford, "Delta Nights: A Singer's Love Affair with Loss," 58.
59	"Life is worth it": Hight, *Right by Her Roots*, 12.
59	"songwriter Blaze Foley": Buford, "Delta Nights," 60.
59	"turn me loose": Lucinda Williams, "Death Came," disc 1, track 5 on *The Ghosts of Highway 20*, Highway 20 Records, 2016, CD.

59	"deep river of life": FOC, "The River," *CS*, 165, 168.
59	"*Readers Under Twelve*": FOC, "The River," *CS*, 163.
59	"You count now": FOC, "The River," *CS*, 168.
60	"forward and down": FOC, "The River," *CS*, 174.
60	"Kingdom of Christ": FOC, "The River," *CS*, 173.
60	"'very literal' experience": "Lucinda Williams her first-ever music video, 'Copenhagen,'" https://www.rollingstone.com/music/music-news/Lucinda-williams-her-first-ever-music-video-copenhagen-231221/.
60	"you are mist": Lucinda Williams, "Copenhagen," disc 1, track 3 on *Blessed*, Lost Highway, 2011, CD.
60	"deliberate homophone": See for example musixmatch; https://genius.com/Lucinda-williams-copenhagen-lyrics.
60	"God up in heaven": Lucinda Williams, "Heaven Blues," track 10 on *Little Honey*, Lost Highway, 2008, CD.
60	"better place than this": Lucinda Williams, "Doors of Heaven," disc 1, track 6 on *The Ghosts of Highway 20*, Highway 20 Records, 2016, CD.
60	"If there's a heaven": Lucinda Williams, "If There's a Heaven," disc 2, track 6 on *The Ghosts of Highway 20*.
61	"separations and sorrows": FOC to Janet McKane, 16 July 1964, *HB*, 592.
61	"soul-corrupting effects": FOC, *Con*, 58.
61	"world's and flesh's rage": Ben Jonson, "On My First Son," elegiac poem published in 1616.
61	"manner of speaking": FOC, "The Comforts of Home," *CS*, 385.
61	"the 'He' pronoun": Lucinda Williams, "Something Wicked This Way Comes," disc 2, track 1 on *Down Where the Spirit Meets the Bone*, Highway 20 Records/Thirty Tigers, 2016, CD.
61	"psychological tendency": FOC to John Hawkes, 20 November 1959, *HB*, 360.
62	"real spirit": FOC, "On Her Own Work," *MM*, 117.
62	"sinisterly transforming": FOC, *VBA*, 24.
62	"haunts young Tarwater": FOC, *VBA*, 45.
62	"straight from Flannery": Mark Hinson, "Lucinda Williams draws from where the spirit meets the bone," *Tallahassee Democrat*, 22 May 2014, https://tallahassee.com/story/entertainment/2014/05/22/lucinda-williams-draws-spirit-meets-bone/9434901/.
62	"'disagreeable' voice": FOC, *VBA*, 12.
62	"make you his home": Williams, "Something Wicked This Way Comes."
62	"cases of possession": FOC to John Hawkes, 20 November 1959, *HB*, 359–60.
62	"wooded area": FOC, *VBA*, 228–32.
62	"fall from grace": Williams, "Something Wicked This Way Comes."
62	"grinning presence": FOC, *VBA*, 45.
62	"'mighty wicked' force": Williams, "Something Wicked This Way Comes."
62	"overused clichés": Williams quoted in Jewly Hight, *Right by Her Roots*, 21.
63	"get the blues": Williams, "Ugly Truth," disc 1, track 9 on *Blessed*.
64	"turn things around": Williams, "One More Day," disc 2, track 9 on *Down Where the Spirit Meets the Bone*.
64	"one more river": Lucinda Williams, "Temporary Nature (of Any Precious Thing)," disc 2, track 5 on *Down Where the Spirit Meets the Bone*.
65	"good country people"; "displaced person"; "the comforts of home"; "a good man is hard to find"—all are familiar phrases that inform O'Connor's story titles.

65	"stomach it emotionally": FOC to Betty Hester, 28 August 1955, *HB*, 100.
65	"light it yourself": Lucinda Williams, "Everything but the Truth," disc 2, track 6 on *Down Where the Spirit Meets the Bone*.
66	"catchy because cliché-like": Carole K. Harris, "The Echoing Afterlife of Clichés in Flannery O'Connor's 'Good Country People,'" *Flannery O'Connor Review* 5 (2007), 63.
66	"Christ's rebuke to Peter": John Desmond, "Flannery O'Connor's Misfit and the Mystery of Evil," *Renascence* 56, no. 2 (2004), 129.
66	"except God alone": Gospel of Mark 10:18, *New American Standard Bible*.
66	"perished out of the earth": A suggested biblical source that has made its way into college-level commentaries on the story; see for example, *This Thing Called Literature: Reading, Thinking, Writing*, edited by Andrew Bennett and Nicolas Royle (Routledge, 2015), 57.
66	"signifies both": *Matthew Henry's Commentary on the Whole Bible: Complete and Unabridged* (Micah 7), https://www.christianity.com/bible/commentary/matthew-henry-complete/micah/7.
66	"I ain't a good man": FOC, "A Good Man Is Hard to Find," *CS*, 128.
66	"everything off balance": FOC, "A Good Man Is Hard to Find," *CS*, 132.
66	"Almost Rotten": FOC to Elizabeth McKee, 15 October 1952, *HB*, 44.
66	"choice of her friend": FOC to Sally and Robert Fitzgerald, 20 December 1952, *HB*, 50.
66	"Drive carefully": FOC, "The Life You Save May Be Your Own," *CS*, 155.
66	"campaign of road safety": "Repository: Collections & Archives," https://repository.duke.edu/dc/outdooradvertising/BBB2633. [Billboards displaying this message were posted along American highways from 1925 to 1950.]
66	"Shiftlet is 'unredeemable'": FOC to John Hawkes, 13 September 1959, *HB*, 350.
66	"other than his own": FOC to John Hawkes, 26 December 1959, *HB*, 367.
67	"peal of thunder": FOC, "The Life You Save May Be Your Own," *CS*, 156.
67	"voice of the stranger": FOC, "You Can't Be Any Poorer Than Dead," *CS*, 298.
67	"what he gets": FOC, "You Can't Be Any Poorer Than Dead," *CS*, 298.
67	"reducing class": FOC, "Everything That Rises Must Converge," *CS*, 405.
67	"Omega Point": Pierre Teilhard de Chardin, "The Attributes of Omega Point," in *The Phenomenon of Man* (Collins, 1959), 268–72.
67	"O'Connor's preferred translation": FOC to Janet McKane, 25 July 1963, *HB*, 532.
68	"dogma of Incarnation": Brad Gooch, *Flannery: A Life of Flannery O'Connor* (Little, Brown and Co., 2009), 331.
68	"serious errors": "Warning Regarding the Writings of Father Teilhard de Chardin: Sacred Congregation of the Holy Office," https://www.ewtn.com/catholicism/library/monitum-on-the-writings-of-fr-teilhard-de-chardin-sj-2144.
68	"most important Catholic writer": FOC to Father J. H. McCown, 21 March 1964, *HB*, 570.
68	"man of God": FOC to Alfred Corn, 30 May 1962, *HB*, 477.
68	"great mystic": FOC to Betty Hester, 4 February 1961, *HB*, 430.
68	"twelve-inch maxi-single": Lucinda Williams, "Faith & Grace (Voodoo Mix)," side A, *Just a Little More Faith and Grace*, Thirty Tigers, 2016, LP, blue vinyl, issued on Record Store Day 2016.
69	"full on testifyin'": Tom Overby, #Hwy20InsideJobBlog, 5 February 2016, **(site discontinued)**. [Author has a transcript of Overby's blogs in his files.]
69	"all I need": Lucinda Williams, "Faith & Grace," disc 2, track 7 on *The Ghosts of Highway 20*.

70   "without damaging": Miller Williams with Marshall Bruce Gentry and Alice Friman, "Our conversations were in script," 11.

70   "it takes every word": FOC, "Writing Short Stories," *MM*, 96.

70   "mentor to him": Erin Williams, "Q&A: A Conversation with Lucinda Williams," *St Louis Magazine*, https://www.stlmag.com/culture/music/a-conversation-with-lucinda-williams/.

70   "I am where I am": Miller Williams with Marshall Bruce Gentry and Alice Friman, 16.

70   "O'Connor was to you": Lucinda Williams, lyrics booklet, *Down Where the Spirit Meets the Bone*, Highway 20 Records/Thirty Tigers, 2016, CD.

Chapter 3: Mary Gauthier: The Brutal Hand of Grace

71   "big influences": Mary Gauthier, interview by Irwin Streight, 25 April 2009.

71   "works and vision": Vanderbilt University, "Flannery O'Connor roundtable," YouTube Video, 1:04:15, 25 February 2009, https://www.youtube.com/watch?v=rZjKG4jI2_I.

71   "read it all": Mary Gauthier, interview by Irwin Streight, 25 April 2009.

71   "unladylike writer": Mary Gauthier, interview by Irwin Streight, 25 April 2009.

71   "reviewer in *Time*": "Such Nice People," *Time*, 6 June 1955, cited in *Flannery O'Connor: The Contemporary Reviews*, edited by Scott and Streight (Cambridge University Press, 2009), 114.

71   "these experiences": Mary Gauthier, interview by Irwin Streight, 25 April 2009.

72   "mental health disorders": "Review: *The Foundling*," *U.S. Catholic* 75, no. 8 (5 August 2010), 42.

72   "she was thirty-five": Creativity Radio, "Art of the Song," Mary Gauthier interview, show #188, Rocky Mountain Folk Festival, Lyons, Colorado, 4 August 2008. [Transcript of radio interview in author's files.]

72   "looking for the grace": Mary Gauthier, "Camelot Motel," track 6 on *Filth and Fire*, Signature Sounds, 2002, CD.

72   "don't deserve it": Gauthier, "Mercy Now," track 2 on *Mercy Now*.

72   "It's a holy art": Steve Boisson, "Mary Gauthier," *Acoustic Guitar* 21, no. 7 (January 2011), 28.

72   "The mystery deepens": Creativity Radio, "Art of the Song," Mary Gauthier interview.

72   "source in a realm much larger": FOC, "The Nature and Aim of Fiction," *MM*, 83.

72   "comes from God": FOC, "The Fiction Writer and His Country," *MM*, 27.

72   "from a higher place": Mary Gauthier, *Saved by a Song* (St. Martin's Essentials, 2021), 4.

72   "violent means": FOC, "The Fiction Writer and His Country," *MM*, 33–34.

73   "commercial songs": Creativity Radio, "Art of the Song," Mary Gauthier interview.

73   "comfort the disturbed": Vanderbilt University, "Flannery O'Connor roundtable," YouTube Video.

73   "telling the truth": Chris Smith, "Mary Gauthier: The Darker Side of Dixie," *Rock's Back Pages Audio*, 4 September 1999, https://www.rocksbackpages.com/Library/Article/mary-gauthier-the-darker-side-of-dixie.

73   "Truth-tellers are different": Creativity Radio, "Art of the Song," Mary Gauthier interview.

73   "a miracle to me": FOC to Betty Hester, 1 January 1956, *HB*, 127.

73   "weren't supposed to eat it": FOC, *Con*, 60.

73   "not to turn away": FOC, "The Fiction Writer and His Country," *MM*, 35.

73   "clear the room": Mary Gauthier, interview by Irwin Streight, 25 April 2009.

74	"Go back to hell": FOC, "Revelation," *CS*, 500.
74	"what I learned": Vanderbilt University, "Flannery O'Connor roundtable," YouTube Video.
74	"grace without the cross": Dietrich Bonhoeffer, *The Cost of Discipleship*, Revised and Unabridged edition (Macmillan, 1979), 47.
74	"justifies the sinner": Bonhoeffer, *The Cost of Discipleship*, 47–48.
74	"a contrite heart": Bonhoeffer, *The Cost of Discipleship*, 48.
74	"grace of Christ himself": Bonhoeffer, *The Cost of Discipleship*, 49.
75	"find a socket": Terry Gross, "Mary Gauthier De-Romanticizes Romantic Love," NPR, *Fresh Air*, 24 June 2014, https://www.npr.org/2014/06/24/325184074/mary-gauthier-on-de-romanticized-romantic-love.
75	"changed everything": Gross, "Mary Gauthier De-Romanticizes Romantic Love," NPR, *Fresh Air*, 24 June 2014.
75	"the next high": Mary Gauthier, "Karla Faye," track 3 on *Drag Queens in Limousines*, In the Black Records, 1999, CD.
75	"executed in Texas": "Murderpedia," https://www.murderpedia.org/female.T/t/tucker-karla.htm.
76	"Goodbye, Karla Faye": Mary Gauthier, "Karla Faye."
76	"his 'botched' life": FOC, "Parker's Back," *CS*, 514.
76	"authoritarian and empty": Gauthier quoted in Hight, *Right by Her Roots*, 121.
76	"traditional gospel thinking": Gauthier quoted in Hight, *Right by Her Roots*, 122.
76	"come down to woo her": FOC, "Greenleaf," *CS*, 311.
76	"hanged himself": FOC, "The Lame Shall Enter First," *CS*, 482.
77	"acts of 'meanness'": FOC, "A Good Man Is Hard to Find," *CS*, 132.
77	"one of my children": FOC, "A Good Man Is Hard to Find," *CS*, 132.
77	"at the time": Gross, "Mary Gauthier De-Romanticizes Romantic Love," NPR, *Fresh Air*, 24 June 2014.
77	"ashes into flame": Mary Gauthier, "Worthy," track 5 on *Trouble and Love*, Six Shooter Records, 2014, CD.
78	"irresistible grace": [See for example Robert Milder, "The Protestantism of Flannery O'Connor," reprinted in *The Critical Response to Flannery O'Connor*, edited by Douglas Robillard Jr. (Praeger, 2004), 161–75. "The issues of predestination and irresistible grace are particularly acute in Miss O'Connor's two novellas, *The Violent Bear It Away* and *Wise Blood*" (173).]
78	"the last thing": FOC, "The Enduring Chill," *CS*, 376.
78	"price of restoration": FOC, "Some Aspects of the Grotesque in Southern Fiction," *MM*, 48.
78	"O'Connor inspired song": Creativity Radio, "Art of the Song," Mary Gauthier interview.
78	"drew on O'Connor's": Hight, *Right by Her Roots*, 110.
78	"used by her father": Creativity Radio, "Art of the Song," Mary Gauthier interview.
79	"snake bit like me": Mary Gauthier, "Snakebit," track 1 on *Between Daylight and Dark*, Lost Highway/UMG, 2007, CD.
79	"'hissed' imprecations": FOC, "The Comforts of Home," *CS*, 403.
79	"as though a snake": FOC, "A Good Man Is Hard to Find," *CS*, 132.
79	"reject the holy": Jewly Hight, "A Good Writer Isn't Hard to Find," *Georgia Music* (Spring 2009), 50.
79	"parade of souls": Gauthier, "Wheel inside the Wheel," track 3 on *Mercy Now*.
79	"rumbling toward heaven": FOC, "Revelation," *CS*, 508.
79	"bottom rail [is] on top": FOC, "Revelation," *CS*, 507.

79	"white-trash": FOC, "Revelation," *CS*, 491.
79	"vast swinging bridge": FOC, "Revelation," *CS*, 508.
80	"bathed in blue": Gauthier, "Wheel inside the Wheel," *Mercy Now*.
80	"lavender blue to purple": FOC, "Revelation," *CS*, 507, 508.
80	"from the stage": Mary Gauthier, "Wheel inside the Wheel" (Live at the Cambridge Folk Festival, July 2005), track 5 on *Season of Mercy* [For Promotional Use Only], Lost Highway, 2005, CD.
80	"middle of the air": "Ezekiel Saw the Wheel," traditional African American spiritual.
80	"recently died": "Behind the Song: Wheel inside the Wheel," https://www.marygauthier.com/news/behind-the-song-wheel-inside-the-wheel.
80	"abysmal life-giving knowledge": FOC, "Revelation," *CS*, 508.
80	"there is very little drama": FOC, "Novelist and Believer," *MM*, 167.
81	"five years on her first novel . . . her second . . . seven years to complete": Sally Fitzgerald, "Chronology," *CW*, 1242, 1246, 1252.
81	"imaginative (and prayerful) pursuit": FOC to Father J. H. McCown, 4 March 1962, *HB*, 468. [After sixteen years as a full-time writer, O'Connor feels that she has "exhausted [her] original potentiality" for creating stories and asks of her confessor, "pray that the Lord will send me some more."]
81	"not easy for me": Mary Gauthier, interview by Chris Smith, *Rock's Back Pages Audio*, 4 September 1999, "Mary Gauthier: The Darker Side of Dixie," https://www.rocksbackpages.com/Library/Article/mary-gauthier.
81	"what I don't know": Creativity Radio, "Art of the Song," Mary Gauthier interview.
81	"want to tell it big": Steve Boisson, "Mary Gauthier," *Acoustic Guitar* 21, no. 7 (January 2011), 29.
81	"three hundred drafts": Grant Alden, "Mary Gauthier: Late train to mercy," *No Depression* (January–February 2005), 53.
81	"Fish swim birds fly": Mary Gauthier, "I Drink," track 4 on *Drag Queens in Limousines*, In the Black Records, 1999, CD. [Lyrics cited from *Saved by a Song*, p. 10.]
81	"*Theme Time Radio Hour*": David Burke, "Mary Gauthier: Liberty Belle," https://www.rocksbackpages.com/Library/Article/mary-gauthier-liberty-belle.
81	"serious writer": Hight, *Right by Her Roots*, 124.
82	"ironic last line": Mary Gauthier, "The Holiday Inn Again," *Amplified*, edited by Julie Schaper and Steven Horwitz (Melville House, 2009), 83–95.
82	"to create life with words": FOC, "Writing Short Stories," *MM*, 88.
82	"the mystery of personality": FOC, "Writing Short Stories," *MM*, 90.
82	"real heart of the story lies": FOC, "On Her Own Work," *MM*, 111.
82	"for an instant": FOC, "A Good Man Is Hard to Find," *CS*, 132.
82	"I would have no story": FOC, "On Her Own Work," *MM*, 112.
82	"can only be expanded": FOC, "Writing Short Stories," *MM*, 102.
83	"from which they fell": Mary Gauthier, "Camelot Motel."
83	"will 'catch up'": Gauthier, "Drag Queens in Limousines," track 1 on *Drag Queens in Limousines*.
83	"the dirty stage": Gauthier, "Evangeline," track 5 on *Drag Queens in Limousines*.
83	"don't give a damn": Gauthier, "I Drink."
83	"Goddamn HIV" and "Skeleton Town": Mary Gauthier, tracks 4 & 8 on *Dixie Kitchen*, In the Black Records, 1997, CD.
83	"Merry Christmas y'all": Mary Gauthier, "Christmas in Paradise," track 9 on *Filth & Fire*, Signature Sounds, 2002, CD.
83	"Hurricane Katrina": Mary Gauthier, "Can't Find the Way," track 2 on *Between Daylight and Dark*, Lost Highway, 2007, CD.

84	"cowritten with veterans": Mary Gauthier, *Rifles & Rosary Beads*, Proper Records, 2018, CD.
84	"complex and troubled hearts": William Faulkner, *Go Down, Moses* (Vintage, Reissue Edition, 1990), 249.
84	"behind him 100 per cent": FOC, *Con*, 83.
85	"wandering and rootlessness": Hight, *Right by Her Roots*, 129.
85	"*The Foundling* is my story": Mary Gauthier, insert/cover plate, *The Foundling*, Razor & Tie, 2010, CD.
85	"adoptee identity crisis song": Mary Gauthier, "The Foundling Notes," personal correspondence, January 2010.
85	"agonizing twenty-six seconds": Gauthier, "Blood Is Blood," track 6 on *The Foundling*.
85	"further six months": Gauthier, "The Foundling Notes," personal correspondence, January 2010.
86	"too much for her": Gauthier, "The Foundling Notes," personal correspondence, January 2010.
86	"that's why I called. Goodbye": Gauthier, "March 11, 1962," track 7 on *The Foundling*.
86	"fundamental tone and harmonic": Gauthier, "Walk in the Water," track 8 on *The Foundling*.
86	"considerable courage": FOC, "The Fiction Writer and His Country," *MM*, 35. [O'Connor concludes her essay/manifesto with this statement: "it requires considerable courage at any time, in any country, not to turn away from the storyteller."]
86	"universal and big": T Bone Burnett quoted in Harold De Muir, "T Bone Burnett: Mad Hatter," *Pulse* 107 (August 1992), 41.
86	"action of mercy": FOC, "The Artificial Nigger," *CS*, 269.
86	"than I understand myself": FOC to Father J. H. McCown, 20 February 1956, *HB*, 140.
87	"he felt he knew *now*": FOC, "The Artificial Nigger," *CS*, 269.
87	"*through* me not *from* me": Mary Gauthier interview by Sheilah Kast, "Mary Gauthier Brings Dark Past to 'Mercy Now,'" *NPR Weekend Edition*, 20 March 2005, https://www.npr.org/2005/03/20/4539873/mary-gauthier-brings-dark-past-to-mercy-now#.
87	"the hand of grace": Gauthier, "Mercy Now."
87	"strong stone cross": Mary Gauthier, illustration in lyrics booklet insert, *Mercy Now*, Lost Highway, 2005, CD.
87	"Jesus or the devil": FOC, *VBA*, 39.
87	"hell and hallowed ground": Gauthier, "Mercy Now."
87	"everything [is] off balance": FOC, "A Good Man Is Hard to Find," *CS*, 132.
87	"walk through the fire": Gauthier, "Walk through the Fire," track 1 on *Filth and Fire*, Signature Sounds, 2002, CD.
87	"applies to songwriting": Gauthier, *Saved by a Song*, 49–50.
87	"because I am called to": Gauthier, *Saved by a Song*, 2.

Chapter 4: Kate Campbell: "Equal Parts Emmylou Harris and Flannery O'Connor"

88	"familiar with Flannery O'Connor": Kate Campbell quoted in Robert K. Oermann, "Songs of the South: Kate Campbell's Music Tells It Like It Is," *Tennessean*, 29 January 1997, D3.
88	"in the liner notes": [See lyrics booklet insert with CD in liner note headed "For inspiration": Kate Campbell, *Moonpie Dreams* (Compass Records, 1997).]
88	"mix of believability and darkness": Kate Campbell quoted in Chris Flisher, "Country Charm: Kate Campbell Writes What She Knows," www.worcesterphoenix.com/archive/music/97/04/25/CAMPBELL.html.

88	"with the late Guy Clark": Oermann, "Songs of the South," D3.
88	"played major venues": "Bio," https://www.katecampbell.com/bio.
89	"equal parts": Craig Harris, "Kate Campbell Biography," https://www.allmusic.com/artist/kate-campbell-mn0000855282.
89	"the same the world over": Kate Campbell quoted in Chris Flisher, "Country Charm."
89	"in a universal light": FOC, "The Regional Writer," *MM*, 58.
89	"a gateway to reality": FOC, "The Regional Writer," *MM*, 54.
89	"jeopardizing his preaching job": Kate Campbell in *Solo: Women Singer-Songwriters in Their Own Words*, 330.
89	"the violence between them": Kate Campbell in *Solo*, 330.
90	"And freedom rang": Kate Campbell, "Crazy in Alabama," track 4 on *Visions of Plenty*, Compass Records, 1998, CD.
90	"junior high school": Kate Campbell in *Solo*, 332.
90	"if the view has changed": Kate Campbell, "Bus 109," track 7 on *Visions of Plenty*.
90	"on March 26, 1961": Sally Fitzgerald, "Notes on the Texts," *CW*, 1258.
90	"violence-wracked journey": [The original group of Freedom Riders, seven Black Americans and six whites, left Washington, DC, on 4 May 1961 in two buses en route to New Orleans. "Freedom Rides," https://www.britannica.com/event/Freedom-Rides.]
90	"Hollywood Baptist Church": Kate Campbell in *Solo*, 330.
91	"mule to fly": FOC to Maryat Lee, 25 April 1959, *HB*, 329.
91	"stained her literary reputation": [See for example, Paul Elie, "How Racist Was Flannery O'Connor?" *New Yorker*, 22 June 2020, 82–85.]
91	"one 'topical' story": FOC to Betty Hester, 1 September 1963, *HB*, 537.
91	"at the local YMCA": FOC, "Everything That Rises Must Converge," *CS*, 405.
91	"own side of the fence": FOC, "Everything That Rises Must Converge," *CS*, 408.
91	"bus to ourselves": FOC, "Everything That Rises Must Converge," *CS*, 409–10.
92	"her 'black double'": FOC, "Everything That Rises Must Converge," *CS*, 419.
92	"flag half-mast": Kate Campbell, "Look Away," track 9 on *Rosaryville*, Compass Records, 1999, CD.
92	"implicitly proslavery": See Daniel Decatur Emmett, "(I Wish I Was In) Dixie Land" (1859).
92	"a plague on everybody's house": FOC to Betty Hester, 1 September 1963, *HB*, 537.
92	"race, a sense of place": Kate Campbell, personal interview 18 July 2019.
93	"a way I could talk about": Kate Campbell, personal interview 18 July 2019.
93	"bear it away": Kate Campbell, "Bear It Away," track 7 on *Wandering Strange*, Eminent Records, 2001, CD.
93	"actual life we live": FOC, "The Fiction Writer & His Country," *MM*, 33.
94	"photographs of such signs": See Harold Fickett and Douglas R. Gilbert, *Flannery O'Connor: Images of Grace* (Eerdmans, 1986); Barbara McKenzie, *Flannery O'Connor's Georgia* (University of Georgia Press, 1980).
94	"printed 'Jesus Saves'": FOC, *WB*, 75.
94	"Jesus and tomatoes": Jodi Matthews, "Songwriting as Storytelling: An Interview with Kate Campbell," 15 January 2002, https://www.goodfaithmedia.org/songwriting-as-storytelling-an-interview-with-kate-campbell-cms-186/.
94	"We'll have a BLT": Kate Campbell, "Jesus and Tomatoes," track 3 on *Visions of Plenty*.
94	"finest singer-songwriters": "Campbell, Kate," *Encyclopedia of Popular Music*, 4th edition, edited by Colin Larkin (Oxford University Press, 2006), 153.
94	"for others concrete": Kate Campbell, "Bud's Sea-Mint Boat," track 4 on *Moonpie Dreams*, Compass Records, 1997, CD.

95	"here for the feast": Kate Campbell, "Funeral Food," track 9 on *Visions of Plenty*.
95	"comic funeral instructions": FOC, *VBA*, 13–14.
95	"couldn't think of anything": FOC, *VBA*, 11.
95	"good for the figs": FOC, *VBA*, 22.
95	"feeling embarrassed": FOC to Robie Macauley, 18 May 1955, *HB*, 80–81.
95	"closes her concerts": Kate Campbell, personal interview 18 July 2019.
96	"did hang on the cross": "The Message of the Cross," https://www.blessitt.com/the-message-of-the-cross.
96	"popular consciousness": Arthur Blessitt, "Arthur Blessitt: Carrying the Cross," excerpt adapted from *The Cross* by Arthur Blessitt (Authentic), https://www2.cbn.com/article/salvation/arthur-blessitt-carrying-cross.
96	"meant sincerely": Kate Campbell, "God Bless You Arthur Blessitt," track 9 on *1000 Pound Machine*, Large River Music, 2012, CD.
96	"list of people": [See lyrics booklet insert with CD in liner note headed "For inspiration": Kate Campbell, *Moonpie Dreams*.]
97	"sentenced by jury": Jeanne McDonald, review of *The Serpent and the Spirit: Glenn Summerford's Story* by Thomas Burton, *Appalachian Heritage* 33, no. 2 (Spring 2005), 79.
97	"will not bite": Kate Campbell, "Signs Following," track 9 on *Moonpie Dreams*.
97	"Signs Following practitioners": Hight, *Right by Her Roots*, 19.
97	"kiss the diamondback": Lucinda Williams, "Get Right with God," track 9 on *Essence*.
97	"holy-rolling snake handlers": Jodi Matthews, "Songwriting as Storytelling: An Interview with Kate Campbell."
97	"a fine line": James Calemine, review of *Salvation on Sand Mountain* by Dennis Covington, https://www.swampland.com/reviews/view/title:salvation_on_sand_mountain.
97	"newspaper clippings": FOC, "Greenleaf," *CS*, 315–16.
97	"Jesus, stab me": FOC, "Greenleaf," *CS*, 317.
98	"Come to destroy": FOC, "The Displaced Person," *CS*, 210.
98	"attempt to manipulate": FOC, *VBA*, 128.
98	"the prophetic message": FOC, *VBA*, 130–33.
98	"cut off the voice": FOC, *VBA*, 134–35.
98	"hadda hunch": FOC, *VBA*, 124.
99	"distortion . . . that reveals": FOC, "Novelist and Believer," *MM*, 162.
99	"priestly darkness": FOC, *VBA*, 128.
99	"glory of the Lord": FOC, *VBA*, 130.
99	"a burning Word": FOC, *VBA*, 134.
99	"burned clean again": FOC, *VBA*, 5–6.
99	"behind him 100 per cent": FOC, *Con*, 83.
99	"who speaks for me": FOC to John Hawkes, 13 September 1959, *HB*, 350.
99	"both native and alien": FOC, "The Catholic Novelist in the Protestant South," *MM*, 197.
99	"not totally congenial": FOC, "The Catholic Novelist in the Protestant South," *MM*, 207, 206.
99	"religious affinities": FOC, "The Catholic Novelist in the Protestant South," *MM*, 207.
100	"Pray for us": Kate Campbell, "Porcelain Blue," track 2 on *Rosaryville*.
100	"found peace within": Campbell, "Ave Maria Grotto," track 10 on *Rosaryville*.
100	"hear themselves talk": Campbell, "Heart of Hearts," track 5 on *Rosaryville*.
100	"typeset in paragraph form": lyrics sheet insert with CD, Kate Campbell, *Rosaryville*, Compass Records, 1999.
100	"Who will pray for Junior": Campbell, "Who Will Pray for Junior?" track 7 on *Rosaryville*.

101 "Who knows what we will find?": Campbell, "Rosaryville," track 1 on *Rosaryville*.
101 "don't think the record": Matthews, "Songwriting as Storytelling: An Interview with Kate Campbell."
101 "her Protestant faith": Kate Campbell, personal interview 18 July 2019.
101 "your rosary": Kate Campbell, "Miracle of the Rosary," hidden 12th track on *Wandering Strange*.
102 "literally and literarily": lyrics sheet insert with CD, Kate Campbell, *Rosaryville*.
102 "mystery of existence": FOC to Eileen Hall, 10 March 1956, *HB*, 143. [The quotation in context and original form reads, "Art is not anything that goes on 'among' people, not the art of the novel anyway. It is something that one experiences alone and for the purpose of realizing in a fresh way, through the senses, mystery of existence."]
102 "a song about it someday": Kate Campbell, personal interview 18 July 2019.

Chapter 5: Sufjan Stevens: In Flannery's Territory

103 "'idol' Flannery O'Connor": Nick Sylvester, "Without a Prayer," *Village Voice*, 2 August 2005, https://www.villagevoice.com/without-a-prayer/
103 "the most important thing": Sylvester, "Without a Prayer."
103 "post-God society": Sufjan Stevens quoted in Ryan Dombal, "True Myth: A Conversation with Sufjan Stevens," https://pitchfork.com/features/interview/9595-true-myth-a-conversation-with-sufjan-stevens/.
104 "Michigan's version": "Sufjan Stevens Fan Page," https://www.soofjan.tumblr.com/post/126416642009/sufjan-stevens-was-born-in-detroit-michigan-and.
104 "the Next Flannery": Sylvester, "Without a Prayer."
104 "New School Chapbook Series": Sufjan Stevens, "We Are Shielded by the Holy Ghost," *New School Chapbook Series*, Spring 2003, 18 pages.
104 "on his Tumblr account": The text of the short story "All the Nonsense of Suffering" can be found at https://www.tumblr.com/soofjan/113724149314/all-the-nonsense-of-suffering; the full text of "An Oboist with So-So Vibrato" can be found at https://www.tumblr.com/soofjan/113589155904/an-oboist-with-so-so-vibrato.
104 "A fourth story": Sufjan Stevens, "My Mother, King Tut," *Image* 39 (Summer 2003), 41–49.
105 "signals 'the added dimension'": FOC, "The Church and the Fiction Writer," *MM*, 150.
105 "largely by the devil": FOC, "On Her Own Work," *MM*, 118.
105 "specific personality": FOC, "On Her Own Work," *MM*, 117.
106 "comical side": FOC, "Novelist and Believer," *MM*, 167.
106 "hunched form of Satan": All quotations from the story are taken from Sufjan Stevens, "We Are Shielded by the Holy Ghost," *New School Chapbook Series*, Spring 2003, 1–18.
106 "bird-shaped water stain": FOC, "The Enduring Chill," *CS*, 382.
106 "Stevens's Tumblr account": See https://www.tumblr.com/soofjan/113724149314/all-the-nonsense-of-suffering.
106 "published on O'Connor": See Rene Steinke, "Engine of Grace: Review of Flannery O'Connor's *A Prayer Journal*," *Bookforum* (December/January 2014), 33.
106 "as much as it obscures": Rene Steinke, headnote to New School Chapbook Series, "We Are Shielded by the Holy Ghost," by Sufjan Stevens, unnumbered page.
107 "once and for all": Sufjan Stevens, "All the Nonsense of Suffering."
107 "the Lord Himself": FOC, *VBA*, 5.
107 "Jesus, stab me": FOC, "Greenleaf," *CS*, 317.
107 "satirical caricatures": Rene Steinke, headnote to New School Chapbook Series, "We Are Shielded by the Holy Ghost," by Sufjan Stevens, unnumbered page.

107	"impenetrable": Sufjan Stevens interviewed by Rick Moody, *PENultimate Lit: An Evening on Music & Literature*, 16 October 2006, https://www.soundcloud.com/penamerican/penultimate-lit-an-evening-on [Stevens cites a *Harpers* editor's comment at 1:02:58].
107	"on to 'Plan B'": Sufjan Stevens interviewed by Jason Crock, http://pitchfork.com/features/interviews/6335-sufjan-stevens/.
107	"Best New Music": "Greetings from Michigan: The Great Lakes State," https://www.pitchfork.com/reviews/albums/7510-greetings-from-michigan-the-great-lakes-state.
108	"Michigan postcard": [Several "Greetings from Michigan" postcards dated from 1969 to the present, displayed on e-Bay in 2023, contain graphics and typographical elements directly incorporated into the cover design of the *Michigan* album and CD, and most evidently in the liner notes with center fold-out included with the CD.]
108	"blinded by the light": Bruce Springsteen, lyrics to "Blinded by the Light," track 1 on *Greetings from Asbury Park, N.J.*, Columbia, 1973, CD.
108	"50 States Project": "Sufjan Stevens," *Contemporary Musicians* 57, 185.
108	"publicity stunt": Luke Howley, "Critical Voices, Sufjan Stevens," *Age of Adz*, The Georgetown Voice, 7 October 2010, https://georgetownvoice.com/2010/10/07/critical-voices-sufjan-stevens-age-of-adz/. ["In 2009, Stevens shamelessly announced that the 'Fifty State Project' [sic] was nothing more than a publicity stunt."]
108	"a mirror image": Frederick Asals, *Flannery O'Connor: The Imagination of Extremity* (University of Georgia Press, 1982), 96.
109	"moral moron": FOC, "The Comforts of Home," *CS*, 385.
109	"bad check": FOC, "The Comforts of Home," *CS*, 386.
109	"no better than": FOC, "The Comforts of Home," *CS*, 392.
109	"each other's arms": FOC, "The Comforts of Home," *CS*, 404.
109	"black double": FOC, "Everything That Rises Must Converge," *CS*, 419.
109	"coming and going": FOC, "Everything That Rises Must Converge," *CS*, 406.
109	"negative image": FOC, "Judgement Day," *CS*, 538.
109	"to greet him": FOC, "Judgement Day," *CS*, 546.
110	"all her life": FOC, "A Good Man Is Hard to Find," *CS*, 126.
110	"repeated six times": Sufjan Stevens, "A Good Man Is Hard to Find," track 9 on *Seven Swans*, Sounds Familyre, 2004, CD.
110	"their common defeat": FOC, "The Artificial Nigger," *CS*, 269.
110	"heart of mystery": FOC, "Revelation," *CS*, 508.
110	"wouldn't shoot a lady": FOC, "A Good Man Is Hard to Find," *CS*, 131–32.
110	"struggles to believe": FOC, "A Good Man Is Hard to Find," *CS*, 132.
111	"reaches to touch": FOC, "A Good Man Is Hard to Find," *CS*, 132.
111	"left me creased": Stevens, "A Good Man Is Hard to Find."
111	"prattling about": FOC, "On Her Own Work," *MM*, 112.
111	"court documents": "Murderpedia," https://www.murderpedia.org/male.G/g1/gacy-john-wayne.htm.
112	"secrets I have hid": Sufjan Stevens, "John Wayne Gacy, Jr.," track 4 on *Come on Feel the Illinoise* [*Illinois*], Asthmatic Kitty Records, 2005, CD.
112	"claim as his own": FOC, "The Artificial Nigger," *CS*, 270.
112	"have both been touched": See the illustrated six-panel, multifold lyric sheet insert, *Come on Feel the Illinoise* [*Illinois*].
112	"finding the will of God": "What is Subud?" https://www.subud.ca/what-is-subud.html.
112	"Stevens reveals in an interview": [Details about Stevens's early life are derived from this interview, recorded at the Festival of Faith and Music, Calvin College, 31 March 2007. For copyright reasons, this recording is no longer available. The author has a personal copy of the recorded interview on cassette.]

112 "converted to Catholicism": Lynsey Hanley, "State Trouper," *The Guardian*, 20 November 2005, https://www.theguardian.com/music/2005/nov/20/popandrock.sufjanstevens.

112 "Christian post-secondary": "Sufjan Stevens," sufjanstevens.us/bio.html.

113 "mystery of the Crucifixion": Stevens, "Concerning the UFO Sighting Near Highland Illinois," track 1 on *Illinoise* and "To Be Alone with You," track 4 on *Seven Swans*.

113 "a spiritual songsmith": *Paste* staff, "The 20 Best Sufjan Stevens Songs," *Paste*, 24 March 2020, pastemagazine.com/music/sufjan-stevens/best-sufjan-stevens-songs/.

113 "It's really a meal": Jeremy Allen, "Adz and It Shall Be Given Unto You: Sufjan Stevens Interviewed," *Quietus*, 12 October 2010, http://thequietus.com/articles/05085-the-age-of-adz-sufjan-stevens-interview.

113 "the bread of life": FOC, *VBA*, 21.

113 "to hell with it": FOC to Betty Hester, 16 December 1955, *HB*, 125.

113 "living and moving and being": David Roark, "How Sufjan Stevens Subverts the Stigma of Christian Music," *Atlantic*, 29 March 2015, https://www.theatlantic.com/entertainment/archive/2015/03/sufjan-stevens-and-a-better-way-to-write-music-about-faith/388802/.

113 "largely by the devil": FOC, "On Her Own Work," *MM*, 115, 118.

114 "to beat you": Sufjan Stevens, "In the Devil's Territory," track 3 on *Seven Swans*.

114 "made to name himself": FOC, "On Her Own Work," *MM*, 117.

114 "identified as the Devil": FOC to John Hawkes, 20 November 1959, *HB*, 360.

114 "one of Hawthorne's 'descendants'": FOC to William Sessions, 16 September 1960, *HB*, 407.

114 "lyric material on *Michigan*": [For example, listen to Stevens's interview by Rick Moody, "PENultimate Lit: An Evening on Music & Literature," 16 October 2006, https://www.soundcloud.com/penamerican/penultimate-lit-an-evening-on. At 1:02:10 Stevens remarks, "a lot of the stories I was writing in my thesis became songs and became part of the *Michigan* record actually."]

115 "social and geographical": See "Chronology" in *CW*, 1240–45.

115 "part to remind me": Stevens, "Say Yes! to M!ch!gan!" track 4 on *Michigan*, Asthmatic Kitty Records, 2003, CD.

115 "I lost my wife": Stevens, "The Upper Peninsula," track 5 on *Michigan*.

116 "her last child": Stevens, "Romulus," track 9 on *Michigan*.

116 "right gesture": FOC, "On Her Own Work," *MM*, 112.

116 "experience of mystery itself": FOC, "Some Aspects of the Grotesque in Southern Fiction," *MM*, 41.

116 "a secret life": FOC, "Revelation," *CS*, 507–8.

116 "monstrance with the Host": FOC, "A Temple of the Holy Ghost," *CS*, 248.

117 "your perfect design": Stevens, "Sleeping Bear, Sault Saint Marie," track 11 on *Michigan*.

117 "the spirit is fine": Stevens, "Jacksonville," track 5 on *Come on Feel the Illinoise* [*Illinois*].

117 "the great I Am": Stevens, "Decatur, or Round of Applause for Your Stepmother," track 7 on *Come on Feel the Illinoise* [*Illinois*].

117 "attributed to the poet": Samuel Taylor Coleridge, *Biographia Literaria* (1817). [The phrase appears in the last sentence of this work in a section headed "Conclusion," as Coleridge contemplates the cosmos and refers to the soul's "pure act of inward adoration to the great I AM."]

117 "American cavalry": "Pulaski Day Parade," http://pulaskiparade.com/father-of-the-American-cavalry/.

117 "a teenage sweetheart": Hanley, "State Trouper," *The Guardian*, 20 November 2005.

117 "collage making": Sufjan Stevens quoted in Evan Rytlewski, "Sufjan Stevens: Narratives, Concepts, and Puzzle Pieces," *American Songwriter* (September/October 2006), 50.

117	"seem personal": Matt Fink, "Sufjan Stevens: Myth and Madness," *Under the Radar* 34 (2010), 67.
117	"O'Connor said that": Hanley, "State Trouper," *The Guardian*, 20 November 2005.
118	"when I see His face": Sufjan Stevens, "Casamir Pulaski Day," track 10 on *Come On Feel the Illinoise* [*Illinois*].
118	"fantasy-cartoonish drawings": 12-page stapled booklet included with CD, Sufjan Stevens, *The Age of Adz*, Asthmatic Kitty Records, 2010.
119	"major museum collections": SAAM Artist: "Prophet" Royal Robertson, https://americanart.si.edu/artist/prophet-royal-robertson-7409.
119	"reference point": Sufjan Stevens quoted in Matt Fink, "Sufjan Stevens: Myth and Madness," 62.
120	"get right with the Lord": Sufjan Stevens, "Get Real, Get Right," track 6 on *The Age of Adz*, Asthmatic Kitty Records, 2010, CD.
120	"Between Hipsters and God": See https://www.fuckyeahsufjanstevens.tumblr.com.
120	"Reviewers compared": See for example Benjamin Naddaff-Hafrey, "Songs We Love: Sufjan Stevens, 'Chicago (Demo),'" NPR, *All Songs Considered*, 25 February 2016, https://www.npr.org/sections/allsongs/2016/02/25/468116881/songs-we-love-sufjan-stevens-chicago-demo.
120	"did not sit well with Stevens": Fink, "Sufjan Stevens: Myth and Madness," 61. ["Having expressed occasional discomfort over the immediate appeal of his most popular albums—once, [Stevens] somewhat embarrassedly singled out *Illinois*' standout 'Chicago' for sounding too much like a Coldplay song—."]
120	"exhaustion of certain possibilities": John Barth, "The Literature of Exhaustion," in *The Friday Book: Essays and Other Non-Fiction* (Johns Hopkins University Press, 1984), 64.
121	"faith in the song": Sufjan Stevens quoted in Kate Kiefer, "Sufjan Stevens: On the Road to Find Out," *Paste*, 2 November 2009, https://www.pastemagazine.com/music/sufjan-stevens/sufjan-stevens-on-the-road-to-find-out/.
121	"death of the album": [For example, in conversation with Warren Zanes in the spring of 2021, asked about his storied resistance to releasing hit singles from his albums, Bruce Springsteen remarked, "I'm always a little suspicious of that stuff, and it wasn't what I was fundamentally interested in, but I didn't mind. It's just that I was an album artist. We remain so to this day." Zanes, *Deliver Me from Nowhere*, 276–77.]
121	"doubt my capacity": FOC to Sister Mariella Gable, 4 May 1963, *HB*, 518.
121	"finger of fire": FOC, *VBA*, 5.
121	"torn by the Lord's eye": FOC, *VBA*, 20.
121	"learned by fire": FOC, *VBA*, 5.
121	"hard facts": FOC, *VBA*, 6.
121	"Even the mercy": FOC, *VBA*, 20.
122	"Fall on me now": Stevens, "Vesuvius," track 8 on *The Age of Adz*.
122	"dangerous volcanoes": Mary Bagley, "Mount Vesuvius & Pompeii: Facts & History," livescience.com/27871-mount-vesuvius-pompeii.html.
122	"Pentecostal hymnology": William J. Henry, "Let the Fire Fall on Me" (1926), https://www.hymnary.org/text/lord_i_would_be_wholly_thine. [Phrases in quotation marks that follow are from the text of this hymn.]
122	"I am fire of fire": Gospel of Bartholomew IV:54, *The Apocryphal New Testament*, trans. and notes by Montague Rhodes James (Clarendon Press, 1924), 178.
123	"favor the ghost/host": Stevens, "Vesuvius."
123	"in the Lord's fire": FOC, *VBA*, 135.
123	"It's the same fire": FOC, *VBA*, 51–52.

123 "flaming 'forked tree'": FOC, *VBA*, 238.
123 "red-gold tree of fire": FOC, *VBA*, 242.
123 "symbolic burning bush": FOC, *VBA*, 238.
123 "which fire he will 'favor'": Stevens, "Vesuvius."
123 "by either fire or fire": T. S. Eliot, "Little Gidding," *Four Quartets* (Faber & Faber, 1941).
124 "conflicted about his calling": Sufjan Stevens interview with Rick Moody, "PENultimate Lit: An Evening on Music & Literature," 16 October 2006, https://www.soundcloud.com/penamerican/penultimate-lit-an-evening-on. [At 1:02:10, Stevens comments, "I made a decision to not be a musician, so I came to [New York] to be a writer . . . music became a serious distraction soon after I graduated. I don't really know what happened. I stopped writing stories and started writing songs."]
124 "baroque pop": "The Sound of Baroque Pop," https://open.spotify.com/playlist/1e3sjciHZnhGYpaVYv6rO1.
124 "the same in songwriting": Sufjan Stevens: interview on Pitchforkmedia.com, 12 January 2006 (unavailable), cited in "Stevens, Sufjan," http://www.encyclopedia.com/education/news-wires-white-papers-and-books/stevens-sufjan.
124 "distortion . . . that reveals": FOC, "Novelist and Believer," *MM*, 162.
124 "deeper kinds of realism": FOC, "Some Aspects of the Grotesque in Southern Fiction," *MM*, 39.
124 "very brief lyrics": Sufjan Stevens, "We Won't Need Legs to Stand," track 8 on *Seven Swans*, Sounds Familyre, 2004, CD.
124 "German novelist": "Thomas Pletzinger interviewed by Sufjan Stevens," *BOMB* 115 (Spring 2011), https://bombmagazine.org/articles/thomas-pletzinger/.
124 "going at it all": Sufjan Stevens, "Size Too Small," *Seven Swans*, Sounds Familyre, 2004, CD.
124 "final copy-edit stage": Sufjan Stevens, *Javelin*, Asthmatic Kitty, 2023, CD.
125 "the kingdom of God": "Jar Jar Binks Fan Club," sufjan.com/page/29.
125 "WARN THE CHILDREN OF GOD": FOC, *VBA*, 242.
125 "appear to lie 'sleeping'": FOC, *VBA*, 243.
125 "slight southern fetish": Stevens interview with Rick Moody, "PENultimate Lit: An Evening on Music & Literature," 16 October 2006, https://www.soundcloud.com/penamerican/penultimate-lit-an-evening-on. [Stevens makes this comment at 21:18.]
126 "nothing left to say of me": FOC, *A Prayer Journal*, 40.
126 "potential chapter titles": "Jar Jar Binks Fan Club," https://www.sufjan.com/post/67361270493/eighteen-lines-extracted-from-flannery-oconnors.
126 "to be the best artist": FOC, *A Prayer Journal*, 29.

Chapter 6: Nick Cave: "In the Bleeding Stinking Mad Shadow of Jesus"

127 "a modern man of letters": Kristine McKenna, "Nick Cave's Song of the South: Brooding Rocker/Author Takes Central Cue from Faulkner, O'Connor," *Los Angeles Times*, 26 February 1989, http://articles.latimes.com/1989-02-26/entertainment/ca-1144_1_nick-cave.
127 "heroes of literate oblivion": Simon Reynolds, "Of Misogyny, Murder and Melancholy: Meeting Nick Cave," in *Nick Cave Sinner Saint: The True Confessions*, edited by Mat Snow (Plexus, 2011), 50.
127 "reading at the time": Nick Cave, "The Flesh Made Word" (BBC Radio lecture, 3 March 1996), [51:30–34 on the recording] transcript published in *King Ink II* (Black Spring Press, 1997), 138.
128 "obsessed with Flannery O'Connor's fiction": Phil Sutcliffe, "Nick Cave: Raw and Uncut 2," in *Nick Cave Sinner Saint: The True Confessions*, 218.

128	"divine essence of things": Nick Cave, "The Flesh Made Word" (BBC Radio lecture, 3 March 1996), transcript published in *King Ink II*, 137.
128	"blood of my father in me": Nick Cave, "The Flesh Made Word," *King Ink II*, 141.
128	"great gaping hole": Nick Cave quoted in Chris Maume, "Nick Cave: Devil's Advocate," *Independent*, 11 March 2006, https://www.independent.co.uk/news/people/profiles/nick-cave-devils-advocate-350562.html.
128	"cruel and rancorous God": Nick Cave, "The Flesh Made Word," *King Ink II*, 138.
128	"on his first novel": Ian Johnston, *Bad Seed: A Biography of Nick Cave* (Abacus, 1997), 161–66.
128	"popular Penguin paperback": Nick Cave, *And the Ass Saw the Angel* (1988) [Revised edition] (Penguin, 2009). All page references are to this paperback edition.
128	"avid collector of curios": Carol Hart, "*And the Ass Saw the Angel*: A Novel of Fragment and Excess," in *Cultural Seeds: Essays on the Work of Nick Cave*, edited by Karen Welberry and Tanya Delziell (Ashgate, 2009), 107.
129	"mostly Mary Flannery O'Connor": Bleddyn Butcher quoted in Ben Beaumont-Thomas, "Bleddyn Butcher's Best Photograph: Nick Cave in Berlin," *The Guardian*, 17 November 2016, hhttps://www.theguardian.com/artanddesign/2016/nov/17/bleddyn-butcher-best-photograph-nick-cave-berlin.
129	"cultural icon Nick Cave": https://www.nickcavemtl.com.
130	"fictional Ukulore Valley": Cave, *And the Ass Saw the Angel*, 4.
130	"in the manner of Flannery": Nick Cave quoted in Kristine McKenna, "Nick Cave's Song of the South."
130	"tall wide-brimmed hat": Cave, *And the Ass Saw the Angel*, 72.
130	"stiff black broad-brimmed hat": FOC, *WB*, 10.
130	"steeped in filth": Cave, *And the Ass Saw the Angel*, 75.
131	"Renew my spirit": Cave, *And the Ass Saw the Angel*, 78.
131	"crying in the wilderness": Cave, *And the Ass Saw the Angel*, 81.
131	"a clean boy": FOC, *WB*, 90–91.
131	"twice insists 'I AM clean'": FOC, *WB*, 91, 95.
131	"you people are clean": FOC, *WB*, 55.
131	"I'm not clean": FOC, *WB*, 223–24.
131	"sacred waters": Cave, *And the Ass Saw the Angel*, 85.
131	"pink caravan of pleasure": Cave, *And the Ass Saw the Angel*, 90–92.
131	"to burn you clean": FOC, *VBA*, 134.
131	"old burnt-out Chevy": Cave, *And the Ass Saw the Angel*, 7.
131	"born in a wreck": FOC, *VBA*, 41.
131	"conscious of the loss": Cave, *And the Ass Saw the Angel*, 8.
132	"celestial mission": Cave, *And the Ass Saw the Angel*, 254, 255.
132	"the Hand of God": FOC, *VBA*, 47.
132	"deranged king": Cave, *And the Ass Saw the Angel*, 182.
132	"demon deed": Cave, *And the Ass Saw the Angel*, 268.
132	"prophet predicted": Cave, *And the Ass Saw the Angel*, 280.
133	"both baptizes and drowns": FOC, *VBA*, 210.
133	"torches his hillbilly home": FOC, *VBA*, 50.
133	"swallowed into the earth": Cave, *And the Ass Saw the Angel*, 274–76.
133	"prophet gone wrong": FOC, "On Her Own Work," *MM*, 110.
133	"intrusions of grace": FOC, "On Her Own Work," *MM*, 112.
133	"*Wise Blood* was projected": Nathan Wiseman-Trowse, "Oedipus Wrecks: Cave and the Presley Myth," in *Cultural Seeds: Essays on the Work of Nick Cave*, edited by Karen Welberry and Tanya Delziell (Ashgate, 2009), 164, footnote 42. ["Cave performed extracts

from *And the Ass Saw the Angel* prior to its publication alongside a screening of John Houston's [sic] film of *Wise Blood* (1980) [sic] on the 23rd and 24th of March 1988 at the Mandolin Cinema in Sydney."]

134 "story of new ancestors": *Wings of Desire*, Dir. Wim Wenders (Bruno Ganz, Solveig Dommartin, Otto Sander, Peter Falk), 1987.

134 "irate drenched crow": FOC, "The Lame Shall Enter First," CS, 453.

134 "the Love Song": Nick Cave, "The Secret Life of the Love Song," in *Nick Cave: The Complete Lyrics 1978–2022* (Penguin, 2022), 7.

134 "From her to eternity": Nick Cave and the Bad Seeds, "From Her to Eternity," track 10 on *From Her to Eternity*, Mute Records, 1984, CD.

134 "flesh, erotics, and violence": Lyn McCredden, "Fleshed Sacred: The Carnal Theologies of Nick Cave," in *Cultural Seeds: Essays on the Work of Nick Cave*, edited by Karen Welberry and Tanya Delziell (Ashgate, 2009), 167.

134 "fleshed or carnal sacred": McCredden, "Fleshed Sacred: The Carnal Theologies of Nick Cave," 168.

134 "Dutch-made biopic": vortexeyes, "Nick Cave: Stranger in a strange land VPRO documentary 1987," YouTube Video, 39:37, 14 December 2015, https://www.youtube.com/watch?v=T5JoaaQbtpU&ab_channel=vortexeyes.

135 "have informed Cave's imagination": [Cave's abiding interest in O'Connor is evident in his "conversation" with music journalist Seán O'Hagen, published as *Faith, Hope and Carnage* (Farrar, Straus and Giroux, 2022). O'Hagen remarks on returning every few years to books that he likes, to which Cave responds, "I don't do that so much. I did go back and re-read Flannery O'Connor recently to remember why we must value her, but that was only because her books had been taken out of a college library in America, due to some skewed and overly harsh charges of racism." Cave then offers three lines of lyrics to a new unnamed song that describes his recent reengagement with her works: "I'm sitting on the balcony / Reading Flannery O'Connor / With a pencil and a plan" (*Faith, Hope and Carnage*, 152–53)].

135 "(misspelled O'Conner)": *Nick Cave Stories*, published in association with *Nick Cave: The Exhibition*, Arts Centre Gallery, Melbourne, Australia, 10 November 2007–6 April 2008, Victorian Arts Centre Trust, 2007, [insert 34/35].

135 "reproduced more extensively": see pages 98–147 in Nick Cave, *Stranger Than Kindness*.

135 "form a narrative unit": Nick Cave and the Bad Seeds, *The Boatman's Call*, Reprise Records, 1997, Remastered ed., 2011, LP.

135 "imprisoned John the Baptist": See Matthew 11:2–3, "And when John heard in prison what the Messiah was doing, he sent word by his disciples and said to him, 'Are you the one who is to come, or are we to wait for another?'" [Revised Standard Version, Anglicized (RSVA)].

135 "most theologically brilliant song": Darcey Steinke, "God Is in the House," in *Nick Cave, Stranger Than Kindness*, 68.

135 "an interventionist God": Nick Cave and the Bad Seeds, "Into My Arms," side A, track 1 on *The Boatman's Call*, Reprise Records, 1997, Remastered ed., 2011, LP.

136 "revealed himself": FOC, "Novelist and Believer," MM, 160.

136 "divine source or balm": McCredden, "Fleshed Sacred: The Carnal Theologies of Nick Cave," 167.

136 "the lost God": FOC, "Novelist and Believer," MM, 159.

136 "be like I am now": FOC, "A Good Man Is Hard to Find," CS, 132.

136 "devil we are possessed by": FOC, "Novelist and Believer," MM, 168.

136 "before grace is effective": FOC, "On Her Own Work," MM, 117.

136 "necessary violation": FOC, VBA, 231–32.

137	"not have been brought off": FOC, "On Her Own Work," *MM*, 117.
137	"nothing else will do": FOC, "On Her Own Work," *MM*, 112.
137	"access to the sacred": McCredden, "Fleshed Sacred: The Carnal Theologies of Nick Cave," 168.
137	"version of his 1999 lecture": transcript of "Nick Cave: The Secret Life of the Love Song," read on 25 September 1999 in Vienna. [This version of Cave's lecture contains passages that do not appear in the text of the same title published in *Nick Cave: The Complete Lyrics 1978–2022*, 2–19, based on a lecture by Cave delivered in 1999 at the South Bank Centre, London. In the Vienna version, he states, "The Song of Solomon, perhaps the greatest love song ever written, had a massive impact on me."]
137	"her hand over mine": Nick Cave and the Bad Seeds, "Lime-Tree Arbour," side A, track 2 on *The Boatman's Call*.
137	"According to scholars": Alina-Maria Tenche-Constantinescu et al., "The Symbolism of the Linden Tree," *Journal of Horticulture, Forestry and Biotechnology* 19, no. 2 (2015), 237–42.
138	"hearts with arrows": FOC, "Parker's Back," *CS*, 512, 514.
138	"haphazard and botched": FOC, "Parker's Back," *CS*, 514.
138	"if he didn't change his ways": FOC, "Parker's Back," *CS*, 519.
138	"yells out 'GOD ABOVE'": FOC, "Parker's Back," *CS*, 520.
139	"all-demanding eyes": FOC, "Parker's Back," *CS*, 522.
139	"his dissatisfaction was gone": FOC, "Parker's Back," *CS*, 527.
139	"*E* is for Elihue": for the Hebrew meanings and significance of the names Obadiah and Elihue, see *The Interpreter's One-Volume Commentary on the Bible*, edited by Charles M. Laymon (Abingdon Press, 1984), Obadiah, 477a; Elihu, 249b.
139	"trees and birds and beasts": FOC, "Parker's Back," *CS*, 513.
139	"Idolatry! . . . crying like a baby": FOC, "Parker's Back," *CS*, 529–30.
139	"People just ain't no good": Nick Cave and the Bad Seeds, "People Ain't No Good," side A, track 3 on *The Boatman's Call*.
139	"Nome, I ain't a good man": FOC, "A Good Man Is Hard to Find," *CS*, 128.
139	"a bent for 'meanness'": FOC, "A Good Man Is Hard to Find," *CS*, 132.
139	"a good woman": FOC, "Revelation," *CS*, 497.
140	"put in a gas oven": FOC, "Revelation," *CS*, 492.
140	"trope of 'good country people'": FOC, "Good Country People," *CS*, 279.
140	"none of the religious 'crap'": FOC, "Good Country People," *CS*, 290.
140	"He thinks he's Jesus Christ!": FOC, "The Lame Shall Enter First," *CS*, 459.
140	"nothing to reproach himself with": FOC, "The Lame Shall Enter First," *CS*, 475.
140	"everything was black before him": FOC, "The Lame Shall Enter First," *CS*, 481.
140	"any contrary assertion": Nick Cave and the Bad Seeds, "People Ain't No Good."
141	"long-suffering shackle": Nick Cave and the Bad Seeds, "The Mercy Seat," track 1 on *Tender Prey*, Mute Records, 1988, CD.
141	"something under construction": FOC, "Introduction to *A Memoir of Mary Ann*," *MM*, 226.
141	"Hail the Pentecostal morn": "Hymnary.org," https://hymnary.org/text/hail_this_joyful_days_return [attributed to fourth-century Saint Hilary of Poitiers].
141	"Where Christ returns": Nick Cave and the Bad Seeds, "Brompton Oratory," side A, track 4 on *The Boatman's Call*.
141	"because he 'wasn't there'": FOC, "A Good Man Is Hard to Find," *CS*, 132.
141	"impossible to endure": Nick Cave and the Bad Seeds, "Brompton Oratory."
142	"nobody believes in the Incarnation": FOC to Betty Hester, 2 August 1955, *HB*, 92.
142	"still on my hands": Nick Cave and the Bad Seeds, "Brompton Oratory."

142 "pure Nick Cave": O'Hagen, *Faith, Hope and Carnage*, 84.
142 "identified only as 'the child'": FOC, "A Temple of the Holy Ghost," *CS*, 236.
142 "version of the author": [See, for example, Howard R. Burkle, "The Child in Flannery O'Connor," who says of O'Connor, "She preserves the child in herself and expresses it in her children" (69).]
142 "a very ancient twelve": FOC to Betty Hester, 11 February 1956, *HB*, 137.
142 "Temple One and Temple Two": FOC, "A Temple of the Holy Ghost," *CS*, 236.
142 "I am a Temple": FOC, "A Temple of the Holy Ghost," *CS*, 238.
143 "she innocently imagines": FOC, "A Temple of the Holy Ghost," *CS*, 243.
143 "the you-know-what": FOC, "A Temple of the Holy Ghost," *CS*, 244.
143 "a man and woman both": FOC, "A Temple of the Holy Ghost," *CS*, 245.
143 "Amen. Amen": FOC, "A Temple of the Holy Ghost," *CS*, 246.
144 "dress-like surplice": FOC, "A Temple of the Holy Ghost," *CS*, 247.
144 "tent at the fair": FOC, "A Temple of the Holy Ghost," *CS*, 248.
144 "O'Connor's 'concrete' fiction": FOC, "The Nature and Aim of Fiction," *MM*, 67.
144 "fleshed or carnal sacred": McCredden, "Fleshed Sacred: The Carnal Theologies of Nick Cave," 168.
144 "incarnational art": FOC, "The Nature and Aim of Fiction," *MM*, 68.
145 "moral law within": Nick Cave and the Bad Seeds, "There Is a Kingdom," side A, track 5 on *The Boatman's Call*.
145 "his musical abilities": John H. Baker, editor, "'There Is a Kingdom': Nick Cave, Christian Artist?" in *The Art of Nick Cave: New Critical Essays* (Intellect, 2013), 223.
145 "And He is everything": Nick Cave and the Bad Seeds, "There Is a Kingdom."
145 "kind of incarnationalism": McCredden, "Fleshed Sacred: The Carnal Theologies of Nick Cave," 173.
146 "mist of tears": Nick Cave and the Bad Seeds, "There Is a Kingdom."
146 "shadows of uncertainty": McCredden, "Fleshed Sacred," 184.
146 "between belief and unbelief": McCredden, "Fleshed Sacred," 172.
146 "imprisoned prophet": Baker, "'There Is a Kingdom': Nick Cave, Christian Artist?" 227.
146 "epigraph to O'Connor's second novel": [It reads, "From the days of John the Baptist until now, the kingdom of heaven suffereth violence, and the violent bear it away." Matthew 11:12.]
146 "Is this how": Nick Cave and the Bad Seeds, "(Are You) The One That I've Been Waiting For?" side A, track 6 on *The Boatman's Call*.
147 "a moral moron": FOC, "The Comforts of Home," *CS*, 385.
147 "the old man": FOC, "The Comforts of Home," *CS*, 393.
147 "guided by his father": FOC, "The Comforts of Home," *CS*, 403.
147 "dogging my tracks": FOC to Cecil Dawkins, 6 September 1962, *HB*, 491.
147 "the dirty criminal": FOC, "The Comforts of Home," *CS*, 403.
147 "invisible currents": FOC, "The Comforts of Home," *CS*, 383.
147 "advances of Star": FOC, "The Comforts of Home," *CS*, 403.
147 "that made her possible": FOC, "The Comforts of Home," *CS*, 403.
147 "about to collapse": FOC, "The Comforts of Home," *CS*, 404.
147 "lacks plausibility": Frederick Asals, *Flannery O'Connor: The Imagination of Extremity*, 110.
148 "noun and adverb forms": "mysteriously" (384); "mystery" (385); "mystery" (388).
148 "various determinations": FOC, "Some Aspects of the Grotesque in Southern Fiction," *MM*, 41–42.
148 "'can't help' but": FOC, "The Comforts of Home," *CS*, 385.

149	"anticipates you": Nick Cave and the Bad Seeds, "(Are You) The One That I've Been Waiting For?"
149	"McCredden's phrase": McCredden, "Fleshed Sacred: The Carnal Theologies of Nick Cave," 168.
149	"O Lord, let it be": Nick Cave, "Just a Closer Walk with Thee," in *Nick Cave: The Complete Lyrics 1978–2022* (Penguin, 2022), 95.
149	"a God-shaped hole": Cave, "There Is a Light," *The Complete Lyrics*, 268.
149	"Nothing matters": FOC, *WB*, 105.
149	"Jesus-seeing hat": FOC, *WB*, 60.
149	"next to her foot": FOC, *WB*, 50.
149	"his first sexual experience": FOC, *WB*, 33.
149	"Haze's epithet 'My Jesus'": FOC, *WB*, 55.
149	"'King Jesus!' he whispers": FOC, *WB*, 85.
149	"not a 'preacher'": FOC, *WB*, 31–34.
150	"in a bathroom stall": FOC, *WB*, 30.
150	"obscene comments": FOC, *WB*, 59.
150	"I got Leora Watts": FOC, *WB*, 56.
150	"absence of you": Nick Cave and the Bad Seeds, "Brompton Oratory."
150	"Do you love me?": Jesus asks his disciple Peter this question three times in succession; see Gospel of John 21:15–17 (NASB and multiple other translations).
150	"I would lose her": Nick Cave and the Bad Seeds, "Do You Love Me?" track 1 on *Let Love In*, Mute Records, 1994, CD.
150	"I don't hold it now": Nick Cave and the Bad Seeds, "Nobody's Baby Now," track 2 on *Let Love In*.
150	"I ain't been delivered": Nick Cave and the Bad Seeds, "Hard On for Love," track 6 on *Your Funeral . . . My Trial*, Mute Records, 1986, CD.
151	"find more pain": Baker, "'There Is a Kingdom': Nick Cave, Christian Artist?" in *The Art of Nick Cave: New Critical Essays*, 230.
151	"'stolen' images from O'Connor": Nick Cave quoted in Peter Murphy, "Love and Death: Nick Cave's Two Decades of the Rosary (Part Two)," *Hot Press* (Dublin), 13 May 1998, 33.
151	"shadowy Jesus": Nick Cave and the Bad Seeds, "I Had a Dream Joe," track 2 on *Henry's Dream*, Mute Records, 1992, CD.
151	"mad shadow of Jesus": FOC, *VBA*, 91.
151	"mov[ing] from tree to tree": FOC, *WB*, 22.
151	"ain't got any God in him": FOC, *WB*, 121.
151	"a man of flesh and blood": Cave, "The Flesh Made Word," *King Ink II*, 139.
151	"new jesus": phrase is from FOC, *WB*, 140–41.
151	"Christ is the imagination": Cave, "The Flesh Made Word," *King Ink II*, 141.
152	"prime motivation as an artist": Cave, "The Secret Life of the Love Song," *The Complete Lyrics*, 6.
152	"And He is everything": Nick Cave and the Bad Seeds, "There Is a Kingdom."
152	"stumbling block": FOC, "Novelist and Believer," *MM*, 161.
152	"standpoint of Christian orthodoxy": FOC, "The Fiction Writer & His Country," *MM*, 32.
152	"calls an 'internal landscape'": Springsteen quoted in Jon Pareles, "Bruce Almighty: The Boss Turns to God," *New York Times*, 24 April 2005, late ed., sec.2: 1+.
152	"the decaf of worship": John H. Baker, "'There Is a Kingdom': Nick Cave, Christian Artist?" in *The Art of Nick Cave*, 223.

272   Notes

152   "far-reaching theological questions": Darcey Steinke, "God Is in the House," in Nick Cave, *Stranger Than Kindness* (HarperOne, 2021), 58.

152   "being a Catholic has saved me": FOC to John Lynch, 6 November 1955, *HB*, 114.

152   "God finds his voice": Cave, "The Flesh Made Word," *King Ink II*, 142.

152   "free of 'obnoxious pieties'": FOC to Robert Giroux, 29 September 1960, *HB*, 409.

153   "leave the uses to Him": FOC to Dr. T. R. Spivey, 30 November 1959, *HB*, 360.

153   "the urge for Jesus in his voice": FOC, *WB*, 50.

153   "fall off a cliff near his home": BBC News, "Nick Cave's son Arthur took LSD before cliff fall, inquest told," 10 November 2015, https://www.bbc.com/news/uk-england-sussex-34779370.

153   "largely completed": ["Skeleton Tree" is the only song written after Arthur's death, says Cave in O'Hagen, *Faith, Hope and Carnage*, 232.]

153   "the long-sustained subtext": See *Nick Cave and the Bad Seeds: One More Time with Feeling*, directed by Andrew Dominik, 2 Disc Set, 2016 & 2017, DVD.

153   "repetition of the 'I need you'": Nick Cave and the Bad Seeds, "I Need You," track 6 on *Skeleton Tree*, Bad Seed Ltd., 2016, CD.

154   "'I Believe' in black letters": See *Nick Cave and the Bad Seeds: One More Time with Feeling*. [The scene with Cave fingering rosary beads is found at 12:18–12:48; Cave briefly appears wearing a T-shirt with "I Believe" in large lettering while doing a voice overdub at a piano; the shirt has been changed to an open-necked white dress shirt in the next cut: 13:54–14:05.]

154   "Psalm 142": [The Hebrew poem "Psalm 142" (ESV translation) repeats the phrase "with my voice" in its opening stanzas.]

154   "I am calling you": Nick Cave and the Bad Seeds, "Jesus Alone," track 1 on *Skeleton Tree*.

154   "the true Love Song inhabits": Cave, "The Secret Life of the Love Song," *The Complete Lyrics*, 7.

154   "artist trying to find his way": [Blurb on the back of the slipcase to *Nick Cave and the Bad Seeds: One More Time with Feeling*, directed by Andrew Dominik, 2 Disc Set, 2016 & 2017, DVD.]

154   "making it in darkness": FOC to Louise Abbot, [undated] Sat. 1959, *HB*, 354.

154   "a little bit of faith": Nick Cave and the Bad Seeds, "Waiting for You," Part 1, track 3 on *Ghosteen*, Awal Recordings Ltd., 2019, CD.

154   "Christian *malgre lui*": FOC, "Author's Note," *WB*, 5.

154   "Breathless, but to you": Nick Cave, "I Come Alone and to You," side A, track 7 on *Seven Psalms*, Cave Things Ltd., 2022, 10" black vinyl, EP.

Chapter 7: PJ Harvey: Uh Huh, O'Connor

155   "from found objects": James Blandford, *PJ Harvey: Siren Rising* (Omnibus, 2004), 117.

155   "paid to *stop* playing": David Peisner, "Let It Bleed: The Oral History of PJ Harvey's 'Rid of Me,'" SPIN, 1 May 2013 https://www.spin.com/2013/05/pj-harvey-rid-of-me-oral-history-steve-albini/.

155   "opening act for U2's": "U2TOURS.COM," https://www.u2tours.com/tours/opening/pj-harvey#tabs-2.

155   "important British female artists": Nigel Williamson, "The Big Interview: Into the Light," *Times Metro* (London), 9–15 January 1999, 1F6.

155   "twice so honored": "Mercury Prize Past Winners," https://www.mercuryprize.com/previous%20shortlists.

Notes

155 "for services to music": "Bradley Wiggins knighted at Buckingham Palace—BBC News," 10 December 2013, https://www.bbc.com/news/uk-england-25315380.

156 "Her personal life": Dorian Lynskey, "Interview: PJ Harvey," *The Guardian*, 24 April 2011, https://www.theguardian.com/music/2011/apr/24/pj-harvey-england-shake-interview.

156 "reading a lot of Flannery": PJ Harvey Fan Archives, "PJ Harvey interviewed by Gary Crowley on BBC Radio London (10/11/2007), Part 1," YouTube Video, 10:58, 24 June 2022, https://www.youtube.com/watch?v=acjrydHiaPg&ab_channel [1:20–1:50].

156 "multiple blogs": [See for example these blogs on Harvey's *Is This Desire?* album: https://fromnovelstonotes.wordpress.com/2013/03/13/pj-harvey/; https://zsidesmusic.medium.com/no-words-so-sweet-pj-harveys-atmospheric-dissent-and-poetic-masterpiece-that-s-is-this-desire-f965e1dd7b66.

157 "Cursed god above": PJ Harvey, "To Bring You My Love," track 1 on *To Bring You My Love*, Island Records, 1995, CD.

157 "Nobody with a good car": FOC, *WB*, 113.

157 "God is here": PJ Harvey, "Working for the Man," track 3 on *To Bring You My Love*.

157 "black and empty heart": PJ Harvey, "The Dancer," track 10 on *To Bring You My Love*.

157 "reading a lot of Flannery O'Connor": PJ Harvey Fan Archives, "PJ Harvey interviewed by Gary Crowley on BBC Radio London (10/11/2007)," Part 1.

157 "deep into O'Connor": Percy, "Rock and Read," 38.

157 "read a proof copy": Blandford, *Siren Rising*, 95.

157 "seeing only darkness": Blandford, *Siren Rising*, 109.

158 "investigating similar things": Blandford, *Siren Rising*, 94.

158 "accidentally *and* deliberately": [See Cave's comments on lyric borrowings from his reading in an expanded interview with Debbie Kruger, "Nick Cave: The Songwriter Speaks," in *Nick Cave Sinner Saint: The True Confessions*, edited by Mat Snow (Plexus, 2011), 134–35.]

158 "our broken condition": FOC, "Novelist and Believer," *MM*, 168.

158 "dark side of one's psyche": Nigel Williamson, "The Big Interview: Into the Light," 1F8.

158 "by shock": FOC, "The Fiction Writer & His Country," *MM*, 34.

158 "even she was shocked": David Peisner, "Let It Bleed: The Oral History of PJ Harvey's 'Rid of Me.'"

158 "songs of morbid intensity": Nigel Williamson, "The Big Interview: Into the Light," 1F6.

158 "dialogues of despair": Sarah Vowell, "PJ Harvey: Is This Desire?" *SPIN* 14, no. 11 (November 1998), 132.

158 "slash-your-wrists music": PJ Harvey quoted in Blandford, *PJ Harvey: Siren Rising*, 111.

158 "Wordsworth or Blake": Mike Boehm, "Four-Star Performers: PJ Harvey *Is This Desire?*" *Los Angeles Times*, 27 September 1998, https://www.latimes.com/archives/la-xpm-1998-sep-27-ca-26893-story.html.

159 "unapologetically Brontë goth": *SPIN* reviewer cited in Blandford, *Siren Rising*, 122.

159 "river Harvey played in": Blandford, *Siren Rising*, 120.

159 "O'Connor and J. D. Salinger": Blandford, *Siren Rising*, 122.

159 "great writers I go back to": PJ Harvey quoted in Dorian Lynskey, "Interview: PJ Harvey," *The Guardian*, 24 April 2011, https://www.theguardian.com/music/2011/apr/24/pj-harvey-england-shake-interview.

159 "a voice that is my own": PJ Harvey quoted in Blandford, *Siren Rising*, 120.

159 "Joy *was* her name": PJ Harvey, "Joy," track 9 on *Is This Desire?* Island, 1998, [includes multifold insert with lyrics and images], CD.

160 "far from these red hills": FOC, "Good Country People," *CS*, 276.

160 "never danced a step": FOC, "Good Country People," *CS*, 274.

160	"to know nothing": FOC, "Good Country People," *CS*, 277.
160	"a deeper understanding": FOC, "Good Country People," *CS*, 284.
160	"real innocence": FOC, "Good Country People," *CS*, 289.
161	"see through to nothing": FOC, "Good Country People," *CS*, 287.
161	"do you love me or don'tcher?": FOC, "Good Country People," *CS*, 288.
161	"without even making": FOC, "Good Country People," *CS*, 288–89.
161	"into the hollow sky": FOC, "Good Country People," *CS*, 287.
161	"reaches into a 'hollow' Bible": FOC, "Good Country People," *CS*, 289.
161	"just good country people?": FOC, "Good Country People," *CS*, 290.
161	"*her own* innocence": PJ Harvey, "Joy."
161	"the same condition": FOC, "Good Country People," *CS*, 279.
161	"No hope or faith": PJ Harvey, "Joy."
161	"sitting on the straw in the dusty sunlight": FOC, "Good Country People," *CS*, 291.
161	"to go blind": [Harvey's line "She wanted to go blind" in the third verse of the "Joy" lyrics reflects O'Connor's description of Joy/Hulga as "someone who has achieved blindness by an act of the will and means to keep it." FOC, "Good Country People," *CS*, 273.]
161	"wanted hope to stay": PJ Harvey, "Joy."
161	"nearly direct quotation": [Harvey's line in the "Joy" lyrics slightly alters Manley Pointer's words in O'Connor's story: "I been believing in nothing ever since I was born!" FOC, "Good Country People," *CS*, 291.]
162	"two silent birds": FOC, "The River," *CS*, 165.
163	"washed away, slow": FOC, "The River," *CS*, 165.
163	"Leave your pain": PJ Harvey, "The River," track 10 on *Is This Desire?*
163	"Like a white light scatters": PJ Harvey, "Joy."
163	"white sun scattered": FOC, "The River," *CS*, 168.
164	"LYRICS TO SONGS PRINTED OR WRITTEN": See the multifold lyrics sheet included with the *Is This Desire?* CD.
165	"the song's title": [O'Connor's "old woman" remarks of her simpleton daughter Lucynell, "No man on earth is going to take that sweet girl of mine away from me!" FOC, "The Life You Save May Be Your Own," *CS*, 151.]
165	"hat pulled down": FOC, "The Life You Save May Be Your Own," *CS*, 146.
165	"angel of Gawd": FOC, "The Life You Save May Be Your Own," *CS*, 154.
165	"and [closed] her eyes": PJ Harvey, "No Girl So Sweet," track 11 on *Is This Desire?*
165	"Took her from Heaven": [At the end of O'Connor's story, after abandoning Lucynell, Mr. Shiftlet recalls his mother and remarks to a hitchhiker he has picked up, "He took her from heaven and giver to me and I left her." FOC, "The Life You Save May Be Your Own," *CS*, 156.]
165	"stories are unmistakably hers": "Readers' panel: What's the greatest PJ Harvey album?" https://www.theguardian.com/music/poll/2011/oct/31/pj-harvey-best-album-readers-panel.
165	"some biographical truth": Blandford, *Siren Rising*, 124.

Chapter 8: *Wise Blood*, Punk, and Heavy Metal

166	"attract the lunatic fringe": FOC to Robie Macauley, 18 May 1955, *HB*, 82.
166	"blasphemy rampant": [unsigned], "Damnation of Man," *Savannah Morning News*, 25 May 1952, 40. Reprinted in *Flannery O'Connor: The Contemporary Reviews*, 11–12.

166 "an unnamed evil": John V. Simons, "A Case of Possession," *Commonweal* 56 (27 June 1952), 297–98. Reprinted in *Flannery O'Connor: The Contemporary Reviews*, 14.

167 "monolith of satanic darkness": Hoke Norris, "A Classic from the Recent Past Is Reissued," *Chicago Sun-Times*, 2 September 1962, sec. 3, p. 2. Reprinted in *Flannery O'Connor: The Contemporary Reviews*, 190.

167 "Jesus wins": William Walsh, "Flannery O'Connor, John Huston, and *Wise Blood*: In Search of Taulkinham," *Flannery O'Connor Review* 9 (2011), 95.

167 "aggressive masculine . . . particular sway": Monica Miller, "'No Man with a Good Car Needs to Be Justified': Preaching Rock and Roll Salvation from O'Connor's *Wise Blood* to Ministry's 'Jesus Built My Hotrod,'" *Flannery O'Connor Review* 12 (2014), 83, 86, 82.

167 "sold 1.5 million copies": Al Jourgenson with Jon Wiederhorn, *Ministry: The Lost Gospels According to Al Jourgenson* (Da Capo Press, 2013), 132.

167 "'high rat-colored' Essex": FOC, *WB*, 69.

167 "Nobody with a good car": FOC, *WB*, 113.

167 "her symbolic use of automobiles": [See Brian Abel Ragen's admirable analysis of the automobile in O'Connor's fiction, chapter 2: "The Automobile and the American Adam," in *A Wreck on the Road to Damascus: Innocence, Guilt, and Conversion in Flannery O'Connor* (Loyola University Press, 1989), 55–105.]

168 "aggressive form of rebellion": Miller, "'No Man with a Good Car Needs to Be Justified,'" 82.

169 "antithetical to Christianity": Jonathan Cordero, "Unveiling Satan's Wrath: Aesthetics and Ideology in Anti-Christian Heavy Metal," *Journal of Religion and Popular Culture* 21, no. 1 (Spring 2009), para 3, https://utpjournals.press/doi/10.3138/jrpc.21.1.005.

169 "darkness and death-dealing": Cordero, "Unveiling Satan's Wrath," para 4 and para 8.

169 "not practicing what they preach": Cordero, "Unveiling Satan's Wrath," para 17.

169 "Do what thou wilt": Cordero, "Unveiling Satan's Wrath," para 10.

170 "tend to agree": Cordero, "Unveiling Satan's Wrath," para 5.

170 "popular Satanism": Cordero, "Unveiling Satan's Wrath," para 10.

170 "the discourse on chaos": Deena Weinstein, *Heavy Metal: A Cultural Sociology* (Lexington Books, 1991), 39.

170 "the gothic and the grotesque": Heather Lusty, "Rocking the Canon: Heavy Metal and Classical Literature," *Latch* 6 (2013), 101–38.

170 "stories of Edgar Allan Poe": Lusty, "Rocking the Canon," 116–17 (see footnote 4).

170 "influence on the darker products": Ministry, "Jesus Built My Hotrod (Redline/Whiteline Version)," Sire/Warner Brothers, 1991, Maxi-Single.

170 "Where you come from is gone": FOC, *WB*, 165.

171 "largely unintelligible lyrics": Ministry, "Jesus Built My Hotrod (Redline/Whiteline Version)."

171 "photographed in Christ-like poses": [Several images of Jourgenson wearing a crown of thorns or with arms outspread in a crucifix pose can be found on Pinterest. See for example https://www.pinterest.ca/pin/139048707230846784/.]

171 "occultist Aleister Crowley": Cam Lindsay, "With 'Psalm 69' Ministry Set the Bar for Depravity," *Noisey*, 14 July 2017, https://www.vice.com/en/article/mbapqa/ministry-psalm-69-25-year-anniversary.

171 "only way to the truth": FOC, *WB*, 148.

171 "loosely based around": Paul Browne, "Wiseblood" review, 18 May 2005, https://www.amazon.co.uk/product-reviews/B0012GMYOQ/ref=cm_cr_arp_d_paging_btm_next_2?ie=UTF8&reviewerType=all_reviews&pageNumber=2.

171 "other sources": "Corrosion of Conformity," corrosion-doctors.org/Arts/conformity.htm.

171	"Go read Flannery": "Sputnik Music: Corrosion of Conformity, In the Arms of God," https://www.sputnikmusic.com/review/6090/Corrosion-of-Conformity-in-the-Arms-of-God/#comments (6810, 4 February 2007).
172	"keep the truth away": Corrosion of Conformity, "Wiseblood," track 3 on *Wiseblood*, Columbia, 1996, CD.
172	"that there is no truth": FOC, *WB*, 165.
172	"You need wise blood": Corrosion of Conformity, "Wiseblood."
172	"many wills conflicting": FOC, "On Her Own Work," *MM*, 115.
172	"holes in my eyes": Corrosion of Conformity, "Goodbye Windows," track 4 on *Wiseblood*.
172	"like two clean bullet holes": FOC, *WB*, 98.
172	"'dark tunnel' holes": FOC, *WB*, 231.
172	"My life is hazy hazy hazy": Corrosion of Conformity, "Born Again for the Last Time," track 5 on *Wiseblood*.
172	"heartless heretic": Corrosion of Conformity, "Wishbone (Some Tomorrow)," track 11 on *Wiseblood*.
172	"delivered from 'nowhere'": Springsteen, "State Trooper," track 6 on *Nebraska*.
173	"What a pity, redemption city": Corrosion of Conformity, "Redemption City," track 10 on *Wiseblood*.
173	"Seven is the most sacred": "Discover How Numbers 1–7 in Scripture Illuminate Bible Truth. ["All sevens are beloved" (*Vayikra Rabbah* 29:9)], https://www.free.messianicbible.com/feature/numbers-scripture-illuminate-bible-truth/.
174	"occult practice": Sarah Bartlett, "All-Seeing Eye," in *The Secrets of the Universe in 100 Symbols* (Fair Winds Press, 2015), 85.
174	"misanthropic exertion of power": "JG Thirlwell . . . Wiseblood: Dirtdish," https://www.foetus.org/content/discography/releases/wiseblood-dirtdish.
174	"demented-electro-avant-jazz": "Foetus—industrial/ Post-Punk-Electro-Avant-Garde-Noise-Rock," http://www.australiangothicindustrialmusic.com/bands/foetus-jgthirlwell-steroid-maximus-band-music-songs-videos.html.
174	"Hazel Motes would feel at home": *CMJ New Music Report* 267 (17 January 1992), cited in https://www.foetus.org/content/discography/wiseblood-pttm-pedal-to-the-metal.
174	"minimalist music experimenters": Anna Station, "JG Thirlwell: Hide and Seek (Foetus interview 2010)," originally published by Brainwashed.com, https://www.reinspired.wordpress.com/2010/07/19/jg-thirlwell-hide-and-seek/.
175	"glutted with images of himself": "JG Thirlwell . . . Images," https://www.foetus.org/content/images.
175	"a frame from the *Wise Blood* film": "*Wise Blood* (1979) Photo Gallery," https://www.imdb.com/title/tt0080140/mediaindex.
176	"nickname given him": Station, "JG Thirlwell: Hide and Seek (Foetus interview 2010)."
176	"it was Jesus all day long": FOC, *WB*, 46.
176	"all-boys Baptist school": Station, "JG Thirlwell: Hide and Seek (Foetus interview 2010)."
176	"beat the be-Jesus into him": FOC, *WB*, 63.
176	"Fornication and blasphemy": FOC, *WB*, 53.
176	"grisly sacrificial slaughter": Wiseblood, "O-O (Where Evil Dwells)," track 2 on *Dirtdish*, K.422, 1987, LP.
176	"I'm God! God! God!": Wiseblood, "Godbrain," track 5 on *Dirtdish*.
177	"checkered flag design": "Wiseblood," www.discogs.com/artist/147291-Wiseblood.
177	"nailing himself to a cross": JG Thirlwell: Images, "cross2" (mouse roll-over label), https://www.foetus.org/content/images, 78/78.
177	"wasn't for you": FOC, *WB*, 55.

177	"insignia of the Church of Satan": JG Thirlwell: Images, "1994-jgthirlwell-thepizz-antonlevey-by-rebeccawilson," (mouse roll-over label), https://www.foetus.org/content/images, 31/48.
178	"fellowship in music": "JG Thirlwell . . . About," foetus.org/content/press/.
178	"Where JG Thirlwell is concerned": Leslie Hatton, "31 Days of Horror 2015: The Music of JG Thirlwell," https://www.biffbampop.com/2015/10/21/31 days-of-horror-2015-the-music-of-jg-thirlwell/.
178	"Fate is in my hands": Gang of Four, "A Man with a Good Car," track 5 on *Hard*, Warner Bros, 1983, CD.
178	"needs to be justified": FOC, *WB*, 113.
178	"anywhere I want to go": FOC, *WB*, 126–27.
178	"not what I meant": Gang of Four, "A Man with a Good Car."
179	"For the author": FOC, "Author's Note to the Second Edition," *WB*, 5.
179	"I'm deep in the mystery": Gang of Four, "A Man with a Good Car."
179	"means of grace": FOC to John Hawkes, 13 September 1959, *HB*, 350.
180	"little bit of everything": "1 Review, rod45, Oct 09 2014," https://www.rateyourmusic.com/release/album/king-swamp/wiseblood/.
180	"parenthetical subtitle": "Wiseblood/Blown Away," https://www.rateyourmusic.com/release/single/king-swamp/wiseblood-blown-away/.
180	"admirable nihilist": FOC to Ben Griffith, 5 March 1954, *HB*, 70.
180	"gothic Southern rock singer": fannishliss, *Livejournal*: "King Swamp: Secret Soundtrack to Supernatural," https://www.fannishliss.livejournal.com/183541.html.
180	"God's own toys": King Swamp, "Wiseblood," track 1 on *Wiseblood*, Virgin/WEA, 1990, CD.
180	"O'Connor identified as 'meanness'": FOC, "A Good Man Is Hard to Find," *CS*, 132.
180	"blow me clean away": King Swamp, "One Step over the Line," track 2 on *Wiseblood*.
180	"Nothing more than shadows": King Swamp, "Floating World," track 3 on *Wiseblood*.
181	"bitterness of [the] empty cup": King Swamp, "Walk the Knife," track 4 on *Wiseblood*.
181	"Was you going anywheres?": FOC, *WB*, 209–10.
181	"in it for the ride": King Swamp, "Can't Be Satisfied," track 5 on *Wiseblood*.
181	"take my hand": King Swamp, "Nightfall Over Eden," track 6 on *Wiseblood*.
181	"no light to take away": William Goyen, "Unending Vengeance," *New York Times Book Review*, 18 May 1952, p. 4. Reprinted in *Flannery O'Connor: The Contemporary Reviews*, 6–7.
181	"looks just like Jesus": FOC, *WB*, 51.
181	"like his daddy": FOC, *WB*, 79.
181	"chiefly a comic character": FOC, "On Her Own Work," *MM*, 116.
181	"what we have instead of God": Ernest Hemingway, *The Sun Also Rises* (Scribner Paperback Fiction [1926], 1995), 249.
182	"matters of life and death": FOC, "Author's Note to the Second Edition," *WB*, 5.
182	"these people's means of grace": FOC to John Hawkes, 13 September 1959, *HB*, 350.
182	"receiving a 'sign'": FOC, *WB*, 92.
182	"form he had to get through": FOC, *WB*, 94.
182	"in a church whisper": FOC, *WB*, 98.
182	"looking for a 'new jesus'": FOC, *WB*, 140.
182	"secret conference with itself": FOC, *WB*, 134.
182	"the whispering night": King Swamp, "Wiseblood."
183	"With your Wiseblood": King Swamp, "Wiseblood."
183	"had a major label": "King Swamp—Press Kit 1989," https://kingswamp.com/press_kit_1989.html.

183	"it's too wise for him": FOC to John Hawkes, 13 September 1959, *HB*, 350.
183	"intellectual dance band": fannishliss, *Livejournal*: "King Swamp: Secret Soundtrack to Supernatural."
183	"quotes Flannery O'Connor": "Interviews: Shriekback Reloaded," www.nemesis.to/shriekbackinterview.htm.
183	"You and I will merge": Shriekback, "Everything That Rises Must Converge," track 2 on *Oil & Gold*, Island Records, 1985, CD.
184	"end of time in Christ": FOC to Dr. T. R. Spivey, 16 March 1960, *HB*, 383.
184	"how incomprehensible God": FOC to Alfred Corn, 30 May 1962, *HB*, 477.
184	"a monitum issued 30 June 1962": "Monitum on the Writings of Fr. Teilhard de Chardin, SJ," https://www.ewtn.com/catholicism/library/monitum-on-the-writings-of-fr-teilhard-de-chardin-sj-2144.
184	"recommend to several correspondents": [See for example FOC to Father J. H. McCown, *HB*, 570–71. O'Connor presents to her personal priest her view that "The most important non-fiction writer is Père Pierre Teilhard de Chardin, S.J., who died in 1955 and so far has escaped the Index, although a monitum has been issued on him. If they are good they are dangerous."]
184	"known as Medway": "Thee Mighty Caesar's Biography by All Music," https://www.allmusic.com/artist/thee-mighty-caesars-mn0000490541/biography.
184	"primitive garage punk": "Thee Mighty Caesars," damagedgoods.co.uk/bands/thee-mighty-caesars/.
184	"spent under £300": liner notes printed inside the jewel case, Thee Mighty Caesars, *Thee Caesars of Trash & Wiseblood*: "Two Albums on One CD," Damaged Goods, 2013, CD.
185	"British visual art scene": "Interview with Billy Childish," https://www.thewhitereview.org/feature/interview-with-billy-childish-2/.
185	"addressed as 'child'": Thee Mighty Caesars, "The Wise Blood," track 17 on *Thee Caesars of Trash & Wiseblood*.
185	"uses most frequently": [See for example seven uses of "child" in reference to Sabbath Lily on pages 39–42 in *Wise Blood*.]
185	"to identify Sabbath Lily": FOC, *WB*, 118. [This character's name is not introduced until midway through the narrative.]
185	"An old man's using you": Thee Mighty Caesars, "The Wise Blood."
186	"he begs on the street": FOC, *WB*, 168–69.
186	"What I gave to you": Thee Mighty Caesars, "The Wise Blood."
186	"I'm sick and tired of you child": Thee Mighty Caesars, "The Wise Blood."
186	"like a 'harpy'": FOC, *WB*, 215.
186	"Finally you'll be through": Thee Mighty Caesars, "The Wise Blood."
186	"detention home": FOC, *WB*, 216.
186	"is still alive": FOC, "Author's Note to the Second Edition," *WB*, 5.
186	"more or less 'a failure'": FOC to Betty Hester, 10 November and 25 November 1955, *HB*, 116, 117.
186	"appalled by the adaptation": FOC to Denver Lindley, 6 March 1957, *HB*, 206.
186	"mildly aghast": FOC to William Sessions, 11 October 1956, *HB*, 178.

Chapter 9: Everything That Rises

188	"only southernness": cited in Monica Miller, "Only Southernness: Flannery O'Connor and R.E.M.," 116.

188 "quoting her title terms": U2, "One Tree Hill," track 9 on *The Joshua Tree*, Island Records, 1997, CD.

188 "Critics have suggested": Ben Child, "Raised in the Country, Working in the Town: Temporal and Spatial Modernisms in Bob Dylan's *Love and Theft*," *Popular Music and Society* 32, no. 2 (May 2009), 202.

188 "I'm puttin' out your eyes": Bob Dylan, "High Water (For Charlie Patton)," track 7 on *Love and Theft*, Columbia, 2001, CD.

188 "body shipped out by train": Patty Griffin, "Don't Let Me Die in Florida," track 2 on *American Kid*, New West Records, 2013, CD.

188 "a lapsed Catholic": Molly Finnegan, "For Patty Griffin 'Downtown Church' Opens a Door to Gospel," https://www.pbs.org/newshour/arts/patty-griffin-sings-the-gospel-on-downtown-church.

189 "famous cousin": "Frank Brannon: singer-songwriter," frankbrannonmusic.com.

189 "what made her tick": Frank Brannon, notes to recordings formerly available on CD Baby, forwarded in an email to the author, 23 March 2023.

189 "delivered God's grace": Frank Brannon, "Flannery's Waltz," track 3 on *Dance on the Wind*, independent, produced and mastered in Nashville, 2015, CD.

189 "come from a spiritual place": Frank Brannon, notes to recordings formerly available on CD Baby, forwarded in an email to the author, 23 March 2023.

189 "have those angels keep sending": Frank Brannon, "When Heaven Speaks," track 10 on *Dance on the Wind*.

189 "my capacity for doing": FOC to Sister Mariella Gable, 4 May 1963, *HB*, 518.

189 "appears to have been aware": [Particularly in the latter months of her life, while in hospital with failing kidneys, O'Connor would ask her Catholic correspondents to pray for her. To Sister Mariella Gable she writes, "I'll count on your prayers" (*HB*, 591); to Thomas Stritch she observes, "Thanks for the prayers . . . It must be doing some good" (*CW*, 1213).]

189 "Christian orthodoxy": FOC, "The Fiction Writer & His Country," *MM*, 32.

190 "premier contemporary Delta bluesman": "John Campbell," *Encyclopedia of Popular Music*, 4th edition, edited by Colin Larkin (Oxford University Press, 2006), 151–52.

190 "spooky side of the blues": Thom Jurek, "One Believer Review," https://www.allmusic.com/album/one-believer-mw0000265390.

190 "the church of no religion": John Campbell, "Wiseblood," track 9 on *Howlin' Mercy*, Electra, 1993, CD.

190 "The only way to the truth": FOC, *WB*, 148.

190 "Jesus was a liar": FOC, *WB*, 105.

190 "Jesus don't exist": FOC, *WB*, 54.

190 "don't foul with redemption": FOC, *WB*, 105.

190 "The lame are still crippled": Campbell, "Wiseblood." [Haze tries to found a "Church Without Christ" where, as he preaches, "the blind don't see and the lame don't walk and what's dead stays that way." FOC, *WB*, 105.]

190 "too wise for him": FOC to John Hawkes, 13 September 1959, *HB*, 350.

190 "Wiseblood's there to stay": Campbell, "Wiseblood."

191 "evangelist (and powerlifter!)": Cindy Howes, Basic Folk Podcast, "Basic Folk 91—Samantha Crain," https://www.cindyhowes.net/2020/10/22/basic-folk-91-samantha-crain/ [00:0905–00:1030].

191 "gave Crain her calling": "Samantha Crain," https://myspace.com/samanthacrain/bio.

191 "three Native American Music Awards": Tara Low, "Samantha Crain: Emotional Healing Is like Having a Cat," 27 November 2022, https://www.gutargirlmag.com/featured/samantha-crain-emotional-healing-is-like-having-a-cat.

Notes

191 "toured extensively": "Samantha Crain," livesessions.npr.org/artists/samantha-crain.

191 "people's stories of loss": Samantha Crain, "Introducing Samantha Crain," YouTube Video, 5:56, 9 December 2008, https://www.youtube.com/watch?v=r1wdypBDkHQ&t=11s&ab_channel=SamanthaCrain.

191 "written in direct response": Hilary Langford, "Behind the Wheel with Samantha Crain," *Style Weekly*, 11 March 2009, https://www.styleweekly.com/richmond/behind-the-wheel-with-samantha-crain/Content?oid=1384478.

191 "drowns a man he's baptizing": *Paste Magazine*, "Samantha Crain—'The River,'" YouTube Video, 2:16, 27 October 2008, https://www.youtube.com/watch?v=Mn7HIJY2XMA&ab_channel=PasteMagazine.

191 "printed on the CD's label": Samantha Crain, "The River" (cited lyrics), track 1 on *The Confiscation: A Musical Novella*, Ramseur Records, 2007, EP.

192 "near the end of O'Connor's second novel": FOC, *VBA*, 202–3.

192 "she wrote short stories": Andy Jones, "The Literate Vitality of Samantha Crain's Music," *Taos News*, 14 January 2016, https://www.taosnews.com/the-literate-vitality-of-samantha-crains-music/article_e594153d-60be-5423-a665-f1e9d05f4eff.html.

192 "O'Connor-influenced literary piece": "Bio & Press," anniecranemusic.com.

192 "I'm glad he's dead": Annie Crane, "Ghost Body," track 7 on *Jump with a Child's Heart*, Constant Clip Records, 2011, CD.

193 "he felt his ghost body": Crane, "Ghost Body."

193 "he *saw* his wife's narrow face": FOC, CS, 143.

193 "every goddam thing to hell": FOC, CS, 140.

193 "until the blade touched bone": FOC, CS, 143.

193 "what God's love becomes": FOC to Louise Abbot, [undated] Sat. 1959, *HB*, 354.

193 "his eternal night": Crane, "Ghost Body."

194 "divine burning through": Colin Cutler, "Tarwater: Making Flannery O'Connor's Stories into Songs," https://www.kickstarter.com/projects/colincutlermusic/tarwater-making-flannery-oconnors-stories-into-songs/description 3/7.

194 "wry lyricism and fiery sermons": "PressKit," colincutlermusic.com/epk.

195 "She just isn't": FOC, "The Lame Shall Enter First," CS, 461.

195 "attempting to 'save'": FOC, "The Lame Shall Enter First," CS, 474.

195 "give the evidence": FOC, "The Lame Shall Enter First," CS, 461.

195 "dead to get there": FOC, "The Lame Shall Enter First," CS, 462.

195 "I'll be there with you": Colin Cutler, "Momma, Don't Know Where Heaven Is," track 2 on *Peacock Feathers*, digital album, Bandcamp, 2018, https://www.colincutlermusic.bandcamp/com/album/peacock-feathers, EP.

195 "a bad man's easy": Cutler, "Bad Man's Easy," track 1 on *Peacock Feathers*.

195 "different breed of dog": FOC, "A Good Man Is Hard to Find," CS, 128.

195 "into everything": FOC, "A Good Man Is Hard to Find," CS, 129.

195 "going to hell": Cutler, "Bad Man's Easy."

196 "can't say he didn't": FOC, "A Good Man Is Hard to Find," CS, 132.

196 "I don't know": Cutler, "Bad Man's Easy."

196 "up in heaven, too": Cutler, "Momma, Don't Know Where Heaven Is."

196 "after the ineffable": FOC, "The Enduring Chill," CS, 378.

196 "Like the prodigal son": Cutler, "The Cold That's Forever," track 4 on *Peacock Feathers*.

196 "far beyond you": Cutler, "The Cold That's Forever."

196 "ever cut a switch": Cutler, "Save Your Life and Drive," track 3 on *Peacock Feathers*.

197 "be dead at 39": Faggot, "Flannery O'Connor," track 7 on *A Good Man Is Hard to Find*, digital album (Bandcamp, 2014), https://www.faggottheband.bandcamp.com/track/flannery-oconnor, EP.

Notes

197   "a voracious reader": Andrew Dansby, "Less Is More for Fleet Foxes Drummer J. Tillman," *Houston Chronicle*, 25 November 2009, https://www.chron.com/entertainment/article/Less-is-more-for-Fleet-Foxes-drummer-J-Tillman-1589751.php.

197   "one of the 'key influences'": "J. Tillman: About," https://www.open.spotify.com/artist/21XbnrbEMUTZelIfoV12hC.

197   "disclaims . . . directly influenced": Eileen Tilson, "Q&A with J. Tillman (of Fleet Foxes)—Playing @ The Earl, November 21," *Atlanta Music Guide*, https://www.atlantamusicguide.com/qa-with-j-tillman-of-fleet-foxes-playing-the-earl-november-21/.

197   "fan of O'Connor's *Wise Blood*": Mikael Wood, "At Home with Father John Misty: 'I'm basically a meme at this point'": *Los Angeles Times*, 30 March 2017, http://www.latimes.com/entertainment/music/la-et-ms-father-john-misty-20170330-story.html.

197   "wearing a dark blue suit": [See for examples Misty's live performances available on YouTube: Floyd Perez, "Father John Misty Only Son of the Ladiesman on Letterman 5.01.12," YouTube Video, 7:36, 16 August 2016, https://www.youtube.com/watch?v=TpC7PDtoyww&ab_channel=FloydPerez , and CBS Television and Spartina Productions, "Father John Misty, 'Holy Shit' on The Late Show w/ Stephen Colbert-1/14/16," YouTube Video, 4:02, 22 April 2017, https://www.youtube.com/watch?v=RYPziRyCTuw. In this latter video, Misty appears wearing dark glasses with a dark blue suit, like the blinded Hazel Motes.]

197   "suit worn by O'Connor's character": FOC, *WB*, 10.

198   "losing his religion": Nick Paumgarten, "Father John Misty's Quest to Explain Himself," *New Yorker*, 19 June 2017, 40.

198   "fierce opposition": Wood, "At home with Father John Misty."

198   "opened his eyes": Wood, "At home with Father John Misty."

198   "all the place you've got": FOC, *WB*, 166.

198   "each other's all we got": Father John Misty, "Pure Comedy," track 1 on *Pure Comedy*, Sub Pop, 2017, CD.

198   "notion of being Christ-haunted": See for examples, John J. Thompson, "Guess who's still haunting David Bazan," 7 January 2015, thinkchristian.net/guess-whos-still-haunting-david-bazan; Christopher Stratton, "David Bazan: Artist, Sinner, Christian," explorefaith.org/music/bazan.html.

198   "stopped being a Christian": Kurt Armstrong, "A Conversation with David Bazan," *Image* 82, p. 57.

198   "Christ-haunted indie rock": Thompson, "Guess who's still haunting David Bazan," https://www.thinkchristian.net.

198   "formed by the church": FOC to John Lynch, 6 November 1955, *HB*, 115; Armstrong, "A Conversation with David Bazan," *Image* 82, 61. [Bazan: "Whatever cultural expertise I have is in the subculture of evangelical Christianity . . . It's a lens that I am continuing to write through now, but not as a believer."]

198   "stopped believing in Him": Thompson, "Guess who's still haunting David Bazan," https://www.thinkchristian.net.

199   "the urge for Jesus in his voice": FOC, *WB*, 50.

199   "mope rock balladry": Marc Hogan, "Headphones: Pedro the Lion's David Bazan Goes Postal Service," 10 May 2005, https://www.pitchfork.com/reviews/albums/4008-headphones/.

199   "I never have done before": FOC, *WB*, 13.

199   "If you've been redeemed": FOC, *WB*, 16.

199   "Then I wouldn't want to be": Headphones, "Wise Blood," track 9 on *Headphones*, Suicide Squeeze, 2005, CD.

199   "faithful and the blind": Simon Joyner, "Flannery O'Connor," track 18 on *Beautiful Losers: Singles and Compilation Tracks*, Jagjaguwar, 2006, CD.

200 "compared to the Birthday Party": "Mark's Record Reviews: Killdozer," https://www.markprindle.com/killdoza.htm.

200 "moronically offensive lyrics": "Reader Comments," thepublicimage79@hotmail.com, quoted in "Mark's Record Reviews: Killdozer," https://www.markprindle.com/killdoza.htm.

200 "resemble the late Sidney Poitier": Killdozer, "Lupus," track 3 on *Twelve Point Buck*, Touch and Go Records, 1989, CD.

200 "The road of excess": See Killdozer, *Twelve Point Buck*, track 9, "Free Love in Amsterdam," and track 8, "Seven Thunders."

200 "Southern Renaissance man": Luke Bauserman, "The Vine That Ate the South: An Interview with J.D. Wilkes," 21 April 2017, https://www.medium.com/@lukebauserman/the-vine-that-ate-the-south-an-interview-with-j-d-wilkes-79ea954bb714.

200 "God-fearing Southern boy": Tom Dumarey, "Features: The Legendary Shack Shakers," 17 February 2008, https://www.punkrocktheory.com/interviews/legendary-shack-shakers.

201 "pays homage to Flannery O'Connor": Hight, "A Good Writer Isn't Hard to Find," 49.

201 "The original group was formed": Red Barn Radio, "JD Wilkes," YouTube Video, 1:22:46, 14 October 2020, https://www.youtube.com/watch?v=ab9fGvIskb0&t=153s&ab_channel=RedBarnRadio (show # 708) [56:00–56:34].

201 "opened for Robert Plant": "The Legendary Shack Shakers," https://www.badearl.com/show/the-legendary-shack-shakers/.

201 "songs have been featured": Jacque Day, "Legendary Shack Shakers: extended feature," WKMS News and Music Discovery, Morning Edition, 30 December 2010, https://www.wkms.org/2010-12-30/legendary-shack-shakers-extended-feature.

201 "miniature short stories": "Two Dollar Radio Presents *The Vine That Ate the South*," https://twodollarradio.com/products/the-vine-that-ate-the-south# [02:50–03:10].

201 "the kind of distortion . . . that reveals": FOC, "Novelist and Believer," *MM*, 162.

201 "instrumental equivalents": Hight, "A Good Writer Isn't Hard to Find," 49.

201 "musical violence": Hight, "A Good Writer Isn't Hard to Find," 50.

202 "a little further into": Hight, "A Good Writer Isn't Hard to Find," 50.

202 "what I'm trying to draw": WKU PBS, "J.D. Wilkes: Handshake from History," YouTube Video, 3:50, 18 April 2018, https://www.youtube.com/watch?v=eAYDFUi7c_4&ab_channel=WKUPSB, [02:50–03:10].

202 "graphically signalled": "Legendary Shack Shakers—Sing a Worried Song," https://www.youtube.com/watch?v=J9V2RcUXyHQ&ab_channel=LegendaryShackShakers.

202 "O'Connor is singled out": "Legendary Shack Shakers—Sing a Worried Song," https://www.youtube.com/watch?v=J9V2RcUXyHQ&ab_channel=LegendaryShackShakers. [See quick cut at 02:34–35.]

203 "Guess I'm a little noncommittal": Legendary Shack Shakers, "Born Again Again," track 8 on *Swampblood*, YepRoc, 2007, CD.

203 "complicit in the murder": FOC, "The Displaced Person," *CS*, 234.

203 "The Devil is the master": Legendary Shack Shakers, "Jumblyleg Man," track 11 on *Swampblood*.

203 "held largely by the devil": FOC, "On Her Own Work," *MM*, 118.

203 "the naked truth": Legendary Shack Shakers, "Preachin' at Traffic," track 14 on *Swampblood*.

203 "gravel and broken glass": FOC, *WB*, 221–22.

203 "not clean": FOC, *WB*, 224.

203 "You must believe in Jesus": FOC, *WB*, 225.

204 "very innocent speller": FOC to Ben Griffith, 3 March 1954, *HB*, 69.
204 "the correct spelling": FOC to Betty Hester, 24 March 1956, *HB*, 148.
204 "Wilkes's favorite of O'Connor's works": "Two Dollar Radio Presents *The Vine That Ate the South*," https://twodollarradio.com/products/the-vine-that-ate-the-south# [09:50]. [As the camera pans the bookshelves in Wilke's modest home in rural western Kentucky, where he is indeed a Kentucky Colonel for his cultural contributions to the state, among the books are Melville's *Moby-Dick*, Harper Lee's *To Kill a Mockingbird*, Faulkner's *As I Lay Dying*, and evidently the embossed spine of a library copy of *Wise Blood*, with the author's name misspelled "O'Conner."]
204 "False propheteerin'": Legendary Shack Shakers, "Cussin' in Tongues," track 7 on *Believe*, YepRoc, 2004, CD.
204 "a key expression in O'Connor's story": FOC, "The Lame Shall Enter First," *CS*, 454. [O'Connor's juvenile delinquent prophet figure, Rufus Johnson, remarks of the hypocritical humanist social worker Sheppard, "I don't care if he's good or not. He ain't *right!*"]
204 "title and refrain to a song": Legendary Shack Shakers, "He Ain't Right," track 12 on *Swampblood*.
204 "Before the cock crows": Legendary Shack Shakers, "Cussin' in Tongues."
204 "posted on the band's website": See comment in Hight, "A Good Writer Isn't Hard to Find," 49.
204 "you draw large and startling figures": FOC, "The Fiction Writer & His Country," *MM*, 34.
204 "curled on a couch reading": *A Love Song for Bobby Long*, directed by Shainee Gabel (Elcamino Pictures/Destination Films, 2004), DVD [59:53–1:02:50].
205 "a God who has not given up": *A Love Song for Bobby Long* [1:19:34–36].
205 "Praise Flannery O'Connor": Grayson Capps, "Love Song for Bobby Long," track 16 on *A Love Song for Bobby Long: Original Motion Picture Soundtrack*, Hyena Records, 2005, CD.
205 "Southern trash rock": "The Moaners *Dark Snack* (Yep Roc) reviewed by Kate X. Messer," *Austin Chronicle*, 18 March 2005, https://www.austinchronicle.com/music/2005-03-18/263035/.
205 "best piece on the recording": The Moaners, "Elizabeth Cotten's Song," track 4 on *Dark Snack*, Yep Roc Records, 2005, CD.
206 "any poorer than dead": FOC, *VBA*, 3.
206 "her novel-in-progress": FOC, "You Can't Be Any Poorer Than Dead," *CS*, 292–310.
206 "that's what Flannery said": The Moaners, "Flannery Said," track 5 on *Dark Snack*.
206 "inside of the bifold insert": see insert to *Dark Snack* CD packaging.
206 "hymn-like melody": The Moaners, "Chasing the Moon," track 12 on *Dark Snack*.
206 "trunk of a derelict car": *Searching for the Wrong-Eyed Jesus*, directed by Andrew Douglas (Lonestar Productions / BBC, 2003) [1:06:04–1:07:35].
206 "I'm a Christian and a Catholic": Jay Anderson, "The Flannery O'Connor of Singer-Songwriters," *Pro Ecclesia*Pro Familia*Pro Civitate*, 23 May 2007, http://proecclesia.blogspot.com/2007/05/flannery-oconnor-of-singer-songwriters.html.
207 "friend and correspondent": Stuart C. Hancock, "Making Light of It: A Conversation with Pierce Pettis," *Mars Hill Review* 7 (Winter/Spring 1997), 114, http://www.leaderu.org/marshill/mhr07/pettis1.html.
207 "three critically acclaimed recordings": "Pierce Pettis: Bio," https://www.sonicbids.com/band/piercepettis/.
207 "Windham Hill's William Ackerman": liner notes in lyrics booklet, Pierce Pettis, *Tinseltown*, High Street Records, 1991, CD.
207 "reprise of the melodic theme": Pierce Pettis, "Flannery's Georgia," track 5 on *Tinseltown*.

207 "reach platinum status": Eric Harvey, "R.E.M.: America's Greatest Band," *The Atlantic*, 22 September 2011, https://www.theatlantic.com/entertainment/archive/2011/09/rem-americas-greatest-band/245525/.

208 "fables about the South": See J. Niimi, *Murmur* [Bloomsbury 33 series] (Continuum, 2005), 86–87; Monica Miller, "Only Southernness," 115.

208 "Stipe refers to *Wise Blood*": R.E.M. Video Archive, "R.E.M. 1985-08-16-MuchMusic, Toronto, Canada (Interview with Peter Buck & Michael Stipe)," YouTube Video, 7:05, 16 August 1985, https://www.youtube.com/watch?v=EdsqSnGwX6U&ab_channel=R.E.M.VideoArchive [1:15–1:32].

208 "O'Connor's title choice": "Notes," *MM*, 235.

208 "fascination with the mysterious peacock": FOC, "The King of the Birds," *MM*, 18.

208 "a pensive reflection": Miller, "Only Southernness," 122–23.

208 "unfurled map of the universe": FOC, "The King of the Birds," *MM*, 14.

208 "on the shoulders of giants": R.E.M., "King of Birds," track 10 on *Document*, I.R.S. Records, 1987, CD.

208 "Stipe's 'foggy lyricism'": Harvey, "R.E.M.: America's Greatest Band."

208 "appropriating and exploiting": Tony Fletcher, *Perfect Circle: The Story of R.E.M.* (Omnibus Press, 2013), 92.

208 "significant influence on the band": Miller, "Only Southernness," 139.

208 "New South orientation": Matthew Sutton quoted in Miller, "Only Southernness," 120.

209 "don't quite make the connection": Peter Buck quoted in Miller, "Only Southernness," 122.

209 "about some derelicts": Craig Rosen, *R.E.M. Inside Out: The Stories behind Every Song* (Carleton Books, 1997), 89.

209 "the mysteries and inspirations": book jacket blurb, Rosen, *R.E.M. Inside Out*.

209 "third novel-in-progress": "Notes," *CS*, 554–55.

209 "began the novel as a satire": Virginia Wray, "Flannery O'Connor's *Why Do the Heathen Rage?* and the Quotidian 'larger things,'" *Flannery O'Connor Bulletin* 23 (1994–95), 25–26.

209 "its last word": FOC, "Why Do the Heathen Rage?" *CS*, 487.

210 "Wash *off* the blood": R.E.M., "Oddfellows Local 151," track 11 on *Document*, I.R.S. Records, 1987, CD.

210 "a highly personal tribute": "In the Course Of . . . An interview with Richmond's Sonorous South," Home: *Virginia Music Flash*, unsigned blog, **accessed August 2018**, no URL **(site discontinued)**. [Author has a hard copy of the webpage in his files.]

210 "surround, pull me down": South, "Flannery," track 6 on *South*, Jagjaguwar, 1998, CD.

210 "swiftly forward and down": FOC, "The River," *CS*, 174.

210 "the color of pecan shells," FOC, *WB*, 10.

210 "green bottle glass": FOC, *WB*, 42.

211 "clear fresh ice": FOC, *WB*, 208.

211 "an insider in the U2 organization": Maddy Fry, "U2 Lists: Top 5 U2 Literary Moments," @U2, 21 June 2009, **accessed 4 May 2018**, @U2 **(site discontinued October 2020)**. [Author has a hard copy of the webpage in his files.]

211 "never felt such sympathy": "The Enduring Chill: Bono and the Two Americas," *Propaganda* #4, 1 December 1986, reprinted in *U2: Best of Propaganda* (Thunder's Mouth Press, 2003), 63.

211 "songwriting by accident": Robert Hilburn, "Where Craft Ends and Spirit Begins," *Los Angeles Times*, 8 August 2004. https://www.latimes.com/archives/la-xpm-2004-aug-08-ca-hilburn8-story.html.

Notes

211 "feeds his songwriting": Hilburn, "Where Craft Ends and Spirit Begins."
212 "by a writer called": "Bono and the Two Americas," *Propaganda #4*, reprinted in *U2: Best of Propaganda*, 63.
212 "famed City Lights Bookstore": Bono, *Surrender: 40 Songs, One Story* (Doubleday Canada, 2022), 217.
212 "favorite book of hers": "Bono and the Two Americas," *Propaganda #4*, 63.
212 "was Flannery O'Connor": Recording Academy / GRAMMYs, "Watch U2 Accept Their First-Ever GRAMMY in 1988 | GRAMMY Rewind," YouTube Video, 2:33, 7 August 2020, https://www.youtube.com/watch?v=nypK7pzGAnI.
213 "dedicated to his memory": Editors of *Rolling Stone*, *U2: The Rolling Stone Files* (Hyperion, 1994), 66.
213 "the cold, enduring chill": U2, "One Tree Hill," track 9 on *The Joshua Tree*, Island, 1988, CD.
213 "that begins slowly": "Bono and the Two Americas," *Propaganda #4*, 64.
213 "any man's death diminishes me": John Donne, "Meditation XVII," *Devotions Upon Emergent Occasions* (1624).
213 "break my heart": U2, "One Tree Hill."
213 "intended as a memorial": Heritage New Zealand: "One Tree Hill Obelisk," https://www.heritage.org.nz/list-details/4601/One%20Tree%20Hill%20Obelisk.
213 "twist and tragic": Steve Stockman, *Walk On: The Spiritual Journey of U2*, Revised edition (Relevant Books, 2005), 76.
214 "oh my love": U2, "Exit," track 10 on *The Joshua Tree*.
214 "pure idiot mystery": FOC, "The Comforts of Home," *CS*, 385.
214 "like nails in the night": U2, "Exit."
214 "moves in mysterious ways": U2, "Mysterious Ways," track 8 on *Achtung Baby*, Island, 1991, CD.
214 "spearmint-flavored sighs": FOC, "The Comforts of Home," *CS*, 395.
214 "deeper into black": U2, "Exit."
214 "kills his mother": FOC, "The Comforts of Home," *CS*, 403–4.
214 "The hands of love": U2, "Exit."
214 "acknowledges the influence": Maddy Fry, "U2 Lists: Top 5 U2 Literary Moments," @U2, June 21, 2009, **accessed 4 May 2018**, @U2 (**site discontinued October 2020**). [Author has a hard copy of the webpage in his files.]
214 "most Christian set of songs": See for example, Ted Trost, "Transgressing Theology: Locating Jesus in a 'F—ed-Up World,'" 25 June 2013, https://www.u2interference.com/15749-transgressing-theology-locating-jesus-in-a-f-ed-up-world/.
215 "a fucked-up world it is too": U2, "Wake Up Dead Man," track 12 on *POP*, Island, 1997, CD.
215 "your sermon on the mount": U2, "Please," track 11 on *POP*.
215 "while standing on": FOC, *WB*, 104.
215 "title to this DIY CD": Velma and the Happy Campers, *Lo-Fi Therapy No.1: Songs about Flannery O'Connor* (2013), [CD-R in author's personal collection], https://www.velmaandthehappycampers.bandcamp.com/album/lo-fi-therapy-no-1-songs-about-flannery-oconnor.
216 "Southern Gothic strain": Barney Hoskyns, *Low Side of the Road: A Life of Tom Waits* (Faber and Faber, 2009), 393 note.
216 "attempts to evangelize": Patrick Humphries, *The Many Lives of Tom Waits* (Omnibus Press, 2007), 246.

Notes

216 "fed on Kerouac": Hoskyns, *Low Side of the Road*, 25.
216 "all the evangelists": Hoskyns, *Low Side of the Road*, 7.
216 "took refuge in reading": Hoskyns, *Low Side of the Road*, 44.
216 "a book under his arm": Humphries, *The Many Lives of Tom Waits*, 30.
216 "'devoured' southern fiction": Humphries, *The Many Lives of Tom Waits*, 30.
216 "an old Flannery O'Connor story": Hoskyns, *Low Side of the Road*, 392.
216 "newspaper clippings": Corinne Kessell, *The Words and Music of Tom Waits* [The Praeger Singer-Songwriter Collection] (Praeger, 2009), 8.
216 "a surreal aesthetic": Kessell, *The Words and Music of Tom Waits*, 119.
217 "The sky turned black and bruised": Tom Waits, "Murder in the Red Barn," track 11 on *Bone Machine*, Island, 1992, CD.
217 "a bruised violet color": FOC, "A Temple of the Holy Ghost," *CS*, 240.
217 "murder in the red barn": Waits, "Murder in the Red Barn."
217 "borrows its story title": "A Good Man Is Hard to Find," https://www.tomwaitslibrary.info/theatre/woyzeck/lyrics-4/#12, Notes: (1).
217 "included in a compilation": Tom Waits, "A Good Man Is Hard to Find," track 12 on *Songs Inspired by Literature: Chapter Two—Artists for Literacy*, The SIBL Project, 2003, CD.
217 "a soldier who suffers from delusions": "Woyzeck: Introduction," https://www.tomwaitslibrary.info/theatre/woyzeck/introduction-4/.
217 "Life's mean as a needle": "A Good Man Is Hard to Find" (Woyzeck theater version, 2000), https://www.tomwaitslibrary.info/theatre/woyzeck/lyrics-4/#12.
218 "perhaps to steal their car": [Among The Misfit's first words when coming upon Bailey and family after the car they are riding in has rolled "Oncet," is a quiet directive to one of his henchmen, "Try their car and see will it run, Hiram." FOC, "A Good Man Is Hard to Find," *CS*, 126.]
218 "And my favorite color is red": Waits, "A Good Man Is Hard to Find," track 13 on *Blood Money*, ANTI-, 2002, CD.
218 "feel good inside": Waits, "Chocolate Jesus," track 12 on *Mule Variations*, ANTI-, 1999, CD.
218 "Hollywood be thy name": Tom Waits, "Jesus Gonna Be Here," track 7 on *Bone Machine*.
218 "intensified gracelessness": Rowan Williams, *Grace and Necessity: Reflections on Art and Love* (Bloomsbury Academic, 2006), 105.
219 "'often shockingly' revealed": *Faith and Theology*, "Tom Waits: theologian of the dysangelion," posted by Ben Meyers, Sunday, 30 December 2007, https://www.faith-theology.com/search?q=tom.
219 "decadent southern evangelist": See Tom Waits, "Tom Waits—Way Down in the Hole," YouTube Video, 4:33, 16 February 2007, https://www.youtube.com/watch?v=Xw2MjRcVO4g.
219 "I'll never let go of your hand": Waits, "Never Let Go," disc 2, track 9 on *Orphans: Brawlers, Bawlers & Bastards*, ANTI-, 2006, CD.
219 "blood of the lamb": Waits, "Down There by the Train," disc 2, track 17 on *Orphans*.
219 "wanderers, strangers, and misfits": Kessell, *The Words and Music of Tom Waits*, 36.
219 "come on up to the house": Waits, "Come on Up to the House," track 16 on *Mule Variations*.
219 "thrown everything off balance": FOC, "A Good Man Is Hard to Find," *CS*, 131.
220 "soulful, sacred, and profane South": *Searching for the Wrong-Eyed Jesus*, directed by Andrew Douglas (Lonestar Productions / BBC, 2003), [83 mins], blurb on DVD case.

Notes

220 "it's alive, and it's awake": *Searching for the Wrong-Eyed Jesus* (BBC) [1:15:07–1:15:32].
220 "central to human life": FOC, "The Catholic Novelist in the Protestant South," *MM*, 204.
220 "get it in your blood": *Searching for the Wrong-Eyed Jesus* (BBC) [1:18:18–1:18:36].
220 "it was Jesus all day long": FOC, *WB*, 46.
220 "got saved": Evan Schlansky, "Jim White," *American Songwriter* [20 March 2012], https://www.americansongwriter.com/jim-white/.
220 "personality disorders": vpro Vrije Geluiden extra, "Jim White: 'I Stalked David Byrne,'" YouTube Video, 23:19, 8 December 2017, https://www.youtube.com/watch?v=eIiUeuaBWsA&ab_channel=vproVrijeGeluidenextra, [2:32–3:00].
220 "names of two friends": "Jim White," gothiccountry.se/articles/south/jim-white.html.
221 "a place in the world": Jim White, interviewed by Steve Almond, *Believer* 4, no. 4 (May 2006), 64.
221 "cannot say much": FOC, "The Catholic Novelist in the Protestant South," *MM*, 199, 198.
221 "we weren't alone": Jim White, "Still Waters," *The Mysterious Tale of How I Shouted Wrong-Eyed Jesus!* (Luaka Bop/Warner Bros, 1997).
221 "go to another world": Jim White quoted in Hight, "A Good Writer Isn't Hard to Find," 49.
221 "made a field recording": Jim White, personal correspondence with the author, 24 July 2019.
222 "Living on the fruit of the vine": White, "Fruit of the Vine," track 5 on *Transnormal Skiperoo*, Luaka Bop, 2007, CD.
222 "the 'handshake' to his first album": White interview, *Believer*, 64.
222 "reading of O'Connor's fiction": Hight, "A Good Writer Isn't Hard to Find," 49.
223 "mad with their singing": "The Mysterious Tale of How I Shouted 'Wrong-Eyed Jesus!' A True Story by Jim White," [booklet included with CD package], White, *Wrong-Eyed Jesus*, Luaka Bop/Warner Bros, 1997, CD.
223 "black wall of woods . . . invisible cricket choruses": [The first phrase appears in O'Connor's novel a few pages after the scene of Tarwater's violation in the woods by a predatory homosexual (*VBA*, 239); the second phrase is found in the concluding sentences of O'Connor's story "Revelation" after Ruby Turpin has experienced her transforming vision (*CS*, 509)].
223 "two ragged holes in the paper": "The Mysterious Tale of How I Shouted 'Wrong-Eyed Jesus!' A True Story by Jim White."
223 "cost you plenty": FOC, "Parker's Back," *CS*, 522.
223 "all-demanding eyes": FOC, "Parker's Back," *CS*, 522.
223 "forever on his back": FOC, "Parker's Back," *CS*, 527.
224 "wrote between the lines?": Jim White, "Static on the Radio," track 1 on *Drill a Hole in That Substrate and Tell Me What You See*, Luaka Bop, 2004, CD.
224 "Ain't no yours or my way": White, "If Jesus Drove a Motorhome," track 6 on *Drill a Hole in That Substrate*.
225 "in them specters": White, "Phone Booth in Heaven," track 10 on *Drill a Hole in That Substrate*.
225 "hillbilly nihilist": FOC to Robie Macauley, 18 May 1955, *HB*, 81.
225 "I jumped around with the Jesus hat on": vpro Vrije Geluiden extra, "Jim White: 'I Stalked David Byrne,'" YouTube Video, 23:19, 8 December 2017, [3:56–4:10].
225 "a church where they serve beer": Jim White, "Jim 3:16," track 5 on *A Funny Little Cross to Bear*, Luaka Bop, 2008, EP, live recording.

225 "slippery slope toward true heresy": "Song Premiere: Jim White vs. The Packway Handle Band 'Jim 3:16,'" 31 October 2014, https://www.relix.com/blogs/detail/song_premiere_jim_white_vs_the_packway_handle_band_jim_316/.

225 "the Devil is in the details": *Searching for the Wrong-Eyed Jesus* (BBC, 2003) [1:19:27–1:20:45].

225 "most certainly Christ-haunted": FOC, "Some Aspects of the Grotesque in Southern Fiction," *MM*, 44.

226 "ethereal synth-pop music": author interview with Ken Harrison of Wild Strawberries, 8 April 2013, L'Espresso Bar Mercurio, Toronto, Canada.

226 "gave us quizzical looks": personal email from Roberta Carter Harrison, 18 July 2012.

226 "altered the way we see": author interview with Ken Harrison of Wild Strawberries, 8 April 2013.

226 "Some things never change": Wild Strawberries, "Postcard from a Volcano," track 3 on *Carving Wooden Spectacles*, Wild Strawberries Publishing, 1989, CD.

226 "What you see through those glasses?": FOC, "Judgement Day," *CS*, 539.

227 "some intruding intelligence": FOC, "Judgement Day," *CS*, 538.

227 "humor and the absurdity in things": author interview with Ken Harrison.

227 "What I oughta know": "Wild Strawberries official, Wild Strawberries—A Good Man Is Hard to Find [Official lyric video]," 3:24, 25 April 2018, https://www.youtube.com/watch?v=UbX1qLZje6c.

227 "sales of over fifty thousand": "Wild Strawberries," https://www.encyclopedia.com/people/literature-and-arts/music-popular-and-jazz-biographies/wild-strawberries.

228 "catchy chorus": author interview with Ken Harrison, 8 April 2013.

228 "This is my country": Wild Strawberries, "Everything That Rises," track 10 on *Heroine*, Nettwerk, 1995, CD.

228 "one 'topical' story": FOC to Maryat Lee, 26 March 1961, *HB*, 436.

228 "can also take meaning from them": author interview with Ken Harrison.

228 "on the *Heroine* recording": [Listen carefully after the "fla-fla-fla" scat that sets up the first syllable in the name "Flannery," sung deep in the mix at 3:43.]

228 "a bit of 'mischief'": email to the author, 12 April 2013.

228 "mischievous hope": author interview with Ken Harrison.

Coda: "Gonter Rock, Rattle and Roll"

229 "a self-described 'good man'": FOC, "The Lame Shall Enter First," *CS*, 475.

229 "dim-witted child": FOC, *VBA*, 23.

229 "one of Tarwater's terrible cousins": FOC to John Hawkes, 28 November 1961, *HB*, 456.

229 "hair hung in a flat forelock": FOC, "The Lame Shall Enter First," *CS*, 449.

229 "coiffed rock 'n' roll teen idols": [American teen idol Fabian and Canadian idol Bobby Curtola, for example, often appear with a forelock in publicity photos from the late 1950s and early 1960s, as do the young Frank Sinatra in the mid-1950s and Elvis before sporting his legendary pompadour. An accentuated curly forelock was the signature hairstyle of Bill Haley. It must be noted, however, that O'Connor adds that Rufus wore his forelocked hairstyle "not carelessly like a boy's, but fiercely like an old man's" (*CS*, 449).]

229 "likely saw Elvis's first appearance": [Nancy Davis Bray, Director for Special Collections at Georgia College and State University—where the Flannery O'Connor Archives are housed—notes in an email, "It has been my understanding that Flannery and Mrs.

O'Connor would drive into town and watch pertinent television shows at a relative's house." Email to the author, 28 January 2013.]

230 "Gonter rock, rattle and roll": FOC, "The Lame Shall Enter First," *CS*, 456.
230 "approaching Apocalypse": FOC, "The Lame Shall Enter First," *CS*, 456–57.
230 "embarrassing scream of 'Daaaaddy'": David Remnick, "We Are Alive: *Bruce Springsteen at Sixty-two*," *New Yorker* (30 July 2012), 44.
230 "mother is serving time": FOC, "The Lame Shall Enter First," *CS*, 446–47.
230 "fanatic intelligence": FOC, "The Lame Shall Enter First," *CS*, 449.
230 "Satan . . . He has me in his power": FOC, "The Lame Shall Enter First," *CS*, 450.
230 "nobody can save me but Jesus": FOC, "The Lame Shall Enter First," *CS*, 474.
230 "Jesus or the devil": FOC, *VBA*, 39.
230 "between hell and hallowed ground": Mary Gauthier, "Mercy Now."
231 "internal landscape": Springsteen quoted in Jon Pareles, "Bruce Almighty: The Boss Turns to God."
231 "I believe it!": FOC, "The Lame Shall Enter First," *CS*, 477.
231 "Gauthier calls a 'truth-teller'": Creativity Radio, "Art of the Song," Mary Gauthier interview.
231 "the sounder of hearts": FOC, "The Lame Shall Enter First," *CS*, 481.
231 "sounds like the Beatles": FOC to Betty Hester, 15 February 1964, *HB*, 566.
232 "more than seventy million Americans": "The Beatles' First Appearance on 'The Ed Sullivan Show,'" *Smithsonian Snapshot*, 9 February 2012, https://www.si.edu/newsdesk/snapshot/beatles-first-appearance-ed-sullivan-show.
232 "among them, presumably, O'Connor": [O'Connor mentions in a letter being gifted a portable television in 1961, from a group of Dominican Sisters in gratitude for her assistance in publishing *A Memoir of Mary Ann* (FOC to Cecil Dawkins, 22 March 1961, *HB*, 435). Craig Amason, former executive director of the Flannery O'Connor Andalusia Foundation, confirmed that O'Connor had a television set in her room in 1964, and adds, "The Beatles would have been difficult to miss or ignore, even by O'Connor." Emails to the author, 28 and 30 January 2013.]
232 "the Original Tin Ear": FOC to Betty Hester, 25 January 1964, *HB*, 563.
232 "resolved to 'educate [herself] if possible'": FOC to Thomas Stritch, 22 January 1964, *HB*, 562.
232 "both classical and pop records": [Reference to the box of records that Thomas Stritch has sent, which O'Connor indicates she is systematically listening to—"haven't got to the bottom of the pack yet" (*HB*, 564)—occasions her remark that "all classical music sounds alike to me and all the rest of it sounds like the Beatles" (FOC to Betty Hester, 25 January 1964, *HB*, 563). The "all the rest of it" might well be presumed to be contemporary pop music of some kind.]
232 "the first time I've listened to music": FOC to Thomas Stritch, 11 February 1964, *CW*, 1200.
232 "left fifteen years before": See "Chronology," *CW*, 1249.
232 "where the peafowls join in": FOC to Thomas Stritch, 28 June 1964, *HB*, 589.
232 "Catholic Meistersinger": Andrew Greeley, "The Catholic Imagination of Bruce Springsteen," *America*, 6 February 1998, 110.
232 "swans she ordered instead": FOC to Thomas Stritch, 22 January 1964, *HB*, 562. [O'Connor confesses, "I never bought the record player. I saved up the money and then I thought this [is] a lot of money to spend for something you don't already appreciate and no guarantee that you ever will, so I ordered me a pair of swans instead."]
232 "Eternity Street": Mary Gauthier, "Wheel inside the Wheel."
233 "the last word will be theirs": FOC, "The King of the Birds," *MM*, 21.

Bonus Track: Stage Names from O'Connor's *Wise Blood* and Characters

234 "never thought about it again": "Weyes Blood interview by Tobias Carroll," *BOMB*, 13 January 2015, https://www.bombmagazine.org/articles/weyes-blood/.

234 "woozy, inward pop songs": Tom Breihan, "Rising: Wise Blood," *Pitchfork*, 27 August 2010, https://www.pitchfork.com/news/39773-rising-wise-blood/.

234 "melodic sound collages": Emilie Friedlander, "Stream Wise Blood's Get 'Em Mixtape," *Fader*, 9 January 2014, https://www.thefader.com/2014/01/09/stream-wise-bloods-get-em-mixtape.

234 "He feels destined": Breihan, "Rising: Wise Blood," *Pitchfork*.

234 "noise-pop artist": Chris Kelly, "Noise-pop artist Wise Blood opens up about debut album Id; stream it now," *FACT*, https://www.factmag.com/2013/06/18/noise-pop-artist-wise-blood-opens-up-about-debut-album-id-stream-it-now/.

235 "what I deserve": Chris Laufman/Wise Blood, "Penthouse Suites," https://www.genius.com/Wise-blood-penthouse-suites-bonus-lyrics.

235 "no evidence of citations": See multifold CD packaging, *Wiseblood vol. 1*, Bootstrap Productions / weownthesky, 2008, EP.

235 "love-hate relationship": Mary Colurso/Birmingham News, "weownthesky.org/label/archive," https://www.wots.bandcamp.com/album/wiseblood-vol-1-ep.

235 "outcast characters": Maura Callahan, "Q&A: Weyes Blood Discusses Her Time in Baltimore, Flannery O'Connor, and Early 20s Disillusionment," *Baltimore Sun*, 9 January 2015, https://www.baltimoresun.com/citypaper/bcp-weyes-blood-interview-20150109-story.html.

235 "deeply religious Pentecostal family": James Kim, "Natalie Mering Taps into Christian Roots on Weyes Blood's Latest Album," *Frame*, 20 October 2016, https://www.kpcc.org/show/the-frame/2016-10-20/natalie-mering-taps-into-christian-roots-on-weyes-bloods-latest-album.

235 "esoteric spirituality": Aly Comingore, "An Older, Wiser Weyes Blood," Interview, 21 October 2014, interviewmagazine.com/music/weyes-blood. [Mering comments in the interview, "I'm not a dogmatic Christian and I don't believe in the Bible literally, but I realized that Jesus is basically a very Zen dude. And I'm into a lot of Eastern philosophy. It's kind of like theosophy; it's about finding the relationships between all the great religions and focusing in on the good stuff."]

235 "not-so 'good car' . . . not going 'anywheres'": FOC, *WB*, 126, 209–10.

235 "my journey to nowhere": Maxwell Williams, "Pop Music for an Uncertain Future: A Conversation with Weyes Blood," *The Hundreds*, 13 January 2017, https://www.thehundreds.com/blogs/content/weyes-blood-interview-2017.

235 "existential anxiety": Charlotte Gush, "weyes blood is searching for meaning in the chaos of modern life," *i-D* (Vice Media), 4 January 2019, https://i-d.vice.com/en/article/wjm34n/weyes-blood-natalie-mering-titanic-rising-interview.

236 "Something to believe": Weyes Blood, "Something to Believe," track 4 on *Titanic Rising*, SUB POP, 2019, CD.

236 "may never find": Weyes Blood, "Andromeda," track 2 on *Titanic Rising*.

236 "'crow-filled tree' of O'Connoresque grace": FOC, "On Her Own Work," *MM*, 113.

236 "from jazz to country": [The author has a promotional poster for the band sent by his dear friend and coeditor, the late R. Neil Scott, who heard the band Mason Tarwater play in a Murfreesboro pub. In August 2018, the band's bio was available on a website, https://www.gigmasters.com.]

Notes

236 "legendary Pinto Bennett": "Country Legend, Reckless Kelly Songwriter Pinto Bennett Has Died," 30 June 2021, https://www.savingcountrymusic.com/country-legend-reckless-kelly-songwriter-pinto-bennett-has-died/.

236 "the band's former website": [https://www.tarwaterband.com was active in August 2018 but is now discontinued.]

236 "novelist and musician Clyde Edgerton": "Clyde Edgerton," https://www.clydeedgerton.com/the-short-version.

236 "on cassette": "Walking across Egypt: Clyde Edgerton/Tarwater Band," https://www.allmusic.com/album/walking-across-egypt-mw0000859011/releases.

236 "rock band Love": "Tarwater: Chronicle," https://www.tarwater.de/beispiel-seite/.

236 "2012 Olympics": "Davis Tarwater '02—Swimmer/Olympian," https://www.webbschool.org/davis-tarwater.

236 "Monroe's final film": James Greene Jr., *This Music Leaves Stains: The Complete Story of the Misfits* (Scarecrow Press, 2013), 13.

237 "moniker from Red Sammy Butts": "Red Sammy," redsammy.com/about.

237 "FAMOUS BARBEQUE": FOC, "A Good Man Is Hard to Find," *CS*, 121.

237 "self-declared 'good man'": FOC, "A Good Man Is Hard to Find," *CS*, 122. [The social worker Sheppard in "The Lame Shall Enter First" *thinks* himself "a good man" (*CS*, 475) but does not make his self-righteousness audible, as does Red Sammy.]

237 "who have inspired him": "Red Sammy," redsammy.com/about.

237 "haunting indie band": Darryl Sterdan, "Kele Fleming Shares the Latest Meme in New Single & Video," *Tinnitist*, 25 January 2021, https://www.tinnitist.com/2021/01/25/kele-fleming-shares-the-latest-meme-in-new-single-video/.

237 "charted on college radio": "Kele Fleming Musician," youtube.com/@KeleFlemingMusician/about.

238 "downloads on Bandcamp": "Hazel Motes," https://www.hazelmotes2.bandcamp.com.

238 "draws imagery from *Wise Blood*": [Email to the author, 18 July 2019.]

CREDITS

Portions of this work first appeared in the *Flannery O'Connor Review* and in *Approaches to Teaching the Works of Flannery O'Connor*, edited by Robert Donahoo and Marshall Bruce Gentry. Reprinted by permission of the review editor and copyright owner, The Modern Languages Association of America (www.mla.org).

"Highway 29"
Words and music by Bruce Springsteen
Copyright © 1995 Sony Music Publishing (US) LLC and Eldridge Publishing Co.
All Rights Administered by Sony Music Publishing (US) LLC, 424 Church Street, Suite 1200, Nashville, TN, 37219
International Copyright Secured All Rights Reserved
Reprinted by permission of Hal Leonard LLC

"Straight Time"
Words and music by Bruce Springsteen
Copyright © 1995 Sony Music Publishing (US) LLC and Eldridge Publishing Co.
All Rights Administered by Sony Music Publishing (US) LLC, 424 Church Street, Suite 1200, Nashville, TN, 37219
International Copyright Secured All Rights Reserved
Reprinted by permission of Hal Leonard LLC

"Devils & Dust"
Words and music by Bruce Springsteen
Copyright © 2005 Sony Music Publishing (US) LLC and Eldridge Publishing Co.
All Rights Administered by Sony Music Publishing (US) LLC, 424 Church Street, Suite 1200, Nashville, TN, 37219
International Copyright Secured All Rights Reserved
Reprinted by permission of Hal Leonard LLC

"Reason to Believe"
Words and music by Bruce Springsteen
Copyright © 1982 Sony Music Publishing (US) LLC and Eldridge Publishing Co.
All Rights Administered by Sony Music Publishing (US) LLC, 424 Church Street, Suite 1200, Nashville, TN, 37219
International Copyright Secured All Rights Reserved
Reprinted by permission of Hal Leonard LLC

"A Good Man Is Hard to Find (Pittsburgh)"
Words and music by Bruce Springsteen
Copyright © 1998 Sony Music Publishing (US) LLC and Eldridge Publishing Co.
All Rights Administered by Sony Music Publishing (US) LLC, 424 Church Street, Suite 1200, Nashville, TN, 37219
International Copyright Secured All Rights Reserved
Reprinted by permission of Hal Leonard LLC

"Jesus Was an Only Son"
Words and music by Bruce Springsteen
Copyright © 2005 Sony Music Publishing (US) LLC and Eldridge Publishing Co.
All Rights Administered by Sony Music Publishing (US) LLC, 424 Church Street, Suite 1200, Nashville, TN, 37219
International Copyright Secured All Rights Reserved
Reprinted by permission of Hal Leonard LLC

"Leah"
Words and music by Bruce Springsteen
Copyright © 2005 Sony Music Publishing (US) LLC and Eldridge Publishing Co.
All Rights Administered by Sony Music Publishing (US) LLC, 424 Church Street, Suite 1200, Nashville, TN, 37219
International Copyright Secured All Rights Reserved
Reprinted by permission of Hal Leonard LLC

"Matamoros Banks"
Words and music by Bruce Springsteen
Copyright © 2005 Sony Music Publishing (US) LLC and Eldridge Publishing Co.
All Rights Administered by Sony Music Publishing (US) LLC, 424 Church Street, Suite 1200, Nashville, TN, 37219
International Copyright Secured All Rights Reserved
Reprinted by permission of Hal Leonard LLC

"Get Right with God"
Words and music by LUCINDA WILLIAMS
© 2001 WARNER-TAMERLANE PUBLISHING CORP.
All Rights Reserved
Used by Permission of ALFRED MUSIC

"Atonement"
Words and music by LUCINDA WILLIAMS
© 2003 WARNER-TAMERLANE PUBLISHING CORP.
All Rights Reserved
Used by Permission of ALFRED MUSIC

"Car Wheels on a Gravel Road"
Words and music by LUCINDA WILLIAMS
© 1998 WARNER-TAMERLANE PUBLISHING CORP.
All Rights Reserved
Used by Permission of ALFRED MUSIC

"Copenhagen"
Words and music by LUCINDA WILLIAMS
© 2011 WARNER-TAMERLANE PUBLISHING CORP.
All Rights Reserved
Used by Permission of ALFRED MUSIC

"Everything but the Truth"
Words and music by LUCINDA WILLIAMS
© 2013 WARNER-TAMERLANE PUBLISHING CORP.
All Rights Reserved
Used by Permission of ALFRED MUSIC

"Ugly Truth"
Words and music by LUCINDA WILLIAMS
© 2013 WARNER-TAMERLANE PUBLISHING CORP.
All Rights Reserved
Used by Permission of ALFRED MUSIC

"One More Day"
Words and music by LUCINDA WILLIAMS
© 2014 WARNER-TAMERLANE PUBLISHING CORP.
All Rights Reserved
Used by Permission of ALFRED MUSIC

"Faith and Grace"
Words and music by LUCINDA WILLIAMS
© 2016 WARNER-TAMERLANE PUBLISHING CORP.
All Rights Reserved
Used by Permission of ALFRED MUSIC

"Louisiana Story"
Words and music by LUCINDA WILLIAMS
© 2016 WARNER-TAMERLANE PUBLISHING CORP.
All Rights Reserved
Used by Permission of ALFRED MUSIC

"Bus to Baton Rouge"
Words and music by LUCINDA WILLIAMS
© 2001 WARNER-TAMERLANE PUBLISHING CORP.
All Rights Reserved
Used by Permission of ALFRED MUSIC

"Karla Faye"
By Mary Gauthier and Crit Harmon
© 1999 Mary Gauthier Songs and Crittunes
ALL RIGHTS RESERVED

"Worthy"
By Mary Gauthier and Beth Nielsen Chapman
© 2014 Mary Gauthier Songs and Songs of Prismlight Music
ALL RIGHTS RESERVED

"Snakebit"
By Mary Gauthier and Joshua Hayes Carll
© 2007 Mary Gauthier Songs and Highway 87 Publishing
ALL RIGHTS RESERVED

"Mercy Now"
By Mary Gauthier
© 2005 Mary Gauthier Songs
ALL RIGHTS RESERVED

"A Good Man Is Hard to Find"
Words and music by Sufjan Stevens
Copyright © 2004 Sufjan Stevens Music
All Rights Administered by BMG Rights Management (US) LLC
All Rights Reserved Used by Permission
Reprinted by permission of Hal Leonard LLC

"In the Devil's Territory"
Words and music by Sufjan Stevens
Copyright © 2004 Sufjan Stevens Music
All Rights Administered by BMG Rights Management (US) LLC
All Rights Reserved Used by Permission
Reprinted by permission of Hal Leonard LLC

"Get Real, Get Right"
Words and music by Sufjan Stevens
Copyright © 2010 Sufjan Stevens Music
All Rights Administered by BMG Rights Management (US) LLC
All Rights Reserved Used by Permission
Reprinted by permission of Hal Leonard LLC

"Vesuvius"
Words and music by Sufjan Stevens
Copyright © 2010 Sufjan Stevens Music
All Rights Administered by BMG Rights Management (US) LLC
All Rights Reserved Used by Permission
Reprinted by permission of Hal Leonard LLC

"Lime-Tree Arbour"
Lyrics by Nick Cave
All rights reserved and used by permission of Mute Song Limited

"Brompton Oratory"
Lyrics by Nick Cave
All rights reserved and used by permission of Mute Song Limited

"There Is a Kingdom"
Lyrics by Nick Cave
All rights reserved and used by permission of Mute Song Limited

"Hard On for Love"
Lyrics by Nick Cave
All rights reserved and used by permission of Mute Song Limited

"Ghost Body"
By Annie Crane
© 2011 Annie Crane Music & Annie Get Your Gun Publishing
ALL RIGHTS RESERVED

"Exit"
Words and music by Paul David Hewson, Dave Evans, Larry Mullen, and Adam Clayton
Copyright © 1987 UNIVERSAL MUSIC PUBLISHING INTERNATIONAL B.V.
All Rights Administered by UNIVERSAL - POLYGRAM INTERNATIONAL PUBLISHING, INC.
All Rights Reserved Used by Permission
Reprinted by permission of Hal Leonard LLC

"One Tree Hill"
Words and music by Paul David Hewson, Dave Evans, Larry Mullen, and Adam Clayton
Copyright © 1987 UNIVERSAL MUSIC PUBLISHING INTERNATIONAL B.V.
All Rights Administered by UNIVERSAL - POLYGRAM INTERNATIONAL PUBLISHING, INC.
All Rights Reserved Used by Permission
Reprinted by permission of Hal Leonard LLC

"Come On Up to the House"
Written by Tom Waits, Kathleen Brennan
(C) 1999, Jalma Music
Used by permission. All rights reserved.

"Murder in the Red Barn"
Written by Tom Waits, Kathleen Brennan
(C) 1992, Jalma Music
Used by permission. All rights reserved.

"A Good Man Is Hard to Find"
Written by Tom Waits, Kathleen Brennan
(C) 2002, Jalma Music
Used by permission. All rights reserved.

"Fruit of the Vine"
Words and music by Jim White
Copyright © 2007 BMG Rights Management (UK) Ltd.
All Rights Administered by BMG Rights Management (US) LLC
All Rights Reserved Used by Permission
Reprinted by permission of Hal Leonard LLC

INDEX

Ackerman, William, 207
"Adam Raised a Cain" (song), 26
After You're Gone (Legendary Shack Shakers), 202
Age of Adz, The (Stevens), 108, 118–20, 122
Alabama, 90
"Alabama Department of Corrections Meditation Blues" (song), 88–89
Allen, David, 183
"All I'm Thinkin' About" (song), 34–35
"All the Nonsense of Suffering" (Stevens), 106–7
"All You Need Is Love" (song), 86
alternative rock, 4, 15, 127, 155, 166, 207
American Kid (Griffin), 188
Anderson, Sherwood, 104
And the Ass Saw the Angel (Cave), 7, 14, 128–33, 140; influenced by *Wise Blood*, 176, 185
"*And the Ass Saw the Angel*: A Novel of Fragments and Excess" (Hart), 129–30
"Another Day Borrowed" (song), 86
aporia, 136
Archer (TV series), 178
"(Are You) The One That I've Been Waiting For?" (song), 135, 148; sacred and profane, 146
Armstrong, Louis, 80
"Artificial Nigger, The" (O'Connor), 8, 86–87, 110
Asals, Frederick, 32, 108, 147–48
Asthmatic Kitty (record label), 103, 107
"Atlantic City" (song), 28
"Atonement" (song), 6–7, 12, 46, 68–69; influence on *Wise Blood*, 41; O'Connoresque ending, 47
Australia, 88, 127–28, 152
Avalanche (Stevens), 108
"Ave Maria Grotto" (song), 100
Avett Brothers, 191
Awakening, The (Chopin), 86

Back, Christina, 135
Badlands (film), 19
"Badlands" (song), 221–22
"Bad Man's Easy" (song), 195
Bad Religion, 201
Bad Seed (Johnston), 157
Baldwin, James, 91
"Ballad of Hollis Brown" (song), 78
Bandy, Stephen C., 33–34
Barth, John, 120
Batman Forever (film), 127
Bazan, David, 198–99
Beach Boys, 113–14
"Bear It Away" (song), 93
Beatles, the, 3, 86, 207, 231–32
Beaver, Ninette, 19–20
Beck, Jeff, 201
"Before I'm Over You" (song), 52
Believe (Legendary Shack Shakers), 201, 204
Bellissimo, Zach, 202
Bennett, Pinto, 236
Berquist, Karin, 71
Between Daylight and Dark (Gauthier), 78
Bible Belt, 4, 13, 43, 65–66, 69, 93, 98, 104, 107, 110, 119, 122, 178, 188, 200–201, 219, 220–22; Bible Belt Catholics, 99–101; road signs, 125
Bick, Susie, 153
"B.I.G.E.G.O." (song), 234–35
Bill Haley and His Comets, 229–30
Birmingham, Alabama, church bombing, 92–93
Birthday Party (band), 127, 200
"Black Cowboys" (song), 37
Blake, William, 9, 158, 200
Blandford, James, 159, 165
Blessed (L. Williams), 48, 60, 63, 68
"Blessed" (song), 68
Blessitt, Arthur, 95–96
"Blinded by the Light" (song), 18
"Blood Is Blood" (song), 85

Blood Money (Waits), 218
Bloom, Harold, 10
"Blowin' in the Wind" (song), 86
Bluebird Café, 51, 88
Boatman's Call, The (Cave), 14, 134–35, 137–39, 141, 144, 146, 148, 150, 157
Boggs, Dock, 202
Bone Machine (Waits), 216, 218–19
Bonhoeffer, Dietrich: costly grace, 76; costly grace vs. cheap grace, 74
Bono, 155, 158, 176, 188, 212–13, 216; influence on *Wise Blood*, 214–15; introduction to O'Connor's work by Springsteen, 211
"Born Again Again" (song), 203
"Born Again for the Last Time" (song), 172
"Born in the USA" (song), 115
Born in the USA (Springsteen), 17, 22
Born in the USA: Bruce Springsteen and the American Tradition (Cullen), 23
Born to Run (Springsteen memoir), 6, 17, 35
"Borrowed Wings" (song), 221
"Bowl-A-Rama" (song), 95
BQE (Stevens), 103
Brannon, Frank, 189–90
Brennan, Kathleen, 217
"Brompton Oratory" (song), 145–46, 148–50; sacred and profane, 141–42, 144
Bruce Springsteen: Songs (Springsteen), 22
Büchner, Georg, 217
Buck, Peter, 208, 209
Buddhism, 112
"Bud's Sea-Mint Boat" (Campbell), 94
Buford, Bill, 53
Bukowski, Charles, 40, 216
Burkle, Howard, 49, 51
Burnett, T Bone, 86, 230
"Burning Bridges" (L. Williams), 64
Bush, George W., 75
"Bus 109" (Campbell), 90
"Bus to Baton Rouge" (L. Williams), 50, 53–55
Butcher, Bleddyn, 128–29
Byrne, David, 201, 220–21

Cage, John, 174
Cale, J. J., 64
Callari, Frank, 60
Call Me by Your Name (film), 103
Calloway, Cab, 202
Cambridge Folk Festival, 88

"Camelot Motel" (song), 72, 82
Campbell, John, 190
Campbell, Kate, 4, 6, 12, 90, 102, 207; background of, 89; Birmingham church bombing, 92–93; Catholic belief and practice, 101; commercialization of religion, 94; influence on O'Connor, 13, 102; narrative songs, 88–89; and race, 92; as regional writer, 89; religious eccentrics among southern Catholics, 99–101; sympathy for southern gospel of the grotesque, 95
Canada, 228, 237, 238
"Can't Be Satisfied" (song), 180–81
"Can't Find the Way" (song), 83
Capps, Grayson, 205
Caril (Beaver), 19–20
Carlile, Brandi, 191
Carll, Hayes, 78
Carpenter, Karen, 235
Carpenter, Mary Chapin, 42, 77
Carrie and Lowell (Stevens), 116
Carroll, Greg, 213
Carter-Harrison, Roberta, 225–26, 228
Carving Wooden Spectacles (Wild Strawberries), 226
Car Wheels on a Gravel Road (L. Williams), 41–42, 45–46, 50, 52, 55, 62
"Car Wheels on a Gravel Road" (song), 50–52
Cash, Johnny, 80, 219
"Casimir Pulaski Day" (song), 117–18
"Catholic Imagination of Bruce Springsteen, The" (Greeley), 24
"Catholic Novelist in the Protestant South, The" (O'Connor), 99
Cave, Arthur, 153
Cave, Nick, 3–4, 8, 13–14, 125, 155, 158, 172, 174–76, 185, 197–98, 200–201, 211, 217, 219–20; background of, 127; as Christ-haunted, 7, 127, 151; clean as righteous, 131; death of son, 153; evil, 140; fallen human nature, 140; hovering between belief and unbelief, 146; incarnational art of, 144–45, 148–49; influence of Bible on, 127–28; influence of O'Connor on, 128–30, 133, 136; interest in extreme human behavior, 133; intrigued by John the Baptist, 146; as irreligious religious writer, 152; lectures of, 151; literary aspirations, 129; as living O'Connor character, 151; medium of

"the Love Song," 148, 152, 154; obsession with *Wise Blood*, 128, 130–31, 157; as pop prophet, 151; redemption, 141, 146; religious beliefs of, 151–52; as sacred and profane, 134–35, 137–38, 141–42, 144, 146, 148–51; similarities between Waits, 215–16; Song of Solomon, 137; in *Wings of Desire*, 134
"Chasing the Moon" (song), 206
Chestnutt, Vic, 59
"Child in Flannery O'Connor, The" (Burkle), 49
Childish, Billy, 185
"Chocolate Jesus" (song), 218
Chopin, Kate, 86
"Christmas Day" (song), 225
"Christmas in Paradise" (song), 83
"Church and the Fiction Writer, The" (O'Connor), 38
Church of Satan, 169–70, 177
Ciardi, John, 40
"Circle in the Fire, A" (O'Connor), 142
Clark, Guy, 13, 88, 94, 189
Clash, the, 184
Clearmountain, Bob, 183
Cockburn, Bruce, 211
Cohen, Leonard, 199
"Cold Day in Hell" (L. Williams), 64
Coldplay, 120
"Cold That's Forever, The" (song), 196
Coleridge, Samuel Taylor, 117, 170
Columbia Records, 42
"Come on Up to the House" (song), 219
"Comforts of Home, The" (O'Connor), 14, 31, 34, 79, 109, 213; divine *caritas*, 147; erotic sacramentalism in, 147; as morality tale, 148; mystery in, 148; Star Drake, 32–33, 109, 147, 214
"Compassion" (M. Williams), 69
Compass Records, 88
concept albums, 114, 120; decline of, 121
"Concerning the UFO Sighting near Highland, Illinois" (song), 113
Confiscation, The (Crain), 191
Cope, Sally Virginia (character), 142
"Copenhagen" (song), 60
Cordero, Jonathan, 168–70
Corrosion of Conformity, 15, 169, 171, 174–77; as Christ-haunted, 172
"Counting Numbers in the Air" (song), 221

Covington, Dennis, 45–46, 96–97
Crain, Samantha, 191–92
Crane, Annie, 192–93
"Crazy in Alabama" (song), 89
Crowell, Rodney, 13, 94
Crowley, Aleister, 171
Cullen, Jim, 23–24, 29
Cutler, Colin, 193–96

Damaged Goods (record company), 184
Dance on the Wind (Brannon), 189–90
"Dancer, The" (song), 156
Darkness on the Edge of Town (Springsteen), 16, 26, 121
Dark Snack (Moaners), 205–6
Dawkins, Cecil, 32
"Death Came" (song), 59
"Decatur, or Round of Applause for Your Stepmother!" (song), 117
desegregation, 91–92
Desmond, John, 66
Detweiler, Lindford, 71
"Devils & Dust" (song), 34–36
Devils & Dust (Springsteen), 11, 24, 28, 37; bonus DVD, 34; Catholic imagery in, 25, 35
Dickey, James, 40
Dirtdish (Wiseblood), 174, 176–77
"Displaced Person, The" (O'Connor), 98, 203, 216, 229
Document (R.E.M.), 207–9
Dominican Sisters, 99
Donne, John, 213
"Don't Let Me Die in Florida" (song), 188
Don't Tell Anybody the Secrets I Told You (L. Williams), 41
"Doors of Heaven" (song), 60
Dostoevsky, Fyodor, 185
Douglas, Andrew, 220
Dourif, Brad, 175, 197
Downey, Barbara, 16
"Down There by the Train" (song), 219
Down Where the Spirit Meets the Bone (L. Williams), 48, 61–65, 69–70
"Do You Love Me?" (song), 150
Drag Queens in Limousines (Gauthier), 75–76, 83
"Drag Queens in Limousines" (song), 83
Drake, Star (character): erotic sacramentalism, 147; "intimate grin," 32–33; as "moral

moron," 214; as nymphomanic, 32; as symbolic twin of Thomas, 109
Drill a Hole in That Substrate and Tell Me What You See (White), 221, 224
"Drunken Angel" (song), 59
Dürer, Albrecht, 173
"Dust" (M. Williams), 69
Dylan, Bob, 3, 35, 40, 78, 81, 86, 188, 211–12

Earle, Steve, 42
Edge (U2 guitarist), 3, 212
Edgerton, Clyde, 236
Ed Sullivan Show, The (television show), 229, 231–32
Eliot, T. S., 123, 235
Elizabeth, Tania, 85
"Elizabeth Cotten's Song" (song), 205
Elizabeth II (queen), 155
Ellis, Warren, 127
Elvis Now! (Presley), 101
"Enduring Chill, The" (O'Connor), 3–4, 78, 105–6, 196, 209, 213–14; grace in, 148
England, 180
Enya, 235
Eponymous (Hazel Motes), 238
Essence (L. Williams), 42–43, 50, 63
E Street Band, 19, 35, 37, 211
"Eternity Street" (song), 232
Eucrow, Euchrid (character), 130–31, 133; hearing voices, 132
Europe, 88
"Evangeline" (song), 83
"Everybody Hurts" (song), 207
"Everything But the Truth" (song), 65, 68
"Everything That Rises (Must Converge)" (Shreikback song), 183
"Everything That Rises Must Converge" (O'Connor), 65, 67–68, 90–92, 124, 227–28; double figures in, 109; informing of Teilhard, 184
Everything That Rises Must Converge (O'Connor), 4–5, 68, 102, 204
"Everything That Rises Must Converge" (Wild Strawberries song), 227–28
"Exit" (song), 213–14

"Fade to Blue" (song), 100
Faggot (band), 196–97
"Faith and Grace" (song), 39, 68–69

"Fancy Funeral" (song), 58
Faulkner, William, 84, 91, 191, 202, 216
"Fiction Writer and His Country, The" (O'Connor), 5, 73
Filth and Fire (Gauthier), 82
Finster, Howard, 209
First Aid Kit, 191
Fitzgerald, Benedict, 167
Fitzgerald, Michael, 167
Fitzgerald, Sally, 66, 114–15
"Flannery" (song), 210
"Flannery O'Connor" (Faggot song), 196–97
"Flannery O'Connor" (Joyner song), 199
Flannery O'Connor: Collected Works (O'Connor), 5
Flannery O'Connor's Georgia (McKenzie), 93–94
Flannery O'Connor: The Complete Stories (O'Connor), 5, 16, 160, 162, 164–65
Flannery O'Connor: The Imagination of Extremity (Asals), 32, 108
"Flannery Said" (song), 205–6
"Flannery's Georgia" (song), 207
"Flannery's Waltz" (song), 189
Fleming, Kele, 237–38
"Flesh Made Word, The" (Cave), 151
"Floating World" (song), 180
Foley, Blaze, 59
For the Love of It All (Brannon), 189
Foundling, The (character), 84–86
Foundling, The (Gauthier), 72, 84–85, 121
Four Quartets (Eliot), 123
Freedom Riders, 90
Frisell, Bill, 68–69
From Her to Eternity (Cave), 149
"From Her to Eternity" (song), 134
"Fruit of the Vine" (song), 221–22
"Fruits of My Labor" (song), 63
Fugate, Caril, 19
"Funeral Food" (song), gothic humor in, 94–95
Funny Little Cross to Bear, A (White), 225

Gable, Sister Marietta, 121
Gacy, John Wayne, Jr., 111–12
Galerie de la Maison du Festival, 129
Gang of Four, 178–79, 183
Gauthier, Mary, 3–4, 7–8, 13, 88, 121, 124, 221, 230–32; background of, 72, 75;

confessional lyrics, 74; creative process, 72; grace, 12, 72, 74–75, 77–78, 87; identification with socially marginalized people, 83; influence of O'Connor on, 12, 71, 74; jailhouse experience, 75, 77; longing for home, 72; narrative songs as collection of soul drama, 80; redemption, 72; as serious writer, 81; songwriting style of, 81–83, 87; spiritualty as grounded in Twelve Step program, 76; themes of, 72; as truthteller, 73; writing process of, 81; uncomfortable songs, 84
Gentry, Marshall Bruce, 69–70
Georgia, 91, 93–94
Georgia College & State University: O'Connor Collection, 81
Georgia Writers' Association, 89
Gerald, Michael, 200
"Get Real, Get Right" (song), 119–20
"Get Right with God" (song), 6–7, 12, 39, 42, 46–47, 68–69, 119, 232; influence on *Wise Blood*, 41, 45, 232; recalling of Hazel Motes, 44–45
"Ghost Body" (song), 192
Ghosteen (Cave), 154
Ghost of Tom Joad, The (Springsteen), 11, 28–30, 35, 37
Ghosts of Highway 20, The (L. Williams), 39, 42, 48, 55–56, 59–60, 62–64, 68–69
Gibson, Mel, 96
Ginsberg, Allen, 40, 216
Gioia, Dana, 41
Gladwell, Malcolm, 25
Glass, Philip, 174, 210
Glory Days (Marsh), 35
"God Bless You Arthur Blessitt" (song), 95–96
"Godbrain" (song), 176
"Goddamn HIV" (song), 83
"God Is in the House" (Steinke), 152
"Goodbye Windows" (song), 172
"Good Country People" (O'Connor), 105, 124, 159–60, 215
"Good Man Is Hard to Find, A" (O'Connor), 5, 20, 33, 34, 65–67, 208, 221, 237; costly grace, 77; meanness in, 6, 21, 58, 77, 131, 139; The Misfit, 6, 21, 58, 77, 82, 109–11, 131, 136, 139, 195, 217–18, 227
Good Man Is Hard to Find, A (O'Connor), 4, 152, 155, 196–97, 217; original sin, 11, 19

"Good Man Is Hard to Find, A (Pittsburgh)" (song), 34
"Good Man Is Hard to Find, A" (Stevens song): double motif in, 109; Misfit character, 110–11
"Good Man Is Hard to Find, A" (Waits song), 217–18
Good Souls, Better Angels (L. Williams), 42
"Good Vibrations" (song), 113–14
Gospel of Saint Bartholomew, 122
grace, 179, 204, 205; cheap, 74; costly, 74, 76–77; in Gauthier, 12, 72, 74–75, 77–78, 87; irresistible, 77–78; in O'Connor, 78, 87, 103, 105, 116, 148, 172, 182, 218–19; paradoxes of, 78; shock of, 79; in Springsteen, 24, 27; in Stevens, 103, 105, 111
Grace (Wild Strawberries), 227
Greeley, Andrew, 24–25, 232
Green, Eddie, 66, 217
"Greenleaf" (O'Connor), 6, 31, 76, 97–98, 107, 216
Greetings from Asbury Park, N. J. (Springsteen), 18, 108
Greetings from Michigan (Stevens), 107
Griffin, Patty, 188
Griffith, Nanci, 13, 94
Gross, Terry, 75, 77
Gush, Charlotte, 235
Guthrie, Woody, 73, 108

Habit of Being, The (O'Connor), 125
Hall, Rebecca Jordan, 53
Happy Woman Blues (L. Williams), 42
Hard (Gang of Four), 178, 180
Harmon, Crit, 75, 81
Harris, Carole K., 65–66
Harris, Emmylou, 13, 42, 58, 88–89, 94
Harrison, Ken, 225–28
Harry Potter and the Deathly Hallows—Part I (film), 127
Hart, Carol, 129–30
Harvey, PJ, 3–4, 134; debt to O'Connor, 14, 155–57, 159; found lyrics of, 155, 162; influence on Salinger, 159; interest in extreme human behavior, 158; introduction to O'Connor by Cave, 158; lyrics drawn from O'Connor, 160–64
Hawkes, John, 32, 61, 114, 182, 190, 229
Hawthorne, Nathaniel, 114

Hazel Motes (band), 237–38
Headphones (band), 199
Heard, Mark, 207
Heart Is a Lonely Hunter, The (McCullers), 204
"Heart of Hearts" (song), 100
"Heaven Blues" (song), 60
heavy metal, 4, 15, 166–67, 171, 180, 186–87, 200, 230; anti-Christian rhetoric, 168–69; discourse of chaos in, 170; influence on science fiction literature, 170
Hell or High Water (film), 127
Hemingway, Ernest, 181
"He Never Got Enough Love" (song), 57
Henry, Matthew, 66
Henry's Dream (Cave), 151
Heroine (Wild Strawberries), 227–28
Hester, Betty, 27, 65, 73, 125
"He Woke Me Up Again" (song), 112
Hight, Jewly, 59, 201
"High Water (For Charlie Patton)" (song), 188
Highway 61 Revisited (Dylan), 40
"Highway 29" (song), 30–31
Hilburn, Robert, 211
Hinduism, 112
"Holiday Inn Again, The" (Gauthier), 82
Hollywood Baptist Church, 90
"Home You're Tearing Down, The" (song), 52
Hoskyns, Barney, 216
Howlin Mercy (Campbell), 190
Hunt, Holman, 36
Hurricane Katrina, 83
Huston, John, 11, 15, 40–41, 133, 167, 197

"I Drink" (song), 81, 83
"If I Was the Priest" (song), 27
"If Jesus Drove a Motorhome" (song), 224
"If There's a Heaven" (song), 60
"If Wishes Were Horses" (song), 63
Iggy Pop, 127, 201
"I Had a Dream, Joe" (song), 151
Illinois, 108, 118
Illinois (Stevens), 103, 107–8, 111, 114, 117, 120
Images of Grace (Fickett and Gilbert), 93–94
"Imagine" (song), 224
"I'm a Honky Tonk Girl" (song), 52
Immaculate Consumptive, 176
"Impossible Soul" (song), 108

Indonesia, 112
"I Need You" (song), 153
"Inescapable Jesus" (song), 238
"In the Devil's Territory" (song), 113–14
"Into My Arms" (song), 135–36, 145, 148
Iraq War, 83–84
Is This Desire? (Harvey), 14, 155, 158, 160, 165; borrowing from O'Connor stories, 157; as haunted by O'Connor, 159
"I Think I'm a Mother" (song), 156
"It's Hard to Be a Saint in the City" (song), 24
"It's the End of the World as We Know It (And I Feel Fine)" (song), 207
"I Wish I Was in Dixie" (song), 92

Jackson, Andrew, 117
"Jacksonville" (song), 117
Jagjaguwar (record label), 199, 210
James, Henry, center of consciousness, 48–49
Javelin (Stevens), 124
Jennings, Waylon, 236
"Jesus Alone" (song), 153–54
"Jesus and Tomatoes" (song), 94
"Jesus Built My Hotrod" (song), 167, 170–71
"Jesus Was an Only Son" (song), 36
"Jim 3:16" (song), 225
Johansson, Scarlett, 204
"Johnny 99" (song), 28, 31
John Paul II, 75, 100
Johnson, Robert, 41, 229
Johnson, Rufus (character), 49, 134, 140, 195, 229, 231; as Christ-haunted, 230
Johnston, Ian, 128, 157
"John Wayne Gacy, Jr." (song), 111–12
Jonson, Ben, 61
Joshua Tree, The (U2), 3, 212–13
Jourgensen, Al, 167, 169, 171
"Joy" (song), 158, 163, 165; connection to "Good Country People," 159–60
Joyner, Simon, 199
"Judgement Day" (O'Connor), 68, 105, 188, 200, 209, 226; double figures in, 109
"Jumblyleg Man" (song), 203
Jump with a Child's Heart (Crane), 192
"Just a Little More Faith and Grace" (song), 68

"Karla Faye" (song), 75–76
Keaton, Buster, 202

Index

Keenan, Pepper, 171–72
Kennedy, X. J., 41
Kerouac, Jack, 216
Kessel, Corinne, 216, 219
Killdozer (band), 200
Kimmell, Tom, 207
King, Martin Luther, Jr., 3, 90, 212
King, Stephen, 201
"King of Birds" (song), 208
"King of the Birds, The" (O'Connor), 208
King Swamp (band), 180–83
Kronos Quartet, 175
Kubrick, Stanley, 225

"Lame Shall Enter First, The" (O'Connor), 4, 49–50, 57, 194, 204, 229; *caritas* kind of love, 76
Landau, Jon, 16, 19
"Land Called Home" (song), 224
"Land of Hope and Dreams" (song), 219
"Last Song, The" (song), 101
"Late Encounter with the Enemy, A" (O'Connor), 192–93
Laufman, Christopher (a.k.a. Wise Blood), 234
Laveau, Marie, 80
LaVey, Anton, 177
"Leah" (song), 36
"Learning How to Live" (song), 58
Led Zeppelin, 174
Lee, Julie, 71
Lee, Maryat, 209
Legendary Shack Shakers, 200; Christ-haunted, 204; "musical violence" of, 201–2
Lennon, John, 224
Lennon and McCartney, 211
Let Love In (Cave), 150
"Letter to You" (song), 37
Letter to You (Springsteen), 27
Lewis, Jerry Lee, 201
Lewis, John, 90
"Life You Save May Be Your Own, The" (O'Connor), 65–67, 163, 186–87, 196
"Lime-Tree Arbour" (song), 137–38, 144–45
Literature: An Introduction to Fiction, Poetry, Drama, and Writing (Kennedy and Gioia), 41
"Literature of Exhaustion, The" (Barth), 120

"Little Gidding" (Eliot), 123
Little Honey (L. Williams), 60, 63
Lo-Fi Therapy No. 1: Songs about Flannery O'Connor (Velma and the Happy Campers), 215
Lolita (Nabokov), 128, 147
"Long Time Coming" (song), 34–35
"Look Away" (song), 92
"Losing My Religion" (song), 207
Lost Highway (record company), 48
"Lost in the Flood" (song), 27
"Louisiana Story" (song), 50
Love (band), 236
Love Song for Bobby Long, A (film), 204; Christ-haunted, 205
"Love Song of J. Alfred Prufrock, The" (Eliot), 235
Lowry, Beverly, 75
Luaka Bop (record label), 221, 224
Lucinda Williams (L. Williams), 42
Lunch, Lydia, 175–76
"Lupus" (song), 200
Lynch, John, 24
Lynn, Loretta, 40, 50, 52

Macht, Gabriel, 204
"Magnolia" (song), 64
Malick, Terrence, 19
"Mama You Sweet" (song), 58
"Mamma, Don't Know Where Heaven Is" (song), 194–95
Manfred Mann and His Earth Band, 18
Mann, Aimee, 224
"Man with a Good Car, A" (song), 178–80
"March 11, 1962" (song), 85
"Maria's Bed" (song), 36
Marsh, Dave, 16, 22, 35
Marzuki (band), 103
Mason Tarwater (band), 236; jukebox approach of, 236
"Matamoros Banks" (song), 8, 34–37
Mauriac, Francois, 153
McCarthy, Cormac, 127
McCredden, Lyn, 134, 136–37, 144, 145–46; "carnal sacred," 149–50
McCullers, Carson, 88, 216
McDowell, Mississippi Fred, 68
McKane, Janet, 61

McKenzie, Barbara, 93–94
McLachlan, Sarah, 227
meanness, 32, 58, 111, 139; meaningless, 21, 28; meaning of, 21, 208; The Misfit, 6, 28, 30, 33–34, 77, 131, 218; mystery of, 29, 38; O'Connor on, 8, 31, 131, 180; "no pleasure but meanness" credo, 21, 33; in Springsteen's work, 21–22, 28–31, 34; as theme, 22
Memoir of Mary Ann, A (O'Connor preface), 141
"Mercy" (song), 146
Mercy Now (Gauthier), 79, 81, 87
"Mercy Now" (song), 72, 87, 230, 231; as signature song, 86
"Mercy Seat, The" (song), 140–41
Mering, Natalie (a.k.a. Weyes Blood), 234, 235
Merlefest, 88
Merton, Thomas, 9
Michigan, 13, 103–4, 108, 125
Michigan (Stevens), 13, 108, 114–15
Miller, Buddy, 94
Miller, Monica, 167–68, 171, 176–77, 208–9
Mills, Mike, 15, 188
Ministry (band), 15, 167, 169–71, 174, 176–77
"Miracle of the Rosary" (hymn), 101
Misfit, The (character), 14, 66, 79, 84, 172, 195–96, 236; in "A Good Man Is Hard to Find," 6, 21, 58, 77, 82, 109–11, 131, 136, 139, 195, 217–18, 227; evil impulse of, 30, 33–34; and meanness of, 6, 21, 28, 30, 33–34, 77, 131, 139, 218; in "Nebraska," 21, 131; in Springsteen, 21–22, 28–31, 34; in Stevens, 110–11; struggle to believe, 136; unbelief of, 141
Misfits (band), 236
Misfits, The (film), 236
Mississippi, 89
Misty, Father John: as Christ-haunted, 198; Hazel Motes-like stage persona, 197
Moaners (duo), 205–6
Moments (Pettis), 207
Monroe, Marilyn, 236
Moonpie Dreams (Campbell), 88, 94, 96
Morrison, Van, 69
Mosimann, Roli, 174
Motes, Hazel (character), 21–22, 41, 43, 55–56, 156–57, 174–75, 185–86, 188, 190, 198, 209, 215, 235; anti-Christian rhetoric, 168, 170–71; as Christ-haunted, 154; Christ-less existence, 178; "clean boy," 131; eyes of, 210; "good car" statement, 167–68; "Jesus-seeing hat," 149–50; liaison with prostitute, 149–50, 170; persona of street evangelist, 130; self-mortification of, 44–45, 151, 153, 170, 203
Motorslug (Wiseblood), 174, 176–77
Mule Variations (Waits), 218–19
"Murder in the Red Barn" (song), 216–17
"My Father's House" (song), 26
"My Mother, King Tut" (Stevens), 115
Mystery and Manners (O'Connor), 113, 181, 208
"Mystery of Love" (song), 103

National Association of Independent Record Distributors, 88
"Nature and Aim of Fiction, The" (O'Connor), 72
"Nebraska" (song), 22, 31; influence on *Badlands*, 19; "meanness" quote, 21, 131; The Misfit, 21, 131; as monologue, 20; O'Connor influence, 140
Nebraska (Springsteen), 7, 11, 17, 20–21, 26, 28–29, 34–35, 37, 84, 115, 124, 172, 180; meanness, 78–79; O'Connoresque characters, 19, 157. *See also* meanness
Nelson, Willie, 236
Nemerov, Howard, 40
"Never Let Go" (Waits), 219
New Agrarians, 207
Newman, John Henry, 141
New Orleans, Louisiana, 80
"New York Comeback" (song), 42
Nick Cave and the Bad Seeds, 14, 127–29, 133–34, 176
Nick Cave Stories (scrapbook), 135
Nick Cave: The Complete Lyrics, 1978–2022 (Cave), 149
"Nightfall over Eden" (song), 181
"Nobody's Baby Now" (song), 150
"No Girl So Sweet" (song), 159, 163; borrowings from "The Life You Save May Be Your Own," 164–65
North America, 228
Norton, Edward, 16
"Novelist and Believer" (O'Connor), 14, 80, 106

O'Connor, Flannery, 12, 15, 35, 37, 40–42, 44–45, 56, 66–70, 73, 79, 83, 86, 88, 90, 102, 112, 117, 126–29, 134–35, 151, 155–57, 161–65, 170–71, 176, 178–79, 181, 183, 185–86, 190–97, 199, 202, 204–7, 212–17, 220, 222–23, 226, 234–38; acts of grace, 76; allusion to Pentecostal fire, 122–23; alter ego, 109; Andalusia (family farm), 39, 189, 208, 221; artistic crisis of, 121; art of storytelling, 115–16; Bible Belt and Catholic faith, 99; biting satire of, 203; Calvinist doctrine of "irresistible grace," 77–78; Catholic doctrine, 50; Catholic faith, 23, 27, 57–58, 65, 72, 113, 152–53; Catholic imagination of, 24–25; Catholic vision of, 17; central theme of, 136; child characters, 49–51; as Christ-centered, 6; Christ-haunted fiction, 4, 6–7, 13, 55, 130, 154, 198; clean as righteous, 131; commitment to place, 103; concern with mystery, 148; as controversial, 4; costly grace, 77; death of, 4, 200; the Devil, 61–62, 105; as devout Catholic, 4–5; double figures, 108–9, 111, 119; epiphanic devices, 110; erotic sacramentalism, 147; explanation of wise blood symbol, 182; exploration of evil, 28–30, 104, 114, 140; exploration of meanness, 8, 31, 131, 180; eyes, 210–11; fallen human nature, 139–41; gothic comedy of, 95, 105–6; grace, 78, 87, 103, 105, 116, 148, 172, 182, 218–19; grotesques, 95, 104, 133; heaven, 60–61; heightened consciousness of, 48; incarnational art of, 144; incarnation as central to, 6, 142; influence on pop stars, 4–5; at Iowa Writers' Workshop, 9, 114–15; interest in extreme human behavior, 133, 158; interest in Teilhard, 184, 227–28; intrigued by John the Baptist, 146, 229; nod to sanctified imagination, 152; original sin, 10–11, 26, 103; peacocks of, 39, 47, 208, 232–33; on popular music, 231–32; on race, 91–92; redemption, 152; as regional writer, 89, 103; religious beliefs and practices, 125, 152; religious eccentrics, 95–101, 107, 208; religious hypocrisy, 203; revelation, 140; rewriting, 81; rhetorical strategy, 65; road signs, 93; sacramental view of, 38; sacred and carnal, 144; sacred shock, 8; short fiction informed by the personal, 119; short story as "complete dramatic action," 82; skewering of southern manners and eccentricities, 94; southern grotesque, 46; the South's Protestant traditions, 99; tin ear of, 3, 187–89, 232; unbelieving searchers, 136; unfinished novel, 209; use of clichés, 62–63; violent characters, 27–33, 71, 82, 137, 201; *Wise Blood* correspondence, 166; wise-blooded characters, 230; *wisdom* writings, 188–89; writing method of, 124

"Oddfellows Local 151" (song), as Christ-haunted, 209, 210
O'Hagen, Seán, 142
Oldham, Spooner, 13, 101–2
"One I Love, The" (song), 207
"One More Day" (song), 64
One More Time with Feeling (film), 153–54
"One Step over the Line" (song), 180
1000 Pound Machine (Campbell), 90, 95
"One Tree Hill" (song), 3–4, 188, 213, 214
"On Her Own Work" (O'Connor), 28, 71, 111
"On My First Son" (Jonson), 61
On the Road (Kerouac), 216
"O-O (Where Evil Dwells)" (song), 176
original sin, 98, 183; doctrine of, 26, 98; in *A Good Man Is Hard to Find*, 11, 19; and O'Connor, 10–11, 26, 103; and Springsteen, 10–11, 17, 26
"Orphan King, The" (song), 86
"Our Lady of the Shooting Stars" (song), 76
"Out of Touch" (song), 63
Overby, Tom, 55–56, 69
Over the Rhine (band), 71

Pandelerium (Legendary Shack Shakers), 201
Pareles, Jon, 25
Parker, O. E. (character), 29–30, 76, 216, 231; revelation of, 223; tattoos of, 138–39
"Parker's Back" (O'Connor), 7, 29, 58, 102, 105, 138–39, 196, 223; grace, 148
"Parker's Reprise" (song), 196
Parks, Rosa, 90, 228
Pascal, Blaise, 149
"Passionate Kisses" (song), 42
Passion of the Christ, The (film), 96
Pate, Ashby, 235
Peacock Feathers (Cutler), 193–94, 196
Pedro the Lion (band), 198, 199
Pentecostalism, 12, 101

"Penthouse Suites" (Laufman), 234
Percy, Walker, 17, 25–26, 232
Percy, Will, 17–18, 21, 25
Pettis, Grace, 207
Pettis, Pierce, 206–7
Phelan, Patrick, 210–11
Phenomenon of Man, The (Teilhard), 184
"Phone Booth in Heaven" (song), 221, 224–25
Pilgrim's Progress, The (Bunyan), 14, 135
Plant, Robert, 171, 201
"Please" (song), 214
Pletzinger, Thomas, 124
Poe, Abie (character), 131; as street evangelist, 130
Poe, Edgar Allan, 109, 130, 170, 202
POP (U2), as Christ-haunted, 214–15
"Porcelain Blue" (song), 100
"Postcard from a Volcano" (song), 226
Pratt, Michael Davis, 220
Prayer Journal, A (O'Connor), 125–26
"Preachin' at Traffic" (song), 203
Presley, Elvis, 101–2, 127–28, 229, 230
"Price You Pay, The" (song), 26
Prine, John, 13, 94, 225
Promise, The (documentary), 16
Promised Land, 26, 36–37, 181
Psalm 69 (Ministry), 171
PTTM (Wiseblood), 174, 177
punk, 4, 155, 166–67, 174–75, 184, 186, 196–97, 201–2, 205–6, 230, 236; post-punk, 15, 127, 134, 178, 180, 185, 187, 207
"Pure Comedy" (Misty), 198

racism, 91
Ragen, Brian Abel, 167–68
Ragnarok (Hazel Motes), 238
Ramones, the, 184
Ramseur (record label), 191
"Reason to Believe" (Springsteen): images in, 22, 26; misinterpretation of, 23
"Red Clay after Rain" (Campbell), 88
redemption, 5, 7–8, 32, 33, 93, 149, 152, 181, 190, 198, 213, 225; in Cave, 141, 146; in Gauthier, 72; in Springsteen, 24–27, 35; in Williams, 47–48, 68–69
"Redemption City" (song), 172
"Red Right Hand" (song), 127
Red Sammy, 237

Reich, Steve, 174, 210
R.E.M., 3, 5, 15, 188; gothic southernness, 208; O'Connor references, 207–10
"Reno" (song), 34–35, 37
"Revelation" (O'Connor), 29, 58, 73, 80, 110, 139; religious hypocrisy, 203; Ruby Turpin, 116, 203, 223; shock of grace, 79
Rid of Me (Harvey), 158
Rifles and Rosary Beads (Gauthier), 83–84
Rinaldi, Stacey, 194–95
Rising, The (Springsteen), 24–25, 35
"River, The" (Crain song), 191–92
"River, The" (Harvey song), 159, 162–63, 165
"River, The" (O'Connor), 50, 57, 59, 162–65, 191–92, 196, 210, 221
River, The (Springsteen), 11, 16, 19, 22
"River, The" (Springsteen song), 26
Road, The (film), 127
Road, The (McCarthy), 127
Robertson, Royal, 118, 120; as Mason Tarwater figure, 119
"Romulus" (song), 115–16
Rosaryville (Campbell), 13, 92, 102; Bible Belt Catholics, 99–101
"Rosaryville" (song), 101
Rosaryville Spirit Life Center, 99–100, 102
"Rose for Emily, A" (Faulkner), 91
Rosen, Craig, 209
Rubin, Rick, 25

Salinger, J. D., 159
Salomé (Cave), 146
Salvation on Sand Mountain (Covington), 45–46, 96
Saved by a Song (Gauthier), 12, 87
"Save Your Life and Drive" (song), 196
"Say Yes! To M!ch!gan!" (song), 114
Scialfa, Patti, 42
Scott, R. Neil, 236
Scream (film), 127
Searching for the Wrong-Eyed Jesus (film), 206, 220, 222; CD booklet, 223–24; as Christ-haunted, 225
"Secret Life of the Love Song, The" (Cave lecture), 137
"Seeing Black" (song), 59
Selby, John, 41–42
Selma march, 90

Sessions, Bill, 207
Seven Psalms (Cave), 154
Seven Swans (Stevens), 13, 109, 113, 124–25
Sex Pistols, 201
Shriekback (band), 183
"Signs Following" (song), 96–97
"Sing a Worried Song" (song), 202
Siren Rising (Blandford), 159
"Size Too Small" (song), 124
"Skeleton Town" (song), 83
Skeleton Tree (Cave), 153
"Sleeping Bear, Sault Saint Marie" (song), 116
Smith, Bessie, 66, 217
"Snakebit" (song), 78–79
"Some Aspects of the Grotesque in Southern Fiction" (O'Connor), 48, 78, 147–48
"Something to Believe" (song), 235–36
"Something Wicked This Way Comes" (song), 61–62
Songs from the Levee (Campbell), 12–13, 88
Songs Inspired by Literature: Chapter Two, 217
SongwritingWith:Soldiers program, 83–84
South (musical collective), 210
Southern Christian Leadership Council (SCLC), 90
"Spare Parts" (song), 24, 26–27
Sparks, Minton, 71
Springsteen, Bruce, 3–5, 7, 41–42, 53, 76, 78–79, 81–82, 84, 88, 108–9, 115, 121, 124, 131, 140, 155, 157, 172, 176, 180, 183, 185, 211, 214, 216–17, 219–22, 230, 232; Catholicism of, 23–24, 27, 36–37; Catholic themes, 26; characters of as being Christ-haunted, 22; as Christ-haunted, 6, 11; exploration of meanness, 29, 31, 34, 37–38; exploration of mystery of evil, 29–30; grace, 24, 27; internal landscape, 152, 231; narrative songwriting style, 37; O'Connor's influence on, 10–11, 16–19, 36; original sin, 10–11, 17, 26; redemption, 24–27, 35; sacramental view of, 38; songwriting as "incarnational art," 37; as spiritual songwriter, 25; as storyteller, 37; themes of, 24; use of biblical language, 26; use of Catholic imagery and symbolism, 24–25, 35; use of religious terms, 24; violent characters, 27–31, 33
Springsteen on Broadway, 37
Stanford, Frank, 58–59

Starkweather, Charles, 19, 140
"State Trooper" (song): echoing of Hazel Motes, 21–22; narrator of, 21–22; O'Connor's influence on, 21–22
"Static on the Radio" (song), 224
St. Augustine, 9
Steinbeck, John, 211
Steinke, Darcey, 152
Steinke, René, 106–7
Stevens, Carrie, 112
Stevens, Rajid, 112
Stevens, Sufjan, 3–4, 6, 13, 81–82, 118, 155, 185, 195, 217, 221, 230; aesthetics of, 124; allusion to Pentecostal fire, 122–23; artistic crisis of, 120–21; background of, 103–4, 112; baroque pop, 124; comedy, 105–6; commitment to place, 103; the Devil, 105–7, 114; evil, 104, 111–12, 114; "50 States Project," 108; grace, 103, 105, 111; identity shaped by Michigan, 114–15; informed by Christian faith, 103, 113; MFA thesis, 103–4, 125; narrative songs informed by the personal, 119; as "Next Flannery," 104; O'Connor's influence on, 117, 124–26; original sin, 103; parabolic song narratives, 114; post-God society, 103; as postmodern prophet, 125; redemption, 114; as regional writer, 103; song cycles, 107–8; songwriting style as collage making, 117; sympathy for Robertson, 119; use of double motif, 109, 111, 119–20; use of ecstatic exclamation, 116–17
"Still Waters" (song), 221
Stipe, Michael, 208–10
Stockman, Steve, 213
Stories from a Rock n Roll Heart (L. Williams), 42
St. Paul, 67, 69, 123, 145
"Straight Time" (song), 29–31
Stranger in a Strange Land (film), 134–35
Stranger than Kindness (book), 152
Stranger than Kindness (installation), 129, 135
Stritch, Thomas, 232
Stumbo (Wiseblood), 174, 177
Subud (cult), 112
Suicide Squeeze Records, 199
Summerford, Glenn, 97
Swampblood (Legendary Shack Shakers), 201; "bob-wire" in printed lyrics, 203–4

Sweet Old World (L. Williams), 42, 57–58
"Sweet Old World" (song), 58–59
"Sweet Words" (song), 86
Swingle, Melissa, 206

Tarantino, Quentin, 31
Tarwater (Cutler), 193, 196
Tarwater (German duo), 236
Tarwater (Texas band), 236
Tarwater, Craig, 236
Tarwater, Davis, 236
Tarwater, Francis Marion (character), 57, 67, 113, 132–33, 136, 151, 206, 230–31
Tarwater, Mason (character), 46–47, 84, 96, 99, 107, 119, 123, 125, 131–32, 136; touched by "finger of fire," 121
Tarwater Band, 236
Teilhard, Pierre de Chardin, 227–28; "everything that rises must converge" phrase, 184; Omega Point, 184
"Temple of the Holy Ghost, A" (O'Connor), 8, 14, 49–50, 116, 142, 196, 217; dream-vision, 143; juxtaposition in Catholic doctrine of transsubstantiation, 144; sacred and carnal as conjoined, 144
"Temporary Nature (Of Any Precious Thing)" (song), 64–65
Tender Prey (Cave), 140
Tent Show Trilogy (Legendary Shack Shakers), 201, 204. See also *Believe*; *Pandelerium*; *Swampblood*
Thee Mighty Caesars, 184–85
Theme Time Radio Hour (radio program), 81
"Theology of Bruce Springsteen, The" (Yamin), 24
"There Is a Kingdom" (song), 144–46
Thirlwell, JG, 15, 177, 197, 234; as Hazel Motes figure, 174–75; Wiseblood persona, 176, 185, 234. See also Wiseblood (band)
36 of His Greatest Hits (H. Williams), 52
Thornton, Billy Bob, 201
Through the Farmlands & the Cities (Crane), 192
Tillman, Joshua. See Misty, Father John
Tinseltown (Pettis), 207
Titanic Rising (Mering/Weyes Blood), 235–36
To Bring You My Love (Harvey), 156; as Christ-haunted, 157
"To Bring You My Love" (song), 157

Tracks (Springsteen), 34
Travolta, John, 204
Trice, Adam, 237. See also Red Sammy
Trouble and Love (Gauthier), 77
Trump, Donald, 42
"Two Faces" (song), 24
Tucker, Karla Faye, 75–76
Tucker, Sophie, 66
"Tunnel of Love" (song), 24
Tunnel of Love (Springsteen), 24
Turpin, Ruby (character), 29, 66–67, 73–74, 79, 116, 139–40, 232
Tutu, Desmond, 3, 212
Twelve Point Buck (Killdozer), 200

"Ugly Truth" (song), 63
"Under the Linden Tree" (lyric), 137
"Unsuffer Me" (song), 39; as song of redemption, 47–48
"Upper Peninsula, The" (song), 115
U2, 3, 5, 176, 183, 207; collaborative songwriting method, 211; Elevation tour, 155; O'Connor's influence on, 211–15

"Valentine's Day" (song), 24
Vancouver (British Columbia), 238
Van Zandt, Townes, 224
Vaughan, Stevie Ray, 190
Velma and the Happy Campers, 215
"Vesuvius" (song), invoking of "fire of fire," 122–23
VH1 Storytellers (TV music series), 6, 18, 36
"View of the Woods, A" (O'Connor), 29, 49, 57
Violent Bear It Away, The (O'Connor), 4, 9, 46, 57, 62, 81, 93, 95, 98, 107, 113, 121, 123, 130–31, 151, 192, 205–6, 223, 229–30; epigraph of, 146; gothic comedy in, 95; reference to John the Baptist, 146; response from "stranger," 205–6
Virgin Records, 183
Visions of Plenty (Campbell), 89–90, 94
"Visions of Plenty" (song), 88–89

"Waiting for You" (song), 154
Waits, Jesse Frank, 216
Waits, Tom, 3, 155, 201, 217, 220, 237; "lyrical theology" of, 218–19; similarities between Cave, 215–16
"Wake Up Dead Man" (U2), 215

Walking across Egypt (Tarwater Band), 236
"Walk in the Water" (Gauthier), 86
"Walk the Knife" (King Swamp), 180–81
Wallace, George, 90
Walsh, Tim, 199
Wandering Strange (Campbell), 93, 101
Washington, Booker T., 91
"Way Down in the Hole" (song), 219
"We Are Shielded by the Holy Ghost" (Stevens), 104–7
Weinstein, Deena, 170
Wells, Junior, 202
Welty, Eudora, 41, 88, 191
"Wendell Gee" (song), 209
Wenders, Wim, 133–34
West (L. Williams), 39, 47–48, 58, 63
Western Stars (Springsteen), 11
"We Won't Need Legs to Stand" (song), 124
"Wheel inside the Wheel" (song), 8, 83, 232; influence on "Revelation," 79–80
"When Heaven Speaks" (song), 189
"When the Saints Go Marching In," 80
White, Jim, 81–82, 201, 206, 220–24, 230; as "hillbilly nihilist," 225
White, Steven, 221
"Why Do the Heathen Rage?" (O'Connor), 209
Wild Strawberries, 225–28
Wilkes, Colonel J. D., 200–202, 204; biting satire of, 203
Williams, Hank, 39, 51–52
Williams, Hank, III, 201
Williams, Lucille, 52–55
Williams, Lucinda, 3–4, 52–54, 65, 81, 84, 97, 104, 119, 121, 124–25, 185, 214, 219–20, 230, 232, 237; background of, 40; child characters, 56–57; as Christ-haunted, 6, 46; confessional songs, 39; death as theme, 58–61; on the Devil, 61–62; fundamentalist upbringing, 56; hybridity of, 42; interest in snake handling, 45–46; narrative songs, 51; O'Connor's influence on, 11–12, 40–41, 46, 48, 70; perfectionism of, 42; redemption, 47–48, 68–69; "The River," 50; song sermons, 68–69; southern gothic sensibility of, 40; southern identity of, 40; suffering of children, 55; themes of, 43; use of clichés, 6, 63–64; visiting O'Connor, 39, 41

Williams, Miller, 11, 40, 51, 52–53, 56, 58, 69; friendship with O'Connor, 39, 41, 70
Williams, Rowan, 218
Williams, Tennessee, 56
Windham Hill (record label), 207
Wind River (film), 127
Winesburg, Ohio (Anderson), 104
Wings of Desire (film), biblical resonance in, 133–34
Wiseblood (Alabama band), 235
Wiseblood (band), 15, 174, 177. *See also* Thirlwell, JG
Wiseblood (Corrosion of Conformity), 171–72, 176; cover art, 173–74
Wise Blood (film), 11, 15–16, 40–41, 133, 167, 170, 175, 197
"Wise Blood" (Headphones song), 199
Wiseblood (King Swamp), 180–81, 183
"Wiseblood (Mote's Rave 12)" (song), 180, 183
Wise Blood (O'Connor), 4, 5, 7, 11, 13–14, 17, 19, 21–23, 40–45, 55, 81, 94, 98, 128, 130–31, 151, 153, 156–57, 171–72, 174–76, 185, 187, 190, 197–99, 203–4, 208, 210–12, 214–15, 218, 225, 232, 234–35, 238; appeal to aggressive form of male rebellion, 167–68; attraction of "lunatic fringe," 166; author's note, 181–82, 186; bleakness of, 181; critical reaction to, 166–67; Enoch Emery's "wise blood," 182–83; influence on extreme musical genres, 167; influence on punk, heavy metal, and alternative rock, 15, 166, 170; irony in, 178–79; misinterpretations of, 166–67, 178, 180; reissue of, 178; sacral-sexual association, 149; shortcomings of, 181. *See also* Motes, Hazel (character)
Wise Blood (Thee Mighty Caesars), 184–85
"Wishbone (Some Tomorrow)" (song), 172
"With God on Our Side" (song), 35
"Wooden Leg" (song), 215
Woolf, Virginia, 86
Wordsworth, William, 158
"Working for the Man" (song), 157
World in Reverse (Fleming), 238
World without Tears (L. Williams), 43, 46, 63, 84
"Worthy" (song), 77
Woyzeck (musical), 217
"Wrap My Head around That" (song), 63
Wray, Virginia, 209

Wray, Walter, 180
Wrecking Ball (Harris), 58
Wrecking Ball (Springsteen), 24–25
Wrong-Eyed Jesus (The Mysterious Tale of How I Shouted) (White), 220–22; as Christ-haunted, 223

Yamin, George, 24
"You Ain't Woman Enough (To Take My Man)" (song), 52
"You Can't Be Any Poorer Than Dead" (O'Connor), 65, 67
"Your Cheatin' Heart" (song), 52
"You're Gonna Change (Or I'm Gonna Leave You)" (song), 52
Your Funeral, My Trial (Cave), 150

Zanes, Warren, 23

ABOUT THE AUTHOR

Photo by Steve Lukits

Irwin H. Streight is full professor in the Department of English, Culture, and Communication at the Royal Military College of Canada. He is coeditor of *Flannery O'Connor: The Contemporary Reviews* and *Reading the Boss: Interdisciplinary Approaches to the Works of Bruce Springsteen*. He is cofounder and coeditor of an online journal devoted to Springsteen studies, *BOSS*.

Printed in the United States
by Baker & Taylor Publisher Services